10 essential herbs

LALITHA THOMAS

HOHM PRESS

November 1, 1992 First Edition

Printed in The United States of America
ISBN: 0-934252-26-2

Library of Congress Card Number: 92-054953
Published by Hohm Press P.O. Box 2501 Prescott, Arizona 86302
602-778-9189

The theories and formulae presented in this book are expressed as the author's opinion and as such are not meant to be used to diagnose, prescribe, or to administer in any manner to any physical ailments. In any matters related to your health please contact a qualified, licensed health practitioner.

Design, Illustrations and Typesetting:
Kim Johansen
Pièce de Résistance Ltée.

CONTENTS

FOREWORD

A DECADE ago, the author of this book contacted me by mail. At that time, I wondered about her single name (*Lalitha is the author's legal, one-word, and preferred name, although for ease of listing we have attached the second name, Thomas, to this publication. —Editor.*) and the term she kept using: "herbistry," which for me was tantamount to having one of my students run his or her fingernails across a chalkboard. But I gave her the information she wanted and heard no more from her until now.

Some things still haven't changed, but a lot else has. She still goes by one name only, and likes to drag her fingernails across the blackboard: "herbistry" keeps popping up throughout her book. But aside from this, her extensive knowledge relative to the botanicals she has elected to write about is quite impressive to say the least. If I, as a respected medical anthropologist and author of numerous books on medicinal plants myself, have used the logo "give dignity to weeds" to describe my work, then she is entitled to the handle "someone who gives plants personality *and feeling!*"

It shows in *how* as well as what she writes about. These various herbs come alive on the pages, colored not only by her own sensitivities, but also fully endowed with the dynamic energy of her very capable expertise. Lalitha has no sheepskin diploma from the usual North American herbal correspondence school (of which there are several). But she graduated from the hills and dales, forests and mountains, and meadows and prairies of Mother Nature U. These were the classrooms in which she studied ardently and diligently, applying herself well to the tasks at hand.

In clear and concise terms she takes the guesswork out of herbs. Under her reliable tutelage even the most novice users of botanicals will soon become qualified enough to use those she covers in a safe and effective way. This is saying *a lot* considering just how many other herb books are out there at present. Even myself, who can claim an even three dozen books on the same topic to date, must reluctantly admit that I've had my share of "dogs" along the way. But for Lalitha, this being her first book is a true winner in every sense of the word! A reliable gem for consumers to place confidence in, and a marketing reward for the publishing house which decided to issue her work.

My congratulations to you Ms. Thomas (yes, she does have a last name!) on a job well done! Botanical medicine in this country will benefit from your book for years to come.

John Heinerman, Ph.D.,
Medical Anthropologist,
Director, Anthropological Research Center,
Salt Lake City, UT 84147

INTRODUCTION

ATTENTION READER! If you are a book skimmer who avoids Introductions, you will want to make an exception in this case. There are some important opinions here (all mine) about the nature of the material in this book, that will definitely help any hopeful, do-it-yourself home herbalist to proceed with confidence and the proper mood.

How It All Started

TASOLE*: I began in my early twenties experimenting with herbistry while in college. That put me in touch with large groups of people almost every day. All of us, strangers and friends alike, seemed to get ill and stressed out frequently, and we automatically responded either by going to a doctor (if we had funds), or riding out the health storm on our own (if we had no funds). In either case the typical colds and flu seemed to last the same amount of time and re-occur at all-too-familiar intervals.

**The word is "TASOLE" (pronounced as in 'tassle') and it stands for "True Actual Stories Of Lalitha's Experiences." In each chapter there are many places where I tell stories about my herbal adventures in order to help the reader easily learn how to begin using the Ten Essentials quickly and confidently. Skip them if you are having a crisis and need immediate instructions for application. But do come back to the TASOLE later.*

I was especially frustrated with the money spent and the lack of real results gained from allopathic health care.

One winter a nasty flu started knocking my friends out by the class-loads, and many of us were losing much-needed work hours. I was in the mood to do something definitive for my own health, especially something that was not the usual allopathic approach. So I went to a local herb store and bought small packets of three well-known healing herbs — goldenseal, myrrh, and Cayenne.* I had read a lot about these herbs and felt confident that my first serious experiment would be a success. What I lacked in knowledge at that time (since I had not yet begun my serious apprenticeship as an herbalist) I made up for in enthusiasm. Besides, I was a little desperate, feeling ill from the usual flu symptoms of fever, body ache, nausea, congestion and intestinal upset.

I mixed the herb powders together and began taking half-teaspoon doses in a little water every three hours or so. It tasted very bitter (and was hot from the Cayenne) but I didn't let that stop me and it was a good thing too, because I started feeling better by the end of the first day and I noted that, in any case, this was a much faster response than the usual medicines produced.

The next day I felt so good that I decided to try out the formula on my friend Bob who had the same symptoms. I gave him a packet of the mixture and told him how to take it, without bothering to tell him what it was. Just like me, he also began feeling much better by the end of the first day. When he took some of the powders to work and began giving them out to sick buddies, they too got the same results and some even suspected that my friend was giving out illegal drugs!

One friend finally asked what this seemingly magical potion was. Because I felt a little mischievous I pretended to have a secret family herbal formula, and declared that the ingredients couldn't be divulged. Yet no one believed me, and I kept hearing rumors all around campus and at various work places about a "miracle drug powder."

A week later when Bob returned to ask for more powders, I found out that he was selling my remedy to his work

---

**The Ten Essential Herbs are capitalized throughout the book.*

partners for a fee befitting a "secret miracle drug." Even at a high price it was substantially cheaper than the usual fees for doctors and prescriptions that his buyers were used to, and it seemed to work much better too.

Although this experiment was totally unscientific, the results were widespread enough to cause me to investigate herbistry further. It was a great feeling to have successfully taken my health into my own hands, and I wanted to find out more about how it all worked.

In my 15 years as a professional herbalist (I didn't start counting until I knew what I was doing), I have learned the medicinal uses of dozens of plants from whatever climate I found myself in, from New England to Arizona. I have owned my own herbal remedy company, called Weeds of Worth, which marketed formulas I prepared myself. I have taught and lectured about herbs and their uses to hundreds of students and professionals, and have herbalized myself and others in first-aid offices, kitchens, at the scene of highway accidents, in classrooms, forests, deserts, foreign countries, and on restaurant floors. I have seen people and pets of all ages and descriptions with health needs from life-threatening to humorous be helped substantially with herbistry. (Am I sounding like the proverbial snake-oil salesman yet?) Through all this adventure I have found that there are Ten Essential Herbs that can take care of almost any of the usual health needs that arise in daily life and travels.

These Ten Essential medicinal herbs are, for the most part, readily available anywhere in the world, from American grocery stores to the open-air markets of India or Mexico. So even if you find yourself in a remote village in Nepal and need help for infected bug bites, food poisoning, colds, flus, cuts, scrapes, foul moods or whatever — you can almost always find some of the Ten Essential Herbs and be back on the trip in good shape. At home the Ten Essentials can be kept on hand at all times. When visiting friends who are inexperienced or unprepared in these matters, you may be amazed to find out how many of the Ten Essentials are already in their spice cabinet or refrigerator.

Limiting the choices of herbs to the Ten Essentials makes this approach to health and beauty-care a simple and practical one. Like many of my students, you may have been intimidated about learning any herbistry in the past because of a fear of being overwhelmed with the sheer number of herbal choices offered in most herb books, seminars and lectures.

Another hesitation about learning to use herbs for health stems from our upbringing in a culture that emphasizes the allopathic medical model and the "giving over" of health care to professionals who, we are taught, are always more "in-the-know." (Any trip to a pharmacy in my growing-up years, especially if I were ill, tended to reinforce in me the idea that there were simply too many choices among all those pills, powders, lotions, liquids, etc., for me to be trusted with. It seemed clear that handling my own health was an impossibly complex and possibly dangerous thing — and what could I know about it anyway?) These learned health attitudes persist and often show up particularly strongly when we first entertain the idea of learning a little self-help herbistry.

Ten Essential Herbs is based on the holistic approach to health care — one which views individual symptoms in relationship to the whole bodily system. The allopathic medical model, on the other hand, uses a specific drug to suppress or alleviate a specific symptom while often ignoring the need to balance the body systems as a whole. For example, a painkiller is commonly prescribed for a headache, regardless of its cause. In herbistry we would look to discover whether the headache was caused by indigestion or a congested liver, etc. We would use herbs to relieve the congestion or balance the digestion, thus quickly relieving the headache without undesirable side effects.

The approach I take in my system of Ten Essential Herbs is simple enough for children to use. Children have been a particularly inspiring group of students for me. I have worked extensively with teaching them how to begin identifying and using the medicinal plants that grow in their own back yards. Insect bites, scrapes and bumps are quite common, and children love the feeling of confidence they get from knowing how to handle these situations as a part of their daily activities rather than as a big scary problem. Even a two-year-old toddler can learn to tape a slice of Onion onto an insect bite or bruise, or to get out the People Paste (a powdered herbal mixture; see People Paste Appendix A) and mix a bit for a cut or small burn.

TASOLE: I did volunteer work once for a group of 15 children ages two through eleven and most of our activities took place out of doors. Even the youngest of the children quickly learned to rub a bit of raw Onion on an insect bite or to chew a fresh Comfrey leaf (growing in the yard) into a pulp for a personal poultice on any cut or scrape. Children from about five years old on up began to learn how to make simple herb tea for soothing a stomach or helping a fever to pass. I always kept a fresh raw Onion in an "Onion bag" on the playing field and almost daily I would hear a child call out "Onion bag, Onion bag," which was the signal for a friend to get a bit of the onion for an insect bite that was itching or to prevent a new bruise from forming. The Comfrey plants were also well-used as were the rest of the Ten Essentials in the herb cabinet in the house. The children delighted in teaching parents and new playmates how to take care of themselves with the herbs.

It is common to take the allopathic medical model and simply try to transfer it onto this new exploration of medicinal plants. In herbistry, although we may speak of symptoms, we are thinking in terms of balancing the body systems as a whole and in relationship to each other. This Ten Essentials system is geared toward addressing your health and beauty concerns in a very intuitive style. As you begin trying out the suggestions with which you feel most comfortable, you build experience. Meanwhile, as you read and practice, you can expect to be imbibing what may be an *entirely new mood*—a sense of self-confidence and organic (i.e. intuitive) understanding of which herbs to use and when, together with an equally important sense of humor about your daily bodily needs. As a result, your next experience of a caffeine headache, for instance, may change from a hair-pulling, eye-crossing dash for pain killers or more caffeine, to a confident step toward the spice cabinet for a dash of Cayenne.

It is this overall intuitive approach that makes this book unique. My major intention is to give you a strong taste of how I have approached and taught herbistry, and how I gained confidence in evaluating and responding to my own physical health needs and those of my family and students. I want you to be inspired to do the same. In giving you numerous examples of the possible uses of each herb and explaining how I have handled the many different types of people and personalities encountered, I am constructing for you the mood, or atmosphere, of thoughtful and creative experimentation that is really *the way* to proceed.

In addition, I include scientific data on HOW and WHY the herbs work (a detail often missing in many herb books). I also simply explain some details of how the body functions and how to discern your health needs. For a more detailed understanding of herbal chemistry and body functionings, I provide a thorough Resource Guide (Appendix C).

In summary, my theory — Lalitha's Theory — goes like this: ***If you grasp the general characteristics, mood, actions, and "personality" of an herb first, then you can use that friendly relationship to apply the herb in an intelligent and effective manner while still maintaining the mood of creative experimentation.***

This book will guide you in that process.

How To Use This Book

FOR EMERGENCY USE:

Look in the Index or the General Use Chart (Appendix F) for the references related to your need and go straight to that information. Then, while you are taking care of your muscle ache, or cold, or whatever, you can begin to enjoy yourself in learning Ten Essentials herbistry by following the steps I will outline below.

FOR ENTERTAINMENT AND LEARNING

—Developing the Intuitive Approach:

STEP #1: *Browse through the book.*

- Enjoy the rhymes.
- Read the TASOLES. These are all True Actual Stories Of Lalitha's Experiences (TASOLE) which will inspire you to ***take action*** with your own self-help needs.
- Understand the layout. Each chapter has a list entitled "APPLICATIONS and ATTRIBUTES (Quick Reference List)." This is a list of all the applications within that chapter. Major uses of that chapter's herb are emphasized within the list. Learning these major uses of each herb is a fast way to begin becoming familiar with each of the Ten Essentials.

At the end of each application within a chapter are several headings that should help you efficiently find the most complete input about that application. These headings are:

ALSO SEE: This will point out other applications *within that same chapter's list* which would give an additional point of view or topic related to the application you have looked up.

ALTERNATIVE OR SUPPLEMENTARY SELF-HELP: All the herbs pointed out here are others among the Ten Essentials that are good *supplementary* herbs which could be used in *addition* to the main herb of the chapter and for the application being studied. The herbs *marked with a "star" (*)* can actually be good *alternatives*, as well as supplements, for the application being studied. To make a decision about which additional herb/herbs, if any, you might want to use, review related applications in those other chapters.

DOSAGE: Most often the dosage of an herb for any application will follow the General Dosage guidelines given at the beginning of each chapter. However, if there are any additional dosage guidelines for a particular application, I will list them here.

STEP #2: *Make yourself a cup of tea.* See the complete instructions on how to do this in the Applications list (under Tea) in Chapter I, Lesson #2. Peppermint is a tasty herb to start with. Since tea preparation is so integral to herbistry, when you can make a cup of tea you are ready to begin using this book for hundreds of needs. As you go along and gain confidence you can add the other skills of preparation such as Honeyball, Infusion, Decoction, etc. (all described in Chapter I, Lesson #2).

STEP #3: *Read Chapter I.* Basic herbistry information is presented in this chapter in the form of six Lessons, the basics of a course in Introductory Herbistry. You will be referring back to this chapter frequently for general information, especially for easy instructions in Application Methods and Definitions given in Lesson #2.

STEP #4: *Learn the "CORE FIVE."* Within the Ten Essentials are a Core Five group of herbs which make an efficient place to begin your learning. These **core five** herbs are CAYENNE, COMFREY, GARLIC, GINGER, and PEPPERMINT. Even with just these five herbs it is quite possible to handle ***most*** common health needs effectively. Each of the Core Five herbs is marked by the *symbol of an Apple Core* on the first page of that herb's chapter.

Pick one of these five that is attractive to you. For instance, you might choose to learn about Garlic first. Read its rhyme, Personality Profile and TASOLES. The rhymes are especially good memory joggers and I have used them with children ages six and up with great success.

Next, choose one or two major uses of that herb, especially one you might currently need to learn about, such as the nervine/tonic uses of Garlic. Read them over, referring back to Chapter I (especially Lesson #2) as necessary for elaboration and clarification. When an herb has a tonic use, this is often the most practical application to start with as it gives a good overview.

If at all possible try to find a situation in which to apply what you are learning, even if it is simply an ear infection on your cat. It really helps to use an application soon if you can.

STEP #5: *Start making connections. Experiment.* Depending on whether you are the type who likes learning many facets of a subject at once, or one who likes to stick to one part until it is mastered, you would now proceed to either:

a) Start cross-referencing the application you have picked,with others of the Ten Essentials that have similar applications. See how each herb is used *singly* and then in combination for that same application.

Review Chapter I, Lesson #6, for brief instruction in using herbs singly and in combinations.

or

b) Continue studying one herb of the Core Five, (or any of the Ten Essentials), and its applications, one by one, until you have a good grasp of "who" the herb is and what it does. Then proceed to study another one.

I want to emphasize again that it is easily within our means to overcome our past fears about taking care of our own health and our feeling that we must rely upon others to "heal" us. This Ten Essentials System is a focused and powerful way to start.

CHAPTER I

GENERAL "HOW-TO" OF HERBISTRY

In this chapter you will receive six easy lessons in basic herbistry:

- Use the Four Big Questions
- Application Methods and Definitions
- Utensils for Herbal Preparations
- Potency of Herbs and the Forms They Come In
- How to Store Your Herbs
- Use the Ten Essentials Separately or in Combinations

Don't be afraid of making a mistake. The Ten Essentials were chosen for their potency and safety.

Throughout your use of the Ten Essential Herbs, you will be continually referring back to this chapter to hone your herbistry skills and build understanding in herbal vocabulary.

LESSON #1: USE THE FOUR BIG QUESTIONS

Four questions need to be answered in each situation you encounter. These are:

- What are the first priorities?
- What herbs address the priorities?
- What herbs do I have on hand?
- How are the herbs best applied in this case?

If you keep these questions in mind and consistently apply them as you learn the Ten Essentials System, you will quickly develop an easy and confident approach that will automatically click in when you need it.

Keep in mind that the great charm of this system is flexibility. Usually there will be more than one good choice among the Ten Essentials for any need you will face. Another charm is practicality. Many of the Ten Essentials can be found day or night at the 24-hour supermarkets that are omnipresent these days. Although it won't take much effort to keep all ten in stock, there is rarely a cause for concern if you find yourself, on occasion, without your "favorite" herb. With this system you will understand how to make do with whatever is available.

Let's begin. I will "talk" you through the general process involved with each of the questions. Using these questions you will be developing a consistent style or approach — a framework through which you will think out each health situation and determine the practical applications, methods, and herbal actions needed.

Question #1: "What Are the First Priorities?"

**Use Observation and Past Experience.*

When faced with a health need, begin the evaluation (often done in moments) through careful observation of general symptoms. Also use common sense and whatever growing knowledge you have so far acquired of how the body works. With family and friends you will have the additional benefit of your past observations of them in their "normal" state, and so you will easily assess whether there is cause for concern or not. (I often laugh when I think of what I consider "normal" for myself, family, and friends. Think about it. Don't you just want to laugh out loud?)

TASOLE: Fred, a new acquaintance, began to have a choking fit during a lecture we were attending at a friend's house. He staggered out of the living room and into the kitchen where he stood gripping the sink while struggling for breath. The situation worsened (in my eyes) when he slowly sank to the floor, gasping out the words, "I can't breathe." It all happened so suddenly, and I felt I had every reason to suspect that he might die on the spot if I didn't act quickly.

I was about to give him a big dose of Cayenne and start mouth-to-mouth resuscitation as first aid prior to taking him to the hospital, when a woman friend of his walked through the kitchen and saw us on the floor. Fred was still gasping mightily, turning white and blue by turns, and the look on my face must have revealed my approaching panic. This other woman, however, seemed unconcerned and casually said, "Oh, this often happens to him when certain touchy subjects are talked about such as in the lecture this evening. Just take him completely outside for a minute or two and he'll be fine right away." Fred seemed to relax a bit after her remarks and although he was still gasping and choking, he got up and stumbled out the door onto the porch. In about one minute he was totally back to normal, breathing easily. Together we went back to the lecture, and the subject matter had conveniently changed. That was it! No hospital bill, no ambulance, no mouth-to-mouth resuscitation, no herbs, just a change of scenery! This is an example of the benefit of past observation of what is "normal" for a particular person!

Take A Broader View

In discerning the priorities we begin to broaden our ways of viewing symptoms. To facilitate this understanding I have included a category at the end of every herbal application called "ALSO SEE." This category specifies other applications within that same chapter that you should "Also See" for a broader understanding of the circumstance you are investigating. For instance, in addition to seeing a headache predominantly as a pain to be relieved, your thinking might run along broader lines: a *headache* could be seen as a restriction of *circulation* to the head, perhaps from a known cause such as *anxiety*, *caffeine withdrawal*, or *digestion* upset. *Menstrual* cramps might be seen as a *muscle spasm* (in this case of the uterus), as are leg cramps, spastic *colon*, or dry heaves of the *stomach*, all variations of muscle *spasm*. A honeybee sting can be viewed in the broader sense of poisonous *insect bites* as could the stings or "bites" of wasps, spiders, etc. If a cut were bleeding profusely the first priority would be *bleeding*, yet that application might also refer you to additional priorities in helping the cut such as *wounds*, *skin*, and *infection*. (The italicized words are some of those you might find in the "Also See" category at the end of an application to which you have referred.)

Taking a broader view allows you to see the commonalities underlying bodily symptoms and how these correspond to the helping actions of the herbs. This is not to say that every case that involves spasms of any kind (for instance), should always be followed through in exactly the same way. Many spasms or cramps of varying types can be relieved through use of herbal anti-spasmodics or nervines, yet the follow-up for menstrual spasms (cramps) might involve nutritional supplementation such as calcium, whereas stomach spasms (vomiting) may involve a follow-up of a simple soothing broth, or sucking on ice chips to relieve dehydration. Going to a "bottom line" in this way and starting your self-help from there is a very effective way to begin.

"Broader View" thinking helps to simplify things and encourages you to get to the root cause of a self-help need efficiently and with confidence. What some students have started off seeing as a scary, unique, and mysterious health crisis necessitating a drastic remedy with possible unhealthy side effects, now is seen as easily handled *causes and effects*. For example, without using Broader View thinking our reaction might be, "Quick! Get me a painkiller! I have a sudden headache and nausea for 'no apparent reason.'" When we begin to use Broader View thinking, the fear and mystery lessen, we make more reasonable and healthy choices, and our mental scenario might go like this: "Oh yeah! I ate three hamburgers and two banana splits which resulted in a headache from indigestion. I need some Peppermint oil to help my digestion and relieve this type of headache." We begin to learn and observe that *what apppeared as disjointed and unconnected symptoms are all connected through the functionings of the body and emotions as a whole.*

Question #2: "What Herbs Address the Priorities?"

I find this a very entertaining question to answer. In this Ten Essentials System there are many ways to respond to any given situation, each quite effective yet each possessing a quality, a creative nuance of its own, that compares somewhat to the choice of colors and materials in painting.

Look in the Index or in a specific chapter under a major symptom or health need such as bleeding, vomiting, headache, burn, nausea, toothache, etc., or refer to the General Use Chart, Appendix F. This chart focuses on the most potent uses for each herb, whereas the general Index and each chapter list a much greater variety and flexibility in each herb's use. You most likely will find more than one choice listed amongst the Ten Essentials for any application, so at this point, especially if quick action is called for, your first choice will be the most-potent-for-the-job herb that you already have on hand. These first-choice herbs are specified by large and small dots on the General Use chart in Appendix F, and by applications printed in bold type within each chapter in the Applications and Attributes (Quick Reference List).

If the situation has flexibility as to the time frame for taking action, you may find yourself wanting to experiment with more than one of the choices or with mixing herbs together for the enhancement of each other and increased potency. (This is described further in Lesson #6.) At the end of each application in every chapter, there is a separate category called "*ALTERNATIVE OR SUPPLEMENTARY SELF-HELP.*" Here is where I have listed other herbs among the Ten Essentials that either have similar action to the herb you are reading about (good alternatives, indicated with a star "⋆") or that have actions that could give additional yet different help along with the herb you are reading about (supplementary herbs, no star). I always suggest to my students to take advantage, whenever possible, of opportunities to try different herbs or a complementary mixture of herbs for similar needs. This leads to a basis for comparison of the herbal actions and gives first-hand experience of the creative nuances I mentioned earlier. An example of this is the choice between Cayenne or Comfrey root for bleeding. Although they are both very effective for bleeding, upon using them you may discover Cayenne to be your choice for immediate first aid in bleeding wounds while Comfrey, with its mucilaginous qualities and tissue-healing capabilities, may be your long-term choice for wounds that bleed intermittently while the tissue needs help regenerating over a period of time. Also, although Cayenne stops bleeding fast, it may not be practical in some instances, such as for children or invalids who may touch a wound with some Cayenne on it and then touch their eyes or other sensitive areas inadvertently. In these cases you have the potent alternative of Comfrey root. It often happens that simple practical considerations such as these may determine the choice of herb.

Question #3: "What Herbs Are Readily Available?"

"Readily available" means which herb or herbs (of the choices suggested in a given application) do you have access to "right now." For example, you may need emergency help in stopping the bleeding of a wound and see that Cayenne and Comfrey root are both good choices. You may have developed a preference for Cayenne, yet if Cayenne is not right at hand and Comfrey root is, then of course you grab the readily available Comfrey root. When you have flexibility in a situation, such as in planning to make a cough syrup for future use, you will find all of the Ten Essentials readily available at a store or through mail order.

If you are really serious about giving this Ten Essentials System a firm place in your self-help repertoire, you will want to have all ten herbs on hand as a matter of habit. However, I have handled many health needs with the herbs gotten from a grocery store on the spur-of-the-moment when I have found myself in unprepared circumstances. This is comforting to keep in mind. Also, if you cannot quickly get one or more of the herbs needed, this is rarely a cause for concern. Many of the herbs have overlapping uses — a great convenience of this system. Simply look under the heading "Alternative or Supplementary Self-Help" at the end of an application. The herbs that can be used as alternatives are clearly marked with a star (*).

Always keep herbs labeled with ink or marker that won't rub off or smear easily. It won't do any good to have the Ten Essentials on hand if you forget what's what and find them unlabeled!

Question #4: "How Are the Herbs Best Applied in This Case?"

Since there are so many ways to apply an herb, you will want to narrow down the choices by deciding first whether an internal or external application is called for. Each chapter has internal and external dosages listed separately. Even if you will be needing both internal and external applications, just take it one step at a time. After having fun practicing with my suggestions you may well be able to invent some applications of your own.

For those of you who may want to progress to more advanced techniques of herbal preparation and application such as the making of complex tinctures and the treatment of more serious illness, refer to one of the two-starred (**) reference titles in the Resource Guide, Appendix C.

Go on to Lesson #2 to begin learning the details of application methods for internal and external use. Go to Lesson #6 for further instruction in mixing an herbal formulation.

LESSON #2: APPLICATION METHODS AND DEFINITIONS

This lesson is one with which you will want to become very familiar, so that you have the knowledge to act with firm confidence when handling a self-help need.

Determine whether you are needing an internal or external application and then proceed to that list. If you are needing both internal and external applications, make the applications step by step in the order of your priority. For instance, with a bleeding wound, your first priority is to stop the bleeding. That would be an external application. Then you might proceed to an internal application of a tea or encapsulated herb for additional help in the prevention of infection or to help soothe pain.

APPLICATION METHODS - INTERNAL USE:

BOLUS
CAPSULES
CHILDREN'S IDEAS
DOSAGE EQUIVALENTS
DECOCTION
EAR DROPS/WASH
ENEMA
GARGLE
HONEYBALL
INFUSION
LOZENGE
NASAL RINSE
RICE PAPER
SUPPOSITORY
SWEETENERS
SYRUP
TEA
TINCTURES

BOLUS: A bolus is a convenient suppository for inserting herbal help into the vagina. Powdered herbs are made into a thick clay-like consistency using melted cocoa butter, water, or honey, and are then rolled and patted into small shapes and dosages convenient for inserting into the vagina. When cocoa butter is used (usually the best idea), warm it enough to just melt the cocoa butter, mix the cocoa butter with your powdered herbs to a stiff consistency and form it into convenient bolus shapes. Put the formed boluses into your refrigerator where the cool temperature will make the cocoa butter firm. Keep the cocoa butter boluses stored in your refrigerator until used, as they will become soft at room temperature. When water is used, place the formed boluses on a cookie sheet in the oven at a low temperature of 120 degrees or so. When they are dry and hard you may store them in an airtight jar. When inserting a water-based bolus into the vagina, use a little lotion or petroleum jelly as a lubricant for easy insertion. When honey is used as the moistening agent, simply mix a small amount of it with the herbs to make a very stiff clay-like consistency. Form it and then stiffen by storing it in the refrigerator. Although a honey bolus can work very well, it will not be as firm as the two other types, yet is usually firm enough for vaginal use.

CAPSULES: Powdered herbs are often put into gelatin capsules as a convenience in taking them. You can buy capsules in most health food stores and even in an ordinary pharmacy, although they are a little more expensive there. Capsules come in varying sizes from "000" (fairly large to swallow) down to size "0," which are the smallest I have found commonly available. Most herbs can be purchased already encapsulated in size "0" capsules, yet it is much more economical, and herbs are probably fresher and more potent, if you buy the herbs in bulk, by the ounce, from the best source you can find and then fill the capsules yourself. I have found that three very full size "00" capsules (the size I prefer when it is up to me) are the equivalent of about one teaspoon powdered herb. There are some drawbacks to using capsules, however. I often prefer not to use gelatin capsules as there is a very potent process that is initiated in the mouth, brain, and digestive tract by having the herbs interact directly with the saliva and enzymes in the mouth. Capsules prevent this initial important process that happens in the mouth and can slow the herb's effect in the digestive tract. Also, I have often seen encapsulated herbs come out, capsule intact, from either end of the body, and this does not encourage my confidence in them as an herbal conveyer, especially if a person has any digestive weakness. You will just have to use your own judgement with respect to convenience and taste in deciding this question for each circumstance.

Some good alternatives to capsules in many situations are herbal Honeyballs, Rice Paper or Tinctures (see these applications). The simplest method is to put the required dose of herb into the mouth and wash it down with water, juice, or tea. Children and people who have trouble swallowing capsules often find these ideas helpful.

Always remember to drink plenty of water to help with the dispersion of the herbs, encapsulated or otherwise. Occasionally I find a person who has what I call a "burp back" effect soon after swallowing encapsulated herbs. This is characterized by a burping that has the flavor of the herbs that were in the capsules. If this happens it means that the capsules are causing slight digestive upset. The situation can often be remedied by drinking an additional glass of water (warm water works best). Other tricks to possibly prevent "burp back" are 1) poke a pinhole in each end of the capsule before swallowing it (this is a bit of a hassle if you must take capsules very often) or 2) take the capsule together with a small bit of light food such as a bite or two of fruit, or 3) take the herbs out of the capsule altogether and drink with some water or juice.

Review Dosage Equivalents in this list to determine equivalents between teas, decoctions, infusions, and capsules, and for hints on adjusting an herbal formula to minimize digestive stress.

CHILDREN'S IDEAS: There are several ways to make it easier to offer herbs and herbal preparations to children. Most of them are described separately in this list under Honeyball, Syrups, Lozenges, Decoction or Infusion (ways to offer herbs in concentrated and therefore smaller doses). Check the Dosage Equivalents and Sweeteners sections in this list, too.

Here are a few more ideas:

1) Make a decoction or infusion of an herb or herbs and soak dried raisins in it. The raisins soak up the herb liquid, automatically adding the raisin sweetness, and make it easy for children to ingest the herbs. You will need to measure the amount of liquid before you soak the raisins, so you can figure out how many raisins need to be eaten for a dose of herbal brew.
2) Small amounts of powdered herbs can be mixed with a spoonful of applesauce and then followed with one or two more spoonfuls of plain applesauce if needed.
3) Raw Garlic (usually crushed) and other fresh or dried herbs can be offered mixed in honey. Honey buffers the spiciness of Garlic and enhances the assimilation of any herb. (See Honey, Appendix B.)

DECOCTION: A decoction is a concentrated brew made by gently simmering "tougher" forms or parts of herbs such as roots, barks, and woody stems (either fresh or dried). It is different from an infusion which is a concentrate made by steeping (not simmering) the more delicate parts of the herb such as leaves, flowers, light stems, etc. (See Infusion in this list.) A decoction is a concentrated version of an herbal tea, commonly made by gently simmering one ounce of herb in 2 cups of water for 20 to 30 minutes. A decoction is usually taken 1/4 to 1/2 cup at a time as needed. If you are a beginner, practice with the tea form of preparation first before going for the decoction or infusion.

If you are combining herbs that call for different preparation methods (i.e., steeping and simmering), simply prepare the simmered herbs first, strain them out when their preparation is finished, and steep the "steeping herbs" in that hot brew for the allotted time.

Start with the purest water possible and avoid using aluminum or cast iron pans in preparing herbal mixtures. (See Lesson #3: Utensils.)

Don't make the mistake of thinking a stronger brew such as a decoction or infusion must always be better than the strength of a simpler, ordinary cup of tea. My new students are often surprised at the results from an average-strength cup of tea and consequently change their "stronger is better" thinking. As you gain experience, you will be able to recognize those situations that do call for a stronger brew such as a decoction, infusion, or tincture. Sometimes it may be more convenient to take fewer doses of an herb or sometimes a situation does call for stronger and more concentrated action than a simple cup of tea provides.

Review Dosage Equivalents in this list to make the proper substitutions between a cup of tea and a decoction.

DOSAGE EQUIVALENTS: Here are some equivalents that will come in handy when you are trying to figure out the most convenient way to administer an herbal preparation. These are approximate equivalents to give you a general idea of where to start and are not meant to be rigid rules or to replace common sense.

1 cup tea = 2 size "0" capsules

1 cup tea = 2 oz. (4 Tbsp.) decoction or infusion

1 cup tea = 1/2 tsp. powdered or 1 tsp. crushed/chopped herbs (either taken plain in mouth or made into a honeyball, etc.)

1 cup tea = tincture as per manufacturer's suggestion for dosage (usually drops per 1/2 cup of water)

For the most efficient action of the herb, unless otherwise specified, take it on an empty stomach as a tea, or, for other forms such as capsules, with a full glass of water. This allows the herb to have maximum impact rather than to be diluted and buried in the digestive action of a stomach full of food.

Occasionally an herb or herbal formula is uncomfortable to an empty stomach. If this is the case, it is a good idea to add 1/2 to 1 part buffering and/or stimulating herb to the formula, such as Ginger, Slippery Elm, or Comfrey, or take the herb with a small bite or two of simple food such as fruit. These ideas almost always work well, yet you can take the herbs with a meal or light snack if you must.

Review additional preparation and dosage details in this list under Capsules, Children's Ideas, Decoction, Gargle, Honeyball, Infusion, Rice Paper, Syrups, Lozenges, and Tinctures.

Also see Lesson #6 in this chapter called *Use the Ten Essentials Separately or in Combinations.*

EAR DROPS/RINSE: Most commonly, herbal oils such as Garlic oil are used for ear drops. For an ear rinse, a tea or decoction or infusion is used. This can be followed with a drop or two of olive oil or Garlic oil to aid in lubrication. Usually 2 to 4 drops of oil is a good amount to put into an ear. Hold it in by putting a bit of cotton in the ear. A bulb syringe can be used to gently inject an herbal tea of the proper temperature (body temperature or slightly warmer) into the ear to help relieve an ear wax congestion. Always treat both ears even though only one ear may be in distress. Ear difficulties may "travel" from one ear to the other, especially if you are dealing with an infection.

ENEMA: During any illness it is important to help the body eliminate toxins as quickly and easefully as possible. The colon is a major eliminative channel. Using an enema at the proper time will help the colon cleanse and renew the body. The colon can also help distribute an herbal action throughout the body. (Some of the most commonly used herbs for enemas are Garlic, Slippery Elm, and Yarrow. See Chapters VI, X, and XI.)

Do not use enemas consistently or casually. Frequent use can lead to a habit which would be harmful. But when you are ill with any of a number of inconveniences, from flu to colds to dysentery to mononucleosis, an enema can help to end the misery and speed your way to well-being. It gets impressive results and is quite simple.

The herbal brew for an enema can be a decoction, infusion, or tincture. It should be a little warm to approximate the internal body temperature. To make the brew, use 1 Tbsp. herb per cup of boiling hot water, steep or simmer 15 minutes, then cool to desired temperature. Fill an enema bag with two quarts of the concoction for an adult, or one quart for younger children under 10 years old.

For babies or infants, use a bulb syringe to gently insert the liquid into the rectum. Do this repeatedly until one or two cups of liquid have been injected or until their automatic intestinal reflex causes their bowels to evacuate, whichever comes first. With a baby the scenario is often that you give the bulb syringe injection of liquid (perhaps 1 to 4 oz. gets in), then it is automatically evacuated, then you repeat the injection, then it is evacuated, three to five times. In this way the colon is helped to empty completely. Remember that with infants or small babies, the colon evacuates automatically and fairly quickly as soon as any pressure builds up as they have not yet learned bowel control. It is wise to have the child in a tub or basin of some kind and to have the enema bag or bulb syringe fairly low to the body to insure milder water pressure. Before beginning the enema, fill a tub or basin with hot water and then empty and dry it to warm it up for its occupant.

If you have no experience with administering enemas, you can begin to develop your own technique by trying the following: Hang the enema bag one or two feet above your body where it (your body, of course) will be reclining perhaps on a clean rug or towel spread on the floor (probably in a bathroom), or in a dry tub or basin (usually for very young children) in a warm room. A primary idea with an enema is to administer it into the colon slowly and gently. If the bag is hung very high up, this makes the water pressure too strong for best efficiency and comfort. Enema bags come equipped with a hand-operated clip that opens and shuts the tubing, thus regulating the flow of liquid as you decide. Cover the enema tube tip (or bulb syringe tip, for babies) with an unscented mild cream or lotion such as baby cream or petroleum jelly and insert it gently into the anus as you lie on your left side. (For babies you should opt for what is most comfortable for the child.) Lying on the left side facilitates the entry of the enema into the descending colon. Allow perhaps one cup of liquid to enter the lower part of the colon and then pinch off the tubing so that you may take the enema tip out of the anus temporarily and sit on the toilet to evacuate this small amount of fluid. The point here is to clear the anus of any fecal matter that may have accumulated at the anal opening. This helps the rest of the enema to flow into the colon more comfortably. If you are using an enema to help a case of diarrhea or dysentery, this first step won't be necessary. Add a little water back to the enema bag so that you still have the full amount you planned for the enema. Continue as before, being careful to monitor the flow of the liquid with the hand-operated clip. It is usually best to allow the enema to flow into the colon in small (perhaps one cup) amounts. Continue to lie on your left side at first; then rotate onto your back or other side to help the enema flow more easefully. Whenever you feel pressure building up in the colon, clip off the water flow and relax — perhaps gently massaging the abdomen while the liquid makes its way inside the colon. When the pressure slackens somewhat, you will then open the tubing clip and continue administering the enema. Two quarts of enema solution is not the entire holding capacity of the colon in an adult and this amount is usually held easily by adults. After the enema is administered, it is then evacuated into the toilet. It is important to stay warm while taking an enema as this facilitates relaxation.

Occasionally an enema will not evacuate easily. This is often due to a spastic colon which holds the liquid in until the colon relaxes, or to dehydration in the body which can result in the body actually absorbing most of the enema liquid so that there is not much left to be evacuated. In either case there is no cause for worry as the body naturally balances itself either by evacuating the enema when the colon relaxes or by using the water it has absorbed.

After an herbal enema (especially a garlic enema) it is sometimes a good idea (usually for adults) to follow it, perhaps an hour to a day later, with an enema of plain water that contains a double or triple dose of liquid or powdered acidophilus (double or triple what the manufacturer suggests for oral use). This will immediately replenish the healthful digestive bacteria in the colon that are usually very depleted during illness. The acidophilus enema hastens the return of healthy bowel action, especially in those whose intestinal action is easily disturbed.

EYEWASH: Always rinse both eyes even if only one eye seems to need help. Put a well-strained herbal tea in an eye dropper, and keeping your eyes open, gently squeeze a few drops into each eye. At this point your eyes will start blinking and this is fine. Sometimes I have dipped a lint-free cotton cloth in an herb tea and then squeezed the tea slowly off the cloth into the eye of a person lying down to receive it.

GARGLE: A gargle is used when you are needing help with a sore, dry, infected, or strained throat. Crushed or powdered herbs can be made into a tea, decoction or infusion for this purpose, or two to four drops of herbal oil such as Clove or Peppermint can be mixed in a cup of warm water and used. The temperature of your gargle is up to you. Additional additives for gargles are 1/2 to 1 tsp. sea salt per cup of herbal mixture or 1/8 to 1/4 cup alcohol-based mouthwash per cup of cooled mixture.

HONEYBALL: It is most efficient to make enough honeyballs to last one or two days at a time instead of making them singly. Measure an amount of powdered herbs to start with, perhaps one or two days' worth. For example, if you wanted to take 1 teaspoon of an herb powder four times a day, one day's amount would be 4 teaspoons. If you wanted to measure an amount to last two days, in this example, you would then pre-measure 8 teaspoons of the herb. Having previously measured your herb powders, mix them with just enough raw, uncooked, "un-anythinged" honey (whatever is the best you can find) to make a stiff clay-like consistency which can be rolled into a long "rope" of perhaps 1/2-inch thickness. Take this "honey roll" mixture and cut it into single doses. In my present example, this would mean that if you mixed 8 teaspoons of herb with honey, this would equal 8 doses and therefore you would divide that particular "honeyball rope" into 8 pieces. This would give you one dose four times a day for two days. Got it?

Each dose can be chewed briefly or pinched apart and rolled into tiny honey balls for swallowing like pills. It usually takes much less honey than you think, so knead it in carefully and patiently as you mix. If on your first try you get a mixture that is a bit too loose, or even runny, you can either add an additional *measured* amount of dry herbs to stiffen it some or simply spoon up a proper dose and take it like a wonderful honey elixir. Take a day's worth of the honeyballs in a little packet along with you to work, school or wherever, and *store the rest in the refrigerator.*

In addition to being a binding agent, the honey serves the purpose of enhancing the digestion and assimilation of the herbs and it will also have antiseptic action if it is good raw honey. Usually it is best to make no more than two days' worth at a time to insure the best potency. (See Honey, Appendix B.)

Honeyballs are a favorite way to administer herbs to children. A variation on the honeyball method is to soak dried raisins in an herbal decoction or infusion and then give these "herbal raisins" to the child to eat. For most herbs among these Ten Essentials, the flavors mix well with the raisins.

Honeyballs can be made equally well using light or dark unsulphured molasses or glycerin (available at health and drug stores). An essential oil, such as Peppermint or Clove oil, could be added for flavor or herbal action, if needed, according to your taste buds.

INFUSION: An infusion is a concentrated version of an herbal tea, commonly made by steeping (usually covered) one ounce of herb in 2 cups of water for 20 to 30 minutes. (To steep, bring the water to a boil and then turn off the heat *before* adding the herbs.) An infusion is usually taken 1/4 to 1/2 cup at a time as needed. If you are a beginner, practice with the tea form of preparation first before going for the infusion or decoction. An infusion is made from the more delicate forms or parts of herbs such as flowers, leaves, powdered herbs of any type, and delicate, thin stems (either fresh or dried), all of which need to be steeped (as opposed to simmered) to extract them. If you want to make a concentrate of a plant part that is "tougher," such as roots, barks, nut shells, woody stems, etc., this would be simmered (not steeped) and is called a decoction (see Decoction heading in this list).

If you are combining herbs that call for different preparation methods (i.e., steeping and simmering) simply prepare the simmered herbs first, strain them out when their preparation is finished, and steep the "steeping herbs" in that hot brew for the time called for.

Start with the purest water possible and avoid using aluminum or cast iron pans in preparing herbal mixtures. (See Lesson #3: Utensils.)

Beware of "stronger is better" thinking which says that a decoction or infusion must always be better than the strength of a simpler ordinary cup of tea. My new students are often surprised at the results from an average strength cup of tea. However, as you gain experience you will be able to recognize those situations that do call for a stronger brew such as a decoction, infusion, or tincture. You may find it is more convenient to take fewer doses of an herb (which is accomplished with a stronger brew), or that a situation does call for a stronger and more concentrated action than a simple cup of tea provides.

Review Dosage Equivalents in this list for help in making the proper substitutions from a cup of tea to an infusion, etc.

LOZENGE: If you want to make throat (or cough) lozenges, first make an herbal syrup as a base. Begin by heating 1 cup honey or molasses to the "hard-crack" stage on a candy thermometer. The next step is to add 1/4 cup powdered or chunked herbs for about 10 minutes of simmering or steeping. At this point if powdered herbs were used, they are left in the lozenge. If chunked herbs were used, they are usually strained out for aesthetic reasons. It won't matter if the honey cools off somewhat when the herbs are added if the syrup was already brought to the "hard-crack" stage of heat. The reason you add the herbs second is that it takes a good while (perhaps half an hour or more) to get the honey or molasses hot enough and sometimes this is long enough to overcook the herbs. Spread (or place in small blobs) this hot mixture onto a buttered cookie sheet to cool into tasty bits to suck on. As the mixture cools part way it is easy to score it with lines to facilitate breaking it up later. Don't forget to butter the cookie sheet as this tasty idea can stick onto an unbuttered cookie sheet in an extreme manner that you don't want to experience. (Do you?)

Use these lozenges freely as desired and experiment with the proportions of herb to syrup, and with cooking methods, once you have the basic idea. Good herbs to start with are Onion or Slippery Elm. See the Cough or Congestion applications in those chapters (Chapters VIII and X).

NASAL RINSE: Using a well-strained herbal tea of a comfortable temperature, gently breathe the tea up one nostril (hold the other one closed) until the tea begins to drain down into the back of your throat. Spit out the tea from the mouth and blow your nose as needed. You might use a cup to hold the tea up to the nostril for this procedure. Do the procedure on the other nostril. Repeat the nasal rinse, one nostril at a time, as needed.

PILLS: See Honeyball and Bolus sections in this list. If you are following the bolus instructions, use the *water method* and form the herbs into a convenient pill size.

RICE PAPER: You can buy small packets of this special paper, made of rice starch, at many health or herb stores. It is a good alternative to capsules for taking herbal powders. A dose of herb powders is simply wrapped in the rice paper and swallowed with water as a pill or capsule would be.

SUPPOSITORY: A suppository is for insertion into the anus, often for help with hemorrhoids. To make a suppository, see the Bolus application above and follow the instructions for making a bolus using the *cocoa butter or water* methods. Shape the suppository for easy insertion into the anus. A bolus and a suppository are essentially the same thing. It is only their names which are different to indicate their use.

SWEETENERS: Good sweeteners to use in herbal preparations, when they are needed, are raw honey, unsulphured blackstrap molasses (light or dark), glycerin (from a drug or health store), or barley malt (from a health food store). Additionally, powdered herbs could be mixed in a sweet spoonful of applesauce or honey. Also see Children's Ideas above. (Review Honey, Appendix B.)

Please avoid using processed sugar and synthetic sweeteners (sugar substitutes) in herbal preparations as these do not have positive results for physical and emotional well-being.

SYRUP: A Syrup is a great form of herbal preparation for administering to children, for making cough syrups or for preparing herbal elixirs and tonics. Here is a basic syrup recipe from which you can continue to create potions. (Also see Lozenge, in this list.)

BASIC HERBAL SYRUP

Mix 1/4 cup (4 Tbsp.) powdered or chunked herb or herb mixture with 1 cup raw honey or light unsulphured molasses in a saucepan. Heat the mixture and simmer gently or steep for 20 minutes while stirring occasionally. Strain. Use freely by the teaspoon for younger children (under 8) and by the tablespoon for older children and adults as often as every hour if it is for a cough. That's it! If you want it thinner, feel free to add a little water. If you started with powder, it will be a thicker brew as you do not (cannot) strain it out. If you started with the herbal chunks, you will get a juicier brew as the chunks are strained out after brewing. Some people really like having the herb powder left in for extra potency and some find the texture not to their liking and prefer to strain the herb out. It is an esoteric and

personal decision. Of course this recipe is a basic starting place and I expect you to experiment freely with proportions to suit your needs.

Slippery Elm or Onion make a great herbal syrup. Look in the Cough or Congestion applications in those chapters to get started (Chapters VIII and X).

TEA: To make an herbal tea, the rule of thumb is 1 teaspoon of herb per cup of water, steeped or simmered for 10 to 15 minutes. Flowers, leaves, powdered herbs, and delicate stems are steeped. Fresh green, (undried), herbs or heavier plant parts such as roots, bark and woody stems should be simmered slowly (not a fast hard boiling, please). Steeping and simmering are both done with a lid on the pan to preserve volatile oils and plant nutrients from evaporating. An exception to this is if you intentionally want to evaporate, and thereby concentrate, a tea. In this case use no cover (for quickest evaporation), or leave the cover somewhat loose (for slowest evaporation).

If you are combining herbs that call for different preparation methods (i.e., steeping and simmering) simply prepare the simmered herbs first, strain them out when their preparation is finished and steep the "steeping herbs" in that hot brew for the time called for.

Start with the purest water possible and avoid using aluminum or cast iron pans in preparing herb teas. (See Lesson #3: Utensils.)

TINCTURES: These are herbal concentrates most often prepared in an alcohol, glycerin or vinegar base. They can be bought commercially or often made at home. Tinctures are sometimes used in place of capsules, tea or other application forms for convenience or more concentrated effect. For the purposes of this book, the art of tincture-making is not discussed in depth. However I have starred several good sources of instruction in the Resource Guide, Appendix C, at the back of this book. One good source is *Natural Healing With Herbs*, by Humbart Santillo. Also see the Yarrow Tincture application in the Yarrow chapter (Chapter XI) for a simple basic recipe.

APPLICATION METHODS - EXTERNAL USE:
BATH
FOMENTATION/PACK
LINIMENT
PEOPLE PASTE
POULTICE/PLASTER
POWDERED HERBS
SALVE
SOAK

BATH: For an herbal bath I make 2 to 4 quarts of decoction or infusion (see Decoction or Infusion applications, above), strain it, and add that to a tub of bath water. When adding a powdered herb directly to a bath, I generally start with 1/4 cup of herb because this is usually mild enough for anyone and then I may work up from there. Sometimes I take the powdered herb and steep it on the stove for 10 or 20 minutes for extra activation and then add the whole mixture to the bath. Powdered herbs rinse down the drain easily — no problem. Yet another method is to take chopped fresh or dried herbs, wrap them in cheesecloth, and put this herbal package directly into a bath of hot water as it is filling up. This makes a mild "tea" right in the tub and is fine in cases where you want a milder brew in the bath. Many herbs among the Ten Essentials make great baths, including Ginger, Peppermint, Yarrow, and Comfrey.

FOMENTATION: This method is very similar to a poultice; however in this case a cloth is soaked in an infusion or decoction (see Decoction and Infusion applications above, in the Internal Use list) from which all the herb has been strained. The soaked cloth is then applied to the body. A fomentation has no herb fiber present whereas a poultice does. It is sometimes helpful to keep the fomentation warm by covering it with a heating pad or hot water bottle. Be sure to also look at the instructions under the "Poultice" application below.

LINIMENT: A liniment is a liquid preparation that is generally rubbed into sore muscles and joints or into areas needing improved circulation such as in chillblains and frostbite. Liniments are easily made by making a decoction or infusion and then adding 1/4 to 1/2 part olive oil and/or rubbing alcohol to get the consistency desired (also see Lesson #6). Another method would be to soak herbs, using infusion or decoction proportions, in rubbing alcohol for one or two weeks, strain the mixture, and then add the desired amount of olive, sesame, or almond oil into the herbal rubbing alcohol for a liniment.

Powdered herbs such as Cayenne or Ginger could be soaked in the rubbing alcohol as above, and then left in the alcohol and used as part of the liniment.

PEOPLE PASTE: See People Paste, Appendix A.

POULTICE/PLASTER: A poultice, generally, is a preparation of the fresh, dry, ground, or powdered form of an herb or herbal mixture that is applied directly to skin or wrapped in thin cotton or wool cloth and then applied.

There are many words that basically mean poultice and some herbalists use them interchangeably. For your information I will describe them separately here because it is good to know how the terms will be used in resource materials.

Poultices can be made from dried or fresh herbs. Usually the more tender parts such as leaves or flowers are used in a poultice, as roots are too rough and are generally made into a fomentation (herbs strained out).

To make a poultice, with dry herbs, activate them in a small amount of boiling hot water, steeped or simmered (see Decoction of Infusion applications) 10 to 30 minutes and applied to the body part as needed. (Apply very warm or at room temperature.) When getting the herbs activated and moistened for a poultice, use enough water to have a wet and pliable preparation but a smaller amount of hot water than you would use for actually making a decoction or infusion. This is a practical detail to learn or you'll end up with a soupy mess. A soupy mess will still work fine, but you may want to strain it a bit.

To keep a poultice damp, when this is called for, I cover the poultice with plastic wrap or a cut-up plastic bag and tape the edges all around onto the skin with breathable surgical tape. Any tape will do in an emergency, but many types of tape will very quickly cause a rashy irritation on the skin. I have found that breathable surgical tape (purchased at drug stores) usually prevents this. To help keep a poultice warm, when this is called for, you may try a hot water bottle or a heating pad held or wrapped over the damp poultice. An additional cloth may be laid over a wet poultice to prevent a heating pad from contacting the wetness.

In the case of a fresh herb poultice such as raw Onion or fresh Comfrey leaves, simply slice, grind, or pulverize the plant material into a convenient form, adding a small amount of hot water to the poultice if needed to achieve the proper activation or consistency (e.g., fresh, ground up Comfrey leaves will require a little hot water).

If a bruise, bite, etc., is not too large, I will probably tape a conveniently-sized slice of Onion or Garlic over it. This "slice poultice" is quick, and easy to hold in place. For more serious situations like an open wound, I generally prepare the appropriate poultice in a form that provides a thick and potent herbal pulp that will mold to contours more effectively. For a bug bite, poison ivy, or small wound, an almost instant poultice can be made outdoors by identifying and collecting a few leaves of a convenient herb (such as Yarrow or Comfrey), chewing them into a pulp, and applying them immediately.

A plaster is quite similar to a poultice (and I use the words interchangeably) yet specifically the word "plaster" is used to refer to powdered herbs moistened into a paste and then spread (like frosting on a cake) about 1/8 to 1/4 inch thick onto a natural fiber cloth which is then applied to the skin, sticky side down. Use a moistening agent such as aloe vera gel (great for burns and skin rejuvenation as well as being a natural antiseptic), honey (full of minerals and enzymes, and good as both a tissue rejuvenator and a natural antiseptic), glycerin (an emollient, a good carrier, and extremely soothing), water, unsulphured blackstrap molasses (has lots of healing minerals and iron), olive oil (or other healing oil like sesame or almond), etc.

Which moistening agent you choose, as well as the temperature of it, depends upon the application. Honey works great on just about everything, so if you are in doubt, go for the honey when making this type of plaster or poultice. (See Honey, Appendix B.)

Another word you may sometimes hear or read is fomentation. A fomentation is a a type of poultice (herbs strained out) in which a cloth is soaked in a decoction or infusion and applied to the area of need. (Please review the Fomentation application in this list.)

Poultices/plasters/fomentations can be left on from 20 minutes to overnight depending on need. In severe cases they can be used continuously as long as the affected area is washed regularly with an antiseptic herb (Yarrow, Chaparral, Garlic water, Clove) or other antiseptic wash. In such cases the poultice is changed at regular intervals, perhaps two to four times a day, to keep it fresh. When leaving a poultice on overnight, change it first thing in the morning.

POWDERED HERBS: Powdered herbs can be applied directly onto a wound, rash, insect bite, etc., or can be mixed with an appropriate moistening agent to form varieties of paste-like poultices. Some common moistening agents, used according to the need of a particular circumstance, are: aloe vera gel, honey, olive oil, water, glycerin. (See People Paste, Appendix A, for additional examples of powdered herb use.)

SALVE: Any of the Ten Essentials can be made into the convenient form of an herbal salve by preparing them in olive oil. A common proportion is 3 or 4 Tbsp. of herb(s) per cup of oil. Depending upon the herb's texture, steep or very slowly simmer (see Tea application in this list) the herb/oil mixture for about one hour. This concentrated herbal oil can be used as is, or thickened with beeswax to the consistency of a lotion or salve by regulating the amount of beeswax added. Start with 4 Tbsp. of melted beeswax added to 1 cup of the warm herbal oil and stir while the salve cools and thickens. If the preparation is too loose you can always warm it up and add more beeswax.

SOAK: Bruises, sprains, rashes, insect bites, infections, etc., often require or benefit from soaking. The soaking liquid is a decoction or infusion (see Decoction or Infusion applications) made of the desired herb(s) for the purpose. To help soothe and heal the effects of a trauma, strain or stress, a rash, etc., for the entire body, an herbal bath is the greatest! (See Bath application.)

LESSON #3: UTENSILS FOR HERBAL PREPARATIONS

In preparing any herbal substance it is wise to pay attention to the type of utensils used. For brewing concoctions, such as tea, on the stove, it is always best to avoid using aluminum or cast iron pots. These metals often disintegrate with cooking and boiling, thereby becoming an unhealthy part of the herbal preparation. Stainless steel, glass, or ceramic pots and bowls are good choices for making herb tea, mixing powdered formulas and making other preparations. Use stainless steel stirring spoons whenever possible or, as I do, keep a set of clean wooden spoons aside that are used for nothing else except making your herbal preparations. For a tea strainer, it is best to get stainless steel or bamboo reed as, again, these materials will act in a positive way with the herbs.

LESSON #4: POTENCY OF HERBS AND THE FORMS THEY COME IN

For the most efficient action of the herb, unless otherwise specified, take it on an empty stomach as a tea, or, for other forms such as capsules, with a full glass of water. This allows for maximum impact of the herb without its being diluted and buried in the digestive action of a stomach full of food.

Occasionally an herb or herbal formula is uncomfortable to an empty stomach. If this is the case it is a good idea to add a buffering and/or stimulating herb to the formula, such as Ginger, Slippery Elm, or Comfrey, or to take the herb with a small bite or two of simple food such as fruit. This almost always works well, yet you can take the herbs with a meal or light snack if you must.

Here is some input on the quality and potency of the herbs you keep on hand. In herbistry we are always on the look-out for the freshest, most potent, properly harvested and dried, and least contaminated materials available. In the U.S., spices (a category which includes many medicinal herbs) are one of the most commonly irradiated, sprayed, and fumigated foods (especially the imported ones, which most of them are). Whenever possible, therefore, many herbalists prefer to grow and dry their own plants to insure potency and purity. There is also a growing availability in the U.S. of "wildcrafted," organic medicinal plants, which are plants grown and/or gathered wild within the country. These are usually unsprayed, un-irradiated, carefully dried in smaller batches, and generally handled in ways that ensure they retain a strong potency. At most herb and health food stores the most commonly available medicinal herbs come from growers/importers whose methods range from "good" to "terrible." (See Herb Buyers Guide, Appendix D.)

You can begin to become an educated buyer simply by drying small amounts of fresh herbs, or any plants for that matter, in a dry and "darkish" place (a dim room, cupboard, well-shaded patio). You will see first-hand what carefully dried plant material should look like. Ideally it should keep much of its color, be free of mold, have the fresh smell of the plant and plant oils especially when rubbed or ground up, and be free of obvious contaminations such as insects and dirt. As a consumer you should know what to look for and if you see, for instance, dried Comfrey leaves that are brownish instead of a good green color, or Clove powder that looks pale and has no aroma—don't buy it. Grocery stores are usually the last choice as a source of dried herbs for medicinal purposes except in an emergency. Grocery stores usually offer spices (many used medicinally) which are often irradiated or fumigated by the large importers to kill insects and ensure indefinite shelf life. These herbs tend to be on the shelf longer than the higher turn-over products of an herb store. However, I have handled many an emergency with what I could find at a grocery store, so consider these a possible source for getting what you need on short notice.

When you go to shop for herbs you will quickly see that they come in many bulk forms and commercial preparations, each having its practical uses. For our purposes throughout this book I am going to be referring to the commonly available bulk forms from which everything else is prepared. Dried bulk herbs generally come whole, chopped, shredded, or powdered. Fresh herbs can come from the live plant, a grower, or often, the grocery store.

Throughout the book I will be suggesting the use of many different forms of each herb for particular applications. For example, I might suggest using the dried leaves of Peppermint for making a tea, the Peppermint oil for a quick digestion tonic, a powdered form of an herb for a poultice, or a fresh form for eating as a food. Each herb chapter contains some short instructions on the use of the various forms of that herb. Lesson #2 in Chapter I provides a comprehensive, alphabetical listing of application methods with instructions and definitions. It should be easy, therefore, to determine the best application method for the varied forms of herbs.

LESSON #5: HOW TO STORE YOUR HERBS

In storing herbs, we want to keep them cool (but not frozen), dry, out of direct light, and free of insects and other contaminations. Airtight glass containers are best for prolonging potency with dried herbs, yet brown paper bags or plastic baggies can be satisfactory and are often used for practical reasons even though herbal potency is less protected. Empty 35mm film containers are a great size for storing small amounts of herbs in glove compartments, backpacks, cupboards, workshops, etc. The lids seem airtight and waterproof and these containers are made of a hard and opaque plastic that does not deteriorate into the herbs very easily, even in heat. I have found an endless and free supply of these containers from my local camera shop. I often use them to send herbs home with friends, or to school and job sites for myself and others. There are some herbs among the Ten Essentials that can be used in their "fresh food" state, such as Garlic, Ginger and Onions. These are stored in such a way as to keep them fresh and potent, perhaps in a cool, dry cabinet.

Dried herbs can keep their potency quite well if they start off potent, and are dried and stored properly. For instance, I have kept Comfrey leaves, which I gathered and dried myself, for a year and more. At the end of a year they were still very active in medicinal properties as evidenced by the results I was getting. However, for the average quality of herbs bought in an herb, health, or grocery store, it is best to buy one month's supply at a time. If this is not practical for your circumstance, renew your herbal supplies every three to four months if you are unsure of their source or potency.

An herbal brew can be kept in the refrigerator for a day or two and will still be of medicinal strength. By the end of the second day of storage, even if kept in a refrigerator, in most cases a water-based potion will not be of the best medicinal strength. I say "medicinal strength" because if you made a tea only for drinking pleasure, in that case it would be good as long as the flavor was pleasing. If you make a decoction or infusion and want it to last a week or two, simply add 1/4 part (by volume) of fresh wine to the brew and store in the refrigerator.

Always keep herbs labeled clearly with ink or marker that doesn't rub off or smear easily. It won't do any good to have the Ten Essentials on hand if you forget what's what and find them unlabeled!

LESSON #6: USE THE TEN ESSENTIALS SEPARATELY OR IN COMBINATIONS

The Ten Essential Herbs are often profitably mixed together for their mutual enhancement. As soon as you feel familiar with two herbs that can be used for the same application (for example, Cayenne and Comfrey for ulcers), you will be able to consider the question of what herbs to mix together and when to mix them. In many cases throughout the chapters I give specific suggestions for the mixing of the Ten Essentials, but this is only the beginning of the creative possibilities.

For example, let's say you have a particular interest in learning about self-help for bleeding ulcers. You look up "Ulcers" in the Index. Several references will be listed. Consult these. You will be referred to the Cayenne chapter, for instance, and will learn that Cayenne stops or slows internal bleeding of ulcers while increasing circulation. In the Comfrey reference you will find that Comfrey rebuilds damaged tissues. Peppermint, you will see, breaks up gas in the stomach while assuaging acidity, and Slippery Elm will soothe mucous membranes in the digestive tract while relieving diarrhea. You would choose the herbal actions you want to emphasize (which might be one or all of the ones I have mentioned) and begin by mixing your chosen herbs together as I will explain.

Start your experimentation in combining herbs by simply mixing the desired herbs together in equal parts. As you gain experience you will learn to refine your "mixings" — making one or two herbs the predominant parts of a formula with one or two others in a minor role. For instance, in the present example you might decide to have Comfrey and

Cayenne predominate in the formula as equal parts while adding Peppermint and Slippery Elm in half parts, thereby having them play a more minor role. The *general* formula would be written like this:

1 part Comfrey
1 part Cayenne
1/2 part Peppermint
1/2 part Slippery Elm

For the purposes of these Ten Essentials, a "part" is measured by volume and is whatever you decide it is before mixing the formula. This depends upon how much of the formula you want to make. For instance, a "part" could be 1 tsp. or 1 Tbsp. or 1/4 cup, etc. If you decide to make 1 part equal to 1/4 cup (in the example above) the *specific* formula would look like this:

1/4 cup Comfrey
1/4 cup Cayenne
1/8 cup Peppermint
1/8 cup Slippery Elm

If you want to put this formula into capsules, you would use the herbs in their powdered form. If you want to make a tea, you would mix the herbs in their crumbled or chopped form. Choose a form that is convenient to your purpose.

Two "carrier" herbs in the Ten Essentials are Cayenne and Ginger. Each of these herbs has potent qualities of its own that might call for it to be used as a major part of a formula. These herbs also play the role of carrying, binding, and enhancing the overall actions of any formula in which they are present. Therefore, in any formula in which they are not already present as a major action, they are often added in a small amount. In herbistry we call this a "carrier." In general, in my own formulas, I always add 1/8 to 1/4 parts of Cayenne and/or Ginger as carriers, if they are not already present in a formula in a more prominent capacity.

The purpose of **Ten Essential Herbs** is to give you a strong foundation in using herbs for your own health. When you have progressed to the point of wanting additional specifics about making formulas, tinctures, etc., you will want to investigate detailed references on this information such as are found in *Natural Healing With Herbs*, by Humbart Santillo. However, the information I have outlined in this book, and in these six lessons, provides a fine basis and may be all you will want to pursue.

CAYENNE

TO STOMACH
SUPER DIGESTIVE POWER!
NO NEED TO BE SHOCKED
"CARRIER" HERB
NO U TURN
HEART FEELS GOOD!
SUPERIOR CIRCULATION!
CAYENNE
HEY! THAT'S NOT HOT AT ALL!
KJohansen

CHAPTER II

CAYENNE

Capsicum anuum

Cayenne's for bleeding, Cayenne's for shock
For ulcers, to build blood, don't go into hock.
To strengthen a heart and spiff up circulation
Meet up with Cayenne—it's a healthy sensation.

PERSONALITY PROFILE—Cayenne

In talking about Cayenne, I am talking about the ordinary, hot, red pepper that most people associate with spicy food.

Perhaps you have heard stories of spicy foods contributing to ulcers, along with warnings to avoid hot peppers. You may be wondering why it is a recommended herbal remedy for numerous conditions. In my experience and study, however, the paradox is really quite simple. In herbistry, Cayenne is used in the dry, usually powdered, form and NEVER used in a cooked or raw form. **Cayenne in its *dried and uncooked form* and in the proper dosage is a number one healer of bleeding ulcers in the digestive tract. Cayenne in its *cooked form* is a major irritation to the digestive tract and may contribute to ulcerous conditions. Therefore for purposes of self-help in herbistry one would never inflict cooked Cayenne or raw (undried) Cayenne peppers on one's digestive tract.**

Cooking Cayenne seems to turn the natural plant acids into a very caustic substance that burns the delicate digestive linings. The acids in fresh, raw hot peppers have a similar effect. Drying the hot peppers, however, cures the acids in such a way as to enhance their healing properties while minimizing any caustic effect. In cooking food that calls for hot spices to be added, I have found it best to add dried Cayenne to the food after it is cooked, just prior to serving. In this way one gets a healthy benefit along with the desired flavor and avoids the irritations to the digestive linings.

Over and over again in my years of herbistry I have witnessed friends totally "wowed" by the experience that ingesting dried, uncooked Cayenne on a daily basis, and in the proper dosage, not only helps heal bleeding ulcers, but goes a long way toward strengthening digestion altogether, thus preventing further digestive inconveniences. This has been true even for those friends who had years of history behind them of hugging up to their bottles of anti-acid preparations and stomach ulcer protectors after every meal!

There are a few herbs, Cayenne among them, that have an outstanding personality trait of being quite efficient as a "carrier herb." Cayenne is often mixed, 1/8 part or more, into herbal formulas or with single herbs. The Cayenne will help hasten that formula or herb's being picked up by the blood and dispersed within the tissues and organs where it is needed, while greatly encouraging the body and the herbs to work potently together. Although it is a carrier herb to all parts of the body, epecially via the blood stream, it is particularly effective in carrying and dispersing the healing agents into the upper half of the body (above the waist). This is one reason that we often find Cayenne used with herbs intended to help the heart, stomach, or head, for instance.

You may be interested to know that there are lots of choices of Cayenne purchases out there in the world, including different shades of reds and oranges. In ordinary grocery stores, Cayenne is sometimes labeled as "mild," "medium," "hot." If you have access to herb supplies from an herb or health food store, however, you'll find the hotness of Cayenne is often rated in the thousands of HUs (heat units). This includes everything from the average, Chinese varieties rated in the 40,000 HUs to the "blast-your-tongue" hotness of African Bird Pepper, often rated at 100,000 HU's and more.

In my early days of herbistry I was a bit impatient and often thought "more is probably better, stronger, or at least faster." I quickly wised up to the fact that the hottest Cayennes are overkill—creating torturously hot tongue and bowel experiences, totally unnecessary to the desired healing effect. Now that I am a Cayenne connoisseur of many years' standing, I can confidently advise others to choose a Cayenne of good flavor, color, and hotness that suits their own needs. If you happen to be one of those people who winces at the thought of anything spicy coming near your tongue or stomach, then start with a mild Cayenne and a tiny pinch of a dose in juice, building up from there to the amount and type of Cayenne needed for your purposes. Tolerance can vary a great deal from person to person and Cayenne to Cayenne.

Cayenne is the #1 choice in herbistry for help with shock and internal bleeding, even with pets and livestock. I have saved many a pet and stray animal from an undignified and untimely demise by administering dry Cayenne directly onto the tongue.

TASOLE: Once while out driving to the store, I passed a puppy lying in the road. It had just been hit by a car. Surrounded by helpless bystanders, the poor animal was near death with internal bleeding and shock. In the car with me were a couple of teenage neighbors who recognized some of their friends in the crowd and were trying to convince me not to stop because my herbs and unconventional methods would embarrass them. We compromised. They hid in the back seat while I went to check the puppy.

I learned that the accident had happened minutes ago. A slow trickle of blood from his nose and mouth indicated internal bleeding. His eyes were totally glazed over, and he did not move except for his shallow breathing.

Over a period of about five minutes I administered three or four small pinches of Cayenne directly onto the puppy's tongue with immediate results. The bleeding from the nose and mouth stopped, and the glazed look started lifting from his eyes. He weakly licked the bits of Cayenne off his lips with no sign of noticing any hotness. As the shock wore off (about the third dose) he shook his head, opened his eyes wide, and staggered to his feet as best he could with my help. It was clear he noticed the Cayenne now! One of the teenage bystanders volunteered to take the puppy home, and I instructed him to take my little bag of Cayenne and administer one or two more doses over the next hour or so.

I went home and thought nothing more about it. The next day, however, my teenage neighbors (who had hidden in my car during the dog drama), came over to report that there was an incredible story going around their school about a woman who had cured an almost dead puppy with a miraculous red powder. A policeman, brother of one of the teenage bystanders, had taken the powder to the crime lab to have it analyzed. (No one at the scene had believed it was simply Cayenne.)

My neighbors confessed they had acted appropriately surprised when hearing this story at their school, claiming they had never heard of such a thing, since they were too embarrassed to admit they had been present. Later that year, however, I observed one of them giving Cayenne to another animal in crisis and felt good that some knowledge had been passed on.

An important process is initiated in the mouth, brain, and digestive tract when Cayenne interacts with the saliva and enzymes in the mouth. For this reason, do not choose capsules over plain powder except when you really need to and only when your stomach agrees. Many stomachs do not like to be surprised in this way when the capsules suddenly melt and release their contents.

I have often known students, especially if they are parents, to hesitate to use Cayenne for children's needs for fear of harming them with Cayenne's spicy hotness. My experience has shown me that if the hotness of Cayenne is explained to a child, even an infant, with language that warns him to expect some hotness but assures him that it won't last and it will help his body, the child is able to handle it much more easefully than most adults expect. Sometimes I mix Cayenne with a little honey before giving it to children, and I always have plain juice or water on hand (or the nursing mother for an infant) so that a cooling drink can be offered immediately.

TASOLE: Twice in my life I have lived and worked in situations that included at least 11 children from the age of 2 months to 10 years. In both cases I was amazed to see how fast the children caught on to using Cayenne to help each other whenever they had a shock from falling or roughhousing in some way. Once while supervising the children's playground, I heard the sound of a small body falling from a slide. Upon running over I saw the crying child calling to a friend, "Kaiwen! Kaiwen! Get the Kaiwen!" After two small sips of Cayenne in water, the crisis was over and emotional equilibrium restored.

I never suggest forcing a child to take Cayenne, or any herb for that matter, unless it is a life or death emergency. Usually there is more than one good way to handle a health need and if a child indicates he/she does not want to use Cayenne,there is rarely a need to push it on them.

Since Cayenne is so frequently the herb of choice for first aid in emergencies, I generally do not slow down to measure exact amounts. Rather, I throw an approximate amount of the Cayenne powder in a glass with water or juice (or use it dry) and administer swallows to myself or others every one to three minutes until the desired effect is reached.

For more stories about the use of Cayenne, read through some of the TASOLES under the application headings below. A well known contemporary herbalist named Dr. John R. Christopher has also written an entire 160-page book solely about Cayenne and all its healing uses. The book is entitled simply *Capsicum*. If you are intrigued by my experiences here, then you may want to look at his work later on. See Resource Guide, Appendix C.

APPLICATIONS AND ATTRIBUTES - CAYENNE

(Quick Reference List)

BIRTHS
BLEEDING
BLOOD BUILDER
BREATHING
CAFFEINE WITHDRAWAL
CIRCULATION
COLDS AND FLU
CONSTIPATION
DIGESTION
EYEWASH
FAINTING
FIRST AID
FLU
FROSTBITE
GARDENS
GARGLE
GUMS
HAIR OIL
HEART ATTACK
HEART PALPITATIONS
HEART TONIC
HOME BIRTHS
INTESTINAL BACTERIA
LINIMENT
MOUTH
OVERDOSE OF CAYENNE
PETS
PLANTS
SCALP
SHOCK
SINUS
STIMULANT
THROAT
ULCERS
VARICOSE VEINS

FORM:

Dried powder, dried whole Cayenne pepper

APPLICATION METHODS:

Internally Cayenne is used dry, mixed in juice, water, honey, or made as a tea. A tincture is sometimes used, but I have not found Cayenne tincture to be as potent and efficient for shock, bleeding, or heart attack as the dry powdered herb.

Externally Cayenne is used mostly as a powder to stop bleeding or as a tincture/liniment for sprains or circulation enhancement.

AVAILABILITY:

Grocery store, herb store, health store. Grow and dry your own. Mail order. Open air markets around the world.

HINTS/CAUTIONS:

In learning the doses listed below, please note that *it is not always necessary to take the whole suggested amount or to be limited to the suggested amount*. It is better to start with small amounts and work up, so as not to overstimulate body activities. Review the Overdose of Cayenne application below.

GENERAL DOSAGE: INTERNAL USE

*PLEASE NOTE: *Although in many cases I emphasize using dry powdered Cayenne, there are other forms of herbal preparations such as Capsule, Infusion, Children's Preparations, etc. that are useful to know about. See Dosage Equivalents in Chapter I, Lesson #2.*

Infants to 3 years: A few grains up to a small pinch (less than 1/16 tsp.) of Cayenne directly on tongue or mixed with approximately 1/4 cup water or juice and administered with a dropper, spoon, or cup in small increments to gauge the results "as you go". Adjust the dose according to results. Rarely is a second dose called for in infant usage, yet in an emergency, such as shock or bleeding, a second dose may be needed.

Children 4 to 10 years: 1/8 to 1/4 tsp. usually in 1/2 cup water or juice but can be taken dry in an emergency. Take the needed amount directly into the mouth in small increments (pinches or swallows) to gauge the results "as you go". Adjust the dose according to results.

Children 11 years to Adults: 1/8 tsp. to 1/2 tsp. or more, dry or in 1/2 cup water or juice. Take the needed amount directly into the mouth in small increments (pinches or swallows) to gauge the results "as you go". Adjust the dose according to results.

Pets and Other Creatures: Appropriate size pinch of Cayenne directly on the tongue, under lip, outside of lip (to be licked off), edge of beak, etc. A horse-size animal can take two or more tsp. (for shock or internal bleeding)—with no problem! I haven't found the upper limit but I wouldn't hesitate to give a tablespoonful to a horse in an emergency.

GENERAL DOSAGE: EXTERNAL USE

Same For People And Pets

Externally Cayenne is sprinkled (a light coating up to 1/16 inch or more) into wounds and cuts to help stop bleeding and take the shock out of the wound. Cayenne can also be used as a stimulating liniment. I do not recommend using Cayenne as an ongoing poultice (longer than 5 or 10 minutes) covering larger areas of human skin as this can often be too strong and might leave a temporary red patch that can be uncomfortable.

APPLICATIONS AND ATTRIBUTES - CAYENNE

BIRTHS: See Home Births

BLEEDING: For internal bleeding from accident or ulcers, Cayenne is taken according to general dosages given above. Cayenne is good for first aid prior to medical treatment, especially as internal bleeding from accidents often leads to shock. If fluids can't be given, use small amounts of Cayenne, dry, directly on the tongue.

Externally Cayenne is sprinkled into wounds and cuts (a light coating up to 1/16 inch or more) to help stop bleeding and take the shock out of the wound.

TASOLE: Surprisingly, Cayenne usually doesn't sting when used externally for bleeding. I used to say it *never* stung because I had used it so much, even on axe wounds, with no stinging at all. But one day I cut the tip off my own finger, and when I put Cayenne on it I was hooting around my kitchen like a banshee. This wound had many more exposed nerve endings than your average cut or gash. In any case, now I say it *usually* doesn't sting and there is always Comfrey root powder as a great alternative.

ALSO SEE: *Circulation, Shock, Ulcers*

ALTERNATIVE OR SUPPLEMENTARY SELF-HELP: **Comfrey, People Paste, Slippery Elm*

DOSAGE: *General*

BLOOD BUILDER: The same mixture mentioned below under the Caffeine Withdrawal application is an excellent blood builder tonic. Mix 1/4 tsp. to 1 tsp. Cayenne (or start with as little as you need to and work up from there) in 1/2 cup grape juice and drink this dose one to three times a day. Grape juice (no sugar added is much preferred) is high in vitamin C, iron, and natural fruit sugars. Cayenne is high in vitamin C, and easily assimilated calcium. The circulation and "carrier" qualities of the Cayenne enable these nutritional attributes to be carried quickly into the blood in a form readily used by the body. I have observed this mixture to efficiently build up iron poor, or "tired" blood, often more effectively than standard iron supplements, probably because of its ability to assimilate so easily.

TASOLE: I have observed that lay midwives are often concerned that their clients have a strong iron level in the blood. So, using hemoglobin centrifuges to test the iron count, I once did some experiments comparing normal iron supplements, this Cayenne blood-building tonic, and nothing. Admittedly this was an amateurish adventure, yet in almost every case of the ten or so friends I tested, the Cayenne blood-builder brought the hemoglobin level (iron indicator) up much stronger and faster than either the standard supplements or nothing. This accorded perfectly with my own observations of the tonic's usage over the years, and I was certainly pleased at the machine's verification.

ALSO SEE: *Circulation, Caffeine Withdrawal, Overdose of Cayenne*

ALTERNATIVE OR SUPPLEMENTARY SELF-HELP: **Comfrey, Garlic, Onion, *Yarrow*

DOSAGE: *General and as given*

BLOOD PRESSURE (high and low): Because of Cayenne's great circulation balancing qualities, it is very good for balancing both high and low blood pressure, although it is most commonly used for help with low blood pressure.

ALSO SEE: *Blood Builder, Circulation*

ALTERNATIVE OR SUPPLEMENTARY SELF-HELP: *Comfrey, *Garlic (for high blood pressure), Ginger (for low blood pressure), Onion (for high blood pressure)*

DOSAGE: *General*

BREATHING: I have used Cayenne to help start the breathing function in newborns having initial difficulty. It is also useful for victims of fainting, shock, and emotional trauma. Cayenne can help with difficult breathing due to mucous congestion in head or chest.

ALSO SEE: *Circulation, Shock*

ALTERNATIVE OR SUPPLEMENTARY SELF-HELP: **Comfrey, *Ginger, *Peppermint Oil*

DOSAGE: *General*

CAFFEINE WITHDRAWAL: 1/4 to 1 tsp. Cayenne in 1/2 cup grape juice (could be diluted with water if desired) up to eight times a day for a safe alternative to the caffeine boost. This potion can greatly reduce headache and other common withdrawal symptoms such as shaking and foul mood. Many friends have also found it useful to take 1 gram of calcium ascorbate (a good form of vitamin C—don't use ascorbic acid form) and 3 or 4 calcium lactate tablets every two or three hours for a few days during severe withdrawal.

Watch out! Don't substitute other forms of caffeine, such as caffeinated soft drinks, black tea, or chocolate, when you are trying to stop a coffee habit.

TASOLE: Often I have been asked by truck drivers for help in kicking the caffeine habit. They are concerned, however, about still being able to stay awake on long drives, especially at night. I always suggest carrying the juice and Cayenne tonic in their former coffee thermoses. This mixture can be drunk in swallows as needed while they drive.

Keeping in mind that cooking Cayenne is a no-no, if a hot drink is considered essential, I recommend that the grape juice be warmed (not boiled) prior to putting it into the thermos and *then* the Cayenne could be added.

One or two night-driving friends reported that they overdid it—drinking more than a quart—with the result that they encountered some of those "hot bowel" experiences I mentioned earlier. At my suggestion they took an additional thermos of hot herbal tea to quench their thirst and only used the Cayenne/grape juice mixture every couple of hours or so. This solved the problem.

ALSO SEE: *Blood Builder, Circulation*
ALTERNATIVE OR SUPPLEMENTARY SELF-HELP: *Chaparral, Comfrey, *Ginger, Yarrow*
DOSAGE: *General or as given*

CIRCULATION: Used internally or externally, Cayenne is renowned for helping with circulation.

Internally: Take doses two to four times a day to strengthen the circulatory system, blood vessels and veins; encourage blood to the extremities, and gently dilate capillaries, thereby increasing blood flow and body warmth. This is very good to try for varicose veins, frostbite and other poor circulation problems, such as sinus congestion and many types of digestive distress. Strong, healthy blood circulation to all your body tissues increases your capacity for stamina and recovery from illness.

Enhancing circulation increases the blood's ability to carry out a flushing action in the joints, organs, and other body tissues. This idea comes into play along with the "carrier herb" principle of Cayenne which I described in the Personality Profile. When mixed with other herbs (or when used alone but to a lesser degree), Cayenne excites the other herbs in a formula to greater action and carries them more efficiently into the tissues. I have observed that toxic waste deposits are more efficiently flushed out.

Externally: Sprinkle Cayenne in socks to help stimulate circulation and keep the feet warm while outside on cold winter days. This works somewhat for cold feet while indoors in a stationary position, but it is most effective when one is moving around so the Cayenne works together with the natural blood pumping action. In any case the best treatment of all for cold extremities due to poor circulation is to use Cayenne internally and externally at the same time. Cayenne makes a very effective stimulating liniment.

Remember! If Cayenne is too strong for you by itself, you can mix it with Ginger, which is a milder stimulant, or replace it with Ginger altogether for most of these applications, except perhaps for shock, bleeding and ulcers.

ALSO SEE: *Blood Builder, Caffeine Withdrawal, Heart Attack, Heart Tonic, Liniment, Overdose of Cayenne, Stimulant*

ALTERNATIVE OR SUPPLEMENTARY SELF-HELP: *Garlic, *Ginger, *Peppermint, Yarrow*

DOSAGE: *General*

COLDS AND FLU: Excellent for stimulating circulation and flushing toxins from the system. Cayenne can clear a stuffy head and often perks up a mood from, "This is totally awful, I'm sure I'm on my way to final rest in the herb garden in the sky," to "It's possible I'm recovering; the spots before my eyes are clearing rapidly."

ALSO SEE: *Blood Builder, Circulation, Liniment, Sinus*

ALTERNATIVE OR SUPPLEMENTARY SELF-HELP: **Chaparral, Comfrey, *Garlic, Onion, Peppermint, Yarrow*

DOSAGE: *General*

CONSTIPATION: Because Cayenne can stimulate digestive action in the intestines (peristalsis), one can often help relieve constipation by using Cayenne either regularly or just when an occasional need arises. This is a good remedy to know when you are traveling.

ALSO SEE: *Blood Builder, Digestion*

ALTERNATIVE OR SUPPLEMENTARY SELF-HELP: **Ginger*

DOSAGE: *1/2 tsp. in 1 cup of very warm water as needed.*

DIGESTION: Use Cayenne sprinkled on food and/or in water after a meal, to stimulate digestive fluids and blood flow (circulation) to the stomach. This is good self-help to use when you have overeaten or have eaten food that does not agree with you and that is creating stomach disturbance or digestive headache.

ALSO SEE: *Blood Builder, Circulation, Constipation, Intestinal Bacteria*

ALTERNATIVE OR SUPPLEMENTARY SELF-HELP: *Comfrey, *Ginger, *Peppermint, Slippery Elm, *Yarrow*

DOSAGE: *General*

EYEWASH: Use a few grains of Cayenne in a little warm water, dropped, or washed, or eyecupped through the eyes. Some people like to use more than a few grains, but it is best to start with this small amount. I have found that it usually does the job just fine. The best time to use this eyewash is before sleep so eyes can remain closed several hours, yet I have used it at all times of the day too. This solution tones and strengthens tired, weak eyes. This is an extremely potent tonic for the eyes and yes, it stings somewhat, so I usually pace back and forth a minute before my eyes cool off. After regular use (perhaps every day or three times a week before bed) the stinging dramatically lessens or stops altogether. As the eye tissue is thoroughly cleansed, circulation is greatly increased, and varying degrees of vision improvement with lessening of eye strain may be experienced.

TASOLE: Students and friends have tried this Cayenne Eyewash, but none more effectively than Joan, who had a long history of continually weakening eyes. Her eye doctor could discern no reason for the condition. Just for the adventure of it she decided to try the eyewash each evening for at least a week. After the first three days she noticed less eyeache at her work, but nothing else very dramatic. After the eyewash on the fifth day, she observed some tiny white granules mixed in with the tearing eye fluids that were oozing out from the edges of the eye socket. Joan said that the granules were so minute that she only noticed them because she happened to rub her fingers together after touching her eyes and felt the graininess of the fluids. She thought her hands were dirty and so tested the fluid again and the same graininess was apparent. For the next two evenings the same thing happened to an even greater extent. Because she noticed a definite improvement in her eyesight and eye stamina, she continued this self-help technique. A few nights later she was startled and a bit frightened to find minutely thin slivers of this white grainy substance, about an eighth of an inch long, popping up from the bottom of the eye socket. Yet Joan said she felt a "very great sense of relief" and so she went to bed. This phenomenon did not continue after that although she continued the eyewashes randomly. Her vision and eye stamina remained improved and she was a Cayenne Eyewash advocate from then on.

Of course there are many reasons for poor eyesight and this eyewash should not be considered a cure for physical defects. Yet since some eye weakness is due to toxic build-up of some sort in the eye tissue itself, or chronic eyestrain from a job environment, this eyewash is worth a try for those willing to hop around a bit.

ALSO SEE: *Circulation*

ALTERNATIVE OR SUPPLEMENTARY SELF-HELP: **Comfrey, Slippery Elm, Yarrow*

DOSAGE: *As given*

FAINTING: Use Cayenne to revive an unconscious or fainting person. Since an unconscious person should not be given anything to drink, I simply put a pinch of the dry Cayenne onto the tongue. If this works and the person begins to regain consciousness, you can offer the Cayenne mixed in a little water or juice to continue to help stabilize the system and lessen shock.

ALSO SEE: *Breathing, Circulation, Shock*

ALTERNATIVE OR SUPPLEMENTARY SELF-HELP: *Ginger, *Peppermint oil*

DOSAGE: *General*

FIRST AID: Cayenne is the #1 herb for first aid as it can have a strong stabilizing effect for bleeding, shock, heart attack, and digestive distress. It should always be kept handy in your car, house, workshop, office, or backpacker's knapsack.

ALSO SEE: *Bleeding, Breathing, Fainting, Heart Attack, Home Birth, Shock*

ALTERNATIVE OR SUPPLEMENTARY SELF-HELP: **Comfrey, Onion, People Paste, *Peppermint Oil*

DOSAGE: *General*

FLU: See Colds and Flu application

FROSTBITE: See Circulation and Liniment applications

GARDENS: Blend 1 Tbsp. Cayenne with 2 medium cloves of fresh Garlic in 1 quart soapy water. Use 1 or 2 Tbsp. liquid dish soap to 1 quart of lukewarm water. Use nontoxic soap, especially if this mixture will be used on vegetables. This mixture can be used as a spray bug repellent, fungus fighter, and help for sick plants. It won't harm the plants, even when you are not sure what is wrong with them. It is always worth a try!

ALSO SEE: *None*

ALTERNATIVE OR SUPPLEMENTARY SELF-HELP: **Chaparral, *Garlic, Onion (blend into above mixture)*

DOSAGE: *As given*

GARGLE: See Throat application

GUMS AND ORAL HEALTH: Keep a small container of Cayenne in the bathroom. As a preventive of oral difficulties, dip your wet toothbrush into that Cayenne container and brush gums, tongue and oral surfaces vigorously on a daily basis. A small amount of toothpaste on your toothbrush is fine to mix with the herb (it helps the Cayenne stick on), but don't overdo it. If more than one use is needed in a day, don't use toothpaste every time (just wet the brush). Cayenne stimulates circulation to all the oral tissues, including the gums, which in turn helps flush out accumulations of harmful bacteria and, if used regularly, helps prevent further bacterial build-up.

If gum disease or weak gums are already present, brush with Cayenne as often as necessary—even once every two hours in severe cases. You may be amazed at how fast healthy gums become your constant companion.

For an even stronger tooth and mouth powder, which I have used so far with 100% success on even the most chronic mouth infection problems, mix equal powdered parts of the herbs: Cayenne, goldenseal, and myrrh. (These last two herbs are not among the Ten Essentials but are easily obtained at health stores.) Brush anywhere from twice a day to every two hours in severe cases. What you can expect is that your mouth will certainly sting and tingle temporarily as the great increase in circulation and antibiotic power of the herbs do their job. This sensation lessens greatly as the health of the gums and oral surfaces returns. If you pursue this regime in a disciplined manner, you can expect very noticeable results within hours or at least by the very next day. Continue the regime for at least two more days after outward symptoms are gone.

TASOLE: The worst case of poor oral hygiene I have encountered over the years was in a man in his fifties who, although he no longer smoked, had smoked heavily for most of his life. His dentist pointed out that this had been a major cause of his chronic gum deterioration and very severe bouts of gum infections. This resulted in the need for many gum surgeries, tooth extractions, and frequent use of antibiotics—with all the attendant side effects. Once on a weekend when his dentist was not available, he came to me in a panic because a severe gum infection was flaring up, the pain of eating in this condition was great, and he was afraid of what was to come. His dentist had informed him that any more tooth extractions or gum surgeries at this point would certainly lead quickly to total loss of all his remaining teeth. I mixed him up the stronger version of tooth powder and told him to carry it around with him so that he could brush his gums and all oral surfaces vigorously every two hours even while at work.

The results were fantastic. His gums not only took a dramatic turn toward health within twenty-four hours but, as long as he kept using the powder at least once a day as a follow-up preventive, he reported that he *never* had another oral infection. In fact, in later years he told me that, much to his dentist's surprise, a good deal of his oral deterioration had reversed and his gums were rejuvenating.

In his case a continued use of the tooth powder at least once a day was essential. In other cases where the problem was not so chronic, a temporary use of the herbal tooth powder, or just plain Cayenne, was all that was necessary.

ALSO SEE: *Throat*

ALTERNATIVE OR SUPPLEMENTARY SELF-HELP: *Chaparral, *Clove, Comfrey, Ginger*

DOSAGE: *As given*

HAIR OIL: See Scalp application

HEART ATTACK: Immediately administer 1/4 to 1/2 tsp. Cayenne in water or juice, or apply pinches of dry Cayenne directly on the tongue as necessary. You may repeat the dose again as needed—from once every minute to once every ten minutes—while waiting for medical attention. Of course this does not replace medical treatment, yet on several occasions I have seen it save people's lives by stimulating and balancing the heart and circulation and preventing shock from setting in prior to medical treatment. Cayenne is an important ingredient in many herbal formulas meant for the strengthening and rejuvenating of the heart and circulation.

ALSO SEE: *Circulation, Heart Palpitations, Heart Tonic, Shock*

ALTERNATIVE OR SUPPLEMENTARY SELF-HELP: *Comfrey, Ginger, Peppermint Oil, Yarrow (none of these is as strong as Cayenne for emergency heart attack help)*

DOSAGE: *General or as given*

HEART PALPITATIONS: See Heart Tonic application.

HEART TONIC: Take Cayenne on a daily basis to help strengthen and tone the heart, balance circulation, and as first aid for heart palpitations. Start with an amount of Cayenne that is comfortable for you—a few grains at a time or up to 1/2 tsp. per dose—and add it to your favorite juice. It tastes good in tomato juice. Ideally, take a Cayenne Heart Tonic two to four times a day, to quickly build up increased stamina and overall strength. If you are new to using Cayenne or feel hesitant perhaps because of its hotness, you may want to start slowly with a small amount. If this is the case it is still worthwhile to take a small dose of Cayenne (a tiny pinch) every other day rather than every day and increase the frequency and amount as you feel comfortable. Coincidently you might discover that your digestion and overall energy level improve as Cayenne steadily helps with these also.

ALSO SEE: *Circulation, Heart Attack, Shock*

ALTERNATIVE OR SUPPLEMENTARY SELF-HELP: **Comfrey, Garlic, Ginger, Yarrow*

DOSAGE: *General or as given*

HOME BIRTHS: Don't be without Cayenne! I have used it with moms, dads, bystanders, and myself! With all the excitement you never know who will become faint at a birth. It can also be used for shock or to stimulate delayed breathing in the newborn.

ALSO SEE: Circulation, Shock

ALTERNATIVE OR SUPPLEMENTARY SELF-HELP: **Comfrey, *Peppermint Oil, Yarrow*

DOSAGE: *General*

INTESTINAL BACTERIA: Stimulate the growth of healthy bacteria and the blood circulation in intestines by using Cayenne, 1/2 tsp. three or four times a day, in "live" (containing living cultures) liquid or dry acidophilus culture, buttermilk or plain yogurt.

Another great bit of herbal help for restoring intestinal bacteria and digestive efficiency is to use the "Restorative Elixir" recipe found in the Digestion application in Chapter VI—the Garlic Chapter. To this recipe you can add some Cayenne to enhance its overall action.

ALSO SEE: *Colds and Flu, Circulation, Digestion*

ALTERNATIVE OR SUPPLEMENTARY SELF-HELP: **Garlic, Comfrey, Yarrow*

DOSAGE: *General or as given*

LINIMENT: Rub a Cayenne liniment into sore, strained muscles for penetrating warmth and to increase circulation and relieve tissue congestion. For an "immediate use" liniment, mix 1 Tbsp. Cayenne in 1/2 cup hot vinegar. Steep for 10 to 15 minutes, cool to a comfortable temperature and rub into the strained area. For increased heat, circulation, and penetration, apply the liniment and then cover the affected area with a towel, plastic wrap, heating pad, or hot water bottle.

Another method, which takes a little longer, is to put 1 Tbsp. Cayenne in 1/2 cup rubbing alcohol or vinegar and let it stand at room temperature for a week.

The Cayenne in these liniments can be strained out or left in as you please. If desired, add some good rubbing oil (i.e., olive oil, sesame oil) to a completed liniment mixture. Your liniment will now have added skin soothing properties and is more easily rubbed on the skin for a massage of strained areas.

These liniments are quite useful for varicose veins, as is using Cayenne internally on a daily basis.

ALSO SEE: *Circulation*

ALTERNATIVE OR SUPPLEMENTARY SELF-HELP: **Ginger, Clove Oil, *Onion (for bruising), *Peppermint Oil*

DOSAGE: *As given*

MOUTH: See Gums application.

OVERDOSE OF CAYENNE: Yes, it is possible to overdo it, but the results are not all that annoying and are easily taken care of. Once in a while a person may take too much Cayenne, especially in the beginning when he/she is learning the correct dosage. This may result in hiccoughs or an overstimulated, pulsing feeling in the stomach and some slight nausea. A few swallows of milk, or a few bites of a milk product like yogurt or cottage cheese, will immediately stop these inconveniences and cool off the tongue and stomach.

ALSO SEE: *None*

ALTERNATIVE OR SUPPLEMENTARY SELF-HELP: **Ginger (an alternative and milder stimulant than Cayenne)*

DOSAGE: *As given*

PETS: With animals, Cayenne is mostly used for bleeding, shock, or as a liniment. The liniment application is good for strained muscles in athletic animals such as horses.

Read the TASOLE about a pet application in the Personality Profile above.

ALSO SEE: *Bleeding, Circulation, Shock*

ALTERNATIVE OR SUPPLEMENTARY SELF-HELP: *Comfrey, Garlic, Onion, People Paste*

DOSAGE: *General*

PLANTS: See Gardens application.

SCALP: Stimulate circulation in the scalp, help dandruff, hair growth, and hair health (because of scalp health) with this Cayenne formula. Put 1 to 2 tsp. of Cayenne in 1/4 to 1/2 cup warm olive oil or other good scalp oil such as jojoba, sesame, sunflower, or almond. Massage into the scalp and leave on for 20 to 40 minutes, or make a milder concentration (1 tsp. or less) and leave it on overnight. Shampoo and rinse hair as usual.

This procedure can be used as often as you like, although once a week is usually enough for a good tonifying effect.

ALSO SEE: *Circulation*

ALTERNATIVE OR SUPPLEMENTARY SELF-HELP: *Comfrey, *Ginger, Yarrow*

DOSAGE: *As given*

SHOCK: Immediately administer Cayenne as follows:

Infants to 3 years: A few grains up to a small pinch (less than 1/16 tsp.) of Cayenne directly on tongue or mixed with approximately 1/4 cup water or juice and administered with a dropper, spoon, or cup in small increments to gauge the results as you proceed. Adjust the dose according to results. Rarely is a second dose called for in infant usage, yet in an emergency, such as continuing shock or internal bleeding, a second dose may be needed.

Children 4 to 10 years: 1/8 to 1/4 tsp. usually in 1/2 cup water or juice but can be taken dry in an emergency. Take the needed amount directly into the mouth in small increments (pinches or swallows) to gauge the results as you proceed. Adjust the dose according to results.

Children 11 years to Adults: 1/8 tsp. to 1/2 tsp. or more dry or in 1/2 cup water or juice. Take the needed amount directly into the mouth. Adjust the dose according to results. Repeat if needed.

Pets and Other Creatures: Appropriate size pinch of Cayenne directly on the tongue, under lip, outside of lip (to be licked off), edge of beak, etc. A horse-size animal can take 2 tsp. or more (for shock or internal bleeding)—with no problem! I haven't found the upper limit but I wouldn't hesitate to give a tablespoonful to a horse in an emergency.

All physical shock has both emotional and mental components. When I write "anti-shock agent," please understand I am also speaking of emotional and mental shocks as well as the physical ones. Some of the more obvious **symptoms of shock** are shaking, unusual drop in body temperature, paleness, dizziness, sweatiness (especially cold sweat), and thirst. In the case of emotional and mental shocks, additional symptoms could include: clouding or numbing of the senses, pounding heart, and a temporary loss of touch with reality.

One of the reasons Cayenne works so well in restoring equilibrium in crisis situations is that it balances circulation. This helps to stop the shock responses that alter the body chemistry, change the blood sugar, speed up glandular reactions past a useful level, affect the emotions, and slow blood to the brain, thereby clouding clear thinking and altering the thinking processes.

During shock, Cayenne can assist in an overall calming of the patient. Shaking stops; skin color, body temperature, and blood pressure normalize; emotional and mental responses balance out, and if there is bleeding (especially internally), it will generally slow down or stop completely. Often a person in shock will say that Cayenne tastes sweet and not hot at all. As the shock begins to wear off (symptoms normalizing), the hotness may become more pronounced, at which point only a few more small doses may be needed. If the Cayenne is reported to be extremely hot at the first dose, one dose is probably enough, especially in cases of mild shock. When you know you have had a shock of any sort, even before symptoms of the upset are noticeable, take some Cayenne right away as a potent preventive to shock symptoms.

Also see the TASOLE in the Personality Profile at the start of this chapter. Even though it refers to a pet in shock with internal bleeding, the situation would be similar for a human.

Emotional Shock: Probably everyone has had the experience of hurting oneself, and even though it may be a rather simple cut, scrape, twist, or whatever, we look at it from the emotional or mental point of view saying, "Yikes! Those are *my* body parts hanging out there and it's making me nervous!" When this happens, it can make any situation a little more trying and the body may experience an escalation of possible shock symptoms (however mild) that will delay the start of the healing and rebalancing process. A few sips of Cayenne in water will calm the shock, or potential shock.

Another type of emotional shock is the familiar scenario of "Having A Bad Day." Say you wake up and realize you have overslept and are late to everything! In your rush you break a large jar full of mayonnaise all over the kitchen floor. Just then a friend strolls in and slips on the mayonnaise, saves herself through a lucky grab at the kitchen table, but not before she cuts her heel on the mayonnaise glass, and now you must drive her to a bodily repair technician for a dozen stitches.

Finally you get to your first appointment only to find it's the wrong time and the wrong day, and your keys are locked in your car, and, and, and, I think you get the idea. As you are struggling to calm your emotions and to avoid falling into a totally depressed state, take a few large swallows of Cayenne in water and you will soon feel your head clearing, your circulation balancing and your sense of well-being returning.

Cayenne usage is particularly potent after the upset of an argument, the death of a loved one, or any kind of frightening experience—a skid off the road or a "near miss" car accident. It can be emotionally draining to give first aid to yourself or others at the scene of an accident, so don't forget to use Cayenne to help keep emotional and physical equilibrium, as well as for internal bleeding and prevention of shock, etc.

I am not saying that Cayenne is a cure-all, but it certainly can help a person "get-a-grip" at the opportune moment.

ALSO SEE: *Bleeding, Circulation, First Aid, Heart Attack*

ALTERNATIVE OR SUPPLEMENTARY SELF-HELP: *Comfrey, Ginger, Peppermint Oil (these are all supplementary, not alternatives)*

DOSAGE: *General*

SINUS RELIEF: A few grains up to a small pinch of Cayenne in 1/2 cup water, gently snuffed up each nostril, will clear most sinus congestion very quickly and stimulate circulation to those sluggish sinus areas, helping to flush out any impending infection.

You could use the "gum formula" (listed under Gums application) of Cayenne, goldenseal, and myrrh as a really fine sinus helper. If a milder version is needed, replace the Cayenne in the formula with a little salt. Use a few grains of this salt and herbs mixture in 1/2 cup water, and gently snuff through each nostril. See the complete Nasal Rinse instructions in Chapter I, Lesson #2.

Since this Cayenne Nasal Rinse is quite stimulating, it is mostly used by my students when they are applying self-help for a severe nasal congestion or infection. For a mild congestion a plain salt water nasal rinse (1/2 tsp. salt in 1/2 cup warm water) or drinking 1/2 tsp. Cayenne in 1/2 cup water is often enough.

TASOLE: Many of us have the idea that "more is better." Paul did. When he asked for my advice he had been suffering from severe sinus congestion and resultant headache for several days. I carefully explained the method of taking a few grains or a tiny pinch of Cayenne, mixing in perhaps a half cup of warm water, and gently snuffing through each nostril. I told him to expect it would be quite stimulating and his eyes would probably water. Yet since he was already in such prolonged pain from his sinus trouble, I assured him it would be a great relief.

Paul took the Cayenne into the bathroom to perform his snuffings. Soon I could hear clankings and mixings going on, and it crossed my mind that he might be doing more preparation than the situation called for. Then came a minute or two of silence. I just was about to put the final touches on my lunch-time baked potato when the bathroom door burst open. Out staggered Paul, howling with rage, claiming that I was trying to torture him. His eyes and nose were running like crazy. Although he looked as if he were breathing just fine now, still he was hopping up and down, holding onto his head, and running around me and my baked potato where we were positioned at the dining table. I managed to give him two large spoonfuls of yogurt to swallow (see "Overdose of Cayenne" application) and a cool cloth for his face (after he had calmed down slightly), while I tried to figure out what had happened to him back there in the bathroom.

Paul told me that he had put an entire teaspoon, "or maybe more," he said, of Cayenne in the half cup of warm water. All the noises I had heard were due to his changing his mind and continually stirring in more Cayenne. He felt that his case was a particularly tough one, and in his desperation, wanted to make sure of the results! Finally he proceeded to snort huge nostrils-full of the mixture at a very brave rate and not so gently. It was at that point, I believe, that he came charging out of my bathroom.

He did, on later occasions, use the suggested gentle method with very satisfactory results. Perhaps this gives you a little idea of what may be in store for you as a budding home herbalist in attempting to advise your more heroic friends.

ALSO SEE: *Overdose of Cayenne, Circulation*

ALTERNATIVE OR SUPPLEMENTARY SELF-HELP: *Comfrey, Garlic, *Onion, *Peppermint Oil, Yarrow*

DOSAGE: *As given*

STIMULANT: Cayenne stimulates energy, alertness, circulation, and digestion. When mixed with other herbs it stimulates and improves the efficiency with which they are carried into the blood and tissues.

ALSO SEE: *Breathing, Circulation, Digestion, Heart Tonic, Shock*

ALTERNATIVE OR SUPPLEMENTARY SELF-HELP: *Garlic, *Ginger, Onion, Peppermint, Yarrow*

DOSAGE: *General*

THROAT: Cayenne is a very potent sore throat gargle as it helps clear the toxic mucus from the throat tissues and increases circulation to the area, which helps flush out infection. I sometimes mix Cayenne with a drop or two of Clove oil or Clove powder for additional pain relief and added antiseptic action. I use Peppermint oil if it is more a laryngitis type of sore throat. See Chapter IX, Peppermint.

Cold pineapple juice makes a great base for an herbal gargle because the enzymes and acidity of the pineapple juice contribute to clearing the throat of bacteria and unwanted mucus. In general, I find that cold juice or water is usually the most comforting base for a gargle.

ALSO SEE: *Gums*

ALTERNATIVE OR SUPPLEMENTARY SELF-HELP: *Comfrey, *Garlic, Onion, *Peppermint Oil, Slippery Elm*

DOSAGE: *In 1/2 cup cold water or pineapple juice, I put a large pinch or 1/8 tsp. Cayenne. Sometimes I add a drop or two of Clove or Peppermint oil.*

ULCERS: Start by using 1/4 tsp. or less Cayenne with a view toward building up to about 1/2 tsp. to 1 tsp. Mix the desired amount of Cayenne in a little juice and drink two to four times a day, preferably between meals or up to 15 minutes before meals.

On rare occasions a student with a bad case of bleeding ulcers has taken an entire tablespoon of Cayenne, when the recommended dose of 1 tsp. or less "was not working fast enough." Those students commonly reported that this large dose immediately stopped the internal bleeding and pain while soothing the stomach. Continuing with that dose three times a day for two weeks, and then cutting back to 1 tsp. three times each day for two to four additional weeks, healed the ulcers. Yet for most people a 1 Tbsp. dose could bring on vomiting. I always tell people to start small, even as small as a few grains for some, and build up to the dose and frequency that works for you.

If there is an acute sensitivity to the spiciness of the Cayenne, simply start with as small an amount as a few grains at a time and build up from there. Putting Cayenne in 1/4 to 1/2 cup milk also cuts the hotness, although it will be much more effective if eventually used in plain water or juice. Please re-read the explanation about the hotness of Cayenne and its uses in the Personality Profile for Cayenne. However you use it, you can expect to feel a gentle warmness spreading internally, and of course your tongue may temporarily be a little spiced too.

Don't make the mistake of using Cayenne in gelatin capsules as most stomachs do not like to be surprised in this way when the capsules suddenly melt and release their contents. An important process is initiated in the mouth, brain, and digestive tract by having the Cayenne interact with the saliva and enzymes in the mouth to start off with.

If you ever feel you have taken too much Cayenne, you can immediately counteract it by eating a few mouthfuls of a milk product such as yogurt, cottage cheese or plain milk.

TASOLE: Henry, an older gentleman in his 60's, came to me for help with his bleeding ulcers after years of the usual treatments of anti-acid emulsions, bland diets, and liver acid-reduction pills. He felt his digestion had deteriorated steadily over those years. He wondered if there was "any herbal thing to try" instead of the medicines he suspected might, in the long run, be contributing to his digestive problems. I suggested 1/4 tsp. Cayenne in a little juice, starting off with once a day and building up to three or four times a day over a period of two weeks or so. Henry was afraid to try this as he had always had to avoid spicy foods. His bleeding ulcer had started years before and he didn't really trust (although he wanted to try) "that herbal nonsense". We decided to start with just a few grains of Cayenne (you could hardly see them) sprinkled in juice, one to four times a day as he felt like it, and I left it at that. About two months later, Henry's grandson reported to me that his grandfather was downing a noticeable amount of Cayenne mixed in his morning prune juice.

It often happens that I am the last to hear the outcome of some of these adventures, so in this case I called Henry to see if the rumor was true. He said that after a few days of taking just a few grains of Cayenne in juice, his confidence had built up and he noticed that he had to take less ulcer medicine—but he wasn't sure, ". . . being herbal nonsense and all".

Next he began increasing his dose very carefully and was surprised at how quickly his tolerance for the spiciness built up in spite of all his initial fears. It was clear to him that the Cayenne powder was acting very differently (in a positive way) than the cooked, spicy foods he remembered from his past and he continued to experiment. Within two months there were days when he needed no ulcer or digestive medicines at all, for the first time in years. He thought it might be due to the Cayenne, but still wasn't sure about ". . . all this herbal nonsense". He was now easily taking 1/4 tsp. Cayenne in juice two or three times a day, and asked me for any other advice I might want to "try out on him". I suggested that he might want to clean up his diet slightly—eat more fish and less beef and pork, and avoid fried foods and caffeine as much as possible. I figured he wasn't looking for a major change in life style but perhaps these simple ideas might help.

Henry's whole constitution was obviously being strengthened, and the only thing he had changed was to add Cayenne to his daily program. His grandson was really noticing it too.

Henry said he intended to keep up with the Cayenne indefinitely as he was saving "a bundle of money" by not having to buy his usual medicines. But whether it was the Cayenne for certain or not he couldn't say, ". . . being herbal nonsense and all".

ALSO SEE: *Bleeding, Circulation, Digestion, Intestinal Bacteria, Overdose of Cayenne*

ALTERNATIVE OR SUPPLEMENTARY SELF-HELP: **Comfrey, *Slippery Elm, Yarrow*

DOSAGE: *Start off with a few grains and work up to 1/2 to 1 tsp. Cayenne in 1/2 to 1 cup juice or water, taken two to four times a day.*

VARICOSE VEINS: Use Cayenne two to four times daily, internally, to strengthen and balance circulation and vein integrity. Also take 1 cup Yarrow tea, morning and night, to gently cleanse the blood and liver and hasten rehabilitation and prevention of varicose veins. Hemorrhoids are similar to varicose veins and can be helped by this same method.

See the Liniment application for a recipe to be used for external help on varicose veins.

ALSO SEE: *Circulation, Blood building, Liniment*

ALTERNATIVE OR SUPPLEMENTARY SELF-HELP: **Comfrey, *Yarrow*

DOSAGE: *General or as given*

CHAPARRAL

CHAPARRAL
IMMUNE SYSTEM
CLEAN AND STRONG
RIVER
OF LIFE
INFECTION FIGHTER
POLLUTION AND FUNGUS
INFECTION HAMMER
BUG-STOMPIN' BOOTS
21-DAY CLEANSE

CHAPTER III

CHAPARRAL

Larrea divaricata

Chaparral Captain cleans blood he's quite charming.
To bad parasites, his attack's quite alarming.
For colds, flu, and tumors his help is outrageous;
He can kill off infection even when it's contagious.

PERSONALITY PROFILE—Chaparral

Chaparral has an active ingredient so powerful and special that I can hardly pronounce it and can only spell it correctly if I am paying careful attention. The name is nordihydroguaiaretic acid and it is commonly referred to as NDGA. This chemical is known to have anti-cancer potential particularly for tumors and leukemia. For more specific data, see John Heinerman's *Herbal Pharmacy*, listed in the Resource Guide, Appendix C.

At first taste you will have no doubt in your mind of the potent turpenes present which, as you may have guessed, have the mild yet distinct flavor of turpentine. These turpene resins have strong antiseptic qualities and, along with the NDGA, give Chaparral a powerful antibiotic action. This means that you can expect many types of bacteria, germs, viruses, unhealthy microbes, etc. (most of us use one or more of those words interchangeably) to be inhibited or killed by the actions of Chaparral. This herb also has a well-earned reputation for noticeably strengthening the immune system. There are plant saponins in Chaparral which give the herb a "soapy" cleansing feel, which I liken to a detergent for the blood, and which also lend themselves to helping the blood keep a healthy alkalinity rather than a toxic acidity.

Chaparral and Garlic are the two main herbs to use for infection, including fungus infection or parasite infection/infestation. Because Chaparral and Garlic are each so potent and because their chemistries are quite different, there is hardly a type of common infection that can survive when confronted by either or both members of this amazing pair.

As a blood and lymph purifier, there is none better than Chaparral. In case you are wondering about the necessity of a potent blood-purifier, let me give you a bit of data. Sometimes the blood is referred to as "the river of life" and that is literally the case. If blood and lymph are "clean" and strong, no disease can feel comfortable living there. Often our "river of life" has become a dump for toxic waste that is perpetually ignored and added to. This is not always due to simple, personal neglect. There are many environmental poisons that we breathe in the air and drink in the water which are often difficult to avoid. Our organs, glands and tissues are not given an opportunity to show off their powers of rejuvenation when they are fed by a "river of life" that has lost its pizazz, and, as a result, they age and deteriorate rapidly. Chaparral can work on purifying and actually altering those "sludge components" of the blood accumulated through neglect and pollution. If you can identify and minimize some of your major sources of incoming pollution, then it is entirely possible to put the pizazz back in your "river of life." That is what a blood-purifying herb can do. (See Blood-Purifier and Lymph applications.)

Typically there are two major types of poisons that collect in the blood. First there is the short-term, more immediate variety which leads to lowered immunity, and often results in common colds and flu or a sensitivity or allergic reaction to airborne (i.e. pollen, dust) or food substances. Examples here include: poisonous bites, common parasites, junk food, chemicals like caffeine and alcohol, or pollutants you might have to work with like photographic chemicals. Secondly there are the more long-term poisons and chemical upheavals that are present in diseases like cancer, venereal disease, persistent eczemas, arthritis, and unwanted growths of various kinds. With a blood-purifier such as Chaparral, you will very likely get gratifying results with reversing the effects of the first type of poison. With the second type there are usually more complicating factors, so the results will vary from remarkable to negligible. To maximize your chances of remarkable results, it is always wise to identify and minimize sources of incoming pollution.

Anyone with a long history of regular use of allopathic drugs, junk foods, or common chemicals such as alcohol, caffeine or non-prescription drugs must realize that there are probably so many toxins stored in the blood and body tissues that they must wait in line to be eliminated. When you intend to clean up your blood and thereby regain new energy and a sense of delight in your life, remember that as these toxins are packaged and made ready to go, they have to leave the body somehow. So keep all your eliminative channels open and flowing. Bowels, urinary tract, sweat glands, lymph, skin—pay attention to each of these and help them along in the cleansing process as needed. If toxins do not leave the body as fast as they are recalled and packaged, you may get symptoms of the backlog such as headache, skin eruptions, or bodyache (lymph congestion). Exercising out of doors, sweating, skin brushing, receiving massage, daily bathing, eating only fruits and vegetables, fasting for short periods—these are all ways to facilitate the easeful cleansing of the blood and body tissues. Herbal or plain warm water enemas can be used for immediate help with elimination of a toxic backlog where needed, yet keep in mind this should not be your only approach.

A word here about the distinctive flavor of Chaparral. It has, as I've mentioned, a taste mildly reminiscent of turpentine which can cause a strong response in first-time users. Many people, therefore, prefer to use the herb in capsules or in tincture form, although I find that the tea form is the most readily usable for the body.

I grew up in Arizona, near Phoenix, where Chaparral grows abundantly, which may explain my liking for it. Whenever it rains in this low desert area, the wonderful fresh aroma of the Chaparral permeates the air and is deeply refreshing and rejuvenating. Visitors and locals alike comment upon it. Yet few know that they are appreciating the rain-stimulated release of the volatile oils of Chaparral. To me, far from being unpleasant, Chaparral tea tastes like the desert after a spring shower.

When using Chaparral on a long-term daily basis, with gradual rehabilitation in mind, I recommend one cup of the tea each day since this form is immediately assimilated in the body (see Blood-Purification application below). No fuss, no muss, no capsules, less expense, very efficient, and the flavor will definitely "grow on you". There are several different traditions of how to prepare the tea, depending on the part of the country you are in. Some say that Chaparral should be boiled and some say that you should never boil the water. Others suggest a combination of these or to make it only in the sun. Each group swears that if their particular method is not followed, the effects of Chaparral will be nonexistent or even harmful. I don't believe them. More than 15 years of experience using Chaparral have taught me that different extraction methods emphasize different components or strengths of the herb and every method has its place.

Here are my favorite methods for making this infamous tea:

1. Pour very hot but *not boiling* water over the dry or fresh herb and let it sit out overnight.
2. To make a sun tea, start by pouring room temperature water over the herb in a glass jar and then leave it in the sun for two to six hours. The length of time in the sun depends on how strong the sun is where you live, and how strong you need the final brew to be.
3: Steep the herb in hot (not boiling) water for about 15 minutes. Very hot tap water is often just right (if you have pure tap water).

The hotter the water, the more essential oils will be extracted. While the oil in Chaparral is a potent healing and cleansing factor, it needs to be extracted in a balance with the other properties of the herb, so as to have a powerful yet not overly harsh cleansing effect on the body. Using the more "refined" methods I have suggested above will extract the essential oils in a moderate way that keeps all the other important properties of the herb in balance.

If this tea is prepared so as to be too strong, you will end up with a brew that my students would describe as "gagsville." Once in my enthusiasm I let my Chaparral tea sit out too long in the Arizona sun. The extracted turpenes/oils floating on the top of it looked strong enough to clean a paintbrush. Being the adventurous sort, I thought, "What the heck, I'll drink it anyway," so I downed a cup. Not a good idea! I quickly learned that this concentrated form, in such a substantial dose, did not respect my stomach or my liver. I paid for my "stronger-is-better" thinking with a headache, a few hours of nausea, and (I was told by friends) a wild and crazed look in my eyes until the next day. The moral of the story is: If a strong Chaparral brew is ever needed (an infusion), always take it in small doses (2 ounces or less) at regular intervals.

For blood-purifying, as for a mild cold or flu, where one to three doses per day of Chaparral might be used, tea is usually the answer. Where more frequent doses are needed, such as for serious colds or flu, or when drinking the tea is not an option, Chaparral powder, put into capsules, is often used. (See formulas under the Antibiotic application below and see Dosage Equivalents in Chapter I, Lesson #2.)

To reap the benefits of a daily, yet mild, intake of Chaparral, sprinkle a few of the leaves into another herbal tea mixture that you enjoy. Try Comfrey/Peppermint/Chaparral or Ginger/Slippery Elm/Chaparral. Experiment to find the one that suits you and gradually increase the Chaparral as you please.

Quite frequently Chaparral is mixed with a demulcent herb such as Comfrey or Slippery Elm to buffer and enhance its cleansing properties. This is especially useful when using any Chaparral formula for more than a few days, or for the infrequent occasions of cleansing distress (see HINTS/CAUTIONS below).

Chaparral grows abundantly in arid climates as in the southwestern United States near Phoenix, Arizona (at about a 2000 foot elevation). It can be harvested anytime, yet I favor spring and early summer as I like to mix in the flowers and seed pods available then. The best source I know for potent, properly harvested and dried Chaparral is Reevis Mountain School of Self-Reliance. They sell it by mail order (see Buyer's Guide, Appendix D).

APPLICATIONS AND ATTRIBUTES - CHAPARRAL

(Quick Reference List)

ABSCESS
ALCOHOLISM
ALLERGIES
ANEMIA
ANTIBIOTIC/ANTISEPTIC
ARTERIOSCLEROSIS
ARTHRITIS
ATHLETE'S FOOT
BLOOD POISONING
BLOOD-PURIFIER
BOILS
BURSITIS
CANCER
CHEMICAL POISONING
COLDS and FLU
CONGESTION
CYSTS
DIGESTION
EYES
FEMALE DISCOMFORT
FEVER
FUNGUS
GOUT
GROWTHS
HERPES
IMMUNE SYSTEM
IMPETIGO
INFLAMMATION
ITCHING
KIDNEYS
LIVER
LYMPH
MUCOUS CONGESTION
PARASITES
PETS/ANIMALS
POISONING
POISON IVY/OAK
PROSTATITIS
RHEUMATISM
RING WORM
SCABIES
SCALP
SINUSITIS
SKIN
SORES
STOMACH
STY
TUMORS
URINARY TRACT
VENEREAL DISEASE
VENEREAL WARTS
WOUNDS
YEAST INFECTION

FORM:

Use fresh or dried leaves. (When harvesting your own, "leaves" can include the delicate, thin "connector" stems and flowers; the seed pods are good also if mixed in a proportion that is mostly leaves.) Purchase as whole leaf, powder, or tincture.

APPLICATION METHODS:

Use internally as tea, tincture, or powder. Externally, use as a strong tea (infusion) for washes, soaks, fomentation, etc. Also use as a poultice, salve, or tincture.

AVAILABILITY:

Herb stores, health food stores, mail order, or harvest your own

HINTS/CAUTIONS:

If you have a long history of heavy use of allopathic drugs or nonprescription drugs, including alcohol and/or caffeine, Chaparral's cleansing of these heavy accumulations from the blood and body tissues may result in headache, bodyache, or nausea. Chaparral is quite often mixed, up to equal parts, with a demulcent herb such as Comfrey or Slippery Elm to buffer its cleansing properties when needed. Review my remarks about this in the Personality Profile above.

GENERAL DOSAGE: INTERNAL USE

*PLEASE NOTE: *It is preferable to take Chaparral on an empty stomach for most potent use. Add a buffering herb such as Slippery Elm or Comfrey root if stomach is sensitive to Chaparral. Although I emphasize using tea, there are many other forms of herbal preparation which are quite effective, such as Capsules, Decoction, Infusion, etc. See these headings and Dosage Equivalents in Chapter I, Lesson #2.*

Infants to 3 years: For short-term antibiotic use, get a tincture and follow manufacturer's directions. Chaparral has such a strong flavor that it doesn't lend itself for use as a tea, etc., for this age group. Any use of Chaparral for this age group for longer than two weeks should be supervised by a health professional. Garlic is an alternative choice, especially for use past one week. See the Garlic chapter, Chapter VI.

Children 4 years to 10 years: Use Chaparral powder, 1/4 to 1/2 tsp., as a "honeyball," two to four times a day, with a glass of water after each dose. See Honeyball, Children's Ideas and Dosage Equivalents in Chapter I, Lesson #2. Use as a tincture according to manufacturer's directions.

Children 11 years to Adults: Use Chaparral tea, 1 to 3 cups per day. Or use powder, 1/2 tsp. with a full glass of water, one to four times a day. Or use tincture per the manufacturer's directions. For other alternative forms and their doses, see Dosage Equivalents in Chapter I, Lesson #2.

Pets and Other Creatures: Use powder in pill or honeyball form (See Chapter I, Lesson #2), or use the tincture. Most average-sized dogs and cats get the adult dosage listed above. For animals outside this average range you must make an educated guess. For instance, I would treat a small bird as in the infant category above, and I would probably treat a horse with 1 Tbsp. Chaparral powder four to eight times a day.

GENERAL DOSAGE: EXTERNAL USE

Same For All Humans And Other Creatures

Powdered Chaparral can be sprinkled, 1/8 inch deep or more, onto wounds. Chaparral can be used singly or mixed with other herbs as an antiseptic poultice for any need including insect bites or itching. An infusion is used as a wash, soak, or fomentation. Tincture can be used as a quick antibiotic application, but the powder stays on better and lasts longer for the "bigger jobs." A powerful poultice is created by wetting the Chaparral powder with Chaparral tincture and applying it externally as needed. Add 1/4 part Slippery Elm powder for a better paste and enhanced action. See detailed Poultice and Fomentation instructions in Chapter I, Lesson #2.

APPLICATIONS AND ATTRIBUTES - CHAPARRAL

ABSCESS: Chaparral's strong antibiotic action coupled with its drawing power and blood-purifying effects will draw abscesses out and dry them up quickly. Use one of the formulas listed in the Antibiotic application, keeping in mind that Slippery Elm added to any formula helps make a better and more active paste. Wet the powders with aloe vera gel, raw honey, Chaparral decoction, or other wetting agent and pack this onto the abscess, 1/4 to 1/2 inch thick. Wrap with gauze (see poultice instructions in Chapter I, Lesson #2). Soak the abscess for 15 to 30 minutes in strong, very warm Chaparral (or other appropriate herb) infusion, one or more times a day, changing the poultice each time. If you do not soak the abscess, at least change the poultice and clean the abscess twice a day. Use one of the antibiotic formulas internally.

ALSO SEE: *Antibiotic, Blood Purification*

ALTERNATIVE OR SUPPLEMENTARY SELF-HELP: ***Comfrey, *Garlic, Onion, *People Paste, *Slippery Elm, Yarrow***

DOSAGE: *Use as given.*

ALCOHOLISM: The following plan will help reduce withdrawal symptoms and cleanse the blood of chemical toxins that exaggerate alcohol craving. It does not take the place of professional counseling which is usually essential for stable withdrawal from an addictive substance.

- Ginger Bath three times a week (see Ginger, Chapter VII)
- Vegetarian diet
- Cayenne/grape juice tonic daily as needed (see Cayenne, Chapter II)
- 2 size "0" capsules filled with a powdered mixture made of 2 parts Chaparral and 1 part Comfrey or Slippery Elm. Take with a *full glass of water* every two hours until craving is gone or greatly subsides. This could be from one day to several days.
- Clove tea is good for "shakes" (see Clove, Chapter IV).
- Exercise vigorously daily, outdoors in fresh air as much as possible.

ALSO SEE: *Blood-Purification*

ALTERNATIVE OR SUPPLEMENTARY SELF-HELP: ***Cayenne, Clove, Ginger, *Yarrow***

DOSAGE: *Use as given.*

ALLERGIES: When dealing with allergies, one often finds there is an emotional trigger or stress that is closely linked with the physical symptoms. It is also common that the body is not digesting food properly, resulting in a build-up of toxins (often extra proteins) in the blood. When using a blood-purifying herb such as Chaparral, these emotional triggers are likely to be stirred up along with the physical cleansing. This will provide an opportunity to deal with the emotional aspect more consciously, but it is often quite uncomfortable to face. This circumstance offers a chance to root out subtle causes of the physical symptoms and perhaps to change the allergic responses as well as dietary habits altogether. Psychological counseling can be quite useful here.

If you are seriously inspired to make a change in dealing with severe allergies, there is a wonderful cleansing diet in Humbart Santillo's book *Natural Healing With Herbs* (see the Resource Guide, Appendix C).

ALSO SEE: *Blood-Purification, Inflammation, Skin*

ALTERNATIVE OR SUPPLEMENTARY SELF-HELP: Cayenne, Comfrey, Ginger, *Yarrow

DOSAGE: *Use Chaparral as described in the 21-day program under Blood-Purification. For times of severe symptoms, also use 2 capsules of Chaparral/Comfrey (a mixture of equal parts) two or three times during the day. If this helps but still is "not enough," experiment with a more frequent dosage either in capsules, infusion, or tea. Many times I have found that the infusion or tea works faster for people, perhaps because it is "ready-to-use."*

ANEMIA: Along with blood-purifying properties (NDGA, turpenes, saponins, etc.) which renew the blood and give it a chance to rebuild its strength, Chaparral also contains a small amount of the trace element molybdenum. This trace element is known for enhancing hemoglobin formation and is wise to use in conjunction with easy-to-assimilate iron supplements and with herbs high in iron, such as Comfrey.

For blood-building, as opposed to blood-purifying, Chaparral is most often mixed with other blood-building herbs such as Slippery Elm and Comfrey. A steady program of smaller dosages works best for blood-building. Also see the Cayenne/grape juice tonic in the Cayenne chapter (Chapter II) under the Blood-Building application.

ALSO SEE: *Antibiotic, Blood-Purifier, Cancer*

ALTERNATIVE OR SUPPLEMENTARY SELF-HELP: **Cayenne, *Comfrey, Onion, Yarrow*

DOSAGE: *Ideally, take 2 size "0" capsules along with 1 cup of Comfrey tea, once or twice a day. As an alternative, take 1 or 2 cups mild Chaparral tea per day, either by itself or with an iron supplement.*

ANTIBIOTIC/ANTISEPTIC: Chaparral is one of two major antibiotic herbs among my Ten Essentials. (Garlic is the other one, so be sure to check out Garlic's Antibiotic application also). Chaparral has the strength to kill many types of bacteria, viruses, parasites, and fungus infections.

The formulas below are each made with powdered herb unless otherwise specified. They also make more than you will probably need, so store the leftovers for future use. (See proper storage instructions in Chapter I, Lesson #5.) If you get interested in a more complete understanding of these formulas and their subtle differences, simply go to each herb chapter individually and review the major actions of the herbs.

Try one of these ideas at the first sign of infection, even if it is as small a sign as "that feeling" that comes just before the no-doubt-about-it signs of illness. In turning an illness around, I always prefer a sharp U-turn rather than indefinite turning around and around the block, so to speak, and this quick U-turn is what happens if you catch an infection early with Chaparral or Garlic.

Formula #1 - Take 1 to 3 size "0" capsules of Chaparral with a full glass of water every two to four hours.

Formula #2 - Steep (don't simmer) 1 oz. whole or powdered Chaparral in 2 cups of "almost boiling" water, covered, for 20 to 30 minutes. Strain. Take 1/4 to 1/2 cup every one to three hours.

Formula #3 - Mix 2 oz. Chaparral powder, 1 oz. Comfrey root powder, 1/4 oz. Ginger powder, and 1/4 oz. Cayenne powder. Take 1 to 3 size "0" capsules with a full glass of water every two to four hours.

Formula #4 - Mix 2 oz. Chaparral powder, 1 oz. Garlic powder, 1 oz. Slippery Elm powder, 1/4 oz. Ginger powder, and 1/4 oz. Cayenne powder. Take 2 size "0" capsules with a full glass of water every two to four hours.

The decision on which formula to use is often based simply on which herbs you have on hand, or which formula digests easiest or works best for your type. I prefer the "buffered" formulas, #3 and #4, especially when I want to use frequent doses.

ALSO SEE: *Blood-Purification, Eyes, Fungus, Immune System, Parasites, Sinusitis, Venereal Disease*

ALTERNATIVE OR SUPPLEMENTARY SELF-HELP: *Cayenne, *Comfrey, *Garlic, Ginger, *People Paste, Slippery Elm, Yarrow*

DOSAGE: *General or as given*

ARTERIOSCLEROSIS: This is commonly known as "hardening of the arteries" and is often linked with obesity, smoking, high fat intake, and cholesterol. When fatty deposits on the inside of the artery walls are the main problem, this is sometimes referred to as atherosclerosis. To help clear out fat and cholesterol deposits in the arteries, and clean up toxins (such as nicotine, or chronic undigested food wastes, often found in cases of obesity), that may be contributing to arteriosclerosis, many of my students have reported good results from using equal parts of Chaparral and Garlic powder, taken in 1/2 tsp. doses two to four times a day. I would add 1 part Slippery Elm to 2 parts of the above formula to buffer and enhance the strong Garlic and Chaparral properties. Also a Ginger bath once a week, a vegetarian diet, and Comfrey "green drinks" are quite useful. (See the Comfrey and Ginger chapters, Chapters V and VII.)

ALSO SEE: *Blood-Purification*

ALTERNATIVE AND SUPPLEMENTARY SELF-HELP: **Garlic, Ginger, Onion, Yarrow*

DOSAGE: *Use as given.*

ARTHRITIS: See Blood-Purifier, Chemical Poisoning, and Gout applications.

ATHLETE'S FOOT: This inconvenient annoyance needs to be treated with a fungus-killing herb, and Chaparral is one of the strongest (Garlic is another). Look in the Antibiotic application above and internally take the formula that includes Garlic. Soak your feet in strong Chaparral tea for at least 20 minutes twice a day. During the rest of the day keep your feet dry, use clean cotton socks when necessary, and go barefoot or use sandals whenever possible.

For ongoing foot-care, dust the feet several times a day with Chaparral powder, or make a paste by mixing Chaparral and Slippery Elm powders with aloe vera gel. (Aloe vera gel is gotten from a health food store.) Apply this paste to any particularly annoying areas on the feet.

Refer to the Blood-Purifier application for the 21-Day Chaparral Cleanse. This is also an effective way to use Chaparral for eliminating athlete's foot. Also see the TASOLE in the Venereal Disease application. Curious?

ALSO SEE: *Antibiotic, Blood-Purifier, Fungus, Skin, Venereal Disease*

ALTERNATIVE OR SUPPLEMENTARY SELF-HELP: *Comfrey, *Garlic, Slippery Elm, Yarrow*

DOSAGE: *Use as given.*

BLOOD POISONING: See Blood-Purifier and Chemical Poisoning applications.

BLOOD-PURIFIER: Chaparral is an excellent herbal blood-purifier. (See the Personality Profile.) When the blood is polluted, everything is affected, since the quality of your blood corresponds to the quality of your health. Chaparral is uniquely effective in its ability to cleanse the blood and lymph system of impurities. When the quality of the blood takes a leap forward, so does the efficiency and strength of all the supporting organs, such as the liver, kidneys, lymph, skin, digestive system, etc. When you send good "food" (healthy blood) to all parts of the body, those parts clean up, reorganize, get reinspired, and often surprise you with a sense of well-being that most of us forget is possible.

Many of the "itis" types of illness, such as arthritis, bursitis, prostatitis, and sinusitis, as well as rheumatism, are the result of the build-up of toxins in the blood, perhaps from many years of eating processed foods or addictive substances including caffeine. When the body's eliminative and cleansing systems get overwhelmed and cannot handle a toxic load, the body desperately tries to store these toxins somewhere to keep them out of the way as much as possible. These stored toxins often end up in the joints and tissues, causing various sorts of inflammation, pain, and malfunction or sluggishness. Here is where the knowledge of a potent blood-purifier such as Chaparral is essential.

Review the formulas under the Antibiotic application and use these in the smaller doses, once or twice a day, for steady, long-term (three weeks or longer) cleansing. For short-term needs, such as the immediate symptoms of infection (blood impurities) that accompany a cold, flu, food poisoning, inflammation pain, allergy attack, etc., I recommend using the larger and more frequent dosages. These formulas are best taken on an empty stomach, or if that is not comfortable for you, take with one or two bites of light food, like fruit or raw vegetable. Eating blood-purifying foods such as raw onions, raw garlic, and raw beets is a favorable addition to this application.

The following 21-day Chaparral Cleanse will give your health a superb boost. I use it as a yearly "tune-up" and many of my students swear that using Chaparral in this way once or twice a year keeps their immune systems strong. Any long-term health annoyances such as skin problems, recurring aches and pains, female organ troubles—anything that is the result of an ongoing toxic build-up in the blood—will be positively addressed by this Chaparral Cleanse.

21-DAY CHAPARRAL CLEANSE

Put 1 tsp. Chaparral (not powdered) in a cup. Add 1 cup of very warm, but not boiling, pure water. Cover and let stand overnight, strain out the Chaparral, and drink the remaining liquid on an empty stomach, first thing in the morning. Do not throw the Chaparral away. Cover it again, immediately, with 1 cup of very warm water and leave it until the next morning when you will again strain it and drink the liquid, first thing, on an empty stomach. For a third time, cover the same Chaparral herbs with 1 cup very warm water. Let it sit covered until the next morning, strain out the herb and drink it first thing on an empty stomach. *After this third use, throw the herb away.*

In the evening of that third-cup-day, start the process over with a fresh teaspoon of Chaparral and use that teaspoon of herb for three cups of tea as you did before. Continue this process for twenty-one days.

There is a TASOLE about the use of this cleanse under the Chemical Poisoning application below.

You can expect a slow and steady cleansing and strengthening of the blood and all its support systems, especially the liver, kidneys, and lymph. You will notice that the flavor and aroma of the tea gets lighter on each succeeding day of the 3-day cycle, but don't be fooled into thinking that it is less potent. The properties of the Chaparral are being extracted in different combinations during the cycle, which means a more balanced overall use.

Anytime you are cleansing the body of toxic build-up, especially as in the 21-day Cleanse described here, there are usually emotional counterparts and memories that have been locked into the tissues which are cleansed along with the physical poisons. It is not uncommon to re-experience memories and emotions that were present when the toxins were first introduced into the system.

A student of mine once found himself spontaneously reliving the emotions and memories of a traumatic break-up of a relationship from several years ago. During that critical time he had also indulged in alcohol, caffeine, and tobacco. During the 21-Day Chaparral Cleanse (and this can happen with any potent blood-cleansing) he was surprised with a brief "re-play" of sadness, tears, and frequent memories from that past experience. During this emotional re-play he detected the odors of and cravings for those substances he had abused during that time. My observation was that these substances were now cleansing from his blood and body tissues.

In my teaching of herbistry I call this process "retracing." Chaparral is a prime mover in this process. While retracing is not always observable, I believe it is going on subtly nonetheless, and if you notice it, I recommend just letting the memories and sensations pass on through. Don't pay undue attention to them. By analogy, pus will simply drain from a lanced wound, but you wouldn't mourn the loss of the pus. If extra help is needed to cope with the process, speak with a close friend or professional counselor.

ALSO SEE: *Abscesses, Antibiotic, Cancer, Chemical Poisoning, Female Disorders, Gout, Parasites, Prostatitis, Sinusitis, Skin, Tumors, Venereal Disease*

ALTERNATIVE OR SUPPLEMENTARY SELF-HELP: **Garlic, Ginger, Onion, People Paste (used internally), *Yarrow*

DOSAGE: *General or as given*

BOILS: See Abscess application.

BURSITIS: See Blood-Purifier application.

CANCER: I know of no herb that, by itself, can be touted as a cure for cancer. All disease, especially something as complex as cancer, is multi-causational, involving physical, emotional and environmental factors. Knowing that, however, I will tell you that Chaparral is a prime ingredient in well-known herbal formulas which have a positive history with many types of cancer, including tumors. I highly recommend further investigation of Chaparral for anyone interested in its possible use. (See the two-starred (**) books in Resource Guide, Appendix C.)

ALSO SEE: *Antibiotic, Blood-Purifier*

ALTERNATIVE OR SUPPLEMENTARY SELF-HELP: **Comfrey*

DOSAGE: *General, or see ideas under Antibiotic and Blood-Purifier applications.*

CHEMICAL POISONING: I refer here predominantly to types of poisoning that do not require the stomach to be pumped or vomiting to be induced. Chaparral would be used to help detoxify the blood from ongoing or long-term exposure through handling and breathing toxic chemicals. Milder, short-term "poisoning," like a reaction to MSG in food or mild food poisoning, also responds well to Chaparral. Even if vomiting needs to be induced, it is often wise to use a blood-purifying herb like Chaparral for a few days afterward to help lessen the effects of the poison.

TASOLE: Stephanie, one of my students, was a taxidermist who breathed and handled toxic chemicals daily. Her boss claimed that the chemicals "weren't that bad," and so no precautions were taken. Any one of the employees who mentioned the subject of chemical poisoning was harshly criticized. Over a period of a few years of doing taxidermy, Stephanie noticed a steady increase in breathing difficulties, lung pain, head and eyeaches, as well as skin sensitivities. Since she did not collapse outright, none of these symptoms alarmed her boss, and Stephanie simply put up with it.

Stephanie mentioned her increasing symptoms to me, confiding her suspicion that she was accumulating poisons from the chemicals used in taxidermy. Upon my suggestion she began the 21-Day Chaparral Cleanse listed in the Blood-Purifier application above.

As each day went by she began having more noticeable detoxifying symptoms and her sweat, saliva, breath, phlegm, urine, even tears, had the subtle yet distinct aroma and taste of the taxidermy chemicals she had worked with over the years. By the second week she was expectorating "old-looking" phelgm that had an even stronger chemical smell. By the end of the 21-Day Cleanse she felt a renewed strength that had not been present for a long time, and during her daily jogging exercise she was regaining her wind capabilities as her lungs became clearer and stronger. Stephanie also used an herbal poultice of Garlic and/or Onion and/or Comfrey directly over her lungs and slept with it in place overnight for the final seven days of the cleanse. This, too, increased the rehabilitation of her lungs.

At the end of all this, Stephanie gave up taxidermy work and opted for another career.

If you are in a situation similar to Stephanie's but a change of career is not an option at the moment, the 21-Day Chaparral Cleanse two to four times a year could lessen your "job hazard" while you work on changing your options.

ALSO SEE: *Blood-Purifier*

ALTERNATIVE OR SUPPLEMENTARY SELF-HELP: **Cayenne, *Comfrey, Garlic, Onion, *Yarrow*

DOSAGE: *General or as given*

COLDS and FLU: See Antibiotic and Blood-Purifier applications.

CONGESTION: Use Chaparral especially for the type of congestion (and perhaps infection) that comes from frequent overeating, too many dairy products, and "junk foods." When the mucus piles up in your head and/or chest or you are feeling sluggish and not up to standard, you can be sure you are experiencing what is politely termed congestion. Chaparral helps to break up mucus and other types of congestion and move them out of the system.

While using Chaparral internally, also apply an external poultice directly over the area of congestion, such as the lungs or liver. Be sure to review the Antibiotic and Blood-Purifier applications.

ALSO SEE: *Antibiotic, Blood-Purifier, Skin*

ALTERNATIVE OR SUPPLEMENTARY SELF-HELP: **Comfrey, *Garlic, *Onion*

DOSAGE: *General*

CYSTS: Use Chaparral internally and make a poultice of Chaparral or Chaparral with Comfrey Root powders for direct application to the cyst itself. Poultices left on overnight and/or most of the day can be continued as long as necessary—generally from two days to two weeks with a change of the poultice at least twice a day. The 21-Day Chaparral Cleanse (see Blood-Purifier application) combined with the use of the poultice is my treatment of choice. Yet any of the formulas under the Antibiotic application are valuable

ALSO SEE: *Abscess, Antibiotic, Cancer, Tumors*

ALTERNATIVE OR SUPPLEMENTARY SELF-HELP: **Comfrey, *Garlic, People Paste, Yarrow*

DOSAGE: *General or as given*

DIGESTION: If the digestive trouble is due to infection in the digestive tract, use one of the formulas under the Antibiotic application. If digestive trouble is a constant companion, avoid overeating to relieve the stress on the digestive functions, and complete the 21-Day Chaparral Cleanse listed under the Blood-Purifier application above.

Another effective digestive aid is to mix equal amounts of Chaparral and Comfrey Root powders and take 1/2 tsp. doses of this mixture either with or without capsules (without is best) 1/2 hour before eating anything (average four to six times a day) or at least before the main meals.

When you review the Personality Profiles on Comfrey and Chaparral, you will see why they are such an important combination for a wide range of digestive upsets, from simple gas to colitis, ulcers and mucous accumulations.

For stomach cramps, Chaparral tincture can give immediate relief, while the Chaparral/Comfrey Root formula mentioned above may take a little longer.

ALSO SEE: *Antibiotic, Blood-Purifier, Congestion*

ALTERNATIVE OR SUPPLEMENTARY SELF-HELP: *Cayenne, *Comfrey, Garlic, Ginger, *Peppermint, *Slippery Elm*

DOSAGE: *Ingest Chaparral powder, 1/4 tsp. four to six times a day, especially 1/2 hour before eating. Or mix equal parts Chaparral and Comfrey Root powders and take 1/2 tsp. four to six times a day, especially 1/2 hour before eating. Take all doses with a full glass of water.*

EYES: For a sty, use a Chaparral poultice, wrapped in gauze or thin cotton cloth, laid over the eye. Leave on for at least twenty minutes or, ideally, overnight. Rinse the eyes with a demulcent herb tea such as Comfrey or Slippery Elm after removing the poultice. For an eye rinse with stronger antibiotic action, make a mild tea by combining Chaparral and one of the above-mentioned demulcent herbs (1/2 tsp. of each chosen herb to one cup of water, steeped for 10 minutes). As an eye rinse, Chaparral alone might be irritating or drying to the eyes. The added demulcent herb remedies that.

For severe eye infection also use an herbal antibiotic, such as Garlic or Chaparral, taken internally. (See Antibiotic applications for those herbs, in Chapter VI and in this chapter.)

ALSO SEE: *Antibiotic*

ALTERNATIVE OR SUPPLEMENTARY SELF-HELP: **Cayenne, *Comfrey, Garlic, *Slippery Elm, Yarrow*

DOSAGE: *General or as given*

FEMALE DISCOMFORT: Over the years my students have had very positive results using Chaparral for all sorts of so-called "female complaints" such as chronic yeast infection (Chaparral is a potent fungicide), vaginal infection, irregular menstruation, uterine fibroids, PID (Pelvic Inflammatory Disease), venereal warts, abnormal cervical tissues, cystitis, and many uterine and ovarian difficulties. I have found that Chaparral strengthens and helps the reproductive organs in women as well as in men.

Commonly, I recommend that women begin with the 21-Day Chaparral Cleanse described in the Blood-Purifier application above. Usually that is enough to remedy most situations, yet it could be repeated after a one week "rest period" if the results were initially good but more was needed. Any of the formulas listed under the Antibiotic application above can also be quite useful, especially for immediate and specific infections rather than long-term complaints.

For infections of the bladder, uterus, or vaginal areas—including vaginal yeast infections—the use of vaginal boluses can be wonderful. Herbal actions are absorbed into the lower abdomen through the thin vaginal walls and thus vaginal boluses can be of powerful use for many lower abdomen infections and discomfort. Mix powdered Chaparral with Slippery Elm (2 parts Chaparral, 1 part Slippery Elm) and moisten these herbs with enough warmed cocoa butter to be able to mold them. The mixture is then formed into the proper bolus shape and allowed to become firm in the refrigerator before being used. If cocoa butter is not available at your drug-store or health food store, boluses can be made using water and herbs, formed into shape, and then carefully dried in an oven at its lowest setting (preferably 120 degrees or so). You may want to use a little unscented cream on these water-based boluses when inserting them into the vagina. For even more details of making boluses, review the instructions for Bolus in Chapter I, Lesson #2.

Boluses are commonly inserted into the vagina, left in place overnight and then rinsed out in the morning. They can also be used during the day and replaced two to four times during a twenty-four hour period. A pad or panty-shield is used to absorb the melted herbs as they leave the vagina. In addition to the boluses, a poultice can be placed directly over the affected organ, such as the uterus or bladder, and left on for 30 to 60 minutes or overnight. Chaparral alone or Chaparral and Comfrey mixed together would make a good poultice. Review the instructions for Poultice in Chapter I, Lesson #2, if necessary.

Often in "mild cases" no boluses or poultices are needed. Simply using an oral Chaparral formula (see Antibiotic application) along with a one-time vaginal douche, or the 21-Day Chaparral Cleanse (see Blood-Purifier application) is sufficient.

ALSO SEE: *Antibiotic, Blood-Purifier, Chemical Poisoning, Venereal Disease*

ALTERNATIVE OR SUPPLEMENTARY SELF-HELP: **Comfrey, Garlic, Slippery Elm, *Yarrow*

DOSAGE: *General or as given*

FEVER: Fevers are often caused by various sorts of internal congestion in the head, chest, or any organ or system of the body that is working poorly. These congestions result in a backlog of toxins, and a fever often develops to help burn these off. Chaparral addresses the root of fever by breaking up these congestions and flushing them out of the body. It also acts as a coolant since it dispels internal heat.

ALSO SEE: *Antibiotic, Blood-Purifier, Congestion*

ALTERNATIVE OR SUPPLEMENTARY SELF-HELP: *Cayenne, Clove, Comfrey, *Garlic, Ginger, *Yarrow*

DOSAGE: *General*

FUNGUS: For a long-term struggle with recurring fungus infections such as athlete's foot, nail fungus, ear fungus, vaginal yeast infections, etc., I suggest doing the 21-Day Chaparral Cleanse as described in the Blood-Purifier application above. This may well take care of the problem. If further help is needed, the next step is to proceed with formula #4 described in the Antibiotic application above. Use the suggested dosage. In addition, a poultice made by using formula #4 in the Antibiotic application, applied directly to an external fungus infection and left on overnight, can speed the healing process. This poultice can be used as often as desired.

For less chronic, mild, or first-time fungus infections, take 1 cup Chaparral tea one to two times a day. At the same time soak the affected body part (where possible) in an infusion (very strong brew) of Chaparral tea for 15 minutes, one to three times a day. (See Infusion instructions in Chapter I, Lesson #2.)

For particularly stubborn cases, you can use more frequent and/or slightly larger doses of Chaparral than you started with. If you are using Chaparral internally, it is important to continue for a week to ten days after the outward symptoms of the fungus have disappeared to ensure that the infection is out of the blood.

For external relief on small areas of less serious fungus infection, a Chaparral tincture (from a health food store) is a convenient form to use. Apply a few drops at a time directly onto the affected part.

ALSO SEE: *Antibiotic, Athlete's Foot, Blood-Purifier, Female Discomfort, Venereal Disease, Yeast Infection (vaginal)*

ALTERNATIVE OR SUPPLEMENTARY SELF-HELP: **Garlic, *Yarrow*

DOSAGE: *General or as given*

GOUT: This painful situation is similar to arthritis and is often characterized by swelling of the joints, hands, and feet, particularly the big toe. It is caused by an extraordinary build-up of uric acid salts in the blood. The body is unable to deal with the overload and tries to get it "out of the way" by storing it in all these inconvenient places.

Use the 21-Day Chaparral Cleanse (see Blood-Purifier appplication) to help the body recall and flush out these stored poisons. Of course it would be extremely wise (I am being polite here) to stick to dietary habits that minimize this uric acid overload which commonly results from too much protein, especially animal proteins. Other dietary irritations include fried and processed foods, caffeine, and alcohol. I strongly suggest a vegetarian diet, Ginger baths once or twice a week (see Ginger chapter, Chapter VII), and drinking at least two quarts of pure water or appropriate herb tea (such as Comfrey/Peppermint) each day to help the Chaparral flush out the uric acid crystals and other toxins.

Following the 21-Day Chaparral Cleanse, the next step would be the consistent daily use, internally, of one of the Antibiotic/Blood-Purifying formulas (see Antibiotic application). The Chaparral formula you choose should be used in the smaller amount first and increased gradually over a period of two to three weeks to an intermediate amount that agrees with you. Continue taking at least two quarts of pure water or appropriate herb tea (not more Chaparral) each day to facilitate the cleansing action of the Chaparral formula.

Severe cases of gout will necessitate professional nutritional counseling and supervision. I suggest that you consult a licensed naturopathic physician, especially if you have recently been using allopathic drugs.

Remember, if there is any digestive distress from using Chaparral, you may want to buffer it with the demulcent action of Comfrey Root or Slippery Elm. Use equal parts Chaparral and demulcent, or mix 2 parts Chaparral and 1 part demulcent.

Chaparral or Ginger footbaths can give temporary relief from the pain of gout as more permanent self-help measures are put into action.

ALSO SEE: *Antibiotic, Blood-Purifier, Chemical Poisoning, Digestion*

ALTERNATIVE OR SUPPLEMENTARY SELF-HELP: **Cayenne, Comfrey, Garlic, *Ginger, Peppermint, *Yarrow*

DOSAGE: General or as given

GROWTHS: See Tumor application.

HERPES (simplex, shingles, venereal): The following suggestions predominantly apply to venereal herpes, yet they can be efficiently used for the other forms of herpes as well.

During an active outbreak of venereal herpes, take 2 size "0" capsules of Chaparral powder alternately with 2 capsules of a Comfrey/Clove formula every two hours (could be taken less frequently for less severe symptoms). Take with a full 8 oz. glass of water. This means that every two hours you will be taking one or the other of these two formulas. Wash sores with a concentrated tea of Chaparral, Yarrow, or Clove as often as needed or apply a poultice of one or more of these herbs directly on the affected area.

Clove is particularly good for pain relief, and Clove oil (from health or drug stores) applied directly to a painful sore will have an immediate numbing effect along with its antiseptic action (see Clove chapter, Chapter IV).

If you are dealing with an ongoing herpes infection that is in a latent phase at the moment, the 21-Day Chaparral Cleanse (see Blood-Purifier application) can lessen or even completely stop the outbreaks.

Alternatively, usually for the most severe cases, whether active or not, use the 21-Day Cleanse simultaneously with the herbal formulas mentioned at the beginning of this application. If you use these formulas *with* the 21-day Cleanse, start with 1/2 the recommended dosage two to four times a day (if herpes is not active at the moment), or take the herbs every two hours as recommended (if herpes is active). Each dose is taken with a full 8oz. glass of pure water.

The ideal is to lessen or eliminate the herpes virus in a steady yet non-cathartic way during times when there are no active outbreaks.

Any of the formulas in the Antibiotic application would also be potent for a herpes outbreak. Use internally and also for external poulticing.

My students and clients testify that these recommendations work better if one refrains from any sexual activity during the treatment. Also, since I have found that any type of herpes is strongly affected by food chemicals, it is wise to eliminate processed sugars, meat, caffeine, alcohol, chocolate, and fried foods from the diet. Instead, emphasize fresh fruits and vegetables, seaweed, carrot juice, and anything with lots of chlorophyll such as "green drinks" (see the Comfrey chapter, Chapter V). A chlorophyll supplement is fine too.

This use of herbs for herpes can be combined with other supplements that you may have found to be useful in inhibiting herpes. I occasionally recommend L-lysine and calcium ascorbate.

ALSO SEE: *Antibiotic, Blood-Purifier, Chemical Poisoning, Venereal Disease*

ALTERNATIVE OR SUPPLEMENTARY SELF-HELP: ***Clove, *Comfrey, *Garlic, Ginger, People Paste, Yarrow***

DOSAGE: *General; or 2 capsules every two hours alternating Chaparral with a Comfrey/Clove combination so that you are taking one or the other each two hours. Also see other alternatives for latent or active herpes described in the application.*

IMMUNE SYSTEM: Chaparral will strengthen your immune system through cleansing of the blood and by supporting proper functioning of the organs and lymph system (which are key factors in healthy immunity).

If you have no specific problem but find that you are easily susceptible to colds, flu, allergies, etc., I suggest strengthening the immune system by: using the smaller suggested doses of Chaparral (see General Dosage), or taking one of the Chaparral formulas listed in the Antibiotic application, or completing the 21-Day Chaparral Cleanse (see Blood-Purifier application). Smaller doses will give you a gentle and steady boost of strength especially when there is no present crisis to be overcome.

Larger and more frequent doses are necessary when there is an active health crisis.

ALSO SEE: *Antibiotic, Blood-Cleansing, Chemical Poisoning, Herpes, Parasites*

ALTERNATIVE OR SUPPLEMENTARY SELF-HELP: **Comfrey, *Garlic, Onion. People Paste (used internally), *Yarrow*

DOSAGE: *General or as given*

IMPETIGO: See Skin application.

INFLAMMATION: See Blood-Purifier application

ITCHING: See Skin application.

KIDNEYS: Use Chaparral as described in the Blood-Purifier or Antibiotic applications but be certain your formula includes at least 1 part of a demulcent herb, like Comfrey root or Slippery Elm, to every 2 parts of Chaparral. These demulcent and mucilaginous herbs are essential to use with Chaparral for soothing and rehabilitating the kidneys and urinary tract.

In addition, you may want to use Chaparral, Comfrey, Ginger, or Peppermint as a poultice directly over the kidneys to relieve congestion there. (See poultice instructions in Chapter I, Lesson #2.)

For any low-grade, on-going distress in the kidneys, my students swear by the rehabilitating actions of the 21-Day Chaparral Cleanse (see Blood-Purifier application). When using the 21-Day Cleanse specifically for the urinary tract, it is important to take 1/4 to 1/2 tsp. Comfrey or Slippery Elm powder with each daily dose of the Chaparral tea.

Comfrey is also an herb for kidneys which may be preferred for daily use in ongoing maintenance after the 21-Day Cleanse is over. See the Comfrey chapter, Chapter V.

Since the kidneys and the liver work closely together, be sure to read the liver application as well.

ALSO SEE: *Antibiotic, Blood-Purifier, Chemical Poisoning, Liver, Urinary Tract*

ALTERNATIVE OR SUPPLEMENTARY SELF-HELP: **Comfrey, Garlic, Ginger, Peppermint, *Yarrow*

DOSAGE: *General or as given*

LIVER: Any herb that cleans and strengthens the blood (and Chaparral is a fantastic one for that) does the same for the liver. Since the blood regularly passes through the liver to be cleaned, the health of the blood directly affects the health of the liver and vice versa. If the blood is in good shape, the liver gets a break and in fact rehabilitates itself by building new tissue with the assistance of the healthy blood.

Use Chaparral as described in the Blood-Purifier application, especially the 21-Day Chaparral Cleanse. Remember, if you get your liver working well it could be the end of many of the other nagging health problems you may be struggling with.

Externally, use a poultice made of Chaparral, or one of the alternative herbs, directly over the liver.

The kidneys and liver work closely together, and proper diet will make a big difference in their functioning. Avoid fried foods, fats, caffeine, alcohol and processed foods and sugars. Keeping dietary stress down will give the liver and kidneys a chance to do their job optimally.

For a TONIC to keep your liver in tip-top condition, use one of the following suggestions:

LIVER TONICS

1. Put 1 tsp. Comfrey leaf and up to 1/4 tsp. Chaparral into 1 cup hot water and steep for 10 to 15 minutes. Drink this once or twice a day at least four times a week. Morning and evening are good times. You may sweeten with a little honey if desired.
2. Drink 1 cup Yarrow tea once or twice a day at least four days a week. Do not sweeten.
3. Make 1/2 cup raw Onion and/or two average cloves raw Garlic a part of your daily diet at least four times a week.

It is easy and interesting to make up your own liver tonic creations as you become familiar with the Ten Essentials. For an idea of how to incorporate Chaparral unobtrusively into a daily herb tea of any kind, see the Personality Profile.

ALSO SEE: *Antibiotic, Blood-Purifier, Chemical Poisoning, Immune System, Kidneys*

ALTERNATIVE OR SUPPLEMENTARY SELF-HELP: *Cayenne, *Comfrey, *Garlic, Ginger, *Onion, People Paste, *Yarrow*

DOSAGE: *General*

LYMPH: Lymph fluid surrounds and saturates every cell in the body, carrying nourishment to the cells and bringing away waste products. Lymph fluids are pumped through the lymph system, via physical activity (exercise), to thousands of cleaning stations along the route called lymph nodes or lymph glands. Waste products are collected in these lymph glands and eliminated from the body via blood, sweat, and other eliminative channels.

Regular exercise and therapeutic massage, both effective means of "pumping" the lymph system, are two primary ways to keep the lymph system eliminating properly. Moreover, if the kidneys, liver, and blood are healthy the lymph glands will not become overtaxed and can do an efficient job of removing "extra" toxic substances from body tissues and the blood. This is a must when you are dealing with colds, flu, and environmental pollutants.

Use Chaparral as described in the Antibiotic and Blood-Purifier applications to stimulate more efficient cleansing and functioning of the lymph system. Also, a Ginger bath will encourage sweating and enhance the release of lymph wastes.

ALSO SEE: *Antibiotic, Blood-Purifier, Chemical Poisoning, Kidneys, Liver*

ALTERNATIVE OR SUPPLEMENTARY SELF-HELP: **Cayenne, Comfrey, Garlic, *Ginger, Onion, *Yarrow*

DOSAGE: *General*

MUCUS: See Congestion application.

PARASITES: Parasites include anything from microscopic amoebas to visible pinworms in the stools or mites beneath the skin. Chaparral is especially potent for any skin parasites. It kills and removes many types of parasites along with their effluents. (Did you know parasites leave excrements in your body?) Chaparral is often mixed with other "parasite herbs" such as Garlic to get a wider range of action.

Often a parasite infestation can be at the bottom of a particularly long-standing weakness or debilitation in the system. If you know or have reason to believe that this is the situation, begin using Chaparral either by itself or powdered with an equal part of Garlic and 1/4 part of Cayenne to help "carry" it. The treatments explained in the Antibiotic and Blood-Purifier applications are also good ones to use for a parasite dilemma.

If there are external signs of parasites as in ring worm, or even certain types of mites (scabies) and chiggers, applying a concentrated Chaparral tea, tincture, or poultice will often drive them out of the skin.

Parasites lodge predominantly in the intestines. An enema of Chaparral or Garlic can be quite useful as part of a program to purge them while you are also using internal (oral) means. Any parasite cleansing program should be followed by a repeat of the entire program after a rest period of seven to ten days. In this way you will be sure to eliminate any new infestation that may come from eggs that are left after the first cleansing. Follow through with the program again after one month for the same reason. Parasites are often quite tenacious, can "hide" in all sorts of nooks-and-crannies internally, and may have particularly stubborn eggs and "survivors," so a three-phase program is necessary.

Here is my suggested Parasite Program. For a period of seven days, use either the Chaparral or Chaparral/Garlic formula as listed in the Antibiotic application. Take 2 size "00" capsules of the herb(s) with a full 8oz. glass of water every three to four hours. One to three times during the week, use an enema of Chaparral or Garlic. Add raw Garlic and raw Onions to your diet. Wait one week and repeat the program. Wait one month and repeat the program again.

As Garlic is also an excellent herb for parasites, be sure to review the Parasite application in the Garlic Chapter, Chapter VI.

ALSO SEE: *Antibiotic, Blood-Purfier*

ALTERNATIVE OR SUPPLEMENTARY SELF-HELP: **Garlic, Onion, Yarrow*

DOSAGE: *as given*

PETS/ANIMALS: For this application, Chaparral tincture is most easily administered. For large animals you can try capsules, pill, or honeyball (see Chapter I, Lesson #2 for instructions in these preparations).

I recommend Chaparral for animals whenever an antibiotic is needed externally or internally and in cases where an animal is appearing sickly but is not sick enough to warrant an emergency veterinary visit. I suggest one of the formulas listed in the Antibiotic application.

ALSO SEE: *Use any human applications that are similar to the animal's needs.*

ALTERNATIVE OR SUPPLEMENTARY SELF-HELP: **Comfrey, *Garlic, *People Paste*

DOSAGE: *General*

POISONING: See Blood-Purifier and Chemical Poison applications.

POISON IVY/OAK: See Skin application.

PROSTATITIS: See Antibiotic and Blood-Purifier applications internally; also use sitz baths of Yarrow or Chaparral infusion, alternating very warm water for three to five minutes and cold water (60 to 70 degrees F.) one to two minutes. Do these sitz baths one to three times a day.

ALSO SEE: *Antibiotic, Blood-Purifier*

ALTERNATIVE OR SUPPLEMENTARY SELF-HELP: **Comfrey, *Garlic, *Yarrow*

DOSAGE: *General*

RHEUMATISM: Chaparral is very potent for this. Use as in the Antibiotic, Blood-Purifier, and Gout applications.

RING WORM: See Parasite application.

SCABIES: See Parasites and Skin applications.

SCALP: For dandruff, scalp eczema, rashes, lice, wash the scalp with shampoo and give a final rinse with strong (1 Tbsp. per cup) Chaparral tea. Let the tea dry on the hair and scalp. Do this once a week as a preventive measure or every day for a severe scalp problem. A strong rinse of Chaparral tea can be left on the scalp at night and rinsed with plain water in the morning. As the symptoms subside, lessen the frequency of the Chaparral rinses.

ALWAYS test the Chaparral on a hair swatch, especially for longer treatments or for light-colored hair, to determine that it does not change your hair color. It is a natural dye in cloth—for a beautiful sand color—and although I have never known it to change hair color, better safe than sandy.

For chronic problems it is a good idea to complete the 21- Day Chaparral Cleanse as described in the Blood-Purifier application or use one of the internal formulas listed in the Antibiotic application.

Lymphatic wastes (blood impurities) on the scalp often contribute significantly to scalp problems. Review the Lymph application.

ALSO SEE: *Antibiotic, Blood-Purifier, Lymph, Parasites, Skin*

ALTERNATIVE OR SUPPLEMENTARY SELF-HELP: **Cayenne, *Comfrey, Yarrow*

DOSAGE: *General; use rinses as described.*

SINUSITIS: Use Chaparral internally as described in the Antibiotic and Blood-Purifier applications. In addition, for fast relief, use as a nasal rinse. Prepare 2 parts Chaparral with 1 part Comfrey root or Slippery Elm made into a tea. Strain well and discard the herbs. Slowly breathe the tea up into one nostril at a time, spitting the tea out through the mouth as it comes down into the back of the throat and mouth through the nasal passages. Rinse each nostril in turn, repeatedly, until one half to one full cup of tea has been used.

Frequent rinsings may dry the nasal passages in a way that produces slight discomfort. If that occurs, simply apply a light coating of an herbal salve or olive oil in the nostrils with your finger. The addition of the Comfrey root or Slippery Elm to the nasal rinse will add a mucilaginous quality and should serve to minimize this drying effect.

ALSO SEE: *Antibiotic, Blood-Purifier*

ALTERNATIVE OR SUPPLEMENTARY SELF-HELP: *Comfrey, *Garlic, *Peppermint, Slippery Elm, *Yarrow*

DOSAGE: *General, and nasal rinses as given*

SKIN: In thinking through everything that can commonly go "wrong" with skin, I came up with this partial list: itching, poison ivy/oak, bug bites, rashes, impetigo (staph infection), parasites, scratched and gummy mosquito bites, wounds of all sorts, inflamed splinters, fungus, "liver spots" (those spreading brown blotches, especially on the hands, arms, and face, that often occur as we get older), psoriasis, acne, eczema, dandruff, blackheads and whiteheads .... The list is seemingly endless.

Depending on how annoying the problem is, choose a simpler or more complex method using Chaparral and/or one of the supplementary herbs listed below. Except for the simplest "Skin Thing", it's best to start by cleaning irritating substances out of the blood, so look to using Chaparral, Chaparral/Comfrey, or one of the other formulas listed in the Antibiotic and Blood-Purifier applications above internally. Externally, especially for immediate relief of symptoms such as itching or infection, use a Chaparral soak, wash, poultice or fomentation.

When the blood, eliminative, and cleansing systems are overloaded with toxins, the skin (because it is an exit area for lymph fluid, dead cells, etc.) will commonly handle the excess. With long-term overload on the body's systems, chronic complaints such as psoriasis, eczema, acne, etc., are often the result. When poisons are stored in the skin itself, you might see symptoms such as "liver spots." If the toxins are trying to eliminate through the skin, you will see rashes, dandruff, impetigo, etc. In any case the basic treatment methods are the same. The major difference would be in the length of time the blood-cleansing and rehabilitation would be continued.

It is extremely important to have the kidneys and liver working efficiently when dealing with a long-term skin problem.

Since Comfrey is a major herb for rebuilding new tissues quickly, it is good to review that chapter (Chapter V) and its skin application.

ALSO SEE: *Antibiotic, Blood-Purifier, Herpes, Parasites, Venereal Disease, Wounds*

ALTERNATIVE OR SUPPLEMENTARY SELF-HELP: **Comfrey, Garlic, *Ginger (esp. as a bath), *People Paste, *Slippery Elm, Yarrow*

DOSAGE: *General*

SORES: See Antibiotic and Wounds application.

STOMACH: See Digestion application.

STY: See Eyes application.

TUMORS: Largely because of its NDGA and turpenes (review the Personality Profile) Chaparral has gotten quite a good reputation for lessening or eliminating various types of tumors. I have seen Chaparral work in the removal of fibroids, skin cancers, warts, moles and fatty tumors.

I suggest starting with the 21-Day Chaparral Cleanse as described in the Blood-Purifier application. This helps cleanse the system in a gentle way.

Next, if further self-help is desired, use one or more of the formulas described in the Antibiotic application. I suggest alternating use of straight Chaparral (2 capsules) with 2 capsules of one of the formulas suggested in the Antibiotic application. Take capsules every two to four hours, alternating between the straight Chaparral and the Antibiotic choice. If you find that taking the herbs every two hours is too much, especially at first, then lessen the amount and frequency. Even one capsule of each formula alternated every four hours can be quite useful.

Simultaneously with an internal application, use a Chaparral or Chaparral/Comfrey Root poultice or fomentation applied directly to the unwanted growth. Change the poultice two to three times a day. If the growth is not serious (i.e., a few warts, a benign mole, or a small cyst) a poultice left on overnight or from one to three hours during the day should suffice.

Include seaweeds, foods high in chlorophyll, whole grains, and fresh fruits and vegetables in the diet. Eliminate "high stress" foods from the diet such as caffeine, alcohol, processed sugars and other processed foods, fried foods, and foods high in preservatives, additives, and fats.

Consult *Natural Healing With Herbs* by Humbart Santillo (see Resource Guide, Appendix C) for more specifics concerning tumors, both malignant and benign.

Read the TASOLE under the Venereal Disease application for an example of how benign growths were eliminated.

ALSO SEE: *Antibiotic, Blood-Purifier, Chemical Poisoning, Lymph, Venereal Disease (for venereal warts)*

ALTERNATIVE OR SUPPLEMENTARY SELF-HELP: **Comfrey, *Garlic, Yarrow*

DOSAGE: *General or as given*

URINARY TRACT: When using Chaparral to fight a urinary tract infection or imbalance, always mix it with an equal part of a demulcent herb such as Comfrey root or Slippery Elm to buffer its action. Take 2 capsules of the mixture every two hours until pain stops and then lessen the dosage over a period of seven days until it stops altogether.

With frequently recurring urinary tract infections, complete the 21-Day Chaparral Cleanse as described in the Blood-Purifier application, or use 1 or 2 capsules of a Chaparral/demulcent herb combination one to three times a day as a preventive.

Several students have told me that the use of Chaparral with a demulcent herb was instrumental in lessening or eliminating kidney stones and gravel. However, I have used it mainly for infections, congestion, and sluggishness in the urinary tract.

ALSO SEE: *Antibiotic, Blood-Purifier, Kidneys*

ALTERNATIVE OR SUPPLEMENTARY SELF-HELP: **Comfrey, *Garlic, *Slippery Elm, *Yarrow*

DOSAGE: *As given*

VENEREAL DISEASE: I have seen remarkable results from using Chaparral in cases of herpes, venereal warts, gonorrhea, and various genital infections that were never officially diagnosed.

Internal Formulas: Choose one depending on which herbs you have on hand. If possible, review the Profile on each herb suggested.

1. Steep 1 oz. each of Slippery Elm, Ginger, Comfrey, and Chaparral in 2 cups of boiling hot water, covered, for 20 to 30 minutes. Strain. Drink 1/2 cup of this formula four to six times a day. Continue for five to seven days after all symptoms are gone. Alternatively you could use this formula as a powdered combination and take 2 or 3 capsules every three or four hours with an 8 oz. glass of water.
2. Take 2 capsules of either straight Chaparral, or a Comfrey/Clove combination every two hours, alternating between the two formulas. Continue for five to seven days after all symptoms are gone.
3. Choose two formulas from the Antibiotic application and alternate between these, taking two capsules every two hours. Continue for five to seven days after all symptoms are gone.
4. Complete the 21-Day Chaparral Cleanse as described in the Blood-Purifier application.

Externally: Take a Ginger bath twice a week (see Ginger chapter, Chapter VII). For further symptomatic relief, use Peppermint water made with 15 to 20 drops of Peppermint oil in a shallow tub or basin of water (see Peppermint chapter, Chapter IX) as a rinse for any external eruptions, or use as a sitz bath or soak.

Another excellent sitz bath would be to use Formula #1 above, making an infusion for external use.

Taking 300 mg. calcium/magnesium with 1 gram calcium ascorbate (a form of vitamin C) every hour or two can help greatly with pain and the healing process.

Women can use vaginal boluses as described in the Female Discomfort application or made by using a formula from this application.

TASOLE: My student, Geraldine, went for her yearly health check-up and discovered she had developed venereal warts. She decided to complete the 21-Day Chaparral Cleanse (as described here in the Blood-Purifier application). In addition to using the Chaparral internally, she also used a clove of Garlic as a vaginal suppository once or twice a day (see Vaginal Infection application in the Garlic chapter, Chapter VI).

Ten days into the program she noticed a significant change in the chronic athlete's foot fungus she had had since the age of eight. It was steadily disappearing and by the second week was totally gone, never to return.

Of course, she hoped that the same thing was happening with the venereal warts. Next she noticed that her menstrual cycle was particularly easeful that month and her energy level was noticeably higher than usual. About that time she experienced a day or two of the emotional sensitivity that is often a part of any potent blood-cleansing process. Spontaneously during the day she would recall little traumas or sad moments from the past year that she had forgotten. She would cry, often for no apparent reason, but would still feel a sense of well-being. Within a day or two the phenomena completely stopped and she resumed her normal emotional equilibrium. (This is an example of the "retracing" I described in the Blood-Cleansing application.)

Six weeks after her test had shown the venereal warts, she was retested. The venereal warts were completely gone.

Geraldine now regularly does the Chaparral Cleanse once or twice a year just for a "tune-up" and has never had a recurrence of the previous symptoms.

ALSO SEE: *Antibiotic, Blood-Purifier, Female Discomfort, Herpes, Liver, Lymph*

ALTERNATIVE OR SUPPLEMENTARY SELF-HELP: *Comfrey, *Garlic, Ginger, Slippery Elm, Yarrow*

DOSAGE: *As given*

VENEREAL WARTS: See Venereal Disease application.

WOUNDS: Into a bleeding wound sprinkle a 1/8 to 1/4 inch layer of powdered Chaparral, plain or mixed with an equal part of powdered Comfrey root or leaf. The Comfrey is especially helpful if there is bleeding. Cover the herbs with a sterile gauze pad held in place with a bandage of clean natural fiber cloth.

For a non-bleeding or slightly bleeding wound, apply a moistened herb poultice. Use the powdered herbs as above but moisten them into a paste with raw honey, aloe vera gel, or glycerin. Water will also work temporarily, but it will soon dry and become stiff. Bandage the wound as described above.

Chaparral infusion can be used as an antibiotic soak or wash for the wound when changing the dressings.

For wounds that threaten infection, either locally or of the whole body, use an internal antibiotic formula from the Chaparral chapter or the Garlic chapter (Chapters III and VI).

ALSO SEE: *Antibiotic, Blood-Purifier, Lymph, Skin*

ALTERNATIVE OR SUPPLEMENTARY SELF-HELP: *Clove, *Comfrey, *Garlic, *People Paste, Slippery Elm, Yarrow*

DOSAGE: *General*

YEAST INFECTION (vaginal): For a vaginal yeast infection, Chaparral tea can be used as a douche,one to three times a week for up to two weeks. Additional internal applications of Chaparral, as described in the Fungus application above, can be used if needed. Often the Chaparral douche is enough. Douching can be drying to the vaginal tissues and I only suggest using it on a temporary basis. It is best to mix 1/2 part of a soothing herb such as Comfrey root or Slippery Elm with the Chaparral,especially if douching more than once a week.

ALSO SEE: *Blood Purifier, Female Discomfort, Fungus, VenerealDisease*

ALTERNATIVE OR SUPPLEMENTARY SELF-HELP: **Garlic, *Yarrow*

DOSAGE: *General or as given*

CLOVES

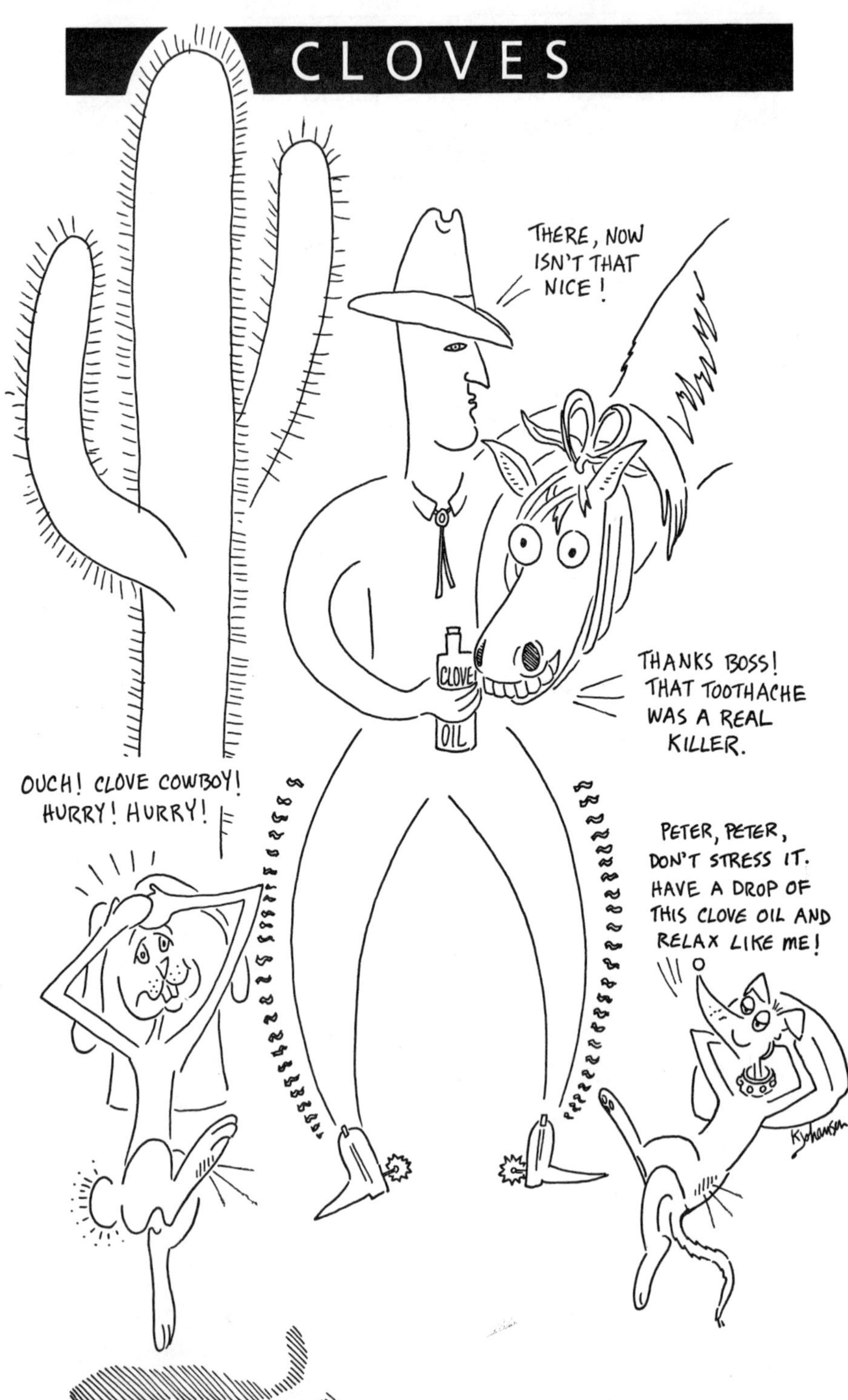
THERE, NOW ISN'T THAT NICE!
THANKS BOSS! THAT TOOTHACHE WAS A REAL KILLER.
CLOVE OIL
OUCH! CLOVE COWBOY! HURRY! HURRY!
PETER, PETER, DON'T STRESS IT. HAVE A DROP OF THIS CLOVE OIL AND RELAX LIKE ME!

CHAPTER IV

CLOVE

Caryophyllus aromaticus

Clove Cowboy's for pain, to relax or sedate
Just make some Clove tea, right now do not wait.
Comes his friend with a toothache to ask for advice
Clove Cowboy says "Clove oil," now isn't that nice?

PERSONALITY PROFILE—Clove

Clove can be an immediate relief for many types of pain.This is a primary reason I have included it among the Ten Essentials.

Did you know that:

- When you go to a dentist and he puts a spot of "something" on your gum to numb it before administering an injection, that "something" is often Clove oil?
- When babies are teething and are fussy from the discomfort in their gums, they can get almost immediate relief from the application of Clove oil?
- The small, yet annoying, pains of bruises, smashed fingers, sore throat, canker sores, cuts and scrapes, etc.,can all be eased with Clove oil?
- The pain of swollen glands, sinus headache, stomach-ache, earache, stress headache, mild anxiety and sleeplessness all respond to Clove?

Pain is often the factor that pushes us "over the edge" into using a toxic, expensive, sometimes addictive, yet often convenient "modern drug" pain reliever. That pain can often be handled instead by reaching for the Clove, in one of its application forms, first.

Clove is actually the dried bud of the Clove plant and many of us are familiar with seeing these buds stuck into the outside of a ham while it is baking for a holiday feast. Or maybe Clove chewing gum is one of our favorites. While Clove is a potent painkiller in many circumstances, it is also a strong antiseptic and a stimulant to the circulation. In fact it is another herb, like Peppermint, that is paradoxical in that it is relaxing and stimulating at the same time. By this I mean that it is soothing and relaxing to the nerves while stimulating to the circulatory system, although not as potent a stimulant as Cayenne or Ginger. Clove helps break up mucous congestion, gets sluggish organs moving (especially when mixed with other herbs), soothes nausea and vomiting and will increase the action of other herbs with which it is mixed. Although Clove is not as major a carrier, stimulant or binder as are Cayenne and Ginger, it is good to remember Clove does have these actions, in milder form, for use in cases where Cayenne and/or Ginger are too strong for the application or person. It is also a good choice when you want to add the nerve-soothing quality of Clove and want only mild stimulating action present.

Much of the strength of Clove resides in its volatile oil. This oil is a convenient form to use especially for external pain relief. It can be purchased in most drug or health food stores in a small vial, and I recommend that you take some along for travel. The oil in the dried buds is also quite easy to access, however, simply by making a tea or decoction of the desired strength. This phrase "of the desired strength" covers a wide range of possibilities, so let me explain this a little further.

To make a cup of Clove tea that would be pleasant to drink as well as relaxing to the nerves, you would take perhaps 1/4 to 1/2 tsp. of the buds and simmer them in a cup of water for about 10 minutes in a covered pot. The cover on the pot is to protect the volatile oils from evaporating more than necessary. Many times I have strained the Clove buds out of the tea and saved them for another brew of tea over the next day or so — that's how potent they are. This average strength of the tea is very tasty and can be flavored with honey, vanilla, and/or the addition of a little milk. The more Clove you use and the longer you (gently) simmer, the stronger it will get in both flavor and action. If you take a teaspoon of Clove buds and simmer them in two cups of water for 15 to 20 minutes, you will usually have a brew strong enough to begin numbing your tongue. This is considered an **average strength decoction** and is taken in 1/4 cup doses (for adults) as needed, rather than drunk in its entirety as a cup of tea. There are occasions when larger doses of a very strong decoction might be used, as when there is an emergency need for knock-out sedative action, yet in general smaller and more frequent doses of this herb are the most useful.

TASOLE: Jerry grew up in an herb-conscious family until he was 18. He then enlisted in the army and was gone from home for several years, during which time the stress level of his life escalated considerably. On one visit home Jerry was so stressed and anxious that he could not sleep. Sitting in the kitchen and reading, he decided to brew up a cup of Clove tea in the hope it might help him relax. Since his family ran mostly on "herb power," there were none of the usual sleeping pills, etc.,immediately available that he might normally have tried. As his tea was brewing he got so involved in the reading that he forgot the tea on the stove and it almost boiled away. Replenishing the water in the tea, he began heating it once more and went back to his reading. Again, however, he forgot the tea and it almost boiled away a second time except for the sludge (now very dark) in the bottom of the pot. He added water to this small amount of dark brew in an effort to start over once again and went back to his reading. This scenario happened three or four times before he finally got a cup of tea in hand, and by then it was so strong that it was not at all pleasant to drink it.

It was very late by now and all others in the house had long since gone to bed, so he half-heartedly decided to try to sleep and impatiently downed the entire cup of quadruple-cooked "Clove Potion" before getting in bed. He fell into a deep sleep and did not stir for hours. Ten hours later his family checked on him to see if he was all right, as no one yet knew of the brew he had drunk. All his vital signs were fine and he seemed to be sleeping peacefully, undisturbed by the sounds of the people in his room. After twelve hours they still thought he was just "extra tired," but after sixteen hours, they began to wonder what was up. Just as they were thinking there might be cause for worry, Jerry stirred and slowly rose from the bed, totally amazed that almost 18 hours had passed! Since he had been unable to sleep and had been stressed out for so long, this extended rest greatly strengthened him, although he did feel a little groggy for a short while longer. At first he said he didn't know why he had slept like that, yet when he described the "trouble" he had in making that cup of Clove tea, everyone understood what had happened.

After that he began to use an average cup of Clove tea at night to help him relax before sleeping and this worked quite well. He learned that the incredibly strong decoction he had made was not the thing for regular use. It was far too overpowering for his body. Not long after this he came to the end of his enlistment and left the army, whereupon his anxiety also left him.

APPLICATIONS AND ATTRIBUTES - CLOVE

(Quick Reference List)

ANESTHETIC
ANTISEPTIC
ANXIETY
APHRODISIAC
AROMA THERAPY
BAD BREATH
BATH
CANKER SORES
CIRCULATION
CLOVE BATH
COUGH
CRAMPS
CUTS/SCRAPES
DIGESTION
EARACHE
FEVER
GAS
GLANDS
GUMS
HANGNAIL
HALITOSIS
IMPOTENCE
INGROWN TOENAIL/ HANGNAIL
INSOMNIA
LUNGS
MOUTH
MUCOUS CONGESTION
NAUSEA
NERVES
PAIN
PERSPIRATION THERAPY
PYORRHEA
SEDATIVE
SEXUAL STIMULANT
SINUS
SKIN
SLEEP
STIMULANT
TEETHING
THROAT
TOOTHACHE
TRANQUILIZER
VOMITING

FORM:

Dried powder, dried whole Clove buds, Clove oil

APPLICATION METHODS:

Internally use tea, decoction, gargle, powder, Clove oil. Externally use decoction, powder, or Clove oil as poultice or soak. The Clove oil is also used as a direct application for pain relief on sores, swellings, bruises, "corns," gums, ears, etc.

AVAILABILITY:

Grocery stores, health and herb stores, mail order (see Buyer's Guide, Appendix D), open-air markets in many countries

HINTS/CAUTIONS:

Do not use Clove when inflammation of stomach or intestines is present, as it can occasionally increase the irritation. Clove oil, when used internally, is given in small, carefully regulated doses by drops as it is possible for it to be too strong in rare cases, causing a temporary irritation of the stomach. I usually prefer the other forms, rather than the oil, for internal use, to be extra safe.

GENERAL DOSAGE: INTERNAL USE

⋆PLEASE NOTE: *Although in many cases I emphasize using the herb in tea, there are many other forms of herbal preparations which can be substituted — such as Capsule, Decoction, Children's Preparations, etc. See these headings as well as Dosage Equivalents in Chapter I, Lesson #2 (General How-To).*

Infants to 3 years: 1 or 2 tsp. of decoction prepared as described in the Personality Profile, as often as every hour or two if needed; up to 1 cup of decoction in twenty-four hours. Could be administered with a dropper and sweetened with honey or light, unsulphured molasses if desired.

Children 4 to 10 years: An average cup of tea as described in the Personality Profile can be taken as desired. Alternatives include:

- 1 to 2 Tbsp. of decoction prepared as described in the Personality Profile, as needed, up to 10 oz. of decoction a day.
- Clove powder, made into a honeyball (see Chapter I, Lesson #2), could be eaten as needed in 1/4 tsp. doses up to approximately 2 tsp. per day.

- 1 drop Clove oil in a little warm water up to six times a day if it is well tolerated by the stomach.

Children 11 years to Adults: 1 cup of tea as described in the Personality Profile as needed. Alternatives include:

- 4 Tbsp. (1/4 cup) decoction prepared as described in Personality Profile, up to six times a day.
- 1/4 tsp. Clove powder in capsule or honeyball (see Honeyball and Capsule in Chapter I, Lesson #2) as often as every hour up to approximately 2 tsp. in each twelve hours.
- 2 drops of Clove oil in a little warm water up to eight times a day if well tolerated by the stomach.

Pets and Other Creatures: Use according to approximate body weight as compared to a person.

GENERAL DOSAGE: EXTERNAL USE

Same For All Humans And Other Creatures

Externally, the main reasons to use Clove are as an antiseptic and for pain relief. The Clove oil works almost immediately in most cases and in my experience the effects can last up to an hour or two (sometimes more). The whole Clove buds can be chewed or ground into a pulp, or powdered Clove can be used for poulticing (add a wetting agent such as honey). A Clove poultice can be wrapped in gauze to hold it together in a convenient size and shape before application. For example, roll a poultice into a cigarette shape to be held in the cheek next to a painful tooth. In any case the poultice needs to be wet (saliva works great for use in your mouth) to activate the strongest action. A fomentation of Clove decoction can also be used. (See Chapter I, Lesson #2, for poultice and fomentation preparation.)

APPLICATIONS AND ATTRIBUTES - CLOVE

ANESTHETIC: See Pain application.

ANTISEPTIC: Besides its strong pain relieving quality, the tannins in the Clove oil make it strongly antiseptic. Say you get an abscessed tooth while on a holiday and must wait to get to a dentist. You can use an antiseptic Clove poultice to help break down the infection while at the same time numbing the bulk of the pain.

The Clove oil concentrate (from the health food store) is great for use as an immediate rub-on antiseptic but may require more frequent reapplication, especially if left uncovered. A good trick for prolonging the antiseptic and pain relief action of any external Clove application is to cover the area with a bandage that retains a little moisture so as to protect the volatile oils from evaporating.

AlSO SEE: *Earache, Mouth, Pain, Sinus*

ALTERNATIVE OR SUPPLEMENTARY SELF-HELP: **Chaparral, *Comfrey, *Garlic, *People Paste, Peppermint, Yarrow*

DOSAGE: *General*

ANXIETY: See Nerves application.

APHRODISIAC: See Sexual Stimulant application.

AROMA THERAPY: The scent of Cloves is famous for its soothing and sensual qualities. Clove oil can be used as a "medicinal perfume" to soothe and relax the physical body as well as the emotions. A pot of Cloves simmering and evaporating slowly on a stove top or over a hearth is a nice way to get the fragrance into a larger environment. Try this in a room where there has been some emotional upset or when you anticipate a volatile meeting of some sort. It can calm the mood. Clove scent is also wonderful in imparting a good-smelling, antiseptic action in the air of a sick-room. In any case it is an aroma to enjoy just for the beauty of it.

ALSO SEE: *Antiseptic, Nerves, Pain*

ALTERNATIVE OR SUPPLEMENTARY SELF-HELP: **Peppermint*

DOSAGE: *Use as given.*

BAD BREATH: Chew on a whole Clove bud to immediately freshen the breath. This is all you will need if the bad breath is from something you just ate or the result of a temporary illness.

To address the deeper cause of bad breath you will need a more long-term approach. Use a blood-cleansing herb such as Chaparral, Comfrey, or Yarrow and work on getting all eliminative channels open and working at peak efficiency. This means that it is a good idea to sweat, have bowel movements, urinate, take baths/showers, skin brush, exercise, and do deep breathing exercises as much as possible. Waste matter trapped in the body becomes the same as a refuse dump that is not tended properly. This is the odor detected in chronic cases of bad breath.

ALSO SEE: *Digestion, Nerves*

ALTERNATIVE OR SUPPLEMENTARY SELF-HELP: *Chaparral, Comfrey, Ginger, *Peppermint, Yarrow*

DOSAGE: *Use one Clove bud chewed in the mouth or 1 tiny drop of Clove oil on the tongue.*

BATH: See Clove Bath application.

CANKER SORES: See Mouth application.

CIRCULATION: Clove has mild stimulating properties that gently enhance circulation to cold extremities, increase circulation to internal organs and help encourage sweat glands to work properly. The stimulating quality of Clove is much milder than the potent stimulation of Ginger or Cayenne. Another difference that Clove has in its stimulating property is that it is coupled with a unique pain relief and nerve-soothing quality.

ALSO SEE: *Digestion, Nausea, Nerves, Pain, Sexual Stimulant*

ALTERNATIVE OR SUPPLEMENTARY SELF-HELP: **Cayenne, Chaparral, Comfrey, *Ginger, Onion, *Peppermint, Yarrow*

DOSAGE: *General*

CLOVE BATH: A bath in Clove tea will calm and sooth the whole body as well as any skin irritation. To prepare this bath, make 2 to 4 quarts of Clove decoction using 1 tsp. whole Cloves per cup of water and slowly simmer (covered) for 20 to 30 minutes. Add this to a bath of warm water. If Clove powder is used in making the decoction, steep the powder in a covered pan instead of simmering.

ALSO SEE: *Nerves, Pain, Skin*

ALTERNATIVE OR SUPPLEMENTARY SELF-HELP: **Ginger, *Peppermint*

DOSAGE: *Use as given.*

COUGH: Use Clove tea, perhaps flavored with honey (refrain from milk during a cough), to help calm a cough and expel mucus from the throat. Clove is especially effective when combined with one or two of the other potent "cough herbs" among the Ten Essentials, such as Slippery Elm, Comfrey, Onion, Peppermint, or Garlic. The Clove adds its soothing, pain-relieving qualities to any mixture. Combine two to four of these herbs into a cough syrup or cough lozenges (see Chapter I, Lesson #2 for syrup and lozenge applications), or use the powdered herbal mixture in capsules, honeyballs, or taken straight in the mouth with water. Two drops of Clove oil in 1/2 cup of water can be sipped as a cough suppressant.

ALSO SEE: *Antiseptic, Lungs, Mucous Congestion, Pain, Throat*

ALTERNATIVE OR SUPPLEMENTARY SELF-HELP: *Cayenne, *Comfrey, Garlic, Ginger, *Onion, *Peppermint, Slippery Elm*
DOSAGE: *General*

CRAMPS (stomach or abdominal): See Digestion application.

CUTS/SCRAPES: For small cuts and scrapes, even paper cuts or rug burns that are simply annoying but not serious, just rub powdered Cloves or Clove oil into the area for quick antiseptic action and pain relief all in one.

For more serious wounds, mix equal portions of Comfrey root powder with Clove powder, and moisten if needed with raw honey, molasses, aloe vera gel, or water for an excellent poultice.

ALSO SEE: *Antiseptic, Circulation, Pain, Skin*

ALTERNATIVE OR SUPPLEMENTARY SELF-HELP: *Cayenne, *Comfrey, *People Paste, *Slippery Elm, Yarrow*

DOSAGE: *General*

DIGESTION: Use Clove decoction prepared as described in the Personality Profile before a meal to stimulate digestive juices, lessen chance of gas and help prepare the stomach. It is also quite good for stomach or abdominal cramps when this is due to tension. Do not use Clove alone if there is a known ulcer or digestive infection present as in rare cases Clove can be a little irritating in this circumstance. If this is the case use an equal amount of Comfrey or Slippery Elm with the Clove to buffer and enhance it while still getting the advantage of Clove's good digestive and cramp-relaxing properties.

A drop or two of Clove oil in 1/2 cup water is also a good digestive aid before or after a meal, as long as it is well tolerated by the stomach (it usually is).

ALSO SEE: *Antiseptic, Circulation, Mucous Congestion, Pain*

ALTERNATIVE OR SUPPLEMENTARY SELF-HELP: **Cayenne, *Comfrey, Ginger, *Peppermint, Slippery Elm, Yarrow*

DOSAGE: *1/4 cup decoction before meals or 1 to 2 drops Clove oil in 1/2 cup water sipped before meals or when there is cramping*

EARACHE: Use a few drops of Clove oil mixed with an equal part of some neutral oil such as olive oil. Put a few drops of this mixture in each ear even if the earache is only in one ear. It is helpful to warm up the oil before putting it into the ears, but is not essential. Also it can be quite useful to rub this Clove oil (diluted or straight) onto the outside of the area just in front of and/or behind the ear, and onto any swollen or painful area near the ear, to enhance pain relief and antiseptic action.

Use Garlic oil in the ears, with the Clove oil, when you need a stronger antibiotic action. Using an Onion poultice, externally, can give additional help in drawing out fluids and infection from the ears.

If an infection in the ear or in the entire body is accompanied by an earache, it is wise to use blood-purifying and/or antibiotic herbs internally in some form. (See the supplementary herbs listed below.)

ALSO SEE: *Antiseptic, Glands, Pain*

ALTERNATIVE OR SUPPLEMENTARY SELF-HELP: **Chaparral, Comfrey, *Garlic, *Onion, Yarrow*

DOSAGE: *General or as given*

FEVER: Drink Clove tea during a fever for its soothing and calming effect. Soothing the body and relaxing the nerves gives the body the "breathing space" it needs to rebalance itself.

If additional help is needed for a more serious illness that involves a fever, look to the supplementary herbs listed below. You might need the stronger antibiotic action found in Garlic or Chaparral.

ALSO SEE: *Antiseptic, Circulation, Pain*

ALTERNATIVE OR SUPPLEMENTARY SELF-HELP: **Chaparral, Comfrey, *Garlic, Ginger, Peppermint, Yarrow*

DOSAGE: *General*

GAS: See Digestion application.

GLANDS: Rub Clove oil directly onto the area over a swollen lymph gland for immediate help with the pain and swelling. Lymph glands become swollen from a build-up of poisons in the body. The lymph glands become overtaxed when not able to eliminate an excessive amount of accumulating toxins by the usual harmonious means. Internal help for returning the system to normal is available by using the blood-purifying and antibiotic herbs listed below under Supplementary Self-Help. Clove could also be used internally for this deeper process either as a tea, a decoction, or mixed with supplementary herbs.

ALSO SEE: *Antiseptic, Circulation, Earache, Pain*

ALTERNATIVE OR SUPPLEMENTARY SELF-HELP: *Cayenne, *Chaparral, *Comfrey, *Garlic, *Ginger, Onion, People Paste (used internally and externally), Peppermint, Yarrow*

DOSAGE: *General and as given*

GUMS: See Mouth application.

HANGNAIL: See Ingrown Toenail application.

HALITOSIS: See Bad Breath application.

IMPOTENCE: See Sexual Stimulant application.

INGROWN TOENAIL/HANGNAIL: You may laugh that I have even listed hangnails and ingrown toenails as something needing help, yet I recently heard of a case in which a man died from an ingrown toenail that finally developed into gangrene! In any case, hangnails and ingrown toenails can be very painful and even become infected, so it is beneficial to know how to treat them. Rub Clove oil into an ingrown toenail or hangnail to stop the pain and help prevent infection whenever it is annoying enough to be worth the trouble.

ALSO SEE: *Antiseptic, Cuts/Scrapes, Pain*

ALTERNATIVE OR SUPPLEMENTARY SELF-HELP: *Comfrey, Garlic, *People Paste*

DOSAGE: *General*

INSOMNIA: See Sleep application.

LUNGS: Clove tea, decoction, and oil can all be used as mild expectorants. At the same time they will sooth and calm irritated lungs. It is quite effective to mix a Clove preparation with an additional "lung herb" such as Comfrey or Garlic in any of the forms listed in Chapter I, Lessons #2 and #6.

If a lung problem is due to constant contamination from pollutants on a job site or in the environment at large, Clove can be used as an ongoing decontaminant and soothing agent (especially when mixed with Comfrey). Of course it is always best to avoid the source of the lung-damaging pollutants altogether,yet I know this is not always possible.

ALSO SEE: *Antiseptic, Mucous Congestion, Nerves, Pain, Throat*

ALTERNATIVE OR SUPPLEMENTARY SELF-HELP: *Cayenne, Chaparral, *Comfrey, *Garlic, Ginger, Peppermint, Yarrow*

DOSAGE: *General*

MOUTH: Clove has many uses for things that can go wrong inside the mouth. These include: Canker sores (inside or out), abscess, pyorrhea, infected or sore gums, toothache, biting parts of the mouth while eating, and dental surgeries or while waiting for dental surgeries, etc. (Use Clove tea for the "waiting" anxiety.)

Apply straight Clove oil directly onto the painful area, or dilute it half and half with plain oil such as olive oil. Another type of application is to soak a bit of cotton with the solution and hold it on the area. Clove powder (or ground or chewed whole Clove buds) can be pressed together as is, or wrapped into a convenient shape inside a bit of gauze to be placed alongside an abscess or sore, or placed directly into an extraction hole. Regarding dental use, some people are very sensitive to using painkilling drugs, or simply don't want to use them, so it is good to know you can put Clove oil or powder directly onto, or into, the gums to numb them, as an alternative to the usual drugs. If it turns out the herbal approach isn't strong enough for you, there are always the drugs to turn to later. You can check with your dentist about the safe use of Clove.

In the case of painful mouth or gum infections such as pyorrhea, herpes simplex, thrush, etc., you will want to use strong antibiotic and blood-purifying herbs internally. These include Chaparral, Garlic, Comfrey, and People Paste. You can take these internally and also mix them with the Clove poultice that you are using inside the mouth.

For an excellent antibiotic and pain-relieving powder that can be used to brush the entire inside surface of your mouth, mix equal parts of Clove, Comfrey root, and Chaparral. Add a little toothpaste if you wish, and brush the mouth surfaces thoroughly several times a day. The more often you do this the faster the result.

In the Cayenne chapter (Chapter II) under the Gums application, there is an excellent formula to use for those suffering from chronic or acute mouth infections. If this is your situation you will want to review that application.

ALSO SEE: *Antiseptic, Pain*

ALTERNATIVE OR SUPPLEMENTARY SELF-HELP: **Cayenne, *Chaparral, *Comfrey, Garlic, Peppermint Oil*

DOSAGE: *General and as given*

MUCOUS CONGESTION: Use a Clove decoction prepared as described in the Personality Profile to help break down and expel accumulations of toxic mucus from the digestive tract and lungs. Powdered Clove can also be used alone or it is excellent when mixed with Comfrey or Slippery Elm for these purposes.

ALSO SEE: *Circulation, Digestion, Glands, Nausea, Pain*

ALTERNATIVE OR SUPPLEMENTARY SELF-HELP: *Cayenne, *Chaparral, *Comfrey, *Garlic, *Slippery Elm, *Yarrow*

DOSAGE: *General*

NAUSEA: Two drops of Clove oil in 1/2 glass warm water, sipped over the period of a few minutes, will often stop nausea and the stomach cramps associated with vomiting. Clove decoction can also be used for this, but since nausea often comes suddenly, it is good to have the immediate help of Clove oil. Small and regular doses of Clove tea or decoction can then be used for continued relief of nausea while the root cause of the problem is being eliminated. This might simply mean waiting for bad food to pass out of the system, or using some blood-purifying and/or antibiotic herb to deal with a stomach flu. (See supplementary herbs listed below).

ALSO SEE: *Antiseptic, Digestion, Nerves, Pain*

ALTERNATIVE OR SUPPLEMENTARY SELF-HELP: *Chaparral, Comfrey, Garlic, *Ginger, *Peppermint, *Slippery Elm, Yarrow*

DOSAGE: *General*

NERVES: Any time a quieting effect is needed, a pleasant way to soothe jangled nerves is to drink Clove tea plain, or flavored with milk and raw honey. In extreme cases use the decoction prepared as described in the Personality Profile. Try Clove when you are dealing with anxiety, tension, pain and nervousness from an illness or accident, sleeplessness, restlessness, or any time a quieting effect is needed.

Try a Clove bath for potent relaxation and soothing of anxiety and tension. See instructions for this in the Clove Bath application.

ALSO SEE: *Pain, Clove Bath, Sleep*

ALTERNATIVE OR SUPPLEMENTARY SELF-HELP: **Garlic, Peppermint*

DOSAGE: *Start with one cup of tea or 1/4 cup of decoction every two hours for adults. A much wider variation of preparation and dosage is described in the Personality Profile and General Dosage intructions.*

PAIN: Internally, for mild pain, drink a cup of Clove tea prepared as described in the Personality Profile. For stronger pain relief you might use the higher doses and stronger preparations given in the General Dosage section above.

Externally, Clove oil can give immediate relief. It is a strong oil and there are those who prefer always to dilute it about half and half and sometimes even more, with a more neutral oil such as olive oil. I like to use it straight unless it is on an area of sensitive skin, or when using on children in which case I always dilute it.

Clove sometimes stings like crazy for 10 to 20 seconds before its numbing properties take effect so I warn people of this ahead of time before applying it. If a Clove application ever stings for more than 30 seconds or so (vary rare indeed), I usually wash it off and dilute it before reapplying. If a Clove preparation ever seems too strong for internal or external use, mix it with an equal portion of a demulcent herb such as Slippery Elm (tastes good for internal use) or Comfrey root. This buffers any possible irritation internally and soothes and protects the skin externally.

Clove seems to work best on pain that is the result of tension, anxiety, temporary illness, or a localized physical injury/discomfort. I have found that its effect is inconsistent (with results ranging from negligible to extravagant) on deeper pain from prolonged illness, or with injuries involving extensive tissue damage. Yet even in these more severe cases, I find it worth trying before I go for a harsher drug because I have seen it work wonderfully when I only expected minimal results.

ALSO SEE: *Clove Bath, Nerves, Sleep*

ALTERNATIVE OR SUPPLEMENTARY SELF-HELP: *Chaparral, Comfrey, Garlic, People Paste, Peppermint*

DOSAGE: *General. In situations of severe pain, if you are getting some results from a mild or regular dose but think you require something more potent, make a stronger decoction and take doses more frequently.*

PERSPIRATION THERAPY: See Circulation application.

PYORRHEA: See Mouth application.

SEDATIVE: See Nerves, Pain, and Sleep applications.

SEXUAL STIMULANT: Occasionally I have had good results with students using Clove on a daily basis to help stimulate the sexual glands, thereby helping with impotency. Some students report to me that Clove tea is sexually stimulating both with its aroma and with its effect on the nerves, yet it doesn't have a harsh or overly dramatic effect.

One of the ways Clove helps impotency is by gently stimulating the circulation in the reproductive organs. It probably relieves congestion there too. Since Clove is for nourishing of the nerves and has such a strong calming action, it can help relieve tension that may contribute to impotency.

ALSO SEE: *Clove Bath, Nerves*

ALTERNATIVE OR SUPPLEMENTARY SELF-HELP: *Chaparral, *Garlic, Ginger*

DOSAGE: *Use a cup or two of the tea each day or 1 to 2 size "O" capsules of Clove powder two to three times a day.*

SINUS: Clove tea or decoction can be snuffed up into the nostrils, one at a time, for antiseptic value and pain relief during sinus infection or congestion. Clove mixed with Comfrey or Slippery Elm gives a more soothing rinse for irritated mucous membranes. (See Nasal Rinse application in Chapter II, Cayenne.)

For more potent draining of the sinuses, use one of the stimulating herbs as a nasal rinse. A few grains of Cayenne or Ginger in 1/2 cup warm salt water or plain salt water or Peppermint tea are good for this purpose. Follow with Clove or Slippery Elm rinse to soothe.

Breathing the steam of Clove tea or Clove oil in hot water can be quite soothing for sinus pain and accompanying headache.

ALSO SEE: *Antiseptic, Circulation, Nerves, Pain*

ALTERNATIVE OR SUPPLEMENTARY SELF-HELP: **Cayenne, *Comfrey, Garlic, *Ginger, *Peppermint Oil, *Slippery Elm, Yarrow*

DOSAGE: *General*

SKIN: Clove tea or decoction is a soothing and antiseptic soak or wash for any painful irritation or bruising of the skin. You could take an entire bath in it which would calm and sooth the whole body as well as the skin irritation. See Clove Bath application.

ALSO SEE: *Clove Bath, Nerves, Pain*

ALTERNATIVE OR SUPPLEMENTARY SELF-HELP: **Comfrey, *Chaparral, *Ginger, People Paste, Peppermint, Slippery Elm, Yarrow*

DOSAGE: *General*

SLEEP: Read the TASOLE in the Personality Profile for an insight into how effective Clove can be for inducing sleep. Usually a brew as strong as the one described in that story is not at all necessary. Generally, a cup of Clove tea before bed is quite enough. Drinking a cup of Clove tea while sitting in a Clove bath or Ginger bath (see those applications) can be a luxurious and relaxing prelude to a good night's sleep.

For severe sleep problems, like insomnia with anxiety, several of my students have had excellent results from using Clove decoction. They sometimes flavor it with milk and honey, and then drink it in 1/4 cup doses every 15 minutes during the hour before sleep. If any nausea results, that means you have had enough, although this rarely happens when the nerves are in great need. This is a strong dose of Clove decoction to take within an hour, yet when the body is in great need the results are generally good. In my experience, no one has reported any ill effects from this treatment except for a temporary numbing of the tongue on occasion.

A blood-purifying herb can also relieve a sleep disorder when the disorder is caused by a toxic build-up in the blood which has put severe wear and tear on the glandular and nervous systems. Of course chronic sleep problems need to be carefully investigated to find their underlying causes, and for this you may need professional help.

ALSO SEE: *Nerves, Pain, TASOLE in Personality Profile*

ALTERNATIVE OR SUPPLEMENTARY SELF-HELP: *Comfrey, *Garlic, *Ginger (bath), Peppermint*

DOSAGE: *General or as given — use higher and more frequent doses when there is greater need.*

STIMULANT: Clove is a mild stimulant to the circulation, digestion, and overall body functioning. It also enhances your energy level while soothing the nerves. Clove is not as strong in this area as is Cayenne or Ginger, but it is active enough to be worth mentioning.

ALSO SEE: *Circulation, Digestion*

ALTERNATIVE OR SUPPLEMENTARY SELF-HELP: **Cayenne, Chaparral, Garlic, *Ginger, Onion, Peppermint, Yarrow*

DOSAGE: *General*

TEETHING: Mix Clove oil with three to five parts olive oil so it won't be too strong for a baby's gums. Dip your finger into the diluted Clove oil and then rub your finger on the teething gums. It may sting a little for about 10 seconds or so and then the numbing effect will begin. It can be reapplied as needed. Also, Clove tea can be given in a bottle to help soothe and calm a teething baby's sensitivities.

One additional method for soothing teething traumas is a homeopathic remedy you can get at most health food stores that is especially for teething. It is made by Hylands company, is easily administered, often works quite well and has no side effects. Between these two items, the Clove oil and the homeopathic tablets, most teething difficulties are "easily" handled.

TASOLE: I have helped deliver several babies for friends and have established a special bond with each child. Then as the children grew up I often took part in their ongoing care. One of these cases involved a first-time mom and dad whose child was experiencing a severe bout of teething upset together with sore and painful gums. They called me after their child had been crying for over an hour or so. They were worried and anxious about what to do for him. The mom, Carolyn, told me that the child was crying so consistently and so hard that she was hesitant to annoy him further by trying to push her finger into his mouth to rub his gums as some books had recommended. She waited instead until I got there with the Clove oil. Since the parents were both so anxious and upset and this had a similarly upsetting effect on the child, I asked to hold the baby myself and then told the parents they could go sit down for a few minutes.

Since this pattern of intense crying had been repeated a couple of times over the previous weeks, they had been to their family doctor, only to be told that this was normal for teething, that the child was not sick, and primarily that there was nothing to worry about. That did not help the child's immediate need, as all parents know. The child was rubbing his gums together, drooling, and rubbing his face while kicking and crying persistently. He had all the signs of teething, so I got out the Clove oil dilution to try on the gums.

It was hard even to hold the child, let alone try to get the oil onto my finger, so several times I missed my goal and ended up with Clove oil on my clothes, the child's cheeks, the floor, etc. At one point everything coordinated for a moment and I got a fingerful of oil into his mouth for a quick yet vigorous rub onto his gums. This made him mad and he screamed louder for about 10 seconds. Then his cries began softening until they finally stopped. I rubbed on a little more oil — this time no resistance. When the room got silent the anxious parents came rushing in to see what had happened. There was a now quiet and wide-eyed child, exhausted from franticness, yet soothed and apparently not in pain. He very quickly fell asleep.

It was all quite dramatic. One minute there there was hysteria, and the next minute the baby was sleeping. The new parents were very relieved, as you can well imagine.

ALSO SEE: *Clove Bath, Nerves, Pain*

ALTERNATIVE OR SUPPLEMENTARY SELF-HELP: *Peppermint Oil [diluted 1:10 (Peppermint to oil) and rubbed onto the gums], Yarrow*

DOSAGE: *General and as given*

THROAT: For antiseptic pain relief put 1/4 tsp. Clove powder in a tablespoon of warmed olive oil (or some other healing oil such as sesame or sunflower). Take tiny sips of this solution and swallow it slowly so as to allow it to coat the throat. The oil helps hold the Cloves onto the throat area. Honey or glycerin (available at drug and health stores) also make great mediums to hold the Clove, but the oil lasts the longest. Gargling with Clove decoction, Clove oil in water, or Clove powder in water can also prove beneficial for pain relief.

Clove is excellent when mixed with Slippery Elm (tastes best) or Comfrey Root as these mucilaginous herbs, with their adhesive actions, keep the Clove action suspended in the throat.

Look in Chapter X, Slippery Elm, under the Cough Syrup and Throat applications to see how to make syrups and lozenges. Then take the methods and apply them to making a throat syrup or lozenge using Clove by itself or with Slippery Elm. Clove throat lozenges really work!

ALSO SEE: *Mouth, Nerves, Pain*

ALTERNATIVE OR SUPPLEMENTARY SELF-HELP: *Cayenne (good gargle), Ginger (good gargle), *Peppermint Oil, *Slippery Elm*

DOSAGE: *As given*

TOOTHACHE: See Mouth application.

TRANQUILIZER: See Nerves, Pain, and Sleep applications.

VOMITING: See Nausea application.

COMFREY

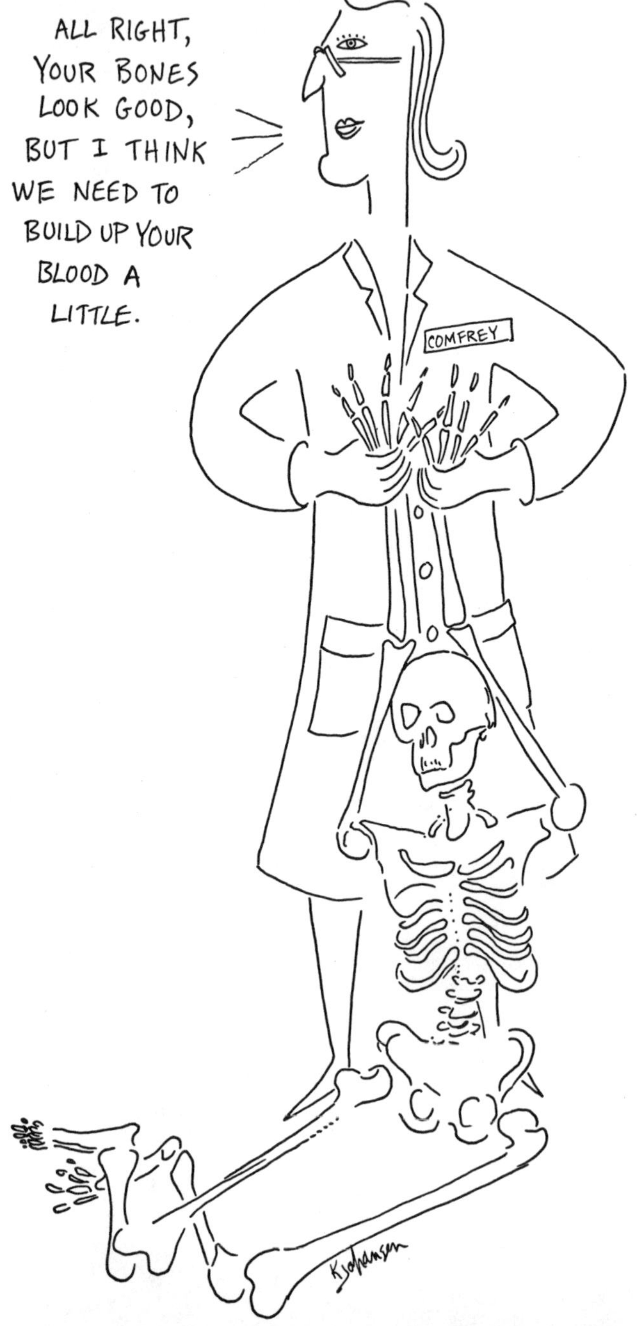
ALL RIGHT, YOUR BONES LOOK GOOD, BUT I THINK WE NEED TO BUILD UP YOUR BLOOD A LITTLE.
COMFREY

CHAPTER V

COMFREY

Symphytum officinale

Miss Comfrey rejuvenates blood and new skin;
Helping inside and out, she's a real gem.
She clears inflammation, works alone or with more
To mend bleeding and burns, broken bones to the core.

PERSONALITY PROFILE—Comfrey

Comfrey has some potent and unique characteristics that are very unusual in the world of plants. Comfrey is famous for its high amount of naturally occurring allantoin, which is found primarily in its roots, but in its leaves as well. Allantoin is a potent "cell proliferant" which means that it actively catalyzes the growth of new cells in all body tissue including bones.

Allantoin also hastens the cleanup of septic, sloughing surfaces (dead, diseased or slow-healing tissues) making way for the fast, new growth of healthy tissues. In healing flesh and bones, it is well known that new cells will not readily grow and rebuild over septic (diseased) surfaces. While allantoin itself is not antiseptic, it catalyzes growth of leucocytes in the blood which are our natural infection-fighters and infection-preventives. Allantoin acts like a hormone in that even small quantities can catalyze large, positive changes in the body's ability to slough off diseased cells and rehabilitate with healthy ones. Comfrey is no ordinary herb!

As early as the 16th century in England, doctors were using and writing about Comfrey's potent cell proliferating qualities. This was long before scientists identified the presence of allantoin. Later, allantoin was found to be an active agent in fetal development and in mother's milk where it helps the baby to grow.

Although allantoin on its own has been proven extremely effective in its healing abilities, there are many other properties of Comfrey that work *with allantoin* to enhance its action. These include Comfrey's strong collection of usable proteins, its rare ability to make available significant amounts of vitamin B12, and the mucilaginous quality of its leaves and roots which make it extremely soothing to irritated mucous membranes and other inflamed areas. Keep in mind that in herbistry every plant has many properties that work together to enhance each other, and that often, when a so-called "active ingredient" is extracted from a plant and used on its own, we lose this valuable interaction.

Comfrey is most potent when properly prepared. Allantoin is much more soluble in hot water than in cold, yet it begins decomposing quickly with prolonged heat, especially past the boiling point. Allantoin is also at its best when it is not prepared in hard water or left standing in its brewed form for more than 24 hours. What all this means is that for the most potent preparation of Comfrey root and leaves, you need to brew the Comfrey in distilled or soft water, bringing it just to the boiling point; steep it with a lid on for the needed length of time (10 minutes to 30 minutes, most commonly), and then use it immediately, or at least within 24 hours. For these reasons it is best to have Comfrey root powdered or chopped in small bits so it steeps easily and quickly. The dried or fresh leaves are easily torn or crumbled for convenient use. The idea is to have the most surface area of the Comfrey parts in contact with the hot water or other extracting medium. Sometimes, if the brew seems not as strong as I think it should be yet it has already cooled off and therefore is not continuing to extract the herb properly, I gently bring it back up to heat and let it sit some more. These "fine points" of Comfrey preparation will definitely enhance the potency of the herb usage yet are not so crucial that they ruin Comfrey's effectiveness if they are not followed. Even if you were to lightly simmer the root in regular tap water (as many people do) you could still expect substantial help from this powerful herb.

TASOLE: Over the years I have noticed in my herbal healing practice that as soon as I would learn to fix something, I would almost immediately get a series of requests from several different people for help with the same problem. This phenomenon was so common that I sometimes had a second thought about learning something new, knowing that I would probably be faced with having to treat several cases of it very soon! That's exactly what happened with a type of skin disease that was regularly diagnosed by doctors as eczema.

I am never sure what the diagnosticians are officially labelling as eczema. Many different-looking skin conditions have been brought to me, each one having been diagnosed as eczema by one health professional or another. In most cases the drug Cortisone had been prescribed in some form, generally as a cream, and the person coming to me would be seeking some alternative, given the known and lengthy list of possible side effects from using that medicine. Once I started getting regular success using Comfrey with many skin ailments, I began getting several requests in a row for help with increasingly painful, stubborn, and vicissitudinous (great word eh?) skin ailments, including eczema.

One memorable case was that of Emily, a young woman in her twenties who had severe eczema on her hands, wrists, eyelids, and randomly on other areas of the body. It was a non-stop eruption which kept her continuously in great discomfort and very isolated socially. Emily had found that the prescribed cortisone creams, as many other people had reported to me, gave dramatic yet temporary relief, but certainly no cure. I knew that over time, stronger and more frequent applications of cortisone would be needed in order to get the same symptomatic relief as initially experienced. Meanwhile, the risks involved in cortisone use would be increasing as well. At the same time, when dealing herbally with a case as long-term as Emily's, I knew we would need to do much more than a simple one-time poultice. I explained to her the commitment needed on a daily basis to help treat the cause of her skin problem.

Emily began to drink four cups of strong Comfrey root or Comfrey leaf tea every day. The intention was to gently cleanse and strengthen her blood while beginning to slough off diseased skin and rebuild new skin cells. She was to use cortisone as little as possible and eliminate stress-producing foods from her diet — processed sugar, caffeine, fried foods, etc. We also made a Comfrey salve to use directly on the skin. (There are several good ones on the market these days.) After about two weeks results were noticeable. Her skin was clearing on its own, with only occasional use of the cortisone cream, and it was staying that way for up to a week at a time instead of having eczema outbreaks as she had experienced previously, every three to five days. The Comfrey salve was soothing and helped the symptoms noticeably, yet not as dramatically as the cortisone had, but Emily felt she could live with this while continuing to work on the overall problem. Her commitment was rewarded within two months. She was able to do away with the cortisone altogether. Whenever she had a setback due to dealing with some of the deeper emotions and psychological issues associated with her skin ailment, she would simply increase the dosage of Comfrey (5-6 cups) for a few days and this proved effective. (We were using the tea form of Comfrey preparation as this puts the herb into the body in a readily usable form along with the extra water needed to flush the eliminative systems and clean the blood. This freed the skin from taking the brunt of this job as it had been.)

This method of self-help went on for three months, at the end of which the skin ailment was not visible except during times of extreme stress, and then only in small patches that cleared quickly. Emily's social life began to change; she felt stronger within herself, and her health took several strides forward. Over the months of dealing with her skin condition, both she and I saw clearly that her improvement was due to a combination of the things we were doing — from dietary changes to relaxation. Yet it was also clear that the use of Comfrey was a crucial factor in the self-help since the symptoms returned in force whenever she stopped it.

After three months of daily use of the Comfrey tea, Emily cut back to only two cups every day. The last I heard (at the end of one year) she was having a daily cup of Comfrey tea as a tonic and "preventive" and hadn't had an eczema outbreak for three months. The side effect of this Comfrey treatment was a noticeable improvement in her overall health as well, as Comfrey strengthened her whole system, not just her skin.

This is only one of many "skin stories." Comfrey is the herb I always think of first when a skin dilemma comes along.

Comfrey grows most easily from root cuttings. It is a plant that you will always want to take with you and start growing—indoors or outdoors—wherever you happen to be living. I have taken Comfrey root "starts" with me from the east coast to the southwest of the United States and have found that it will grow in a wide variety of circumstances. Comfrey roots should be harvested when the highest concentrations of allantoin are present, during the dormant winter months of January through March. At this time the plant is getting ready for renewed efforts of cell growth in spring, and has concentrated all its resources in the roots. Harvest the roots by digging them up, peeling off their rough external layer, and chopping them into smallish bits (you'll need a small hand-axe or large, sharp knife) for quick drying and more efficient preparation in the future. The roots will be quite moist. To guard against mold forming on them during drying, lay them out in thin layers on brown paper out of direct sunlight (this is great in hot and dry climates) or perhaps dry them in a low oven (100 to 120 degrees).

If you are not a plant-growing person, you can always get the dried leaves and roots at an herb store. Properly dried Comfrey leaves keep much of their deep green color, so don't buy them if they look all brown or greyish. Dried Comfrey root should be varying shades of cream to tan. If it looks blackish it may have been processed improperly.

Once Comfrey is planted, it's there for good. Comfrey roots go very deeply into the soil, somewhat like tree roots, and root-portions left in the soil after harvesting will start a new Comfrey plant in the spring.

By April and May, allantoin concentrations in the Comfrey roots are already beginning to lessen. That's when allantoin starts moving up — proliferating cells for the growth of fresh stems, leaves, and springtime flowers. While allantoin concentration in stems and leaves is never as dramatic as the amount the winter roots hold, the leaves (especially) and the stems (to the least degree) still hold significant and usable amounts of allantoin along with vitamins, minerals, and protein which add to Comfrey's healing properties and make it an important food crop for humans (it can be prepared like spinach, fresh or cooked) and farm animals as well (see Nutritional application below). The flowers are beautiful, and can be eaten, yet hold no significant amounts of allantoin. Therefore, the most "finicky" time for harvesting mature Comfrey leaves is anytime before or after the plant flowers. This is when the nutritive and allantoin properties are most potent in the leaves as they are not being directed toward the making of flowers or being withdrawn back into the roots in late fall for winter storage.

To harvest the mature leaves simply pick off a few and use them fresh, or cut leaves off—stems and all—and hang them upside down in bunches in a well shaded and dry area (indoors or out) until the leaves are well dried. Then it is easy to rub the leaves off the larger main stems (small, tender stems often stay with the leaf) into a bag or jar for storage somewhere dark and dry, as in a cupboard. Any leftover larger stems are great to put into the compost.

None of this is meant to intimidate you into thinking that you absolutely must stick to this time schedule of harvesting or must necessarily grow your own plants to get good results with Comfrey. Rather it *is* meant to point out when you can get the maximum potency from your Comfrey. I use any part of my fresh Comfrey plant whenever a need arises, no matter what time of the year it is. But if I am harvesting for later use, then I pay attention to the most potent harvesting times. In the case of using dried Comfrey purchased from an herb store, you have to assume that the commercial harvesters knew what they were doing. (Of course you'll check for proper color anyway, right?) Given the good results that most people have with purchased Comfrey, I would guess that such optimism is quite realistic.

When I first learned about all the ways to use Comfrey, I often got stumped trying to decide which part of the plant—root or leaf—to use for any given situation. Many of my herbalist friends would just say, "Use Comfrey for such-and-such," and if I didn't think to clarify exactly how to prepare it or apply it, I would get home and begin to question how to use it. Often I would be living in such secluded circumstances that it was not possible to make telephone contact when questions arose, so I sometimes felt anxious that I was using roots and leaves interchangeably depending on convenience and not on what might be "the best way," if only I knew what that was. This situation was further complicated by the fact that even when asked directly which part was best for such-and-such, my more experienced friends might give different answers at different times.

After much study and experience with fresh and dried Comfrey roots and leaves, I found that for most average uses—for wounds, digestive ailments, blood tonics, etc.—I got fairly equal and timely results with whatever Comfrey parts were handy. The leaves have enough allantoin for many needs and since they are higher in nutritional components and tastier to most people (when needed internally) they are often the first thing I reach for in "everyday" situations. When a friend or student needs help with internal bleeding, more long-term disease conditions, or old wounds or ulcerations that seem to drag on and on without healing, I usually find the Comfrey root to be what is called for as it is more potent in the allantoin department.

Comfrey leaves, both fresh and dried, are an extremely potent food source for humans and foraging animals, so I want you to be sure to read through the Green Drink, Nutrition, and Pets/Livestock applications in the list below. Years ago I discovered an excellent source book which contained detailed information about the use, nutritional value, and cultivation of Comfrey — *Comfrey: Food, Fodder and Remedy*, by Lawrence D. Hills (see Resource Guide, Appendix C). Although this book is now out of print, it is well worth searching for a copy through a public or university library. Also, check out *Herbal Pharmacy*, by John Heinerman, and *Natural Healing With Herbs*, by Humbart Santillo (see Resource Guide, Appendix C) for further contemporary input on the uses and properties of Comfrey in general.

At present, some researchers claim that Comfrey may contain varying amounts of saturated pyrrolizidine alkaloids (called PA's). For certain individuals, saturated PA's, when taken internally, are found to be harmful to the liver, especially with long-term, daily use. However, many other medicinal-plant educators/authors/users assert that Comfrey's long-standing reputation as a unique, safe, and profoundly healing herb, speaks for itself. I am one of the latter group, and therefore, have not hesitated to include Comfrey as one of my Ten Essentials. However, I am not "closing the book" on this question for my readers. I recommend a cautious approach when using Comfrey internally in some circumstances. (This does not apply to external uses). For children under three years, for pregnant or lactating women, or for those with a history of liver weakness or disease, I suggest using a liquid Comfrey concentrate that is totally free of PA's (thus eliminating the "PA question" altogether). This product is available from a company called "Herb Pharm." Look for it at your local health food store, or order directly from "Herb Pharm" (see Buyers Guide, Appendix D).

If you are not a member of any of the above "caution categories," yet would like to include extra support for your liver during any long-term (three weeks or more), daily, internal use of Comfrey, simply add an equal part of a potent liver-supporting herb, such as artichoke leaf (Cynara scolymus) or milk thistle seed (Silybum marianum) to your Comfrey herb or formulation. And/or, you may want to take one week off of Comfrey use for every three weeks of daily, internal use.

APPLICATIONS AND ATTRIBUTES - COMFREY

(Quick Reference List)

ANIMALS
BATH
BLEEDING
BLOOD-BUILDING
BLOOD-PURIFIER
BONES
BOWELS
BREASTS
BRUISES
BURNS
CANKER SORES
CELL PROLIFERANT
COLDS and FLU
COLITIS
COMFREY BATH
COMFREY WATER
CONGESTION
COUGHS
DIAPER RASH
DIARRHEA
DIGESTION
ECZEMA
EXPECTORANT
EYES
GREEN DRINK
INFECTION
INFLAMMATION
INSECT BITES
INTESTINES
KIDNEYS
LUNGS
MOTHER'S MILK
MUCILAGINOUS
MUCOUS MEMBRANES
NUTRITION
PETS/LIVESTOCK
PNEUMONIA
PROTEIN
REHABILITATION
SINUS
SKIN
SPRAINS
STAMINA
SURGERY
TONIC
ULCERATIONS
WOUNDS

FORM:

Fresh roots and leaves; dried roots, powdered or chopped into small bits; dried leaves, crumbled or powdered

APPLICATION METHODS:

Internally use Green Drink, tea, tincture, capsules, decoction, infusion, gently cooked leafy vegetable, or raw leaves in salad. Chew on a fresh piece of peeled root, or use any of the application methods described in Chapter I, Lesson #2.

Externally use poultice or fomentation of fresh or dried roots and/or leaves (whole or powdered), Comfrey salve, lotion, tincture, etc.

AVAILABILITY:

Herb store; grow your own; or mail order new plants and dried herb (see Herb Buyer's Guide, Appendix D)

HINTS/CAUTIONS:

For internal use during pregnancy and lactation, for children under 3 years old, or for anyone with liver disease or liver weakness, use only PA-free Comfrey concentrate. See details of this caution on p. 111 in the Comfrey Personality Profile.

GENERAL DOSAGE: INTERNAL USE

*PLEASE NOTE: *Although I emphasize using tea, there are many other good forms and ideas for herbal preparations including: Capsules, Children's ideas, Decoction, Infusion, Honeyball, etc. See these headings as well as Dosage Equivalents in Chapter I, Lesson #2.*

Infants to 3 years:

Internally use only PA-free Comfrey concentrate such as the "Herb Pharm" brand. This is available at most health food stores and from "Herb Pharm" directly via mail order. See Buyers Guide Appendix D. Follow manufacturer's directions for dosage.

There are a few more details about PA-free Comfrey on p. 111.

Children 4 years to 10 years:

- Powdered Comfrey root 1/2 tsp., or Comfrey leaf 1 tsp., could be taken every 3 to 5 hours up to five times per day, depending upon seriousness of the self-help need. This could be taken in one of the forms suggested under Children's Ideas in Chapter I, Lesson #2.
- Or, commercial Comfrey tincture could be taken according to manufacturer's directions.
- One cup Comfrey tea, made from root or leaf, could be taken in place of any single dose of Comfrey as suggested above. Green drink or Comfrey Water, (up to 2 cups altogether in a day) could also be used in place of any single dose. Also see Dosage Equivalents in Chapter I, Lesson #2.

Children 11 years to Adults:

- Powdered Comfrey root 1/2 tsp., or Comfrey leaf 1 tsp., can be taken every 3 to 5 hours up to six times a day, depending upon seriousness of the self-help need. This could be taken in any of the forms listed under Capsules, Honeyballs, Children's Ideas, or Dosage Equivalents in Chapter I, Lesson #2.
- Or, commercial Comfrey tincture could be taken according to the manufacturer's directions.
- Instead of any dose of Comfrey powder or tincture above, you could take Comfrey tea (up to 6 cups a day), or 1/2 to 1 cup Comfrey Water, or Green Drink, up to 2 cups a day.

Pets and Other Creatures: Comfrey root "honeyball" (leaves are good too, but I usually use Comfrey root as it is stronger for many animal purposes and therefore you need less to get a result) pushed to back of pet's throat for swallowing. Or, many animals like the flavor and will willingly chew it. Grazing animals eat fresh or dried Comfrey leaves readily and some animals, like pigs, eat the fresh root. To figure out a dosage I make a "guesstimate," taking into account the body weight of the animal and comparing it with adult human doses. I've never had to fix up an elephant, but for a horse I would start with two or three times the adult dosage.

GENERAL DOSAGE: EXTERNAL USE

Same For All Humans And Other Creatures

Prepare a fomentation or poultice of strong decoction or infusion made from fresh or dried Comfrey root or leaf, and apply directly to affected part.

Comfrey decoction or infusion can be used to gently cleanse (rinse off) an external area before applying a poultice or fomentation. For a less serious external need, this Comfrey rinse may be all that is needed.

Fresh green Comfrey leaves can be blended with a little water into a thick paste and applied 1/4 to 1/2 inch thick as a poultice. The fresh leaves can also be chewed into an "instant poultice" for insect stings.

The green juice, strained from fresh leaves ground up with a little water, or fresh leaves put through a juicer, can be applied directly as a fomentation (it is amazingly potent), or used as a healing liquid to rinse a wound or skin irritation.

See the detailed instructions for all these application methods (decoction, poultice, etc.) in Chapter I, Lesson #2.

APPLICATIONS AND ATTRIBUTES - COMFREY

ANIMALS: See Pets/Livestock.

BATH: See Comfrey Bath application.

BLEEDING (internal and external): Comfrey root works to stop bleeding, fast.

Externally, use Comfrey root powder in any situation by putting 1/16 to 1/4 inch, or more, of the powder directly onto the wound. The amount depends on the severity of the case. If a wound is actively bleeding this sometimes washes the Comfrey root powder away before the bleeding stops. Don't get discouraged; just keep putting the powder back onto the area (use direct pressure on the wound if blood is gushing) and the bleeding will usually slow and then stop altogether very quickly. Comfrey doesn't sting and helps any damaged area heal very quickly, so it's well worth having in your traveling first-aid kit. With major, life-threatening bleeding, you would use this method as first aid on your way to getting professional help. Cayenne will also stop external bleeding quickly. See the Cayenne chapter (Chapter II).

Internally, Comfrey, especially Comfrey root, is equally effective at stopping bleeding while it helps repair and replace any damaged tissue. Comfrey is an herb to think of, in addition to or instead of Cayenne (see Cayenne chapter, Chapter II), for many types of internal bleeding including: bleeding of the stomach, intestines, and lungs, from internal ulcerations, infection, inflammation, or after surgery or an accident in which a person may have sustained internal injuries.

For an immediate crisis involving internal bleeding, use 1/2 to 1 tsp. Comfrey root powder straight in the mouth and swallowed with a little water, as frequently as needed. In extreme cases, this dose could be given every five to ten minutes until 4 to 5 tsp. were given, but usually one dose every one to three hours is enough. In an emergency, use your first available free moment to make a strong decoction of Comfrey root or make Comfrey water from the fresh leaves (see Comfrey Water application), and drink this at the rate of 2 to 4 oz. every one to three hours. In most cases it is not necessary to continue the use of plain dried root powder after starting use of the decoction. Decocting the root (see suggestions for most potent preparation techniques in the Personality Profile above) will activate the allantoin more efficiently for the body's immediate use. Although many herbalists will keep on using the dried root powder only, I find that in a crisis situation the body does not always digest and assimilate at its best, and this is why I often switch to using the carefully prepared decoction.

Keep Cayenne in mind as another potent bleeding stopper. Comfrey and Cayenne can be used together effectively, especially after you gain some experience with each herb separately and can thereby determine the useful proportions for different needs.

ALSO SEE: *Colitis, Comfrey Water, Diarrhea/dysentery, Lungs, Skin, Ulcerations, Wounds*

ALTERNATIVE OR SUPPLEMENTARY SELF-HELP: **Cayenne, People Paste, Slippery Elm*

DOSAGE: **Internally:** *1/2 to 1 tsp. Comfrey root powder as needed, or 4 oz. Comfrey root decoction as needed.* **Externally:** *Comfrey root powder applied 1/8 to 1/2 inch thick as needed.*

Also review the specifics within the application above.

BLOOD-BUILDING TONIC: See Tonic application.

BLOOD-PURIFIER: See Tonic application.

BONES (broken, weak, slow-healing): The ideal helper for the fastest healing of bone tissue would, in my opinion, include the following attributes: It would be easily available and affordable; have a good supply of easy-to-assimilate calcium, protein, and other nutrients to provide plenty of "building materials"; contain a strong cell proliferant, such as allantoin, to help optimize the rebuilding of healthy new bone tissue; encourage the growth of white blood cells to prevent and fight infection; strengthen the blood to help the entire body system work at peak healing efficiency; be demulcent and mucilaginous to soothe inflamed parts; be something so simple to use that it could be applied at home, perhaps with the help of a friend or family, and be something that would nicely interface with and possibly enhance the usual allopathic treatment of various kinds of bone damage if a doctor were found necessary. All these attributes are present in the Comfrey herb!

Be sure to review the Dislocation application.

ALSO SEE: *Bruises, Cell Proliferant, Comfrey Water, Dislocation, Green Drink, Nutrition, Tonic*

ALTERNATIVE OR SUPPLEMENTARY SELF-HELP: *Ginger, People Paste, *Slippery Elm*

DOSAGE: **Externally:** *Apply a poultice of either fresh or dried Comfrey leaves, Comfrey root powder, or Comfrey root or leaf decoction. There are further poultice instructions in Chapter I, Lesson #2.* **Internally:** *Use General Dosage.*

In the more extreme situations, as described in the TASOLE in the Dislocation application, 4 oz. Comfrey decoction or infusion, of root or leaf, can be taken internally as often as every hour for the first few days of crisis.

BREASTS **(clogged milk ducts, inflamed glands):** See Inflammation application.

BRUISES: Bruises, commonly seen as the purplish discoloration in the surface skin, are an accumulation of blood within damaged tissue. Some bruises, however, can be so deep in the tissue that they are not visible externally. This is often the case with bruised bones, for instance. Poultices of Comfrey root or leaf, applied externally, are very helpful, as is taking Comfrey root or leaf internally.

Be sure to read the advice about bruising in the chapter on Onion (Chapter VIII), as this herb is also very dramatic in relieving all types of bruising and would be of significant use alone, or mixed in equal parts with Comfrey.

ALSO SEE: *Comfrey Water, Green Drink, Mucilaginous, Skin, Tonic, Wounds*

ALTERNATIVE OR SUPPLEMENTARY SELF-HELP: **Onion, People Paste, Peppermint, Yarrow*

DOSAGE: *General*

BURNS: In addition to using Comfrey, remember to *always administer Cayenne* immediately, internally, to a burn victim to work against possible shock, as this is a common complication with burns. (For adults, give 1/2 tsp. powdered Cayenne in 1/2 cup water, to be taken in swallows as necessary. See the Shock application in the Cayenne chapter (Chapter II). Also, *keep administering water* as dehydration is another common complication with burns, even the mildest sunburn.

Because of Comfrey's cell proliferative, mucilaginous, and nutritional qualities, it is a #1 choice for fast repair of burns, as well as for any body tissue rehabilitation. The self-help technique here is very similar to any of the other applications that involve tissue repair, such as the Bone, Dislocation, and Wound applications, so be sure to review these for additional valuable input.

Honey is a well-known burn remedy that has been used even at traditional burn clinics in the U.S. Sometimes it is all I use to apply to surface burns. Honey is antiseptic, soothing, pain relieving, and has skin rejuvenating qualities. Apply honey directly to the burn, from a thin layer to 1/2 inch thick depending upon severity of the burn, and cover with a clean bandage. Once again a simple remedy is often the best solution. Read more about honey in Appendix B.

Here are some additional burn poultice formulas for use with any burn. These poultice formulas are quite remarkable for many skin and bone dilemmas as well as burns, so don't limit their use only to burns. Poultices are generally 1/16 to 1/2 inch thick depending on need. Review additional poultice details in Chapter I, Lesson #2.

Formula #1: For the most serious burns, mix an equal part of Comfrey root powder with the People Paste mixture (see People Paste, Appendix A) and wet this with raw honey to a smooth, yet thick, paste consistency. Apply 1/4 to 1/2 inch thick directly to the burn surface. Clean with an antiseptic, such as hydrogen peroxide, two to four times a day and apply a fresh poultice. This is a potent skin healing formula, is the strongest antiseptic, and should be your first choice for burns with significant tissue damage.

Formula #2: This is the formula that is most commonly used for the average burn, which might have blistering, a small amount of bleeding, and/or minor tissue damage up to 1/16 inch deep.

Mix 3 parts Comfrey root or leaf powder, 1/2 part Slippery Elm herb powder, enough raw (uncooked) honey to make a paste, and the contents of two or more vitamin E pearles (make a small hole and squeeze out the oil). The amount of vitamin E to add depends upon the size of the area to be covered. Use the Vitamin E in the proportion of 1 pearle of 5000 I.U.'s Vitamin E for each three square inches of skin to be covered. The idea is not to overdo it to the extent that you have a poultice that is markedly oily, since oil is not the best helper for open burns, especially if they are fresh. However Vitamin E is very good for helping the skin heal. Apply the poultice 1/8 to 1/2 inch thick, depending upon severity of the burn. This is a favorite, all-around burn poultice that is simple to use. Clean the burn and replace the poultice as needed.

Formula #3: If you are lucky enough to have access to fresh Comfrey leaves, this is the poultice to choose for common burn situations as described in Formula #2.

Use fresh Comfrey leaf, ground or blended into a wet mush. It will have a slippery (mucilaginous) quality. Add enough honey, while you are blending, to end up with a poultice of fairly thick consistency. Add the contents of a few pearles of Vitamin E if you have some (see Formula #1). Apply this mixture 1/4 to 1/2 inch thick. Cleanse the burn and change the poultice as needed.

■

In each of these formulas, you can mix and match the recommended ingredients depending on what you have on hand and the situation you are facing. There are other herbs among the Ten Essentials, such as Clove, Chaparral, or Yarrow, that you may choose to use in your poultice. For fresh burns I usually avoid using oil in the poultices (except for the small amount of vitamin E) as this can inhibit the fastest healing initially. Later, when the burn shows good progress in healing and is not so open and raw, and is perhaps scabbing over and a little dry, the above herbal poultices can be mixed with a healing oil such as olive, sesame, or almond oil for good results.

It is helpful to know how to evaluate burns as this can guide you in your self-help response. Burns are designated as first, second, third, and fourth degree severity. The higher the number the more serious the tissue damage. For instance, a mild sunburn that reddens the skin and probably hurts but doesn't blister or leave open skin is in the first degree category. If there is skin damage, such as blisters or tissue damage in the topmost layers, this would constitute the second degree category. With serious tissue damage that actually gets to muscles and blood vessels, you are looking at third degree damage. Fourth degree burns involve the most serious damage, even to the bone. I have no experience with this type, and would always advise the help of a burn specialist when faced with a serious burn.

Anytime there is broken skin the risk of infection is much higher, and with the more serious second and third degree burns you must be very attentive to this risk by keeping the burns clean as the dead skin sloughs off, and new skin is being made. A strong antiseptic substance, such as one of the formulas above (#1 is the strongest), is excellent for this purpose. A decoction of Clove herb is a good wound wash to use in between dressings as it is an antiseptic and helps relieve pain.

For the least serious burns, such as a mild sunburn, that involve no breaking of the skin (i.e., no blistering, etc.; do not put vinegar on broken skin), I have found that simply splashing on some ordinary vinegar, and preventing further burn by covering the skin with light clothing, is enough to cool things off and help the body heal itself. If the skin is broken, yet it is still a minor burn, rinsing continuously with cold water for a few minutes will stop the pain prior to the immediate wrapping with one of the formulas above, with plain honey, or with a formula of your own invention.

For the pain of a burn, especially if a burn involves broken skin, keeping it covered with the proper herbal poultice and minimizing its direct exposure to the air greatly minimizes the pain. Also, drinking Clove tea (either hot or cold), using a Clove decoction as a wound wash, adding Clove powder to your poultice formula, or adding several drops of concentrated Clove oil to your poultice formula will increase its strong pain-killing qualities.

Drinking Comfrey tea during any healing process will enhance your body's ability to rehabilitate itself.

ALSO SEE: *Comfrey Water, Mucilaginous, Skin, Wounds*

ALTERNATIVE OR SUPPLEMENTARY SELF-HELP: *Chaparral, Clove, Garlic, *People Paste, *Slippery Elm, Yarrow*

DOSAGE: *General or as given above*

BOWELS: See Intestines application.

CANKER SORES: Drink Comfrey tea, two to six cups a day, to strengthen and cleanse the blood while using a Comfrey poultice externally. Any of the formulas under the Burns application will also work well for canker sores although you may want to use Aloe Vera gel (from health food stores and some supermarkets) and/or a bit of Clove oil as the wetting agent for the powders, since honey can be a bit inconvenient when it gets warm and sticky on facial areas.

ALSO SEE: *Burns, Green Drink, Mucilaginous, Nutrition, Skin, Tonic, Ulcerations*

ALTERNATIVE OR SUPPLEMENTARY SELF-HELP: **Chaparral, Clove, Garlic, *People Paste, *Yarrow*

DOSAGE: *General*

CELL PROLIFERANT: This is one of several really exciting qualities that Comfrey has in its root and leaves, mostly due to the allantoin which is present throughout the plant. I have discussed allantoin in the Personality Profile for Comfrey and I would like to give you an even broader idea of how it is applied. In the Applications list for Comfrey, for instance, there is not one situation in which this cell proliferant quality is not strongly at play. Anytime you have a situation that involves tissue damage of any sort, be it a broken bone, burn, tissue disease, or even an abnormal growth of tissue, you want a substance that can help the body to get rid of the damaged tissue and to effect repairs most efficiently. This is what a cell proliferant can do. Comfrey is a powerful one that is available to people without a lot of mystery and expense.

"Clear out the old and build up the new" would be Comfrey's motto in an herb motto contest!

ALSO SEE: *Bones, Bruises, Burns, Dislocations, Growths, Inflammation, Mucilaginous, Skin, Tonic, Ulcerations, Wounds, and everything on this list!*

ALTERNATIVE OR SUPPLEMENTARY SELF-HELP: *Chaparral, *People Paste, *Slippery Elm, Yarrow*

DOSAGE: *General*

COLDS and FLU: Use Comfrey as in the Tonic application. A clever addition to the use of Comfrey for colds and flus is to take Garlic and/or Chaparral internally, for their antibiotic action.

A possible combination would be to drink 4 cups of Comfrey tea a day while taking a mixture (in equal parts) of powdered Garlic/Chaparral/Comfrey, 1/2 to 1 tsp. three to six times a day.

ALSO SEE: *Mucilaginous, Tonic*

ALTERNATIVE OR SUPPLEMENTARY SELF-HELP: **Chaparral, Clove, *Garlic, Peppermint, *Yarrow*

DOSAGE: *General*

COLITIS: See Intestines application.

COMFREY BATH: Make two quarts of strong Comfrey decoction or infusion (see decoction and infusion instructions in Chapter I, Lesson #2). Use the roots or leaves, dried or fresh, and add to a bath. This is very soothing and helpful for all types of skin irritations and is a good pick-me-up for any occasion.

ALSO SEE: *Colds and Flu, Insect Stings, Skin, Sprains, Ulcerations*

ALTERNATIVE OR SUPPLEMENTARY SELF-HELP: **Ginger, *Peppermint, *Yarrow*

DOSAGE: *Usually 2 quarts of strong decoction is plenty for a regular size bath, yet it is safe to play around with more or less as you please.*

COMFREY WATER (use fresh leaves): To make this fresh-leaf, all-purpose green liquid, blend 4 oz. of room-temperature water packed full (usually one medium to large leaf), with fresh-chopped Comfrey leaf. Or, crush and grind the leaves manually, in the water. Squeeze the green liquid thoroughly out of the leaf pulp. Use this liquid as a powerful healing substance for internal and external uses.

Comfrey Water is especially good when taken daily. Use 1/2 to 1 cup for a dose and use up to 2 cups per day as a tonic to build the blood, or as a persistent healing influence for ulcers. It is a good herbal wash for any wound or other external need. Always use Comfrey Water fresh within an hour or two after preparing and keep it refrigerated as it deteriorates rapidly. Review the Hints/Cautions for long-term use.

See the Green Drink application as this is similar to Comfrey Water and may be tastier for long-term internal use.

ALSO SEE: *Green Drink*

ALTERNATIVE OR SUPPLEMENTARY SELF-HELP: *None*

DOSAGE: *Usually 4 to 8 oz. taken internally up to 2 cups within a day.*

CONGESTION: Next to supporting the healing of bones, the second most famous use for Comfrey is clearing up congestion, especially in the chest or head area. Comfrey tea, decoction, or infusion are the most convenient forms to use for this purpose although a healthy dose of the powdered herb accompanied by at least a cup of very warm water also does the trick just fine. Warm Comfrey poultices applied directly to the chest also help speed the decongestion process, and warm Comfrey decoction is great to slowly rinse up through the nostrils for clearing the sinuses. Comfrey tea, or Comfrey powder, taken alone or with some powdered or fresh Garlic, is a #1 expectorant. Garlic and Comfrey work very well together. Another way to use them for clearing congestion is to take one cup of Comfrey tea, or 1/2 tsp. of Comfrey root powder (with warm water), along with a clove of fresh Garlic or 1/4 tsp. of the Enhanced Garlic Formula (see Garlic chapter, Chapter VI).

Congestion means something is clogged up and this is usually associated with mucus in the lungs and sinuses. However, you should also think in terms of the liver, kidneys, or the intestinal system being congested. These organs are filled with delicate mucous membranes just as the lungs are. Congestion in these systems will cause a backup in accumulating poisons. This accumulation of various toxins in the blood, lungs, sinuses, intestines and elsewhere results in the body having a noticeably lessened ability to cleanse and heal itself. If you review the explanations under the Mucilaginous, Tonic, and Cell Proliferant applications you will see why Comfrey would be so great for any type of congestion of internal organs. Briefly put, Comfrey can soothe inflamed tissues, gather and help eliminate toxic forms of mucus, cleanse and strengthen the blood, and help to catalyze quick new growth of healthy tissues.

Comfrey is also used for self-help in persistent lung troubles such as asthma, tuberculosis, emphysema, and bleeding of the lungs.

ALSO SEE: *Breasts, Cell Proliferant, Mucilaginous, Tonic*

ALTERNATIVE OR SUPPLEMENTARY SELF-HELP: *Cayenne, Garlic, Ginger, Onion, Peppermint, Yarrow*

DOSAGE: *General or as given*

COUGHS: See the Congestion application in this chapter. Also see the cough syrup and throat lozenge instructions in the Onion and Slippery Elm chapters (Chapters VIII and X) which can incorporate the use of Comfrey quite nicely.

DIAPER RASH: See Skin application.

DIARRHEA (INCLUDES DYSENTERY): See Intestines application.

DIGESTION: Drinking a cup of Comfrey tea before meals helps stimulate the liver and pancreas for more efficient digestion. Some students have told me that this also helped to balance their appetites. If there are any ulcerations in the digestive tract that are aggravated while eating, taking 1/2 to 1 tsp. Comfrey root powder with a warm glass of water before eating can be soothing and protective. It is even more effective when you add 1/8 to 1/4 tsp. Cayenne to the Comfrey root powder.

ALSO SEE: *Green Drink, Intestines, Mucilaginous, Tonic, Ulcerations*

ALTERNATIVE OR SUPPLEMENTARY SELF-HELP: **Cayenne, Garlic, Ginger, Peppermint, *Slippery Elm, Yarrow*

DOSAGE: *1 cup tea, or 4 oz. decoction/infusion, or 1/2 to 1 tsp. Comfrey root powder with a little Cayenne (as described above) before meals.*

DISLOCATIONS: All Comfrey's power to rebuild and repair is called into play when dealing with a bone dislocation. A dislocation can be worse than a broken bone because it often involves torn ligaments, muscles, blood vessels, etc., that all have to repair and re-coordinate after such a severe rearrangement. The details of how to use Comfrey are covered in the bone application so I will not repeat them here. However, I will take this opportunity to tell you a true story.

TASOLE: One moment my friend Rita was standing up on a piano stool to reach for something, and the next moment the stool swung around and she was on the floor screaming, holding her suddenly misshapen elbow. I felt my stomach sink—you know the feeling I mean? I knew it was bad. I also knew it was the same elbow that had been badly injured several years ago, and I remembered Rita saying that she had been told that if she ever injured that elbow again, it could mean surgery, pins in the joint, and possible complete loss of use.

Rita and I were living in a household of fellow herbalists and, upon hearing her screams, two more friends ran into the room to see what had happened. The elbow was evidently dislocated — the two main parts of the joint were lying loosely next to each other inside the sack-like covering of the elbow skin which was quickly turning blue as blood started to slowly collect inside. Her arm was literally going in two different directions, right at the joint, and none of us had any experience with putting such a serious dislocation back in its proper place.

We took Rita to the hospital emergency room and were told by the doctors on duty that the dislocation was so serious that they would have to operate. Just at that moment, however, the situation took a turn for the better. Another doctor, a bone specialist, arrived on the scene. He was not on duty, but just "passing through" for some reason. The first doctors seemed relieved to see him. The specialist informed us that he had recently learned a new way to set this type of dislocation. He warned us that there were no guarantees, but said that if it worked it might avoid surgery. Did we want him to try? We said yes! Meanwhile Rita was half unconscious from the pain, moaning and crying. Yet even so, she too knew the amazing healing powers of the body and herbs, and she felt that if the arm could be set in place without surgery, we could then go home and do the rest with our herbs.

The doctor took Rita into another room. After a few moments we heard her let out a yell that made us all turn white. About ten minutes more passed and the doctor brought her out with her arm wrapped carefully in a sling. The procedure had worked. He then explained to us all that this type of injury usually took at least six months before any movement could be expected, and at that point she might start physical therapy. He told us that there was still the option of surgery and/or having the arm casted, yet she could take a few days to think about it and come to his office in a week, unless she changed her mind and wanted a cast before then. Rita had asked him if it would do any harm to go without a cast and he had informed her that if she kept her arm carefully in the sling it would be alright, even though a cast would make it less painful. In any case he emphasized to her that this was a serious injury that would take months to heal at best; that she still might have to have surgery, and that she might never regain complete strength and movement in her arm.

Back at home, we began with Rita the self-help, healing therapies which included immediate use of Comfrey tea internally and Comfrey poultices externally. The external poultice was applied extremely carefully as the pain of any touch or movement was excruciating for her. To lessen the pain we began to use a strong decoction of Clove (see Chapter IV) and this soon relaxed her and thus lessened the pain. We took turns staying with Rita for three days and three nights while we used continuous rounds of Comfrey poultices (changed every three to four hours during waking hours) and used Clove and other pain-killing herbs for the pain. She also drank at least a cup of Comfrey tea or a half cup of Comfrey decoction or infusion every two hours.

Rita was very restless during those first nights, but by the third day there was such a definite improvement that she began to sleep well and the pain greatly lessened.

During this time we had also advised her to take a double dose of calcium lactate and two grams of vitamin C (in the calcium ascorbate form) every three hours. This she had found in the past would support quick healing in her body and greatly help with pain besides. Yet constant use of Comfrey was the major self-help applied.

Rita visited the doctor on the fifth day and he asked her if she needed another prescription for pain medicine as he was sure her arm must still be unbearably painful. She told him that she hadn't filled her first prescription yet, but would let him know if she needed more. When she showed him that she could wiggle her fingers, and pointed out that the bruising was greatly lessened, he was impressed but said not to expect much more than that for several weeks. He warned her again that she should not be alarmed if she had no strength or arm movement for quite some time, and advised her to "just keep the sling on."

We continued the Comfrey use internally and externally, and in addition we now carefully soaked the elbow in warm Comfrey decoction once a day for about 40 minutes and then wrapped it in a fresh Comfrey leaf poultice. The final Comfrey poultice of each day, usually applied in the late evening, was left on overnight. Rita also continued the calcium, Vitamin C and Clove tea supplementation to soothe the pain.

At ten days she was able to gently move the elbow joint with her own strength, and she could clench and unclench her hand. This was not supposed to be possible for a couple of months. She started taking the sling off three or four times a day in order to carefully and slowly move her elbow joint (assisted with her other hand) for a few moments.

At the end of two weeks she had another doctor's appointment, so she put on the sling that she was now wearing a couple of hours on and one hour off, and went to his office. The doctor tenderly took the sling off, for what he assumed was the first time, and began to test for nerve and muscle response which he expected would be very slight. Still hinting that she might want a cast instead of a sling, as it would be more comfortable for her, he talked on about how this type of injury was slow to improve, since the body had to repair all the connective tissues, blood vessels, etc., that were torn up in the dislocation. When he saw the slow but steady movement in her elbow, he was frankly amazed! When she told him all that she had been doing, he was even more amazed! He said that it was a seemingly impossible recovery she was experiencing and that he would support her in continuing whatever she was doing.

After one month Rita no longer needed a sling. Her elbow did not have its full strength but was regaining it quickly, expecially with the help of some therapeutic massage. According to her doctor, this degree of improvement could be expected after at least six months, and would most likely have included substantial time in a cast and/or surgery.

Although Rita no longer did daily poultices, she continued for two more months with a program of 2 to 4 cups of Comfrey tea daily, and 500 mg. of calcium lactate taken with two grams of the calcium ascorbate form of vitamin C four times a day.

I want to emphasize here that if it hadn't been for that particular doctor being in the right place at the right time, Rita might never have been able to have the use of her arm back to the complete degree that she did without having to undergo lengthy, expensive and painful surgery and therapy. It was his expertise and willingness to work with less invasive methods that got her off to such a good start. Then it was Rita's determination to put into practice what she knew about herbs and other healing methods that secured this happy ending. Since this experience, which actually happened at the beginning of my herbal apprenticeship, I have observed that serious dislocations usually take longer to heal than simple broken bones yet the Comfrey process to be used for both is the same. Comfrey definitely earns its common nickname—Knitbone.

ALSO SEE: *Bleeding, Bones, Mucilaginous, Nutrition, Skin*

ALTERNATIVE OR SUPPLEMENTARY SELF-HELP: **Clove, Onion, *People Paste, Slippery Elm*

DOSAGE: *General or as given in Bones application*

ECZEMA: See Skin application; also see TASOLE in Personality Profile of Comfrey.

EXPECTORANT: See Congestion application.

EYES: For an excellent eyewash that is soothing, infection-fighting, and rehabilitating, simply use cool Comfrey tea. For more serious eye trouble, like a scratched eye, or a sty, use a Comfrey poultice. (Review the Eyewash and Poultice instructions under their headings in Chapter I, Lesson #2.)

ALSO SEE: *Cell Proliferant, Mucilaginous*

ALTERNATIVE OR SUPPLEMENTARY SELF-HELP: **Cayenne, Chaparral (as a poultice), Clove, People Paste, Peppermint, *Slippery Elm, Yarrow*

DOSAGE: *General*

GREEN DRINK: This delicious green mixture is an entertaining way to use fresh Comfrey leaves for children and adults alike. It packs a real charge of nutrition, is light on the stomach's digestion, and carries most of the helping qualities of the Comfrey leaves quickly and easefully into the body's systems. I will give you the basic recipe, yet the bottom-line is to develop your own variations, coming up with the strength and combination of ingredients you most prefer.

For instance, because they have special enzymes, pineapple or papaya juice MUST be used to get the best digestive effect when combined with the "greens." Yet you may find, as I do, that straight juice has too strong a flavor and may need to be diluted considerably with plain water. It is also up to you what quantity of greens you like in your mix. Here are the basics:

GREEN DRINK

- 1 cup plain pineapple or papaya juice. (Fresh, frozen, or juice in jars is preferable to canned juice. Try to get the "real thing" without all kinds of sugar and other stuff added.) Don't substitute other juices.
- 2 medium to large-size fresh Comfrey leaves (tear out mid-rib) plus optional greens as you like. Optional greens include fresh spinach, parsley, mint, beet greens, carrot tops (organic from your garden are much the best), green leaf sprouts (alfalfa, sunflower, etc.), kale. Do not use lettuce.
- Blend it all up extremely well in a good blender and drink immediately. Without a blender I have done a passable Green Drink by pulverizing the greens with mortar and pestle or putting them through a juicer, and then mixing in the pineapple or papaya juice.
- Green Drink is incredible even when made without Comfrey leaves for someone in a "caution category" mentioned under Hints/Cautions on p. 113.

Almost everyone loves this stuff, including and especially children. It is a quick pick-me-up if you're having a tiring day or mood, and a good meal for dieters. Drink up to 4 cups a day, and don't be alarmed if your bowel movements turn greenish! If stools get too loose, cut back on your intake. Cayenne and/or Garlic are two adventurous additions that can enhance the whole experience.

ALSO SEE: *Comfrey Water, Nutrition, Tonic*

ALTERNATIVE OR SUPPLEMENTARY SELF-HELP: *Cayenne, Garlic, Slippery Elm*

DOSAGE: ***Drink up to 4 cups a day within the limits of what agrees with your body. See Hints/Cautions on p. 113.***

INFECTION: See Cell Proliferant, Mucilaginous, and Tonic applications; also see background information in Personality Profile of Comfrey.

INFLAMMATION/IRRITATION: See Mucilaginous application.

INTESTINES: One of the most untidy things that can go wrong with intestines is that they can become irritated through poor diet, illness, and emotional stress. For instance, these irritations might show up as diarrhea, colitis, or hemorrhoids. Since Comfrey soothes inflammation, is mucilaginous, is a cell proliferant, and stops bleeding, you can see why it is so well-suited in rehabilitating intestinal tissues.

If the intestinal distress includes irritation of the large intestine, such as in colitis or diarrhea, Comfrey can be used with good effect as an enema. For this purpose you could use Comfrey Water or Comfrey root decoction.

ALSO SEE: *Bleeding, Cell Proliferant, Comfrey Water, Digestion, Mucilaginous, Tonic*

ALTERNATIVE OR SUPPLEMENTARY SELF-HELP: *Garlic, People Paste, *Slippery Elm, *Yarrow*

DOSAGE: ***2 to 4 oz. Comfrey root decoction every hour until discomfort is noticeably improving (or up to 2 cups decoction total in a day), and then you may lengthen the time between doses as needed. Or take Comfrey root or leaf tea as needed. A Comfrey root enema, using 2 quarts of Comfrey root decoction, can have immediate results in stopping inflammation and/or mild intestinal bleeding. See the complete instructions for preparing an enema in Chapter I, Lesson #2.***

INSECT BITES: When faced with these inconveniences I tend to go for a bit of the fresh Comfrey leaf, chewed or mashed into a green wad, and then taped on or rubbed into the sting. Dried Comfrey leaf or root can also be gotten wet and prepared into a poultice. A small poultice is usually all you need, yet if you get in a big mess with lots of bites from something (i.e., mosquitoes, ants, etc.) soak in a bath of Comfrey (Epsom Salts is also a good addition to this) and then poultice the worst bites. Drink Comfrey tea after the bath. Raw Onion is another strong and quick antidote for many stings, so look in the Onion chapter (Chapter VIII) also.

ALSO SEE: *Mucilaginous, Skin, Tonic*

ALTERNATIVE OR SUPPLEMENTARY SELF-HELP: *Clove, Garlic, *Onion, *Yarrow*

DOSAGE: *General and as given*

KIDNEYS: See Congestion and Mucilaginous applications.

LUNGS: See Bleeding, Congestion and Mucilaginous applications.

MOTHER'S MILK: See Tonic application.

MUCILAGINOUS: A mucilaginous plant contains significant amounts of mucilage. Mucilage describes a slippery, sticky and soothing (demulcent) substance, often of high nutritional value (as is the case with Comfrey), that coats and protects an area from infection, inflammation and other irritants while at the same time acting as a further deterrent to many toxic substances, through its ability to absorb them and help them pass harmlessly out of the body. This mucilaginous property is quite useful in any case of inflammation or congestion of mucous membranes in the lungs, digestive tract, or urinary tract including kidneys, and in any ulcerous situation both internal and external.

This mucilaginous property of Comfrey has a good "lasting" effect which means it will not break down or disappear quickly. For example, when you ingest a teaspoon of Comfrey root powder with a glass of water (warm water makes it work fastest), it will immediately start activating its mucilage in your stomach and then spread its slippery healing help all the way down through the digestive tract, so that when you have a bowel movement there is a very good chance it will be slippery too! Think of the possible applications of just this one attribute of "mucilaginous staying power" and combine it with the cell proliferating, nutritional, and blood tonic attributes, and your imagination may take off on how you could use this herb in addition to the list of applications offered in this chapter.

Comfrey's mucilage is soothing to burns, colitis, lungs, kidneys, stomach, and skin rashes of all sorts. It helps balance diarrhea by soothing the inflammations associated with diarrhea and protecting the intestinal linings from further inflammation. For constipation it provides the fiber and mucilage necessary to slip fecal matter out easily. Whenever you use Comfrey, this attribute comes into play.

Mucilage is present both in the Comfrey leaves and in the roots, and even though it is stronger in the roots it is plenty strong enough in the leaves, especially the fresh leaves, to noticeably contribute its action.

There is one possible caution in relation to this mucilaginous action of any herb (including Slippery Elm). If you find yourself needing to use a strong mucilaginous herb in its most potent form, such as plain Comfrey root powder (any tea or fresh leaves are exempt from this caution), daily for a period of three weeks or more, then it would be wise to take a day off from its use once a week. This is because the herb does its job so well that a prolonged use of 3 tsp. or more of the plain root powder per day could, in especially sluggish systems, overcoat the digestive tract, possibly causing a temporary lessening of the assimilation of some nutrients. Simply taking a day off once a week takes care of this. Also, using 1/8 to 1/4 part of Ginger with Comfrey is good help against any temporary over-coating of the intestinal tract with Comfrey's wonderful mucilaginous property during long-term use. Ginger carries and focuses the Comfrey action more potently for any use.

There are some good references to various research around the world on this mucilaginous property of Comfrey in *Herbal Pharmacy* by John Heinerman, and *Comfrey: Food, Fodder & Remedy* by Lawrence D. Hills (see the Resource Guide, Appendix C).

ALSO SEE: ***Bleeding, Burns, Cell Proliferant, Comfrey Water, Congestion, Green Drink, Intestines, Lungs, Skin, Tonic***

ALTERNATIVE OR SUPPLEMENTARY SELF-HELP: ****Ginger (a potent combination with Comfrey), *Slippery Elm***

DOSAGE: ***General; review Hints/Cautions p. 113***

MUCOUS MEMBRANES: See Mucilaginous application.

NUTRITION: Comfrey, especially the leaves, is packed with such amazing nutrition that it has been and is being seriously researched for use as an important food crop in several countries including England and the United States. The highest nutritional content is found in the leaves and is even more concentrated if the stem/rib of the leaf is eliminated during harvest. Research on Comfrey's use as a food for people and animals can be found in *Comfrey: Food, Fodder & Remedy* by Lawrence Hills, and in other materials listed in the Resource Guide, Appendix C. I will briefly summarize some of the major nutrient qualities here.

Comfrey contains:

1) Protein. Many sources agree that Comfrey has substantial protein. Comfrey leaves are usually 20% to 25% protein, which is seven times more protein than is found in soybeans. The juice of the plant is also high in flesh-forming proteins.

2) Calcium
3) Phosphorus
4) Vitamin B12. It should be very good news for vegetarians that Comfrey is a major source of this nutrient which is not commonly found in plants.
5) Carbohydrates. Comfrey contains about eight times more than soybeans.
6) Iron
7) Vitamin A
8) Potash. Comfrey makes a great natural fertilizer and compost additive.

There are many ways for humans to eat Comfrey. You can add the fresh leaves, chopped up, to a salad, or steam them like spinach greens. My favorite way is to blend them with a little pineapple juice and make a Green Drink (see Green Drink application). Whenever you drink a Comfrey leaf tea you are getting good amounts of vitamins and minerals, extracted through steeping. Think of Comfrey leaf tea as a potent vegetable broth.

I've read that pigs will dig up and eat Comfrey roots enthusiastically, yet for animals in general I know that it is the fresh and dried leaves that win attention. I can't keep the deer, horses, and rabbits out of my Comfrey patch without fencing!

ALSO SEE: *Comfrey Water, Green Drink*

ALTERNATIVE OR SUPPLEMENTARY SELF-HELP: **Garlic, *Onion, *Slippery Elm, Yarrow*

DOSAGE: *General and see Hints/Cautions p. 113*

PETS/LIVESTOCK: Primarily I have used Comfrey either externally for wounds on animals or internally as feed. (Chickens eat it as do horses and cattle.)

Comfrey can be given internally for medicinal uses, such as increasing stamina, strengthening weak digestion, stopping internal bleeding, or speeding rehabilitation after an illness. I recommend experimenting with adding the leaves or powdered root to their food or pushing the Comfrey back into the throat (for swallowing inducement) in the form of a lozenge made by adding a little water to the powdered herb. Tincture could be used on smaller animals but it would take a heck of a lot to treat a horse!

Externally I use Comfrey in the same ways for animals as I do for people. I have appplied it as a poultice for broken bones, torn ears, barbed wire injuries, animal bites, strained muscles, etc. It is great mixed with Garlic powder since the Garlic is a strong antibiotic and keeps insects out of wounds.

ALSO SEE: *Nutrition, and any external use for humans that corresponds to an animal use*

ALTERNATIVE OR SUPPLEMENTARY SELF-HELP: *Any of the other herbs in this book applied to the appropriate animal counterpart use*

DOSAGE: *General*

PNEUMONIA: See Cell Proliferant, Congestion, Mucilaginous, and Tonic applications. Also be sure to check out the chapter on Garlic (Chapter VI) for help with Pneumonia. Garlic and Comfrey work very well together for this purpose.

PROTEIN: See Nutrition application.

REHABILITATION: See Cell Proliferant, Mucilaginous, and Tonic applications.

SINUS: Make a decoction of Comfrey root or leaf and use this to gently snuff up through the nostrils one at a time to soothe, cleanse, and enhance healing of tissues, and to stimulate proper sinus function. If you have such a stuffed nose that you can't snuff at all, then I have found that a few grains of Cayenne in 1 Tbsp. of lukewarm water, dropped with a clean medicine dropper into the nostrils (keep your head held back for a few minutes), can really get things moving. Then go back to gently trying to wash out the sinus as best you can with the Comfrey solution. The decoction will go up the nostrils and drain down into your mouth and throat, whereupon you will spit it out and continue the process again. It is sometimes nice to add a 1/2 tsp. of sea salt to 4 ozs. of decoction, as this has an additional drawing and soothing effect.

You may want to add a few drops of Garlic Oil or a drop or two of fresh squeezed Garlic juice to the decoction of Comfrey for an extra strong antibiotic effect when that is needed (see the Garlic chapter, Chapter VI). A good way to add Garlic juice is to smash a clove of Garlic, soak it in the lukewarm Comfrey decoction, and then strain it out.

Internally, especially if infection is present in the sinuses, it is always good to help the body strengthen itself by taking two or more cups of Comfrey tea. Additional antibiotic action can be generated by adding Garlic and/or Chaparral to a powdered formula or tea that includes Comfrey.

ALSO SEE: *Bleeding, Congestion, Mucilaginous, Tonic*

ALTERNATIVE OR SUPPLEMENTARY SELF-HELP: **Cayenne, *Garlic, *Onion, People Paste, Slippery Elm*

DOSAGE: *General and as given*

SKIN: Because of its strong qualities as a nutritive, blood building tonic, cell proliferant, and mucilaginous herb (see Nutritive, Tonic, Cell Proliferant and Mucilaginous applications) I have had many successes with friends and students using Comfrey for skin problems (see the TASOLE in Comfrey's Personality Profile about a case of eczema). In addition to eczema-like skin difficulties, there are many less serious and more common things that go wrong with skin, such as rashes, scrapes, insect bites, and assortments of punctures, cuts, gashes and smashes. In each case think of helping the skin topically with a Comfrey wash, soak, salve, or poultice. Also think of helping the skin internally by taking advantage of the tonic effects of Comfrey to strengthen and cleanse the blood and internal organs, many of which cleanse excessively through the skin when their usual channels for eliminating toxins are clogged or broken down.

To avoid making a war zone out of your skin, always make certain to escape constipation by drinking at least two quarts of pure water daily (which could include cups of Comfrey tea), especially if the body is detoxifying from illness. Ginger is another strong herb to relieve constipation. Also use saunas (if your doctor says OK), skin brushing, and exercise to enhance the health of your skin. The skin is a major eliminative organ in the body and is as crucial in this function as are the kidneys.

Also keep in mind the direct effect that emotions, environmental pollution, hormones, and diet have on the skin.

For a basic skin-fixing mixture, put together equal parts of Slippery Elm powder and Comfrey root powder. This mix can be used as a dusting powder for diaper rash, or moistened and made into a sticky paste for a more heavy-duty poultice as needed for a skin ulceration or wound.

Chaparral powder is a good addition to Comfrey for skin fungus or infection, and is very potent for self-help with eczema, especially when used with Comfrey. Review the Skin and Blood-Purifier applications in the Chaparral chapter (Chapter III).

ALSO SEE: *Bleeding, Cell Proliferant, Green Drink, Mucilaginous, Nutritive, Tonic, Wounds*

ALTERNATIVE OR SUPPLEMENTARY SELF-HELP: **Chaparral, Cloves, Garlic, *People Paste, Peppermint, *Slippery Elm, Yarrow*

DOSAGE: *For chronic skin difficulties, cleanse the blood and strengthen the liver and all eliminative organs. One way to facilitate this is to drink at least four cups of Comfrey (or other blood-cleansing herb such as Yarrow) tea daily, or use a dosage equivalent (see Dosage Equivalents in Chapter I, Lesson #2). In addition, use the Comfrey/Slippery Elm mix externally as described above.*

SPRAINS: Wrap a sprain in a Comfrey poultice of ground fresh leaves and/or Comfrey root powder mixed with a little Slippery Elm powder (to help make it pasty) and some warm water or other wetting agent (see Poultice instructions in Chapter I, Lesson #2). A poultice can be left on a sprain anywhere from 20 minutes to several days. If needed several days for a bad sprain, change the poultice twice a day. If the sprain is accompanied by swelling, add 1/4 to 1/2 part salt to the poultice to draw out the lymphatic fluids that usually cause this. Drink Comfrey tea, 2 or more cups per day, to help with any possible inflammation.

An Onion and Salt Poultice is also quick acting for sprains that involve extensive bruising and/or swelling. You can always alternate between these two types of poultices, or even use the Comfrey, Onion, and salt together in the same poultice if there is a need. Look up Onion Pack application in the Onion chapter (Chapter VIII).

If your whole body is sprained or strained from excessive physical activity, take a Ginger bath (see Ginger chapter,Chapter VII).

ALSO SEE: *Bones, Cell Proliferant, Mucilaginous, Nutrition, Tonic*

ALTERNATIVE OR SUPPLEMENTARY SELF-HELP: *Cayenne (liniment), *Ginger, *Onion, Peppermint*

DOSAGE: *As given*

STAMINA: See Nutritive and Tonic applications.

SURGERY (RECOVERING FROM): See Bones, Cell Proliferant, Green Drink, Mucilaginous, Nutritive, and Tonic applications.

TONIC: Use Comfrey tea, from either leaf or root (I often prefer leaf), on a daily basis during healthy times to help keep you that way, and during times of illness to ensure a quick recovery. The tonic effect of Comfrey helps the body rebalance from a wide variety of inconveniences, from common colds and flu to more long-term annoyances such as colitis. Comfrey's cell proliferant, nutritional, and mucilaginous attributes make it quick-acting. It can keep healthy blood, bone, and tissues strong while bringing strength and well-being to weaker blood, bone, and tissues. Use this herb alone or mixed with another blood tonic herb such as Yarrow for rehabilitation during or after an illness. Comfrey can be used for elderly people to help keep up their strength when nothing else seems to assimilate into or "stay with" the body. These tonic qualities contribute to Comfrey's reputation for enhancing the quality and quantity of mother's milk and for building strength during pregnancy (see Hints/Cautions p. 113). I have often suggested Green Drink as a fast-acting use of Comfrey (and other greens) for building up the iron content in the blood.

A good tonic herb is also often a very efficient blood-purifier and this is certainly true of Comfrey. Something that I mentioned briefly in the Comfrey Personality Profile is the proven ability of allantoin (found in highest amounts in Comfrey root and to a lesser degree in the leaf) to measurably increase the leucocyte (white blood cell) count. White blood cells are our infection fighters and infection preventives par excellence. This property alone should make Comfrey a top choice for healing. Add the great nutritional value of the leaves, and to a somewhat lesser extent the roots, and it is easy to see why herbalists from many countries such as America, England, Japan, and Russia enthusiastically recommend it.

For the most potent tonic effect from Comfrey, be sure to review the preparation suggestions in the Comfrey Personality Profile at the beginning of this chapter. They include using distilled water where possible, using heat just to the boiling point, and avoiding prolonged overheating. If you get bored with tea alone, you can always try a yummy Green Drink. Add a small amount of a "flavor herb" to Comfrey tea, such as Peppermint or Clove, for variety. If you need a sweetener, honey, molasses, or barley malt are the best choices for herb tea. It is always best to avoid highly refined sugars such as white table sugar or artificial sweeteners, especially when you desire the most potent tonic efficiency in the body.

ALSO SEE: *Comfrey Water, Green Drink, Nutrition*

ALTERNATIVE OR SUPPLEMENTARY SELF-HELP: *Chaparral, *Garlic, Onion, Slippery Elm, *Yarrow*

DOSAGE: *Drink 1 to 6 cups Comfrey root or leaf tea each day. It's always a good idea to start slow with a cup or two per day and gradually increase the amount while you monitor your body's response to the preparation. See Hints/Cautions p. 113.*

ULCERATIONS (INTERNAL AND EXTERNAL): To me an ulceration is an open, bleeding, and usually slow-healing sore, big or small, inside or outside the body.

Externally use a fomentation made from a strong Comfrey root decoction or a Comfrey leaf infusion, and change as needed for the situation (usually a minimum of two times a day).

For a stronger application, make a poultice of Comfrey root powder or ground up Comfrey leaf (fresh or dried), using warm distilled water (to optimally activate the allantoin) and apply the poultice directly to the ulceration. (See detailed poultice instructions in Chapter I, Lesson #2.) In addition, cover the poultice with a cloth soaked in Comfrey root decoction (called a fomentation). Replace the outer fomentation cloth with a freshly soaked cloth each hour, and change the underneath poultice every two to six hours depending upon the severity of the situation.

Ulcerations are usually continually "weepy" with all sorts of effluents, and they must be kept cleanly wrapped. Remember that Comfrey will be working to slough off dead tissues and regrow healthy new skin. Help this process along by changing the old poultice and cleaning off the sloughed tissues regularly enough to keep up with the process (perhaps two to six times a day). There are several detailed accounts of Comfrey root's use on serious, long-term ulcers in the book *Comfrey: Food, Fodder & Remedy* by Lawrence Hills. (See Resource Guide, Appendix C).

For internal ulcers, or to use Comfrey internally to support healing of external ulcers, the method is the same. Use the tea or decoction of Comfrey root or leaf or see Dosage Equivalents in Chapter I, Lesson #2. Situations vary greatly, requiring from one cup of Comfrey root or leaf tea daily to 4 oz. of Comfrey root decoction every few hours around the clock, so you will need to be discerning here in determining how serious each case is. For severe ulcerations be sure to read all the supporting applications mentioned in "Also See" below.

ALSO SEE: *Bleeding, Cell Proliferant, Intestines, Mucilaginous, Nutritive, Skin, Tonic, Wounds*

ALTERNATIVE OR SUPPLEMENTARY SELF-HELP: **Cayenne, *Chaparral, *Garlic, *People Paste, Slippery Elm, Yarrow*

DOSAGE: *General or as given*

WOUNDS: In general, wounds can be treated by using a Comfrey poultice made from the dry powdered form of the root, or from the powdered or ground form of the dried leaf. The chosen form of the herb is moistened with warm water or another of the wetting agents suggested in the detailed poultice instructions in Chapter I, Lesson #2. Less common, yet equally effective, is the fresh leaf ground up, or fresh root pulverized, into a poultice paste. Poultices are used for cleaning, protecting, and catalyzing new cell growth in wounds.

Internally, Comfrey tea, decoction, infusion or powder is taken to strengthen the body's ability to generate new tissues and resist infection.

For specific attributes and types of wounds, refer to "Also See" below.

ALSO SEE: *Bleeding, Bones, Burns, Cell Proliferant, Mucilaginous, Nutrition, Skin, Tonic, Ulcerations*

ALTERNATIVE OR SUPPLEMENTARY SELF-HELP: *Cayenne, Cloves, Garlic, *People Paste, *Slippery Elm, Yarrow*

DOSAGE: *General or as given in specific applications*

GARLIC

FIGHTING INFECTION IS MY LIFE!
FUNGICIDE
ANTIBIOTIC
TELEPHONE
HE'S MY HERO!
OH, ISN'T HE AMAZING!
K Johansen

CHAPTER VI

GARLIC

Allium sativum L.

Garlic goodgirl smells great, she is calm and serene,
To high blood pressure, infections, and fungus, she's mean!
She's for people, plants, pets; for both outside and in;
When she soaks in your footbath, you'll wear a big grin.

PERSONALITY PROFILE—Garlic

If I could take only one herb with me to that proverbial desert island, I would take fresh Garlic to use and grow. Chinese texts dating back to 2,000 B.C. speak of the healing potency of Garlic. I don't think there is a country in the world that has not known and researched the powerful medicinal qualities of this amazing herb. If your scientific curiosity gets nudged in reading about Garlic here, there is much more data available in the books listed in the Resource Guide, Appendix C.

Fresh Garlic has many active constituents including alliin,allicin, and sulphur compounds. These ingredients primarily account for Garlic's famous potency as an antibiotic and fungicide and for its use in healing high blood pressure. Allicin is a strong antibiotic agent which means that it kills bacteria and many viruses. Alliin becomes an antibiotic agent, with properties similar to allicin, when it comes into contact with the digestive enzyme alliinase. Sulphur compounds strengthen the immune system, lower high blood pressure, and also fight infections. These three major properties of Garlic make it an infection fighter easily comparable to penicillin. In fact, my experience has shown that Garlic, especially when combined with Cayenne as a "carrier", is often a more potent choice than penicillin. For more data on the chemistry of Garlic, see *Herbal Pharmacy*, by John Heinerman and *Miracle of Garlic and Vinegar*, by James O'Brien, both listed in the Resource Guide, Appendix C. Garlic also contains significant amounts of Selenium (a trace mineral) and vitamin B1. Both of these are important in strengthening the nerves and skin.

Allicin, the major antibiotic property in Garlic, is particularly heat sensitive. For healing purposes, therefore, ***Garlic is used in its raw form*** (first choice), or in its dried and powdered form (a good second choice), or in its home-made Garlic oil form (usually for infants or small children). ***For healing purposes do not cook Garlic***, as this will essentially negate the effect of the allicin.

In purchasing raw Garlic, look for fresh, tightly packed and plump bulbs free of mold or any other contamination. The best Garlic I ever purchased was organically grown by a farmer in Mexico, but usually I buy Garlic at the local grocery store, taking my time to pick out a few of the best bulbs available. I store my Garlic in a ceramic jar on my kitchen counter. In addition I always keep a few ounces of powdered Garlic, from an herb store, and some home-made Garlic oil on hand. I brew the oil from the fresh Garlic (see the Garlic Oil application). With these three forms of Garlic on hand I rarely need anything else to stop or prevent most types of infection, internally or externally.

Sometimes I hear complaints about the strong aroma of Garlic, particularly raw Garlic, or its spiciness on the tongue. Many new Garlic converts lack ideas on how to eat a quantity of raw Garlic in a pleasurable manner, so here are a few simple suggestions.

Fun and Easy Ways to Eat Garlic

1. For pleasure, or to minimize hotness on the tongue or in the stomach, eat slices of raw Garlic simultaneously with bites of raw fruit like apple, peach, or pear, or in fruit sauces such as applesauce. Some people prefer to chop up some Garlic and mix it with a spoonful of honey before chewing. With these methods most children and adults will grow to enjoy Garlic.

2 A "Garlic sandwich" is another pleasurable method for ingesting raw Garlic or for buffering the spiciness. Start with whole grain bread spread with your favorite butter or mayonnaise. Next add as much raw Garlic as you need and maybe some lettuce or tomato slices. The idea here is to eat a lot of Garlic with just enough sandwich around it to buffer the spiciness.

3. There are odorless, commercial preparations of Garlic available, such as the Kyolic brand found at most health food stores. Although they can offer some beneficial results and are convenient when you need them, I still prefer the three forms mentioned above (fresh, dried, or Garlic oil).
4. My all-time favorite Garlic ingestion technique is to make Garlic Popcorn! In a blender, mix:

   • lots of peeled raw Garlic (powdered Garlic is OK as a second choice but not for real Garlic lovers).
   • tamari soy sauce or salt, or any other spices according to taste. I like cumin and dill weed.
   • a small amount of olive oil (or other cold-pressed oil) mixed with one or two parts water — enough oil/water to cover the Garlic and still make a concentrated brew. The water is important so the mix doesn't end up being too oily for a body in the midst of a healing crisis.

   Blend extremely well and dribble heavily over the popcorn you've made. The idea for medicinal use is to have this mixture heavy on the Garlic sauce and lighter on the popcorn, but it's not crucial. Being a Garlic popcorn-lover myself, I usually make it so strong that I can blow your eyelashes off at 100 paces — not that I'd want to but I enjoy the Garlic popcorn immensely nonetheless. (See the TASOLE about Garlic popcorn in the Thrush application.)

■

To transform "Garlic breath" eat a generous mouthful of raw parsley, or chew on a Clove bud or a bit of Cinnamon stick, or put a drop of Peppermint oil on your tongue. You could also rinse your mouth with equal parts of lemon juice and water, or chew on orange peel, or munch on a few roasted coffee grounds for thirty seconds or so.

In addition, or as an alternative to eating raw Garlic, you can always use powdered Garlic or Garlic oil. Garlic oil is especially useful with infants and small children. There are more details on how to prepare these in the Applications list below. Students often ask me about the effectiveness of the commercial Garlic preparations that have been deodorized, concentrated in various ways, and packaged in liquids, pills, and gelatin pearles or capsules. There are a few brands that do have usable healing potency and are worth buying and using, but only as your last choice whenever the raw, powdered, or home-made Garlic oil forms are unavailable or undesirable in a particular case. Often we have to make an herbal choice based on a practical circumstance we can't change, and for times like these the deodorized commercial preparations are certainly an option.

To demonstrate the efficiency with which Garlic enters the blood and begins its work, I have often had my students do an experiment which you may want to try. At the beginning of a two hour class, everyone would peel a clove of Garlic and place it between two toes. Garlic will enter the body through the skin in this way and by the end of the class almost all of them would report they could taste the Garlic in their mouths! Some reported the Garlic taste in their mouths within five minutes. Once in awhile we would have a "tough case" who had to begin with the Garlic clove held under the armpit. That always proved the point.

Garlic is really advantageous for use on animals! In any external wound Garlic kills infection and keeps insects completely away. Many times I have come across stray animals with old infected wounds that often contained maggots and other insects. A few cloves of fresh Garlic blended in a cup of water and used to wash or soak the area removed even the most deeply imbedded insects (see TASOLE under Pets application). Then a Garlic or People Paste poultice (see People Paste, Appendix A) would finish off the job beautifully. Internal use on animals is also quite gratifying. I am always surprised at how quickly pets develop a taste for Garlic and began "asking for it" in their food!

TASOLE: A veterinarian friend once told me about an illness that often struck the Husky breed of dog. It involved a palsy-like shaking and trembling that resembled an epileptic seizure. There was allopathic medicine available for this yet it was expensive and had to be administered every day to prevent the seizures.

A short time later, as happens many times, someone asked my help for her pet Husky who had been diagnosed with this condition. "Is there any herbal alternative to the prescription drug?" she asked.

I had used Garlic advantageously for different types of pet illnesses and I knew the herb's nerve-soothing and immune-building qualities might have some effect, so I suggested using powdered Garlic in the Husky's food. The dog's owner was doubtful that her fussy Husky would eat Garlic, but she added a small dash to his food the next morning. At first the dog took one sniff of the unfamiliar aroma and walked away. Later in the day he sniffed it again but this time took one lick before leaving. A few minutes later the dog returned and began tentatively sampling the food. By the next morning the Husky was eating his Garlic dog food easily, so his owner increased the dosage on the third day. Soon the dog was eagerly consuming a heaping tablespoon of Garlic powder on his food, and showing much more energy and curiosity about life than he had for many months. The seizure medicine was lessened gradually and then finally stopped, and the daily dose of Garlic (at least one tablespoon each day and often more) was continued.

To test if the Garlic was really having any effect, we stopped administering it. Within three days the dog's seizures started again. When the Garlic was added again, the seizures stopped. We did this several times, just to be absolutely sure. The Garlic did not seem to cure the cause of the seizures permanently but totally controlled them. The expensive allopathic medicine, which was known to have unhealthy side effects, was discontinued. I have witnessed this use of Garlic on two other Huskies with the same results. In both cases the owners reported that the dogs' overall strength and stamina also noticeably improved.

I often receive newsletters from herb companies, vitamin companies, health writers, etc., that contain interesting information. Recently (February, 1992), I received a newsletter from a vitamin company (NOVA Inc., in Inglewood, California) reminding me of a couple of facts about two of my Ten Essentials, Garlic and Onion. I love it when I am reminded of these details and so I pass them on here. The newsletter was mentioning that researchers had found more than 30 possible cancer preventives in the Onion family (which includes Garlic). It went on to quote Daniel Nixon, Vice-president of Detection and Treatment for the American Cancer Society, as saying, "There's a lot of potential" in Garlic and its relatives for cancer prevention.

For more stories about the use of Garlic, read through the TASOLES in the Applications list on the following page.

APPLICATIONS AND ATTRIBUTES - GARLIC

(Quick Reference List)

ABSCESSED TEETH
AMOEBIC DYSENTERY
ANIMAL BITES
ANIMALS
ANTIBIOTIC
ANTISPASMODIC
ARTHRITIS
BATH
BITES
BLOOD POISONING
BLOOD PRESSURE
BOILS
COLDS and FLU
CONGESTION
COUGH
COUGH SYRUP
DIARRHEA
DIGESTION
DYSENTERY
EARACHE
ENEMA
EXPECTORANT
FOOTBATH
FUNGUS
GANGRENE
GARLIC BATH
GARLIC ENEMA
GARLIC OIL
GARLIC POULTICE
GARLIC WATER
GUM INFECTION
HEPATITIS
HERPES
HIGH BLOOD PRESSURE
IMMUNE SYSTEM
INFLAMMATION
INSECT BITES
INSECT REPELLENT
KIDNEY INFECTION
LUNGS
MONONUCLEOSIS
MOUTH INFECTION
MUCUS
NERVINE
OIL
PARASITES
PETS
PIMPLES
PLANTS
PNEUMONIA
POULTICE
RASH
REJUVENATING ELIXIR
SINUS
SKIN INFECTION
SLEEP
TEETH
THROAT
THRUSH
TONIC
URINARY TRACT
VAGINAL INFECTION
VERMIFUGE
WARTS
WOUNDS
YEAST INFECTION

FORM:

Dried powder, and commercial preparations

APPLICATION METHODS:

Internal uses: Eat fresh clove of Garlic or dried powder following one of the techniques listed in the Personality Profile. Garlic can also be applied internally using Garlic Oil, Garlic Water, Enhanced Garlic Formula (see Garlic Oil, Garlic Water, and Antibiotic applications), or commercial preparations. Also, one or two fresh Garlic cloves can be juiced with other vegetables as a tasty and healing drink. **Externally,** use a poultice made from fresh Garlic, dried powder or Garlic oil. Also simply rub the juice from a cut piece of Garlic directly onto a small wound, rash, or insect bite.

AVAILABILITY:

Grocery store, herb store, grow your own, open air markets around the world, mail order (See Buyers Guide, Appendix D.)

HINTS/CAUTIONS:

The raw juice of Garlic may raise a water blister when applied to sensitive areas of the skin — like the inner thigh or abdomen or the bottoms of a baby's feet. I generally don't consider this a problem. Yet if it is an inconvenience, or too irritating for any reason, there are easy ways to handle it. Wrap the raw Garlic in a thin layer of gauze or tissue, or cover the area of skin first with a light layer of petroleum jelly. The water blister may still arise under the jelly, yet it will be protected by the jelly and won't be irritated or sore. The water blister can be gently drained by piercing its side if desired. With a little time, however, itwill drain naturally. Do not take the tops off these blisters as this will temporarily make a sore spot. This phenomenon is actually a fairly easeful (and sometimes expected) way for the body to eliminate poisons.

There are a huge variety of types, styles, and sizes of Garlic. Keep this in mind when determining a dosage. Obviously a dose of 1 clove of an average-sized Garlic (about 1 inch long and 1/2 inch wide) will be far less than a dose of one clove of Elephant Garlic which can be inches in diameter! However, I have never heard of an overdose of Garlic. Simply use common sense.

GENERAL DOSAGE: INTERNAL USE

*PLEASE NOTE: *There are some additional forms of usage for Garlic which I do not put here in detail, such as Honeyballs, Capsules, Children's Ideas, etc. See these applications and Dosage Equivalents in Chapter I, Lesson #2.*

Infants to 3 years: Garlic oil is most often used and administered by the dropperful (1/4 to 1/2 tsp.), followed by a few swallows of water or juice or mother's milk (for a nursing infant). Garlic oil can be taken as often as every two hours up to eight times a day, depending upon the seriousness of the condition. 1 tsp. of Garlic oil equals approximately 1 average clove of raw Garlic when using the Garlic oil formula I have listed under that application. I have known many three-year-olds who will chew up a piece of Garlic with a bite of fruit and this method could be used for ingesting up to 5 Garlic cloves a day. A "5 clove" child is a real Garlic lover!

Children 4 to 10 years:

- Garlic oil, 1/2 to 1 tsp., as often as every two hours up to eight times a day, depending upon the seriousness of the condition. 1 tsp. of Garlic oil equals approximately 1 average clove of raw Garlic when using the Garlic oil formula listed under that application.
- Or, powdered Garlic (plain), 1/8 to 1/4 tsp., as often as every two hours up to eight times a day, depending upon the seriousness of the condition.
- Or, powdered Garlic in the form of the "special enhanced formula" (under Antibiotic application), 1/4 to 1/2 tsp., as often as every two hours, up to eight times a day, depending upon the seriousness of the condition.
- Or, fresh raw Garlic (average size 1 inch long by 1/2 inch wide), 1 or 2 cloves, eaten as often as every two hours up to five times a day, depending upon seriousness of the condition.

In mild cases of cold or flu, congestion, cough, etc., generally three to four doses are all that is needed during a day.

Any of these doses of Garlic could be taken with a little juice, fruit, applesauce, honey, cracker, or some other healthy yet small tidbit to lightly buffer the stomach. This will prevent any indigestion that might occur on an empty stomach.

Children 11 years to Adults:

- Garlic oil, 1 or 2 tsp., as often as every two hours up to eight times a day, depending upon the seriousness of the condition. 1 tsp. of Garlic oil equals approximately 1 average clove of raw Garlic when using the Garlic oil formula listed under that application.

- Or, powdered Garlic (plain), 1/4 to 1/2 tsp., as often as every two hours up to eight times a day, depending upon the seriousness of the condition.
- Or, powdered Garlic in the form of the "special enhanced formula" (under Antibiotic application), 1/2 to 1 tsp., as often as every two hours, up to eight times a day, depending upon the seriousness of the condition.
- Or, fresh raw Garlic (average size 1 inch long by 1/2 inch wide), 1 or 2 cloves, eaten as often as every two hours up to five times a day, depending upon seriousness of the condition.

In mild cases of cold or flu, congestion, cough, etc., generally three to four doses are all that is needed during a day.

Any of these doses of Garlic could be taken with a little juice, fruit, applesauce, honey, cracker, or some other healthy yet small tidbit to lightly buffer the stomach. This will prevent any indigestion that might occur on an empty stomach.

Pets and Other Creatures: Administer in the same ways as for humans. Dosage size depends upon body weight. For tiny or baby animals use dosage as for an infant child. A small bird would get 1 or 2 drops of Garlic oil. For an animal the size of a horse the estimate of dosage might be double that for a large man. With large animals I usually add Garlic powder to the feed, or mix chopped Garlic with honey and then gently push this "pellet" down the animal's throat, far enough to have it swallowed. Obviously, the latter method does not work for every large animal. I would be discriminating about trying it on an angry animal, especially one with sharp teeth or claws.

GENERAL DOSAGE: EXTERNAL USE

Same For All Humans And Other Creatures

Use Garlic externally as an antibiotic, insect repellent,fungicide, or against parasites.

Garlic oil can be rubbed into the affected body part, or if an infection is in the ear, the oil can be used as eardrops.

Powdered Garlic (plain, or use the Enhanced Garlic Formula under the Antibiotic application) can be applied topically as a dusting powder for infection, fungus, rash, or mild skin abrasions. Used as a poultice, the powder is moistened with a little water, aloe vera gel, honey (not for outdoor animals, as honey draws insects), or other moistening agent and applied 1/8 to 1/2 inch thick to the affected area. Clean the affected part with Garlic water, or other disinfecting wash, and repack with a fresh poultice two to five times a day depending upon the seriousness of the condition.

Fresh Garlic, chopped, crushed, or sliced, can be used alone or mixed with another herb from the Ten Essentials as a poultice 1/8 to 1/2 inch thick over the area. For a small need, such as a scratch or insect bite, tape a slice of Garlic, juicy side down, onto the area. These poultices will speed healing and prevent or treat infection.

Raw Garlic juice can be rubbed onto an affected body part. Simply cut a clove of Garlic and rub the juicy part onto the area.

Also see Animal Bites and Pets applications.

APPLICATIONS AND ATTRIBUTES - GARLIC

ABSCESSED TEETH: Make a small poultice by wrapping a raw Garlic clove (not cut, the juice would sting your mouth) or Garlic powder in a single layer of gauze to buffer sensitive gum tissue. Position the poultice next to the abscess between cheek and gum. Use Clove oil rubbed directly on the gum for pain relief. Take the Enhanced Garlic Formula (see Antibiotic application) and/or drink 2 to 6 cups per day of a blood-purifying herbal tea such as Chaparral, Comfrey, or Yarrow. Review those chapters (Chapters III, V, and XI) before deciding which one(s) to use.

If you have had an extraction of a tooth where there is or was also infection present, it works well to press Garlic powder or Garlic oil combined with Clove powder or Clove oil into the extraction hole for pain and infection relief. This is an excellent alternative to allopathic drug treatment. This Garlic/Clove poultice is a great trick to know when a tooth problem begins and there is no dental help available.

Garlic will not repair tooth decay, however. You still need a dentist for that!

ALSO SEE: *Antibiotic, Bath, Footbath, Garlic Poultice*

ALTERNATIVE OR SUPPLEMENTARY SELF-HELP: **Chaparral, *Clove, Comfrey, *People Paste, Peppermint Oil, Yarrow*

DOSAGE: *Use externally as given. Internally use the General dose.*

AMOEBIC DYSENTERY: Pay attention to this use of Garlic especially if you travel in places like Mexico, India, Southeast Asia, etc. Garlic can be found almost anyplace in the world at open-airmarkets. The best self-help I know is to eat 1 or 2 cloves of raw Garlic every few hours throughout the day. Take a small bit of mild food to buffer the stomach if needed.

As Garlic is a strong vermifuge (it kills certain parasites), it begins knocking out amoebas almost immediately. The more the body becomes saturated with Garlic, the stronger it works. Use Garlic early on, if possible, before the parasites become solidly entrenched. A Garlic enema is the ideal addition to the regular internal use of Garlic. Even without the enema, however, Garlic is often the answer to amoebic dysentery. After a bout of amoebic dysentery, it is sometimes necessary to use raw Garlic, in lesser doses, for up to a month to make sure the problem does not recur. Also, when possible, continue taking a Garlic enema every two or three days until three enemas have been taken. This is a necessity for stubborn cases of amoebas.

Consult the Diarrhea application to find ways to stop the diarrhea while you continue to work on the amoebas.

As a preventive measure, eat Garlic daily especially when traveling in more primitive areas. In this way, even if you do ingest some amoebas (or other parasites) there is a good chance they will not survive in your digestive tract.

ALSO SEE: *Antibiotic, Bath, Diarrhea, Garlic Enema, Garlic Water, Parasites*

ALTERNATIVE OR SUPPLEMENTARY SELF-HELP: **Chaparral, Comfrey, Sippery Elm*

DOSAGE: *Take the higher doses described in the General Dosage and be consistent about keeping the Garlic pumping through your system.*

ANIMAL BITES: These wounds need to be cleaned at once with a strong antibiotic wash such as Garlic Water (see that application), or a strong infusion of Chaparral or Yarrow herb. Sometimes a bite that is mostly a series of puncture wounds, without much torn skin, needs to be soaked thoroughly in the antibiotic solution to deeply treat the punctures. Depending on the seriousness of the bite, it can then be sprinkled with People Paste herbs or wrapped with a Garlic poultice or People Paste poultice.

For a serious bite, use an internal antibiotic formula such as suggested in the Antibiotic application in this chapter or in the Chaparral chapter (Chapter III). A blood-purifying tea, such as Yarrow, Chaparral, or Comfrey, taken 4 cups a day for three to six days, is an additional preventive for blood-poisoning and infection.

Always remember to take Cayenne for shock following a startling experience such as an animal bite.

To stop bleeding that may accompany an animal bite, use Comfrey root powder or Cayenne powder.

ALSO SEE: *Antibiotic, Blood Poisoning, Garlic Poultice, Wounds*

ALTERNATIVE OR SUPPLEMENTARY SELF-HELP: *Chaparral, Comfrey, *Garlic Water, *People Paste, *Yarrow,*

DOSAGE: *General*

ANIMALS: See Pets/Livestock application.

ANTIBIOTIC: Garlic is the **#1 Herbal Antibiotic** for any internal or external use. Read why this is so in the Personality Profile. The following formula doubles, or even triples, the strength and effectiveness of Garlic alone, while it helps the body to more quickly assimilate the Garlic and thus put it to work. I rarely have to use anything else besides plain Garlic or this Enhanced Garlic Formula when an antibiotic action is demanded.

ENHANCED GARLIC FORMULA

1 part Garlic powder
1 part powdered calcium ascorbate (a form of vitamin C)
1/4 part Cayenne powder

1 part = 1 pinch, 1 oz., 1 Tbsp., etc., depending on the amount of the formula you intend to make. See Chapter I, Lesson #6 for more details about preparing herbal formulas.

The powdered calcium ascorbate vitamin C that I normally use is found at health food stores and has a potency of 1/4 tsp. = 1 gram of vitamin C. If you prefer, you could mix only the Garlic and Cayenne together as powders and take 1 gram of vitamin C (calcium ascorbate) in tablet form with each dose or as needed.

I recommend making a large enough quantity so you always have extra on hand for emergency use. Store in an airtight container in a cool, dry place for best shelf life.

If you are not getting the results you want from the Enhanced Garlic Formula you may have a tough-case "germ" that calls for an additional antibiotic herb such as Chaparral or others among the Ten Essentials. Several additional antibiotic formulas are listed in the Chaparral chapter (Chapter III). Here is another one that uses Garlic:

ALTERNATIVE ANTIBIOTIC FORMULA

Mix together equal parts of Chaparral, Garlic, and Slippery Elm powders for internal and external use.

Begin taking a dose of some form of Garlic at the first signs of an illness. For some of us this first sign is a certain type of grumpiness; for others it is a scratchy throat. One or two doses of Garlic will generally act to prevent these first signs from becoming full-blown illnesses. If more is needed, however, the next step would be to continue the proper doses of Garlic as specified in the General Dosage. For an average cold, a dose of Garlic every two or three hours is good, but even less frequent doses can still work quite well. Feel free to experiment.

When using Garlic as an antibiotic, always drink at least two quarts of pure water and/or herb tea during the day to help flush toxins out of your body. At any stage you may want to consider using a Garlic enema to speed recovery. For stubborn or harsh illnesses such as pneumonia, hepatitis, and virulent forms of the flu, etc., definitely use a Garlic enema (see Garlic Enema application) in addition to the internal doses of Garlic. A Garlic poultice (or a poultice made from another appropriate Ten Essentials herb) applied externally directly over the affected area, or a Garlic poultice applied on the bottoms of the feet, will strongly draw toxins out. (Application to the feet is usually for children but can also work well for thin-skinned adults.) See the Garlic Poultice application.

Review the fun ways to eat raw Garlic and the hints for dealing with "Garlic Breath" in the Personality Profile above. These suggestions really help turn a Garlic resister into an enthusiastic (or at least willing) Garlic ingester.

In cases where an odorless Garlic formulation is absolutely needed, a commercial, odorless variety of Garlic preparation can be used as a second choice.

For small external infections such as an infected mosquito bite, cut a slice of Garlic and rub the spot with the wet, juicy side of the Garlic slice.

ALSO SEE: *Amoebic Dysentery, Garlic Bath, Diarrhea, Digestion, Footbath, Garlic Enema, Garlic Oil, Garlic Poultice, Garlic Water, Gum Infection, Hepatitis, Herpes, Immune System, Wounds, Yeast*

ALTERNATIVE OR SUPPLEMENTARY SELF-HELP: **Chaparral, Cloves, Comfrey, *People Paste, *Yarrow*

DOSAGE: *General or as given in specific application*

ANTISPASMODIC: Taking Garlic internally can act as a potent antispasmodic and nervine — actions which relax tension in the nerves and body tissues (see Nervine application). This soothing and calming action of Garlic is beneficial for relieving spasms in any body part, especially if the spasm is the result of tension or anxiety.

Try Garlic for spasms of the blood vessels to and in the head, resulting in tension headache; for spasms or cramps in the lower abdomen resulting in spastic colon; alone or with a dose of calcium lactate or calcium gluconate for muscle spasms in general.

ALSO SEE: *Blood Pressure, Nervine*

ALTERNATIVE OR SUPPLEMENTARY SELF-HELP: **Clove, Ginger, Peppermint*

DOSAGE: *General*

ARTHRITIS: Many forms of arthritis respond quickly to Garlic because of the anti-inflammatory action in its allicin and sulphur compounds. "Garlic gives me rapid pain relief," many of my friends have told me. I have had good results with some people using the odorless Garlic supplements available commercially, so there is no reason not to use some form of Garlic regularly if you suffer from arthritis pain.

ALSO SEE: *Antibiotic, Antispasmodic, Garlic Bath, Nervine*

ALTERNATIVE OR SUPPLEMENTARY SELF-HELP: **Chaparral, Clove, *Comfrey, Ginger, Onion, Slippery Elm, *Yarrow*

DOSAGE: *General or as given*

BATH: See Garlic Bath application.

BITES: See Animal Bites and Insect Bites applications.

BLOOD-POISONING: Soak the affected part in Garlic Water or a Garlic Bath (see those applications) and take Garlic internally. Drink at least two quarts of blood-purifying tea like Yarrow, Comfrey, or Chaparral each day. You should see signs of poison reversal within twenty-four hours. You can then start decreasing the dosage as the symptoms continue to subside.

Sometimes for a less severe case of blood poisoning, a few doses of Cayenne, perhaps thirty minutes apart, can stimulate your circulation into carrying off the poisons right away. It is still important to drink at least two quarts of water or blood-purifying herb tea to supply the extra body fluids needed to carry off the poisons.

ALSO SEE: *Antibiotic, Gangrene, Garlic Poultice, Garlic Water, Wounds*

ALTERNATIVE OR SUPPLEMENTARY SELF-HELP: **Chaparral, *Comfrey, *Yarrow*

DOSAGE: *General and as given*

BLOOD PRESSURE: Garlic can help both high and low blood pressure problems. I will address high blood pressure(HBP) first.

In 1948, Dr. F.G. Piotrowski of the University of Geneva surprised the medical world with his announcement of the discovery of a natural food that had "astounding results" in lowering high blood pressure (HBP). There had been many similar reports from around the world, including from India, Germany, and Russia. The natural food referred to was none other than Garlic!

Many of my students and friends have kissed their HBP problems goodbye upon discovering the use of Garlic. For one thing, Garlic has a high amount of natural sulphur, which calms the nerves and strengthens the heart. In Dr. Piotrowski's findings he suggested that Garlic had a gently dilating effect on congested and restricted blood vessels. I knew that Garlic worked for HBP and used it regularly on friends for years before I began to find out why it worked. If you have interest in more of the "whys," see Science of Herbal Medicine by John Heinerman, Natural Healing With Herbs by Humbart Santillo, and Garlic by Dorothy Wade; these are all listed in the Resource Guide, Appendix C.

Self-help for HBP is to ingest Garlic on a daily basis. Fresh Garlic, powdered Garlic, or home-made Garlic oil are still my preferred suggestions. However, even commercial preparations of Garlic are often satisfactory. Begin by taking Garlic several times a day in some form, adjusting the dosage until you find the amount right for you. For instance, start with 1/4 tsp. Garlic powder three or four times a day. Or, purchase a commercial preparation of odorless Garlic oil that comes in gelatin "pearles" (similar to a capsule) and start by taking 3 to 5 pearles four times a day. I have never seen or heard of any bad side effects from taking too much Garlic, so you can feel confident in taking regular, healthy doses. You will cut down later as your body heals itself.

There are dietary changes that will augment the reducing of HBP, like eating a no-salt or low-salt diet and avoiding fried foods. A person taking allopathic treatment for HBP is advised to consult his/her doctor before experimenting with taking Garlic as a dietary addition to prescription drugs. It's always best to take differing remedies at separate times during the day. I usually find that fewer and fewer drugs are needed as the Garlic begins its amazing work. I suggest carrying a convenient form of Garlic with you so that as soon as any HBP symptoms begin, you can take an extra dose of Garlic to help rebalance the situation.

Garlic can also help to rebalance low blood pressure problems. The same general principles for determining the dosage apply for low blood pressure as for HBP. In addition the blood building, stimulating, and circulation-strengthening properties of Cayenne and/or Ginger should be incorporated into any program for low blood pressure.

ALSO SEE: *Antispasmodic, Nervine*

ALTERNATIVE OR SUPPLEMENTARY SELF-HELP: *Cayenne, Clove, Comfrey, Onion, Yarrow*

DOSAGE: *Use as given or experiment according to the form of Garlic used.*

BOILS: Take Garlic internally as recommended in the Antibiotic application, or use an alternative antibiotic or blood-purifying herb internally. Use a Garlic poultice on the boil to draw it to a head and encourage it to drain naturally. You may need to open the boil, however, with a sharp, sterile instrument to effectively drain it. Keep the area clean and repack it with a fresh poultice two to three times a day, or as needed. After the boil is thoroughly drained and on its way to healing, you may want to switch to a more soothing poultice of People Paste, Comfrey, or Slippery Elm, since fresh Garlic can be irritating to the newly forming skin.

ALSO SEE: *Antibiotic, Garlic Poultice, Garlic Water, Pimples, Skin*

ALTERNATIVE OR SUPPLEMENTARY SELF-HELP: **Chaparral, *Comfrey, *People Paste, Slippery Elm, Yarrow*

DOSAGE: *General*

COLDS and FLU: See Antibiotic and Congestion applications.

CONGESTION: Congestion can take many forms. You can have toxic forms of mucus (see Mucus application) clogging up just about any part of the digestive system, head, or chest. You can have the sluggish, sometimes painful, internal organs that are congested with various forms of toxic build-up (i.e., from poor diet, addictive substances, heavy medicinal drug use, etc.). Liver congestion is one of the most noticeable types of organ congestion. It results in all sorts of digestive (or should I say indigestive) upsets, besides liver and gall bladder pain. Another place where congestion is obvious is in the lungs.

For all varieties of congestion, a Garlic enema combined with ingesting some form of Garlic is my favorite approach. The Garlic enema breaks up congestion throughout the body and helps the body to eliminate it. The use of Garlic taken orally builds the immune system (see that application) and helps restore equilibrium through its blood-purifying and antibiotic properties.

ALSO SEE: *Antibiotic, Garlic Bath, Cough, Digestion, Footbath, Garlic Enema, Garlic Poultice, Immune System, Mucus*

ALTERNATIVE OR SUPPLEMENTARY SELF-HELP: **Chaparral, *Comfrey, Ginger, *Onion, Slippery Elm, *Yarrow*

DOSAGE: *General*

COUGH: At the first sign of a scratchy throat that may be the precursor to a genuine cough, reach for the Garlic. (See Antibiotic application.) Even if the cough already has some momentum, reach for the Garlic anyway. In that case you will take more frequent doses and perhaps drink some blood-purifying or decongesting tea such as Comfrey or Ginger.

For severe cough and/or congestion, Garlic oil (or Garlic in another form) could be administered as often as every half-hour over a two hour period. Then use less frequently, as needed, perhaps once every two hours. This frequency of dosage can be used with infants and adults alike, but the amounts, of course, will vary.

Review further antibiotic formulas in the Chaparral chapter,(Chapter III).

ALSO SEE: *Antibiotic, Congestion, Cough Syrup, Expectorant, Mucus*

ALTERNATIVE OR SUPPLEMENTARY SELF HELP: *Cayenne, Chaparral, *Comfrey, *Ginger, *Onion, Slippery Elm, Yarrow*

DOSAGE: *For children and adults use 1/4 to 1 tsp. Garlic oil to help stop a cough, taking it as often as needed. For infants and small babies you would use the smaller doses administered by dropper onto the tongue. (See General Dosage, above.)*

COUGH SYRUP: For 20 to 30 minutes, slowly simmer 1 cup chopped raw Onions in enough honey to cover them. Take this brew off the heat and add 4 tsp. powdered Garlic or 6 to 8 crushed cloves of Garlic. (A Garlic press is best here if you have one.) Let this mixture steep (do not cook) in a covered pot until it reaches room temperature. This may take an hour or two. Use in teaspoon doses as needed for cough and as an antibiotic expectorant.

ALSO SEE: *Antibiotic, Congestion, Cough, Expectorant, Immune System*

ALTERNATIVE OR SUPPLEMENTARY SELF-HELP: **Comfrey, *Onion, Peppermint, *Slippery Elm (syrup and lozenges)*

DOSAGE: *For infants to 4 years, 1/4 to 1/2 tsp. as needed; children 5 years to 9 years, 1 tsp. as needed; 12 years to adults, 1 tsp. to 1 TBS. as needed.*

DIARRHEA: If you have diarrhea from a viral or amoebic infection, then Garlic is the herb to try first. Overnight results in stopping or significantly slowing the diarrhea often follow taking a Garlic enema (see Garlic Enema application) as well as taking Garlic in some form orally.

Use a Garlic enema when a strong antibiotic or vermifuge action is called for. If the diarrhea is from nervous tension, poor digestion, or some recurrent intestinal irritation (other than amoebas or infection), then Slippery Elm, Comfrey, or Yarrow, taken orally and/or as an enema, are the alternatives or additions to choose. (See Chapters V, X, and XI.)

When dysentery or severe diarrhea strikes, the "double whammy" approach known to many seasoned world-travelers is to use charcoal. Take a cup of charcoal (yes, I mean the blackened chunks of wood from a fire, not the white-grey ash), pulverize it with enough water to be able to eat it or drink it down somehow, and consume the entire cup of "charcoal soup." Use less charcoal for less serious situations. My traveler-friends and I swear that this "soup" will stop diarrhea and dysentery within three hours, 100% of the time. Charcoal is well known as an absorbent of poisons, gas, undigested substances, and much else. It collects (absorbs) the "bad-guys" and dumps them out of the system before they have time to take hold. This is called for with any kind of intestinal distress. If the distress is connected with a parasite infection, you should still supplement the charcoal with Garlic to insure long-term success.

I have used commercial herb capsules filled with charcoal powder and they work fine for mild intestinal distress. You would have to take a lot of them to equal the cupful of charcoal I am suggesting for extreme cases of dysentery or serious diarrhea.

ALSO SEE: *Amoebic Dysentery, Garlic Enema, Parasites*

ALTERNATIVE OR SUPPLEMENTARY SELF-HELP: *Comfrey, Slippery Elm, Yarrow*

DOSAGE: *General for oral use; use specific directions in theGarlic Enema application or use other herbal enema. (See enema instructions in Chapter I, Lesson #2.)*

DIGESTION, rehabilitation: To rejuvenate an ill or inefficient digestive system and build up healthy digestive bacteria, try drinking this restorative elixir.

RESTORATIVE ELIXIR

Crush or mince one cup (or at least 16 average cloves) of raw Garlic and soak in two quarts of fresh whey (see directions below) for 12 to 24 hours at room temperature. Then strain this mixture and store the liquid in the refrigerator. Drink 1/4 cup of the liquid three to six times a day for one month, or as long as you please. Optional: Add a small amount of Cayenne to each dose to enhance the benefits.

Whey is best made by setting out certified raw cow or goat milk, at room temperature in a covered glass jar, until the milk curdles. This could take from a few hours up to a few days depending on what temperature your room is. (Pasteurized milk is a close second-best choice; homogenized milk is only used as a "last resort" when nothing else is available.) It will be obvious when the whey is ready because you will see white, soft lumps of milk solids (the curds) floating around in a somewhat clearish liquid (the whey). Strain this through a cloth and you'll have curds and whey. Use the liquid whey for this elixir and perhaps make cottage cheese out of the curds by adding a little salt. This whey contains rejuvenating digestive bacteria — sometimes referred to as acidophilus, although this label is somewhat inaccurate. This home-made whey also includes B-vitamins and some digestive enzymes. The Garlic adds all the potent rebalancing properties you have read about in this chapter so far, and even many that I haven't included!

You could make this healthy bacteria-content in the whey more potent (and this step is more essential if you are forced to use pasteurized or homogenized milk) by adding the digestive bacteria cultures from a commercial acidophilus, or "live" yogurt culture, to the milk you start with. With plain, raw milk, no additives are necessary, but make sure the raw milk is certified.

I learned about this elixir from herbalists exposed to methods used at a Swedish health camp and have used the elixir for many years with great results. I have since experimented with soaking the Garlic in a commercial, liquid acidophilus instead of the home-made whey, and have gotten marvelous results.

For those who hesitate to use milk at all, or won't take the time to make whey, try this alternative. To get the acidophilus base, you will have to dilute the commercial product according to its instructions. This elixir is perfect for keeping the immune system strong as well as for rehabilitating the digestive tract. It can be used as a daily tonic for those who want to maintain good health.

ALSO SEE: *Digestion, Immune System*

ALTERNATIVE OR SUPPLEMENTARY SELF-HELP: **Cayenne, Comfrey, *Ginger, Peppermint, Slippery Elm*

DOSAGE: *Start with 1/4 cup, three to six times a day. Experiment with amount and frequency of doses to suit the individual case.*

DYSENTERY: See Amoebic Dysentery and Diarrhea applications.

EARACHE: For earaches or irritations from infection, fungus, water, coldness, etc., Garlic is one of the first herbs to think of. Orally take an antibiotic herbal formula such as the one listed in this chapter or in the Chaparral chapter (Chapter III).

It is best to treat both ears even when there is trouble in only one of them. This greatly lessens the possibility of having the ear problem transfer back and forth from ear to ear.

To remedy an earache use a few drops of Garlic oil, warmed if you like, in each ear. Hold in with a bit of cotton. Another way to use Garlic is to cut a sliver of raw Garlic to the right size, wrap it in one thin layer of soft tissue or gauze to protect the ear tissue from any Garlic juice irritation, and insert it into the ear opening. Change this Garlic sliver at least three times a day. In some cases you will see fluids and perhaps pus clinging to the Garlic when it is changed as the Garlic tends to pull out the infection. For a very painful earache, I suggest the use of Clove oil and/or an Onion pack.

For an earache from wax build-up, persistently and gently flush the ear with a warm stream of water, using a bulb syringe, until the wax begins to break up and wash out in bits. (Do not block the ear opening by pressing the bulb syringe in too far. This could result in harmful water pressure.) Have patience as you may need to keep flushing for 10 to 15 minutes. But the effort is usually well worth it. After such a flushing, soothe the ear canal with a few drops of warmed plain olive oil or Garlic oil which will also help soften and loosen any wax residues. Putting warmed Garlic oil into the ear canal half an hour prior to the flushing helps soften the wax.

ALSO SEE: *Congestion, Garlic Oil*

ALTERNATIVE OR SUPPLEMENTARY SELF-HELP: **Clove oil, *Onion pack*

DOSAGE: *As given*

ENEMA: See Garlic Enema application.

EXPECTORANT: Garlic will help pull mucus out of the lungs at the same time that it is soothing the lung tissues and helping to kill any infection. Garlic oil or Garlic cough syrup (see Cough Syrup application) are particularly good forms to use when an expectorant is needed as they coat the throat and esophagus, which hastens and prolongs the expectorant effect. For infants and small children, just a few drops or a small dropperful of the oil or cough syrup on the tongue can induce expectoration of mucus or fluid and promote healing in the lungs. Garlic in these forms will also relax the child for a good night's sleep and serve as an antibiotic as well. Any form of Garlic can help to clear the lungs very efficiently, and a Garlic Enema (see that application) is one of the best.

ALSO SEE: *Antibiotic, Garlic Bath, Congestion, Cough, Cough Syrup, Footbath, Garlic Enema, Garlic Oil, Garlic Poultice, Mucus*

ALTERNATIVE OR SUPPLEMENTARY SELF-HELP: **Cayenne, Comfrey, *Onion, Slippery Elm*

DOSAGE: *General*

FOOTBATH: Make some Garlic water (see Garlic Water application) and add to a small tub of hot water. Soak your feet for twenty minutes or more. This Garlic footbath will draw toxins from the entire body, soothe tension and anxiety, rejuvenate sore or tired feet and legs, help treat athlete's foot, speed recovery from colds and flu, relieve toxic build-up from a daily job environment that may be physically or emotionally polluted or stressful, and much, much more! And besides, it feels so good.

ALSO SEE: *Garlic Bath, Garlic Water*

ALTERNATIVE OR SUPPLEMENTARY SELF-HELP: *Ginger, *Peppermint, *Yarrow*

DOSAGE: *For each one gallon of water in the footbath, add 10 to 16 cloves of fresh Garlic crushed well or blended with approximately 2 cups of water. No need to strain it for this purpose.*

FUNGUS: Garlic is a potent fungicide internally and externally (as is Chaparral). I have used it profitably on athlete's foot, finger and toenail fungus, ear fungus, vaginal yeast (see Vaginal Infection application), candida, and even plant-leaf fungus! Externally I most often use Garlic powder or Garlic oil as these are generally more convenient to apply topically. For one particularly stubborn case of foot fungus, a student of mine applied crushed, raw Garlic (over a thin layer of petroleum jelly to prevent stinging) as an overnight poultice for two or three nights and this worked extremely well.

Taking Garlic internally helps with both internal and external fungus infections, especially of the yeast variety. It is doubly effective if sugar, alcohol, and products containing yeast (such as bread and beer) are eliminated from the diet. The Enhanced Garlic Formula (see Antibiotic application) is ideal for enhancing internal anti-fungal activity.

Review the Chaparral chapter (Chapter III) as this herb is also a fungicide and can be combined with Garlic or used effectively alone as an alternative to Garlic.

ALSO SEE: *Earache, Footbath, Garlic Bath, Garlic Oil, Garlic Poultice, Vaginal Infection, Yeast Infection*

ALTERNATIVE OR SUPPLEMENTARY SELF-HELP: **Chaparral*

DOSAGE: *General*

GANGRENE: To prevent or possibly retard gangrene or blood-poisoning, pack the entire area thickly with pulverized Garlic directly in and around the wound. Clean out dead tissue and any pus, etc., with strong Garlic water (see Garlic Water application). One way to do this is to soak the area for 10 minutes, and then repack it with fresh Garlic poultice at least three times a day. In some cases I have seen the red lines of blood poisoning actually begin retracting within a few hours, or at least by overnight. At this point in the process the dead gangrenous flesh may start cleaning out of the wound. With that the re-infection cycle is stopped, and the wound begins healing normally.

Once the wound gets to the point where it stays free of the gross infection and blood-poisoning symptoms, you can switch to the more soothing yet strong antibiotic action of a People Paste poultice. (See People Paste, Appendix A.)

These types of infections are *very serious* and must be meticulously tended to with frequent cleanings and repackings while you also take Garlic and Cayenne internally plus a gram of the calcium ascorbate form of vitamin C each hour or two. If this method is carefully followed you should see tangible signs of improvement (such as lowering of fever, lessening of redness and swelling around wound, better drainage of infection and sloughing of dead tissue) after twenty-four hours, in which case you should continue with this program. If there is no improvement, you should seek professional help immediately.

ALSO SEE: *Antibiotic, Garlic Poultice, Garlic Water, Wounds*

ALTERNATIVE OR SUPPLEMENTARY SELF-HELP: **Chaparral, *People Paste*

DOSAGE: *General or as given*

GARLIC BATH: It may sound odd to take a Garlic bath, but don't be too hasty to discard this idea. A Garlic bath is literally a euphoric experience. It is also relaxing, rejuvenating, detoxifying and an enjoyable way to dose yourself with Garlic to make short work of many common colds, flus, and daily stresses.

A Garlic bath is a dynamic form of prevention of illness, especially if you find yourself nursing a sick friend with a contagious disease.

Don't worry about carrying the aroma of Garlic. Unless you soak your whole head in the Garlic bath, in which case your hair will probably carry the scent until it is shampooed, the scent in your skin is generally undetectable. See the Ginger chapter (Chapter VII), or the Yarrow chapter (Chapter XI) for alternative types of herbal baths.

This bath is especially effective on infants and children.

ALSO SEE: *Footbath, Garlic Water, Immune System*

ALTERNATIVE OR SUPPLEMENTARY SELF-HELP: *Comfrey, *Ginger, Peppermint, *Yarrow*

DOSAGE: *Use 1/2 to 1 cup Garlic powder in a full tub of hot water (buy your Garlic powder in bulk at an herb store). Don't hesitate to use more or less as you play around with how it feels to you. Some people use as little as 1/4 cup and the most I ever heard of a student using was 2 cups. I admit I thought that was a bit too much! You could probably use crushed raw Garlic in the tub but it is something I have never tried. I am too lazy to peel all the Garlic if I'm not going to eat it!*

GARLIC ENEMA: Taking an enema of any kind is not my idea of an entertaining activity. Nevertheless, with any number of illnesses from flu, colds and pneumonia to dysentery or mononucleosis, a Garlic enema, with its antibiotic and decongesting actions, can lessen or end the misery quickly.

Fill an enema bag with two quarts of Garlic Water (see Garlic Water application) for adults, one quart for children, or use a bulb syringe for infants. The temperature of the Garlic water should approximate the internal body temperature. If you have no experience with administering an enema, begin to develop your own technique by following the detailed instructions in Chapter I, Lesson #2.

After a Garlic enema (or any enema for that matter) it is a good idea to follow it, perhaps one hour to a day later, with an enema of plain water that contains a double or triple dose of liquid or powdered acidophilus. This will quickly replenish the colon with the healthful digestive bacteria that are usually depleted during illness. This acidophilus enema also hastens the return of healthy bowel action, especially in a person whose intestinal balance and action is easily disrupted.

For short periods of time (usually no more than two weeks) during extreme illness, two or even three Garlic enemas (three being the rare case) per week could be useful.

ALSO SEE: *Antibiotic, Garlic Water, Mononucleosis, Pneumonia, and the Enema application in Chapter I, Lesson 2*

ALTERNATIVE OR SUPPLEMENTARY SELF-HELP: **Chaparral, Comfrey, *Slippery Elm, *Yarrow*

DOSAGE: *As given*

GARLIC OIL: This home-made oil can be used in place of raw Garlic, especially for infants and children. In oil form, Garlic can easily be dropped into ears for almost any ear problem in both humans and pets (see Earache application), given by drops to infants, rubbed into fungus infections, or used whenever you desire a convenient form. Always keep some Garlic oil made up and ready for use. This oil will keep its potency for a few months or longer if stored properly inside a well-sealed glass container (often a dropper bottle) in the refrigerator. One teaspoon Garlic oil equals about 1 average clove of raw Garlic. Instructions for making Garlic oil are on the following page.

HOME-MADE GARLIC OIL

Ingredients: 1/2 cup minced fresh Garlic
1/2 cup olive oil

Blend ingredients *thoroughly* and then add 1/4 cup more olive oil. Stir lightly, put in a covered glass jar in a sunny window, and let stand for 10 days. Shake the jar gently 3 times a day. On the 10th day, press (strain) through a cloth and store the oil in the refrigerator.

THIS IS POTENT STUFF!

After the mixture is strained, there is always a little bit of fine, white residue in the oil. It is O.K. to leave this in as long as it really is a small amount and very fine. Otherwise it will clog up your dropper or cause spoilage, etc.

If you find yourself in need of Garlic oil and you have none prepared, start a fresh batch according to the instructions above but use it immediately as is, unstrained. Do continue the instructions by letting the remainder of the Garlic oil sit for 10 days and then strain it, etc., but also feel free to use it as is in the meanwhile. Sometimes you may find that you have used up the Garlic-oil-in-the-making while it was sitting in your window, before the 10 days have passed. This is OK in a crisis, but it is better to have the properly extracted Garlic oil on hand to use whenever possible.

Don't let the mixture continue standing past the tenth day. It will begin loosing potency and deteriorating if not strained and refrigerated at that time. The Garlic pulp that is strained out can be eaten or used as a cooking condiment.

ALSO SEE: *Antibiotic, Cough, Earache, Expectorant, Fungus*

ALTERNATIVE OR SUPPLEMENTARY SELF-HELP: *Commercial liquid Garlic preparations are O.K. if you find yourself otherwise unprepared. Results may be a little slower.*

DOSAGE: *General*

GARLIC POULTICE: Use crushed raw Garlic or Garlic powder made into a poultice. (See Chapter I, Lesson #2 for poultice instructions.) Apply externally directly over any organ or body part that is experiencing infection or congestion. This would include anything from poulticing the lungs during pneumonia (especially in children), to poulticing the gall bladder/liver area for relief of hepatitis, to poulticing a simple insect bite. Leave the poultice on for at least 30 minutes and up to overnight, depending upon the circumstances. A Garlic poultice will draw infection out of an internal source, break up congestion, and supply antibiotic action through the skin and therefore directly into the spot needed.

You can cover a poultice with a hot water bottle to keep it warm and help it to penetrate more deeply. Sometimes you may need to coat an area of sensitive skin (such as over the liver or lungs) with a light coating of petroleum jelly or plain face cream to prevent any irritation of the skin from the strong Garlic juices. Especially for children and babies, it is a good idea to pack the bottoms of their feet with Garlic to draw out infection or congestion from anywhere in the body. Be sure to coat a baby's delicate feet with the protective jelly mentioned above. Also see the special note about this under "Hints/Cautions" at the end of the Personality Profile.

During and after a Garlic poultice, especially if it is covering a large area, don't be surprised if you get the taste of Garlic in your mouth. Garlic is absorbed into the body through the skin, picked up in the blood and lymph fluids, and soon reaches everywhere in the body. This taste of Garlic is a sign that your body is using the herb. Your sweat may also temporarily have the aroma of Garlic. Chewing on raw parsley or Cloves, or using a drop of Peppermint oil on the tongue, will help to transform the temporary Garlic aroma in your mouth. See many "breath aroma ideas" in the Personality Profile, above.

ALSO SEE: *Antibiotic, Congestion, Fungus, Gangrene, Wounds*

ALTERNATIVE OR SUPPLEMENTARY SELF-HELP: *Chaparral, Comfrey, Ginger, People Paste, Yarrow*

DOSAGE: *Cover the affected area 1/4 to 1/2 inch thick with a poultice made from raw crushed Garlic or Garlic powder (add water). Cover the poultice with a band-aid or clean cotton cloth and wrap the whole thing with plastic or plastic wrap to keep it damp. Cover with a hot water bottle as needed. Leave on for an average of one hour; however the poultice can be left on overnight for severe congestion or infection. See details and cautions within this application.*

GARLIC WATER: Garlic water is made from fresh Garlic crushed or blended well in pure water. Strain out the pulp, or not, according to use. This water can be added to a footbath, bathtub (see Garlic Bath application), enema bag, etc., or used as an antibiotic wash for wounds, as a spray for plant diseases, or as a plant insect repellent.

For an internal use such as an enema, begin with a mild mixture, using one (generally for babies) or two cloves of Garlic for each quart of water. For an external use such as a footbath, it is fine to have a stronger mixture, such as 1 clove of Garlic for each cup of water. To make a large amount of Garlic water it is often simplest to first make a concentrate by blending many cloves of Garlic with two or three cups of water. Then dilute this mixture to the strength desired.

If you plan to put the Garlic water through a sprayer, enema tube, etc., you must first strain it well to prevent small Garlic bits from plugging up any equipment.

ALSO SEE: *Antibiotic, Footbath, Garlic Bath, Garlic Enema, Pets, Plants, Wounds*

ALTERNATIVE OR SUPPLEMENTARY SELF-HELP: *Chaparral, Yarrow*

DOSAGE: *As given*

GUM INFECTION: See Abscessed Teeth application.

HEMORRHOIDS: Use a peeled clove of Garlic (take off "onion-skin" covering but do not break the inner skin) as a suppository and leave in overnight. This helps to calm and disinfect the area. Also drink 3 to 6 cups of unsweetened Yarrow or Comfrey/Yarrow tea each day to continuously cleanse the blood while giving the inflamed blood vessels (hemorrhoids) a chance to heal.

ALSO SEE: *Antibiotic, Tonic*

ALTERNATIVE OR SUPPLEMENTARY SELF-HELP: **Comfrey, *Slippery Elm, *Yarrow*

DOSAGE: *As given*

HEPATITIS: The type of hepatitis to which I am referring is the inflammation of the liver caused by eating contaminated food or water. Taking Garlic daily, especially while traveling, can go a long way toward preventing this liver disease altogether. (See Immune System application.)

However, if you do contract hepatitis, especially if you are in an out-of-the-way place with no reliable medical treatment, take Garlic every one to two hours depending upon seriousness of the case. For the most severe cases use a Garlic enema one to three times a week along with a Garlic poultice (see Garlic Poultice application) externally, right over the liver, when possible. If this seems to be working then continue the treatment, being certain to take any undue digestive stress off the liver by eating only small amounts of simple-to-digest foods and drinking at least two quarts of pure water daily.

ALSO SEE: *Antibiotic, Garlic Bath, Garlic Enema, Garlic Poultice*

ALTERNATIVE OR SUPPLEMENTARY SELF-HELP: *Chaparral, Comfrey, People Paste (use herbs internally and as a liver poultice externally), *Yarrow*

DOSAGE: *General*

HERPES: Garlic taken daily is often good prevention for herpes or herpes outbreaks of the genital or oral variety. It can also be used as a Garlic water wash on active sores, or as a small poultice on active sores if it is mixed with a demulcent herb such as Slippery Elm or Comfrey Root to prevent irritation.

As with any strong outbreak of disease, a Garlic enema is always a good thing to keep in mind to speed results.

Review the Chaparral chapter (Chapter III) as this herb is also specifically helpful with Herpes and mixes well with Garlic and a buffering/soothing herb like Slippery Elm.

ALSO SEE: *Antibiotic, Garlic Bath, Garlic Enema, Garlic Water*

ALTERNATIVE OR SUPPLEMENTARY SELF-HELP: **Chaparral, Comfrey, *People Paste, Slippery Elm*

DOSAGE: *General*

HIGH BLOOD PRESSURE: See Blood Pressure application.

IMMUNE SYSTEM: To strengthen your immune system and greatly decrease your chances of getting colds, flu, etc., simply take a dose of Garlic each day. Keep this approach in mind while traveling, especially in back-country places, as it can also lessen the chances of picking up hepatitis and parasites. Even the commercial Garlic preparations can give good results in this application, although the strongest immune builder is the Enhanced Garlic Formula (see the Antibiotic application).

ALSO SEE: *Antibiotic, Digestion (rejuvenating elixir), Hepatitis, Herpes, Nervine, Parasites*

ALTERNATIVE OR SUPPLEMENTARY SELF-HELP: *Chaparral, *Comfrey, Ginger, Onion, *Yarrow*

DOSAGE: *Use the smaller general dosage perhaps once a day to help maintain good health, or two or three times a day while traveling in more adverse circumstances or tending sick friends.*

INFLAMMATION: See Arthritis application.

INSECT BITES: For most insect bites all that is needed is to rub the cut (juicy) surface of a Garlic clove on the bite a few times. Any itching, swelling, etc., will be prevented or greatly lessened. For an insect bite that seems more serious you may need to tape a slice of Garlic or a full Garlic poultice onto the area to prevent or draw out infection.

ALSO SEE: *Antibiotic, Blood Poisoning, Garlic Poultice, Pets, Skin Infection*

ALTERNATIVE OR SUPPLEMENTARY SELF-HELP: **Chaparral, *Comfrey, *Onion, *People Paste, *Yarrow*

DOSAGE: *General or as given*

INSECT REPELLENT: I learned an old folk use of Garlic that really works for repelling insects. If you wear a necklace of Garlic cloves on the outside of your clothing, no insects will come around! This is a great trick for children or adults who seem to attract insects everywhere.

There is no strong smell to the necklace since the Garlic cloves are not chopped or even skinned, but only pierced on the string. However the insects certainly seem to smell it. They keep away. Try a Garlic hat band.

Use Garlic to repel bedbugs, fleas, and lice when you are traveling under "rustic" circumstances. Make small Garlic pouches or pillows to tuck into bedding, or put Garlic powder or Garlic cloves in strategic places.

These methods also work on pets for insect repelling.

ALSO SEE: *None*

ALTERNATIVE OR SUPPLEMENTARY SELF-HELP: *For some people fresh Yarrow or Chaparral rubbed on the skin at frequent intervals repels insects. Peppermint oil also works for some people, lasts longer than the fresh plants, and smells good.*

DOSAGE: *One Garlic necklace per person! You don't even need to peel them!*

KIDNEY (infection): See Antibiotic, Garlic Poultice, and Vaginal Infection applications.

LUNGS: See Expectorant application.

MONONUCLEOSIS: I was greatly satisfied to discover that Garlic works on overcoming mononucleosis. Here is what to do. As soon as mononucleosis is suspected or confirmed, begin taking about 1/2 tsp. of the Enhanced Garlic Formula (see Antibiotic application) or one to two cloves of raw Garlic accompanied by 1 gram of the calcium ascorbate form of vitamin C and 1/8 tsp. Cayenne, every two to three waking hours. If you awake during the night, take another dose. In addition to this take a Garlic enema (see Garlic Enema application) one day, alternating with an acidophilus enema the next day (also see Garlic Enema application for acidophilus instructions) until a total of three Garlic enemas have been taken. Frequent enemas are *only* used in cases of tenacious illness such as mononucleosis. Generally I recommend using enemas sparingly. You can expect, with this many enemas and this much Garlic, to have the aroma of a Garlic factory. You may, but it will be a small price to pay. Also, you probably won't have regular, if any, bowel movements as your colon will be kept quite empty.

During this time, and for at least a week or two following, eat a diet of predominantly fresh fruits and vegetables and avoid hard-to-digest foods such as processed foods, refined sugars, and fried foods. Use no caffeine, alcohol, or nicotine if you can possibly help it. This diet will greatly enhance your chances for a rapid recovery. Get more rest than usual and drink at least two to four quarts of pure water each day as this helps the body flush itself of the poisons being released.

After the series of Garlic and acidophilus enemas (be sure to end up on an acidophilus-enema day) continue with internal Garlic doses but slowly reduce the amount and frequency. Keep up the water intake and diet suggestions.

Most students who have tried this treatment for "mono" notice improvement in their energy levels and body strength within a day or two, and steady improvement after that. They report that it is helpful to continue a maintenance dose of Garlic—two to three times a day for two to four weeks—following the main program in order to strengthen the immune system and lessen the possibility of any recurrence of the illness.

ALSO SEE: *Antibiotic, Footbath, Garlic Bath, Immune System*

ALTERNATIVE OR SUPPLEMENTARY SELF-HELP: **Chaparral, Comfrey, *Yarrow*

DOSAGE: *As given*

MOUTH INFECTION: See Abscessed Teeth, Antibiotic and Gum Infection applications.

MUCUS: To pull mucous congestion from head, chest, or colon, try a Garlic enema (see that application) for fast relief. For chronic mucous congestion from an allergy or other regular irritation, remember that habitual use of enemas is not recommended. Rather I suggest that you cleanse the blood and balance the diet to strengthen the functioning of the body as a whole.

Garlic is also a well-known expectorant when taken orally, especially as a cough syrup or Garlic oil, although any form will have a beneficial effect.

I have found superb results in clearing the severe congestion of ordinary pneumonia and "walking pneumonia" by using Garlic orally, as an enema and as a poultice directly over the lungs.

ALSO SEE: *Congestion, Cough Syrup, Digestion, Expectorant, Garlic Bath, Garlic Enema, Garlic Oil*

ALTERNATIVE OR SUPPLEMENTARY SELF-HELP: *Cayenne, *Chaparral, *Comfrey, Ginger, *Onion, Slippery Elm, Yarrow*

DOSAGE: *General and as given*

NERVINE: Garlic is often referred to as the "Peacemaker" among herbs because of its ability to soothe, calm, and strengthen the nervous system. Some herbalists, including myself, actually claim that Garlic can change an upset mood that is due to strained nerves. It is similarly effective as an antispasmodic, especially in dealing with spasms caused by nervous tension or anxiety such as certain types of headache, stomachache, abdominal cramps, and nervous muscle tension. I was very skeptical when I first learned of this nervine effect of Garlic, yet it has proved itself repeatedly.

Some people respond more readily to this nervine quality. Young children and vegetarians are, in my experience, the most sensitive groups. For myself and many of my friends, it is enough to eat a little Garlic before bed to ensure us a restful and soothing sleep after a trying day. I observe a stronger nervine and antispasmodic action from Garlic use with people who do not eat Garlic each day and therefore don't ordinarily experience Garlic's nervine action. On the other hand, people who use Garlic on a daily basis are much less likely to build up the kind of tension that can result in illness.

When using Garlic as an antibiotic for a cold or flu that includes an aching body, an additional effect is that those tensions and aches are often eased away. This encourages the high quality of rest that speeds recovery from illness.

Raw or powdered Garlic seems to work fastest for this nervine effect although many students report that they get fairly good results even with the commercial preparations available. For children, Garlic oil works well, and most children I know actually *enjoy* eating the Garlic oil pearles that are available at health food stores.

For hyperactive children and adults, I recommend *daily* use of Garlic in some form along with avoidance of highly processed foods and the elimination of refined sugars. These simple habits are often enough to make a noticeable difference in the stabilizing of a hyperactive nervous system. I know of no side effects to worry about.

ALSO SEE: *Antispasmodic, Blood Pressure, Colds and Flu, Footbath, Garlic Bath*

ALTERNATIVE OR SUPPLEMENTARY SELF-HELP: **Clove*, **Peppermint*

DOSAGE: *Use general dosage, or experiment with commercial preparations starting with their recommended dosage.*

OIL: See Garlic Oil application.

PARASITES: A "parasite herb" (or vermifuge) is an herb that can help eliminate or prevent parasites in the intestines and other body tissues. This is a handy thing to know when you are traveling, especially in more rustic areas where parasites are common. Mexico and India are two places where I have used Garlic in this capacity, yet parasites should not be thought of as only coming from bad food or animal dung in far-away places. Cases of pinworms in American children are so common that many parents and health professionals consider it to be "normal" and not worth treating unless these parasites start causing uncomfortable symptoms. Unless symptoms of the parasites are observed, as in amoebic dysentery, or as in bad cases of pinworms where anal and vaginal sensations such as stinging/itching irritations or "crawly" feelings (the description of a seven-year-old with pinworms) interfere with sleep, most people don't even know they have them. Another common symptom I have noticed with pinworms is that of chronic irritation of the inside of the nose, often resulting in a frequent nose-picking habit especially in children.

In severe cases, tests can sometimes diagnose parasites. In mild cases, parasites are rarely even suspected, much less tested or treated. Pinworms are quite common, fairly harmless, and usually easy to treat by ingesting Garlic.

Garlic is an herb to try for any suspicion of parasites. If you are travelling, be aware that parasites are often airborne, especially in places where the dust contains high levels of animal dung. Use Garlic (and for that matter raw Onions and Ginger as well) as a preventive to help keep any parasites from getting a stronghold. Garlic enemas (see that application), or one of the alternative herbs used as an enema, are another means of handling intestinal parasite problems.

Chaparral is a potent parasite herb to be used with or as an alternative to Garlic for many types of parasites. (See Parasite application in the Chaparral chapter, Chapter III.) Drinking Onion Water—1 cup, three or four times a day, along with a Garlic enema—is an additional or alternative approach to eliminating parasites. (See instructions for making Onion Water in Chapter VIII.)

ALSO SEE: *Amoebic Dysentery, Antibiotic (those formulas are good for Parasites, too), Garlic Enema*

ALTERNATIVE OR SUPPLEMENTARY SELF-HELP: **Chaparral, Ginger, *Onion, Yarrow*

DOSAGE: *Take Garlic two or three times a day as a preventive while travelling. As a preventive, even commercial preparations can be somewhat useful. For pinworms in children, have the child eat 1 clove of Garlic four to six times a day. Use a Garlic enema as needed for severe cases in adults and children, especially if any parasites can be seen in the bowel movements. However, for severe cases in children or adults, professional supervision is advised.*

PETS: Garlic works wonders on external infections and keeps flies and other insects away from pets' wounds, too. Drop Garlic oil or sprinkle Garlic powder directly into the pet's ears to prevent or treat ear mites. Dust Garlic powder on birds to prevent all kinds of feather problems such as mites. Garlic powder in animal feed acts to prevent many illnesses, strengthens the immune system, and repels insects, especially when used internally and externally at the same time. The Garlic antibiotic formulas can be used internally or externally for animals. I "guess-timate" the dosage according to the animal's body weight.

TASOLE: During a time when I lived in a cabin in the woods in upstate New York, I had many occasions to fix up animals, both domestic and wild. One night as I tried to sleep I thought I heard the mournful mewing of a lost kitten, yet I got no response when I called. The sound was so faint, moreover, that I couldn't track it in the dark.

Next morning as I walked on a trail near my home I heard the sound again. This time I found a two month old kitten mewing weakly from far underneath some brush. It was a struggle to get the kitten out of its hiding place and when I finally saw its condition I doubted that it would live one more day. The kitten had been badly chewed up by another animal. The open wounds on its head, belly and legs were already full of maggots and other insects, and there were obvious signs of infection. It was amazing that the kitten had survived at all.

I prepared a warm bath in a plastic dishtub and added a blenderful of strong Garlic Water (see Garlic Water application) made from 6 to 10 cloves of Garlic. I gently held the limp kitten in the water (it struggled lightly for about ten seconds), and kept its whole body immersed for about fifteen minutes, except for the little face. In this case the kitten had so many deeply contaminated wounds that it was wiser and simpler to soak the kitten's whole body at first. In other circumstances this would not be the best plan (usually you don't want a totally wet, wounded animal) ana each wound should be washed and treated separately. During this soaking, all manner of maggots, insects, pus, blood clots, and dirt floated out of each wound. Within a short time the kitten was relaxed, started to breath more regularly, and its painful mewing stopped. I did these soaks three times a day the first two days and then cut down to one a day for another day or two. Between baths I would gently dry the kitten's fur while checking the progress of the wounds. The rest of the time, the kitten would lie swaddled in cotton rags in a box and rest/sleep/fall into unconsciousness. Each day there were longer periods of wakefulness during which the kitten was more attentive and alert, and by the fourth or fifth day it would occasionally stand up and attempt a few steps.

I stopped the Garlic baths and instead packed the major wounds with People Paste (see People Paste, Appendix A) for the duration of the healing process. As long as the kitten was unable to eat for itself, I fed it with droppers of warm milk, and then later switched to softened kitten food in a dish.

After about ten days the kitten was outside playing during the day and eating with a regular appetite. However, its wounds had been so severe, especially to the head, that it had permanently lost the agility and balance common to cats and was retarded in its full growth. This was one of my first lessons in becoming more thoughtful about when and where "helping" might not really be "helping" at all. With pets, as with humans, this is a big question. Definitely not one with a single answer.

ALSO SEE: *Any "human" use in this list that seems similar to an animal need; also see TASOLE in the Garlic Personality Profile.*

ALTERNATIVE OR SUPPLEMENTARY SELF-HELP: **Chaparral, Comfrey, Onion, *People Paste, Yarrow*

DOSAGE: *General, or as given in individual applications for people. In the case of animals, however, you usually need to use a "guesstimate" about the dosage based on body weight rather than age. For tiny creatures the infant dosages are what I use most often.*

PIMPLES: Tape a small slice of Garlic directly onto the pimple overnight (wet side of Garlic covering the pimple) and it will probably be gone by morning! Sometimes just rubbing the juice of a slice of Garlic over a pimple a few times will "fix it".

ALSO SEE: *Antibiotic, Boils, Warts*

ALTERNATIVE OR SUPPLEMENTARY SELF-HELP: **Chaparral, Onion, *People Paste, Yarrow*

DOSAGE: *General, and as given*

PLANTS: Garlic water as a plant spray will repel most insects and will often cure plant fungus and other plant diseases. Sometimes, to make it more potent, I add Cayenne to the mixture (perhaps 1 tsp. per cup) plus a little mild liquid dish soap (not detergent) to help the concoction stick to the plants better.

ALSO SEE: *Antibiotic, Fungus*

ALTERNATIVE OR SUPPLEMENTARY SELF-HELP: *Try plant spray made from strong brews of Chaparral, Onion, Yarrow, or from some of these herbs mixed with the Garlic.*

DOSAGE: *As given*

PNEUMONIA: See Antibiotic, Congestion, Cough, Expectorant, Footbath, Garlic Bath, Garlic Enema, Garlic Poultice, and Mucus applications. Also see the Comfrey, Onion (Onion chest poultice) and Yarrow chapters, (Chapters V, VIII and XI).

POULTICE: See Garlic Poultice application.

RASHES: See Skin Infections application.

REJUVENATING ELIXIR: See Digestion application.

SINUS (infection and congestion): See Antibiotic and Congestion applications.

SKIN INFECTIONS: I most often use Garlic powder for this need. I simply dust on Garlic powder for the lighter skin infections and for more serious ones, especially if they are weeping fluids, I use more Garlic powder and wrap the area with gauze or cotton bandage. Results have been positive with skin infections such as ringworm, impetigo, staph, and many other infectious-looking skin disruptions.

Since raw Garlic is sometimes too irritating to use on skin areas already sensitized with a rash, my first choice in this situation would be the powdered form of Garlic. An herbal poultice such as Garlic is another method to use. When changing the poultices, regularly clean the skin with an antiseptic herbal wash such as Garlic water, Chaparral, or Yarrow in order to speed the cleansing and healing process.

If the skin infection is one of the dry or cracked-skin type, or is located on a particularly sensitive area, I buffer and enhance the Garlic with the addition of 1/2 to 1 part Slippery Elm or Comfrey root powder to every part of Garlic. Sometimes it will be necessary to use a thin coating of herbal salve on the skin before applying the Garlic poultice.

Often, for a small patch of skin infection, all it takes is to rub the juice of a slice of Garlic onto it several times a day.

ALSO SEE: *Antibiotic, Boils, Fungus, Garlic Water, Pimples*

ALTERNATIVE OR SUPPLEMENTARY SELF-HELP: **Chaparral, *Comfrey, *People Paste, Slippery Elm, Yarrow*

DOSAGE: *As given*

SLEEP: See Nervine application.

TEETH: See Abscessed Teeth application.

THROAT: For throat infections, suck on a clove of Garlic during the day, changing to a fresh clove two or more times. If you take off the "onion skin" part of the Garlic but do not pierce the inner skin, the aroma is lessened and the effect is still potent.

ALSO SEE: *Antibiotic, Congestion*

ALTERNATIVE OR SUPPLEMENTARY SELF-HELP: **Clove, Comfrey, Onion, Peppermint, *Slippery Elm*

DOSAGE: *General, and as given*

THRUSH: Thrush is a yeast infection in the mouth and is most troublesome in babies and young children because the mouth and throat tissues become coated, sore, and swollen, causing difficulty in eating or nursing. In a severe case the throat can become so swollen that breathing can become difficult for a small child. In adults a thrush (oral yeast) infection predominantly has the symptoms of a coated tongue and mouth discomfort. In every thrush infection I have seen, the tongue becomes coated with white, starting at the back of the tongue and moving forward in observable sections as it worsens. When you begin taking Garlic for this condition, the tongue often begins clearing in marked sections starting at the tip and moving toward the back of the tongue. While the thrush is active, the rest of the internal oral surfaces may become coated with white, swollen and sore, and may be striped with reddish markings in severe cases. Eating raw Garlic, or using Garlic oil for smaller children, has always had noticeable results. The yeast begins visibly clearing within 24 hours and continues to diminish until totally cleared — usually within one to three days of persistently using the Garlic.

TASOLE: One summer when I worked at a camp, I picked up thrush infection from the children there. At first I thought I must have simply burnt my mouth on some hot food as I noticed my gums were stinging and a little swollen. Later in the day, however, I noticed that the insides of my mouth were turning a pale color and the stinging was increasing. By the end of the day the telltale sign on the tongue appeared—

a white coating proceeding from back to front. The camp nurse explained what it was, and an herbalist friend told me to try Garlic. Since the camp was located far from town and from professional medical care, I agreed that Garlic was worth a try. At that time I didn't have much of a taste for Garlic and the thought of eating lots of it did not appeal to me. However I *did* love popcorn and my herbalist friend had said, "Eat lots of Garlic any way you can." I became permanently "hooked" by Garlic popcorn and it has stayed a lifelong favorite.

Being an impatient sort, I wanted the thrush infection to clear up as fast as possible. I blended about 6 or 8 cloves of Garlic in a little olive oil with some basil, cumin and Cayenne, plus a little water and soy sauce to add liquid volume without the need for more oil. I poured this sauce over a fresh batch of popcorn—a 2-quart-size bowl—and ate the whole thing. The Garlic stung my mouth a little but it actually felt like a positive kind of sting compared to the sensation of the infection.

A bunch of friends around the camp smelled the herbed Garlic sauce from far across the grounds and came to investigate. After tasting what I thought was my "extra-strong medicinal batch," they were so pleased and impressed that we made several more gallons of popcorn and a giant super-strength batch of Garlic sauce. We easily used up an entire bulb of Garlic, which I later learned wasn't necessary (except for love of the taste) since much smaller amounts of Garlic are enough for medicinal purposes.

I ate so much Garlic in this fashion that by the next morning my mouth was 50% better just from that one Garlic feast. I ate a clove of Garlic three or four more times the following day which cleared the infection entirely. But I kept my passion for Garlic popcorn for the rest of my life.

Since Garlic is also a great relaxant (nervine), my friends and I slept very restfully that night. From many points of view that thrush infection was a great success!

Since that time I have regularly worked with infants and children with thrush infection. Although infants don't enjoy Garlic popcorn and this infection is quite uncomfortable for them, I get fine results using Garlic oil every two or three hours. They are usually able to nurse or eat comfortably again within twenty-four hours.

ALSO SEE: *Fungus, Vaginal Infection, Yeast Infection*

ALTERNATIVE OR SUPPLEMENTARY SELF-HELP: **Chaparral, Yarrow*

DOSAGE: *Use Garlic oil, 1/4 to 1/2 tsp., every two hours for the severest cases in young children, or at least three times a day in less severe cases; for older children and adults, eat as much raw Garlic as you can, (ongoingly) during the day, until you have consumed 5 to 10 cloves depending on the severity of the infection. The more Garlic ingested, the quicker the infection leaves. See Garlic-eating ideas in the Garlic Personality Profile.*

TONIC: See the fantastic Rejuvenating Elixir under the Digestion application.

URINARY TRACT: See Antibiotic, Garlic Enema and Vaginal Infection applications.

VAGINAL INFECTION: The method of treating vaginal infection with Garlic is also appropriate for any lower abdominal infection such as in the bladder, uterus, or endometrium.

Use an average-size clove of Garlic and peel off the outer onion-like skin while leaving the inner skin intact. Make sure there are no cuts or scratches on the inner skin of the Garlic clove that would allow raw Garlic juice to seep out onto the delicate inner tissues of the vagina. This will avoid any possibility of a slight, temporary irritation. Insert the clove of Garlic far back into the vagina. Leave this in overnight and/or remove it and exchange it for a fresh one, two to four times a day. The clove of Garlic generally becomes soft and "wilted" as its healing properties are gently emitted into the vaginal tissues (and the tissues and organs of the lower abdomen as well). For stubborn infections you may need to replace the Garlic clove more often and you will want to take Garlic (or another antibiotic herb such as Chaparral) orally as this enhances the body's ability to fight off infection wherever it is in the body.

If the infection is accompanied by a vaginal discharge, as is quite common, a douche using 2 to 3 TBS. apple cider vinegar to 1 quart of water can be very soothing while promoting the proper balance of vaginal bacteria. An alternative to the Garlic clove insertion is to make a vaginal bolus using Garlic powder and Slippery Elm powder in equal parts. (See Bolus instructions in Chapter I, Lesson #2.) This method uses the antifungal and antibiotic properties of Garlic to control the infection in the vagina, whether from yeast or virus.

ALSO SEE: *Antibiotic, Congestion, Fungus*

ALTERNATIVE OR SUPPLEMENTARY SELF-HELP: **Chaparral, Comfrey, *Slippery Elm, Yarrow*

DOSAGE: *As given*

VERMIFUGE: See Parasites application.

WARTS: Tape a slice of raw Garlic to the wart with the wet side of the Garlic covering the wart. Change this dressing at least twice a day until the wart and its "roots" are removed. Usually this takes 5 to 10 days. Sometimes rubbing the wart with Garlic oil or Garlic juice (from a slice of Garlic) will, over time, remove it, yet raw Garlic has the surest results by far. I have used this method to permanently remove warts as big as half an inch in diameter, and 1/4 inch thick.

TASOLE: I once had a wart on one of my fingers and decided to use Garlic on it since I knew this herb was such a potent fungicide and virus eradicator. I sliced a clove of Garlic and taped the slice directly onto the wart (wet side of Garlic slice covering the wart). Once or twice a day I would put on a new slice of Garlic, usually morning and night, until the wart was entirely gone.

The first day there was definitely a strong, tingly sensation in the wart after the first couple of hours. By the evening the top layer of the wart was "missing." Every day I watched the wart disappear, layer by layer, until it was level with the normal skin. When I looked directly into the wart at this point, I could see a few tiny black dots within a lightly marked ring where the wart had been. I understood that these black dots were most likely the "roots" of the wart, from which another wart might grow, so I continued to use the Garlic slices and was delighted to see that, after a day or two more, the black dots also dissolved, layer by layer, until finally (looking like four or five grains of black sand) they popped up out of the bottom of the wart. The wart never came back. I was so pleased that I passed on this approach to the next person who came to me asking about wart removal.

Marty had many warts on his hands and was hesitant to tape on so many pieces of Garlic. He started with a slice of Garlic on three different warts and sure enough the wart removal followed exactly the same stages as mine had. He then taped all the rest of the warts each night before sleeping, and only kept a few of the worst ones taped during the days so as not to have the inconvenience of the aroma and the numerous band-aids to deal with.

Marty's warts began disappearing one by one—the ones that were taped day and night disappeared the fastest.

Over the years I have noticed that if the person gets impatient and does not leave the Garlic on long enough to remove what seem to be the roots (those black dots), the wart usually grows back in a month or so.

I recommend this system to children and adults regularly as it is highly successful in eliminating warts, especially from hands or feet. In a few of the worst cases the person also took Garlic internally. This seems to hasten the process.

For venereal warts, see the Chaparral chapter, Chapter III.

ALSO SEE: *Antibiotic, Fungus, Garlic Poultice*

ALTERNATIVE OR SUPPLEMENTARY SELF-HELP: **Chaparral*

DOSAGE: *As given*

WOUNDS: Wounds of all types are usually treated in a similar manner. I use Garlic immediately to prevent infection, yet it is also effective for wounds that have been neglected, where infection has already set in. To stimulate the pulling together of tissues and to assure minimal or no scarring, I always switch to a powdered Comfrey/Chaparral mix or People Paste after a day or two.

Wash out the wound with Garlic water or other antiseptic rinse such as Chaparral. Apply Garlic powder and/or People Paste. After a day or two dress the wound with People Paste alone or with another antibiotic and tissue-healing mixture such as the Comfrey/Chaparral. Change the wound dressing at least twice a day and rinse the wound with Garlic water or other antiseptic, in between changing of the dressings.

Garlic, or a formula including Garlic, would be the treatment of choice for the long-term in cases of deep, infectious contamination — such as gangrene (see Gangrene application) or other severe ulcerations. Once the active infection is checked and the wound begins to heal normally, People Paste is the herbal formula for the job. (See People Paste, Appendix A.)

Puncture wounds will need special attention to make sure infection does not get started inside the punctured tissue where it is harder to see and clean. These wounds respond well to frequent soaking in strong Garlic water and then poulticing with People Paste, depending on the severity of the wound.

If the body is banged up and bruised all over with many little wounds, remember to try a Garlic bath using some Garlic powder (see Garlic Bath application).

ALSO SEE: *Antibiotic, Blood Poisoning, Footbath, Gangrene, Garlic Bath, Garlic Poultice, Garlic Water*

ALTERNATIVE OR SUPPLEMENTARY SELF-HELP: **Chaparral, *Comfrey, Onion (especially for bruising), *People Paste, Slippery Elm*

DOSAGE: *General, most often using Garlic powder except where specifically suggested otherwise*

YEAST INFECTION: The most common symptoms I see with yeast infection are: vaginal yeast discharge (see Vaginal Infection application), a white (and often stinging or uncomfortable) coating of the tongue and entire inside of the mouth which is often referred to as thrush (see Thrush application), a chronic tiredness accompanied by inefficient action of the immune system, and in men, a chronic irritation of the penis. Because of its strong antifungal properties, Garlic taken on a daily basis goes a long way toward preventing yeast infection and lessening the population of yeast cells in the body.

Anyone who is serious about ending a long-standing yeast/Candida problem should study *The Yeast Connection, A Medical Breakthrough*, by William G. Crook (see Resource Guide, Appendix C). Also review the Chaparral chapter (Chapter III) as this herb is very potent against yeast infection.

ALSO SEE: *Fungus, Thrush (including TASOLE in the Thrush application), Vaginal Infection*

ALTERNATIVE OR SUPPLEMENTARY SELF-HELP: **Chaparral*

DOSAGE: *Eat as much Garlic as possible; consult the General Dosage instructions and see the suggestions for ways to eat Garlic listed in the Personality Profile.*

GINGER

STEP RIGHT UP TO THE GINGERMAN FOR YOUR ACHES AND PAINS, NAUSEA, DIGESTION, CIRCULATION... YOU NAME IT!
BIG BAG OF CURES
LYMPH CLEANSER
OH, WHY DID I DANCE ALL NIGHT?
EXCUSE ME, DO YOU HAVE ANYTHING FOR AN UPSET STOMACH?
KJohnson

CHAPTER VII

GINGER

Zingiberis officinalis

Gingerman runs or dances all night;
He'll take Ginger baths, his muscles get tight.
For chills, flu, or fever, Ginger tea he imbibes
And always, for nausea, to that herb he subscribes.

PERSONALITY PROFILE—Ginger

Think of yourself sinking into a vat of a warm and steamy magic liquid that is able to take away the aches and pains of colds and flu or physical exertions. It gives your skin a healthy glow as circulation rushes through every inch of your body, and its rejuvenating warmth penetrates your bones. As you surrender into this magic liquid, giving yourself an experience of renewed vitality and relaxing bliss, your body is gently stimulated into a cleansing perspiration. Body toxins are rinsed away as you lie back reading, listening to music, or enjoying the silence. Arising from this exquisite elixir you move on to work or sleep still carrying the rosy glow, comforting warmth, and deep sense of well-being. And to think that this secret treasure is available to anyone at the cost of one dollar or less. I call it the Ginger Bath! (See that application.)

Ginger's sensual delights, as great as they are, still don't overshadow its medicinal attributes. Ginger (along with Cayenne) is a "carrier herb." This means that when Ginger is mixed with other herbs, it helps to "bind" their actions together and to "carry" the actions of the entire formula more deeply and efficiently into the body's systems. Often you will see Ginger or Cayenne listed at the end of the list of ingredients of prepared herbal formulas. That indicates that a small part of these herbs (often 1/8 to 1/4 part) have been included in the formula to bind the ingredients, increase their activity, and carry them more efficiently on their way. This is a good technique to know about if you get enticed into preparing some of your own self-help mixtures from among the Ten Essentials in this book. See Chapter I Lesson #6 on using herbs in combinations.

The major active ingredients in Ginger are terpenes (quite similar to the chemical action of turpentine) and an oleo-resin called Ginger-oil. These two, and other active ingredients in Ginger, provide antiseptic, lymph-cleansing, circulation-stimulating, and mild constipation relief qualities along with a potent perspiration-inducing action that is quite effective in cleansing the system of toxins.

The oleo-resin is responsible for Ginger's ability to "bind" and "carry." For instance, suppose you are using Slippery Elm, Garlic, and Comfrey in a powdered mixture intended as an intestinal tonic. This formula is already quite good as it is, yet the (optional) addition of 1/8 to 1/4 part Ginger to the formula would (because of the oleo-resin) serve to "bind" the actions of the Slippery Elm, Garlic, and Comfrey together, enhancing their ability to reach their destination as a cohesive group. In addition, through stimulating the circulation and digestive tract, the Ginger will "carry" the herbal actions more quickly and efficiently into all of the bodily systems.

Of course any herb you ingest will travel into your whole system to varying degrees. In the example just given, even though it was the intestinal tract needing the help, the formula will have a healing and balancing effect on the entire system. Therefore, the idea of "carrier" and "binder" herbs, such as Ginger and/or Cayenne, is to lend an increased efficiency to any formula to which they are added, no matter what the purpose of the formula. This principle applies to external applications as well. I almost always add carrier herbs to my formulas.

For making tea, most people, including myself, prefer using fresh Ginger root. Although dried Ginger root chunks or powder can be used, the fresh root gives a truer flavor. In preparing any of its forms, the Ginger root must be simmered, although the powder is fine enough to work even if it is only steeped. To make fresh Ginger root tea, chop up a small handful of the root, skin and all, and simmer in 2 to 4 cups of water for about 10 minutes (or longer, according to taste and desired strength). Usually the same fresh Ginger root can be re-boiled for a second pot of tea, although it will have to be boiled longer.

For taking a stronger dose of Ginger internally, use the Ginger powder, as it is more concentrated. (See the note about taking this under "Dosage," below.)

Ginger is *the* "Winter Herb" for many people who live in cold climates. In my household, during the winter there is always a pot of fresh ginger root simmering on the stove. I keep it ever-ready to warm the bones of adventurers coming in from the cold, or to speed up the circulation (and therefore warm the cold toes, etc.) of the sedentary writers who inhabit isolated corners of the house.

Speaking of cold toes, Ginger powder can be added to socks to keep feet warm. This works most nicely when the feet in question will be at least slightly active. If you want more heat, simply add Cayenne with the Ginger. The more Cayenne, the hotter the mix. Straight Cayenne is for the coldest toes and coldest climates around. If your feet ever get too warm from these herbal toe-warmers, wash your feet and put on fresh socks.

TASOLE: At a spa, I once talked with a banker about cold feet. I told him about using herbs inside of socks, which was a totally new idea to him, and he said he would mention it to his wife and daughter who both suffered terribly from cold feet while snow skiing. When I met him a few weeks later, he was unhappy about my advice, saying that it did not work. Questioning him I found out this tale.

He and his family left for their ski lodge armed with a mixture of Cayenne and Ginger. His wife and daughter put the herb powders into their socks, but instead of skiing, they sat in the lodge to spectate . . . (first clue). Their feet got cold as usual and they complained about this when the banker-husband-dad returned a few hours later. Meanwhile they had continued adding more and more herbs to their socks thinking that might do the trick.

With the banker's return they all got active, started walking, and soon noticed that their feet began to warm up from the exercise . . . (second clue). Not only did their feet "warm" up, they soon got so hot that wife and daughter ran, half-crazed and screaming, into the wash room, where they quickly ripped off their socks and plunged their feet into cold water. They blamed the banker and the banker blamed me and I began to think some extremely rude things about the feet and skiing habits of his wife and daughter.

The lesson of this tale for those who did not pick up my clues is that the "herbs-in-the-socks" trick does not work so well if you start off with ice-cold feet and don't move them. It takes at least minimal effort, like walking, to kick-start the circulation in the cold area. But once started, wahoo! Then it doesn't take much activity at all (depending on the ratio of Ginger to Cayenne) to keep the warmth going. The more Ginger, the milder the mixture. For sedentary types, I suggest drinking fresh Ginger root tea and taking five-minute walking breaks in addition to seasoning your feet with these spicy herbs.

APPLICATIONS AND ATTRIBUTES - GINGER

(Quick Reference List)

ANTISPASMODIC
ASTHMA
BACKACHE
BATH AND FOOTBATH
BLOOD PRESSURE (low)
BRONCHITIS
CHILBLAINS
CHILLS
CIRCULATION
COLDS and FLU
CONGESTION
CONSTIPATION
COUGH
DIGESTION
FEET (cold)
FEVER
FROSTBITE
GAS
GINGER ALE
GINGER BATH
GINGER POULTICE
HEADACHE
HEART
INFLAMMATION
INSECT BITES
JOINTS (aching)
LINIMENT
LOW BLOOD PRESSURE
LUNGS
LYMPH
MENSTRUATION
MORNING SICKNESS
MOTION SICKNESS
MUCUS
MUMPS
MUSCLE STRAIN
NAUSEA
NERVES
NIGHT SWEATS
PERSPIRATION THERAPY
SINUS
SKIN
STIMULANT
STOMACH
TENDONITIS
THROAT
URINARY TRACT

FORM:

Ginger Root used either fresh or dried. In dried form you will find it whole, in small chunks, and powdered.

APPLICATION METHODS:

Internally: Use as a tea or in capsules. Fresh Ginger root makes the best tea for internal use yet dried can also be used. Powdered Ginger is the thing to use in internal formulas other than tea. **Externally:** Use Ginger as a bath, soak, or poultice. For a bath or soak I usually use Ginger powder. For a poultice it depends on the circumstance as either can well be used.

AVAILABILITY:

Herb store, grocery store, mail order (usually offers only dried Ginger), open air markets around the world

HINTS/CAUTIONS:

Ginger by itself, especially fresh Ginger root, becomes too stimulating for some people if used daily for more than three or four weeks. If this herb becomes too stimulating to intestines, circulation, etc., simply lessen your use. A note of caution: If there is regular bleeding from the colon, as in colitis, it would be wise to check with your health professional before using a Ginger enema.

GENERAL DOSAGE: INTERNAL USE

*PLEASE NOTE: *Although I often emphasize using tea, there are many forms of herbal preparations which are quite effective such as Capsules, Children's Ideas, Decoction, Honeyballs, etc. See those headings plus Dosage Equivalents in Chapter I, Lesson #2.*

Infants to 3 years: Use Ginger tea in a bottle or cup, or given by dropper or teaspoon — 1 to 4 oz. up to four times a day. Or, 1/4 tsp. Ginger powder made into a "honeyball" (see Chapter I, Lesson #2) can be given four times a day for babies of "chewing age." If children like the tea or honeyballs there is usually no problem with letting them have more. If any signs of diarrhea occur from taking Ginger,then you will know to cut down the amount and frequency of use as it is becoming too stimulating to the intestines. The tea or powder may be sweetened with honey or light, unsulphured molasses. See instructions for making fresh Ginger root tea in the Personality Profile.

Children 4 years to 10 years: Ginger tea, 1 to 4 cups a day as desired. Or, 1/2 to 1 tsp. Ginger powder, usually made into "honeyballs" (see Chapter I, Lesson #2) can be given two to four times a day or as needed. The tea can be sweetened with honey or light, unsulphured molasses. See instructions for making fresh Ginger root tea in the Personality Profile above.

Children 11 years to Adults: Ginger tea can be taken at the strength preferred and as often as desired. Ginger powder too can be taken as needed, starting with 1/2 to 1 tsp. The only contra-indication may be more frequent elimination of the bowels. Many people, however, do not mind this. In any case the simple antidote is to lessen or stop the intake of Ginger. If the Ginger is mixed with other herbs in a tea or powdered formula then I have never seen a problem with any amount.

Pets and Other Creatures: I have never used Ginger internally on pets although I do not see why it would be harmful.

GENERAL DOSAGE: EXTERNAL USE

Same For All Humans And Other Creatures

A Ginger bath (see Ginger Bath application), soak, or wash can be used in any situation where you need to increase the circulation, flush the lymph (through perspiration/skin), or lessen pain from sore, stiff muscles and joints.

A Ginger poultice (see Ginger Poultice application) is used as a "walk-around" version of the bath, soak or wash. The poultice becomes a suitable decongestant when laid on the chest. This is helpful even for asthma attacks. Poultices can be kept warm, when needed, using a hot water bottle or by regularly re-dipping them into hot, strong Ginger tea and then reapplying.

APPLICATIONS AND ATTRIBUTES - GINGER

ANTISPASMODIC: Ginger acts as an antispasmodic in the sense that it increases circulation and quiets the nerves. These actions often relieve spasms in the colon, uterus, stomach, lungs, etc.

ALSO SEE: *Digestion, Menstruation, Muscle strain, Nausea*

ALTERNATIVE OR SUPPLEMENTARY SELF-HELP: **Cloves, *Garlic, Peppermint*

DOSAGE: *General*

ASTHMA: See Lungs application.

BACKACHE: See Circulation, Digestion, Ginger Bath, Ginger Poultice, and Joints applications.

BATH: See Ginger Bath application.

BLOOD PRESSURE (low): Use Ginger mixed with an equal part of Cayenne. It doesn't hurt to take it several times a day. If your lifestyle or diet is part of the underlying problem, and it usually is, this should be addressed for any long-term results.

Low blood pressure can often be accompanied by blood-sugar difficulties. Review the use of Yarrow for this.

ALSO SEE: *Circulation, Ginger Bath, Stimulant*

ALTERNATIVE OR SUPPLEMENTARY SELF-HELP: **Cayenne, Garlic, Yarrow*

DOSAGE: *General*

BRONCHITIS: See Lungs application.

CHILBLAINS: See Circulation and Frostbite applications.

CHILLS: See Circulation application.

CIRCULATION: Increasing healthy circulation is often a dramatic turning point in many health-care crises. Think about it for a moment. If you increase circulation to an inflamed joint or tendon, in a feverish body, to a clogged and/or wheezy chest, frostbitten appendages, sluggish internal organs, or especially the lymph system—any of these areas will be flushed with an increase of blood and lymph. These fluids will in turn give their nourishments and pick up poisons to be carried off while imparting the rejuvenating effects of any herbs they are carrying. A famous self-help tool for colds, flu, and other congestive ailments is to encourage a cleansing perspiration so that the body's natural eliminative channels can work at top efficiency to shorten the duration of the illness. Again, this is another example of how increasing circulation directly restores well-being.

What if you don't have an illness but feel like a clogged straw? Such a circumstance calls for a good sweat to open and flush all the eliminative channels which can translate into a need for increased circulation. Increased circulation in the intestines will help empty them. Increased circulation to the lungs will help flush them of unwanted fluids. You see what I'm getting at?

Ginger is the #1 herb to think of for this type of help. A Ginger tea enema can immediately increase circulation throughout the entire body. For a "double-whammy" effect try drinking Ginger tea while sitting in a Ginger bath (see that application). For a milder circulation treatment, use one or the other. I usually choose the bath because it is so delectable.

One of the best ways to take Ginger tea is to make it with fresh Ginger root and then add lemon and honey or light unsulphured molasses. I find that the lemon drives warmth more deeply into the tissues and of course adds vitamin C.

ALSO SEE: *Congestion, Constipation, Fever, Ginger Ale, Ginger Bath, Ginger Poultice, Inflammation, Lungs, Skin, Stimulant, Throat*

ALTERNATIVE OR SUPPLEMENTARY SELF-HELP: **Cayenne, Comfrey, *Peppermint, Yarrow*

DOSAGE: *General*

COLDS and FLU: Drinking Ginger tea and/or taking Ginger as a powder immediately soothes the symptoms of colds and flu, such as chills, fever, aches and pains, and congestion. If you add the remarkable effects of a Ginger bath, you will practically guarantee a less painful trip through the cold/flu carnival. The Ginger tea is enhanced by adding fresh-squeezed lemon juice to it *after* it is brewed, along with honey or light unsulphured molasses if you want sweetness.

With a more serious cold or flu you may need an herbal antibiotic in addition to Ginger. Use the Enhanced Garlic Formula listed under the Antibiotic application in the Garlic chapter (Chapter VI) or a combination of equal parts Chaparral, Yarrow, and Comfrey root, and 1/4 to 1/2 part Cayenne powder as a "carrier." There are more antibiotic formulas listed in the Chaparral and Garlic chapters (Chapters III and VI).

ALSO SEE: *Circulation, Ginger Bath, Ginger Poultice, Lungs, Nausea, Sinus, Throat*

ALTERNATIVE OR SUPPLEMENTARY SELF-HELP: *Cayenne, *Chaparral, Comfrey, *Garlic, People Paste (used internally), Yarrow*

DOSAGE: *General*

CONGESTION: Use a Ginger poultice over the congested area—lungs, liver, kidneys, etc.—and keep it warm with a hot water bottle. Follow the suggestions under the colds and flu application.

Internally Ginger works well all by itself or in combination with Comfrey and/or Slippery Elm, either as a tea or mixed as powders. Ginger breaks up mucus and helps to flush it out, wherever it is—in the lungs, stomach, intestines, etc. The other supplementary herbs listed below could also be considered for making an herbal combination of equal parts for congestion, colds and flu, etc.

ALSO SEE: *Circulation, Colds and Flu, Ginger Bath, Ginger Poultice, Lungs, Stomach*

ALTERNATIVE OR SUPPLEMENTARY SELF-HELP: *Cayenne, *Comfrey, *Onion, Peppermint, Slippery Elm, Yarrow*

DOSAGE: *General*

CONSTIPATION: Ginger taken internally, either as a powder or as fresh Ginger root tea, acts as a stimulant to the digestion and to the action of the intestines. This is how it gets the bowels moving without being a harsh purgative. A natural "side effect" of drinking Ginger tea regularly is that often the intestines evacuate much more efficiently. For the worst constipation, a Ginger tea enema will immediately clear the large intestine while at the same time stimulating peristalsis, relieving gas, and increasing circulation to intestinal tissues. While you should avoid the regular use of enemas and/or laxatives for the elimination of body waste, a Ginger enema, when called for, is an invaluable measure to know about. In the most severe cases you can both do the enema and take the Ginger orally for constipation relief. Often, however, simply taking a generous dose of Ginger powder two or three times during the day with a full glass of water will get the results needed.

For a tasty and more potent laxative formula using Ginger,try this: Finely chop one oz. fresh Ginger root (or about one tablespoon of Ginger powder if fresh root is not available) and mix with 2 Tbsp. whole flax seeds. Gently simmer, covered, in 2 cups of water for about 15 minutes. Sweeten with honey or light unsulphured molasses if you like. Take one to two cups of this warm mixture daily, in 1/2 to 1 cup doses as needed. This formula is safe even for children, although they would generally need half as much.

Since Ginger is not a harsh laxative or purgative, I have never found it to create an addiction as many laxatives and stimulants will.

A note of caution: If there is regular bleeding from the colon, as in colitis, it would be wise to check with your health professional before using a Ginger enema.

ALSO SEE: *Antispasmodic, Circulation, Congestion, Stimulant*

ALTERNATIVE OR SUPPLEMENTARY SELF-HELP: **Cayenne, *Slippery Elm*

DOSAGE: *The General Dosages are applicable here. In addition, for healthy adults, I would not hesitate to take a 1 Tbsp. dose of Ginger powder two or three times in a day for constipation relief. Don't forget to drink at least two quarts of water each day, which includes at least one glass of water with each dose of Ginger powder, as this is crucial to the efficient emptying of the bowels.*

COUGH: See Lungs and Throat applications.

DIGESTION: Ginger stimulates digestive juices to flow in the stomach, liver, pancreas, and gall bladder through increasing blood circulation to the digestive tract. Ginger relieves gas by assisting the movement of food through the intestines so that it doesn't sit still and create what some of my young students like to call "the disgusting sludge monster."

Ginger powder or tea can be used before and after meals to create an enthusiastic digestive environment. Several students have told me that this digestive aid has enhanced their attempts to lose weight.

Sluggish digestion is often the precursor to other seemingly unrelated problems such as backache, headache, kidney pain, and heart stress.

Ginger, Comfrey root, and Cayenne powders, mixed in equal parts, or with less Cayenne, make a dynamic digestion tonic.

ALSO SEE: *Circulation, Congestion, Constipation, Nausea, Stimulant*

ALTERNATIVE OR SUPPLEMENTARY SELF-HELP: **Cayenne, *Comfrey root, People Paste (used internally), *Peppermint, Slippery Elm, Yarrow*

DOSAGE: *General*

FEET (cold): See Circulation and Frostbite applications, as well as the TASOLE in the Personality Profile.

FEVER: Use Ginger internally and externally (see Ginger Bath application) to increase circulation, open the pores, start perspiration, and flush poisons out of the body. These actions diminish the need for a fever thus causing it to leave quickly.

If a fever accompanies an illness that calls for an antibiotic action, use the ideas under the Colds and Flu application and review the Antibiotic applications in the Chaparral and Garlic chapters (Chapters III and VI).

ALSO SEE: *Antiseptic, Circulation, Colds and Flu, Congestion, Lungs*

ALTERNATIVE OR SUPPLEMENTARY SELF-HELP: *Chaparral, Comfrey, *Garlic, Peppermint, *Yarrow*

DOSAGE: *General*

FROSTBITE: First gently rub the frostbitten area with snow or a cold, wet towel until it begins to "thaw" a little. Next soak the part, or the entire body, in a warm Ginger bath for at least 20 minutes or longer. Following the bath, rub the affected part with a stimulating herbal liniment. Review the Liniment application in the Cayenne chapter, Chapter II.

If you are in a climate where frostbite might happen regularly, a good herbal rub to have on hand is made by mixing 1 oz. Ginger powder with 2 oz. Cayenne powder, and then soaking these powders in one pint of some form of alcohol (rubbing alcohol or vodka are two possibilities). This "brew" can sit around indefinitely waiting to be used. This rubbing mixture could also be made with a healing oil such as olive oil, or with unpasteurized apple cider vinegar, in place of the alcohol. This herbal liniment/rub will also increase circulation to an area and relieve strain or soreness after exercising.

Take Ginger tea or Ginger powder internally to normalize circulation.

For a stronger action and to stop shock, administer Cayenne immediately.

ALSO SEE: *Circulation, Ginger Bath*

ALTERNATIVE OR SUPPLEMENTARY SELF-HELP: **Cayenne, Comfrey, People Paste, Peppermint*

DOSAGE: *General*

GAS: See Constipation and Digestion applications.

GINGER ALE: Delectable, bubbly, fun-to-make Ginger Ale! Here is what to do.

Make a batch of fresh Ginger root tea that is at least three to five times stronger than you would normally drink it. Sweeten with honey to taste and let it chill in the refrigerator. When you are ready to serve it, or just before you bottle it, pour in some plain sparkling mineral water both to dilute it and to add the fizz.

A man I knew bottled up a great batch of home-made Ginger Ale and labeled it with his son's picture. What a great gift! Another time I made some myself for a party and, believe me, no one went home the least bit stuffed or constipated from all the food!

Some people like to add a few cinnamon sticks or some sassafras root (an herb), while cooking the Ginger Ale concentrate, to give the brew a more "root-beer-y" flavor.

ALSO SEE: *None*

ALTERNATIVE OR SUPPLEMENTARY SELF-HELP: *None*

DOSAGE: *As given*

GINGER BATH: Before you read any further, review the opening remarks in the Ginger Personality Profile to recall why I am so enthusiastic about Ginger baths. Then read on to see how easily it is done.

Ginger powder works the best for a Ginger bath. It is readily purchased in its freshest and most economical bulk form from an herb or health food store. As you are filling a tub with hot water, you add about 2 Tbsp. (1 oz.) of the Ginger powder. Now, hop in and soak.

Add more Ginger for a stronger bath. I must admit that I never use less than 4 to 6 Tbsp. and I have many friends who regularly use 1/2 cup or more, so you can see that there is much flexibility here. Men tell me that they like to start with smaller (2 Tbsp.) amounts because the stimulation of circulation to their private parts is a bit startling, and even a bit too warm for their comfort at first. Women have never voiced this observation to me. Children should start with 2 Tbsp. in a full tub of water, or less Ginger if the tub is only half full.

As you soak you can expect your skin to start turning pink all over as the circulation increases everywhere. Then you will gently begin to perspire. It is important to drink water or tea while you sit in the bath to help the body replenish the fluids it is releasing through perspiration. Fevers, emotional traumas, athletic injuries, a stress-filled day, colds and flu, all are generally accompanied by symptoms of bodyache and pain along with a sluggish and hampered ability of the body's tissues and glands to cleanse themselves of poisons. A Ginger bath gets the circulation going in these congested tissues and glands, flushes out the toxic wastes accumulated there, and relieves you of the aches and pains.

If you must work in a smoke-filled environment or in the midst of other toxic effluents, regular Ginger baths (usually not more than two or three a week) can help to lessen the accumulation of these substances in the body by stimulating the elimination channels of the lymph, skin, and sweat glands.

A Ginger footbath (hand bath, elbow bath, sitz bath, etc.) is another variation on the Ginger bath. Make the bath the strength you prefer and soak your feet (or whatever) for as long as you like. This is great for chilblains, tired and/or aching feet, injured joints, insect bites, and skin troubles. Take a Ginger bath once or twice a week for general health maintenance or just for the sheer pleasure of it. During an illness a Ginger bath can be used more frequently, four or five times a week or even every day for no more than a week or two. As enjoyable as it is, a Ginger bath does stimulate the elimination of toxins and this can be overdone, or done too quickly, which reminds me of a story.

TASOLE: Beverly, an herbalist friend, was once quite ill. Like many enthusiastic herbalists I have known, she was also extremely impatient. In truth she wanted to get her body back in shape so that she could stress it some more with her heavy workload. Her entire system had become overtaxed, and she was experiencing what she humorously called "near-death symptoms" of fever, bloodshot eyes, total bodyache, stiff joints, skin rashes, smelly perspiration, horrible gas, complete indigestion and nausea. Getting the picture?

Deciding to take a Ginger bath and thinking herself quite hardy, Beverly felt she needed to take extraordinary measures and threw an entire one pound bag of Ginger powder into the tub. She stayed in the tub soaking and drinking fresh water for several hours.

When I didn't hear from her for about a day and a half, I checked in and found her flopped in a chair looking flushed, yet well. I was suspicious of the grin on her face. Here is what she told me.

As she sat in the "Super-Tub," her circulation began racing as if she were exercising in a sauna. Sweat was pouring off her as blood and lymph raced through her body, faster than she thought possible, indiscriminately picking up poisons both ancient and recent. As time passed she got extremely "drunk" on her own toxins and began giggling like a madwoman while her heart pounded at an alarming rate and her skin color turned from a nicely flushed pink to beet red. She didn't remember how she got out of the tub but did recall falling face first onto her bed and waking up, about 15 hours later, feeling immensely well but still a little giddy and "high" as her body emerged from its whirlwindcatharsis.

Beverly never tried this "technique" again. In fact she admitted it was foolish—"a bit harsh and dangerous." I tell the story here as a warning to budding but over-zealous herbalists. I also tell the story because I laugh every time I think of Beverly in that tub sweating her brains out.

ALSO SEE: *Circulation, Congestion, Ginger Poultice, Skin, Stimulant*

ALTERNATIVE OR SUPPLEMENTARY SELF-HELP: *Cayenne, *Garlic, *Peppermint, *Yarrow*

DOSAGE: *As given*

GINGER POULTICE: Using Ginger powder, mix it to a paste with warm water, and spread it about 1/8 inch thick or more on an appropriate-sized natural-fiber cloth (such as cotton or wool). Place the cloth in a pie plate (not an aluminum one), or something like that, to catch water-drips from the next part of the procedure. Gently add enough boiling water to thoroughly wet the poultice, but not so much that the herbs are being washed away. Let the poultice sit until it cools to the warmest temperature that suits the skin it will be touching. When the poultice is the proper temperature you can apply it (herb side down) and lay a hot water bottle on top of it, where possible, to keep the poultice warm and the herbs well activated.

Another way to use Ginger as a poultice, especially on tricky parts like knee or elbow joints, is to mix 2 parts Ginger powder with 1 part Slippery Elm powder. Moisten with a small amount of hot water to form a pliable paste. Apply this warm Ginger paste directly onto the skin and mold it to a perfect fit. Wrap it with gauze or a clean cotton cloth. This poultice can be kept warm with a hot water bottle, or the entire appendage, wrapping and all, can then be soaked in warm Ginger tea. For this I simply put 1/4 to 1/2 cup Ginger powder into a dishpan or washtub filled with 3 to 5 gallons of hot water.

As an alternative for less serious cases, try a "walk-around poultice." This is a poultice you can apply and attach securely so that you can "walk around with it," without having to sit still for soaking or using a hot water bottle.

One more variation on a Ginger poultice is the Ginger fomentation. Finely chop about 6 oz. fresh Ginger root and simmer in 6 to 8 cups water (preferably distilled) for about 20 minutes, covered. Or, make 6 to 8 cups of Ginger decoction using 5 to 7 Tbsp. Ginger powder, steeped 20 minutes. Dip a natural-fiber cloth into this mixture, wring it out slightly, and repeatedly apply it to the area, redipping the cloth into the hot decoction between applications.

These poultices are useful for congestion in any internal area, and for inflamed, sore, strained, irritated or stiff appendages, skin, or muscles.

Any of these poultices should be left on at least 30 minutes, and longer, even overnight, as is needed.

ALSO SEE: *Circulation, Congestion, Ginger Bath, Inflammation*

ALTERNATIVE OR SUPPLEMENTARY SELF-HELP: *(add to the poultice any of the following): Cayenne, *Comfrey, Garlic, *Onion, People Paste, Peppermint, Slippery Elm, Yarrow*

DOSAGE: *As given*

HEADACHE: Soak your feet (yes, that's right) in a very strong Ginger decoction made by simmering about 8 oz. finely chopped fresh Ginger, or 4 oz. (1/4 cup) powdered Ginger in a quart or so of water for 20 minutes. Add this concentrate to a washtub of hot water. Now soak.

Additional help can be accessed by internally taking Ginger or one of the other supplementary herbs below.

ALSO SEE: *Circulation, Colds and Flu, Digestion, Fever, Ginger Bath*

ALTERNATIVE OR SUPPLEMENTARY SELF-HELP: **Cayenne, Comfrey, Garlic, *Peppermint, Yarrow*

DOSAGE: *As given*

HEART: Ginger can be used internally as self-help for heart pain caused by indigestion and/or poor circulation.

Also review the Cayenne chapter (Chapter II) for other suggestions regarding heart pains, palpitations, etc.

ALSO SEE: *Blood Pressure, Circulation, Stimulant*

ALTERNATIVE OR SUPPLEMENTARY SELF-HELP: **Cayenne, Clove, *Comfrey, Garlic, Yarrow*

DOSAGE: *General*

INFLAMMATION: Ginger, used internally and externally, helps prevent or stop inflammation, especially in joints and muscle tissue. If you add to the Ginger one or more of the supplementary herbs listed below, you will have an even more powerful anti-inflammation agent for both internal and external use.

Additionally here is a formula for combatting inflammation. It can be used for pain, sprains, rheumatism, bursitis, tendonitis, etc.

2 parts Ginger
1 part Slippery Elm
1 part Cayenne
1 part Comfrey root

Mix these herbal powders together and take internally, 1/2 to 1 tsp. three to six times a day for adults. For instruction in combining herbs, see Chapter I, Lesson #6.

ALSO SEE: *Circulation, Congestion, Ginger Bath, Ginger Poultice, Tendonitis*

ALTERNATIVE OR SUPPLEMENTARY SELF-HELP: *Chaparral, Clove, *Comfrey, *Garlic, *Onion, People Paste, *Slippery Elm, *Yarrow*

DOSAGE: *General*

INSECT BITES: See Ginger Bath application.

JOINTS: See Circulation, Ginger Bath, and Ginger Poultice applications.

LINIMENT: See Circulation and Frostbite applications.

LOW BLOOD PRESSURE: See Blood Pressure and Circulation applications.

LUNGS: Take Ginger internally and externally to help clear congestion in cases of lung irritations such as asthma, bronchitis, pneumonia, etc. When a stronger effect is needed, add one or more of the supplementary herbs listed below to the Ginger, either for an internal formula or for a quick-acting poultice. With children and the elderly, usually considered more delicate, Ginger is still fine to use.

If there is infection involved in the lung congestion, it is best to add a strong antibiotic herb like Garlic, Chaparral and/or Comfrey. The antibiotic formulas in the Chaparral and Garlic (Chapters III and VI) are highly effective.

ALSO SEE: *Circulation, Congestion, Ginger Bath, Ginger Poultice, Inflammation*

ALTERNATIVE OR SUPPLEMENTARY SELF-HELP: *Cayenne, Chaparral, *Comfrey, *Garlic, *Onion, People Paste, Peppermint, Yarrow*

DOSAGE: *General*

LYMPH: See Circulation and Ginger Bath applications.

MENSTRUATION: Ginger is especially useful for both menstrual cramps and suppressed menstruation because of its antispasmodic properties and its ability to enhance circulation and relieve congestion in internal organs, particularly in the lower abdomen. Use it internally as tea or powder and/or externally as a Ginger bath or poultice.

ALSO SEE: *Antispasmodic, Circulation, Congestion, Ginger Bath, Ginger Poultice*

ALTERNATIVE OR SUPPLEMENTRY SELF-HELP: **Chaparral, Clove, *Comfrey, Peppermint, *Yarrow*

DOSAGE: *General*

MORNING SICKNESS: See Nausea application.

MOTION SICKNESS: See Nausea application.

MUCUS: See Congestion, Ginger Bath, and Ginger Poultice applications.

MUMPS: Mumps involves infection and swelling in the lymph glands, usually in the neck area. Use Ginger baths to help relieve the pressure on the swollen glands and if needed, use a supporting tea or powdered herbal formula internally, such as the antibiotic formulas in the Garlic or Chaparral chapters (Chapters VI and III). Also refer to the Colds and Flu application. Often, just taking Ginger baths and drinking Ginger tea, 4 to 8 cups a day, erases the bumps of the "Mumps Ride."

Drinking Ginger tea assists in stimulating the colon so that natural elimination can take place. If there is significant constipation or a high fever, it is wise to use an herbal enema of Ginger, Garlic, or Yarrow to encourage the body to release its toxins faster.

ALSO SEE: *Circulation, Colds and Flu, Congestion, Ginger Bath, Ginger Poultice*

ALTERNATIVE OR SUPPLEMENTARY SELF-HELP: *Cayenne, *Chaparral, *Comfrey, *Garlic, Onion (as a poultice on swollen glands), *Yarrow*

DOSAGE: *General or as given*

MUSCLE STRAIN: *See Ginger Bath, Ginger Poultice, and Inflammation applications.*

NAUSEA: Ginger is the miracle herb for nausea of any kind and is safe for children, pregnant women, and the elderly. Be cautious, however, if there is severe intestinal inflammation such as in colitis. In such cases of severe intestinal inflammation, consult your doctor first before using Ginger. In rare cases, Ginger is too stimulating.

For mild nausea, often a simple cup of Ginger tea will soothe it away.

For the more persistent nausea of motion sickness, or morning sickness during pregnancy, you should initiate "Plan B," which is stronger. With "Plan B," use Ginger powder in 1/2 to 1 tsp. doses washed down with a glass of water. You may take the Ginger in capsules if you must, yet the capsules are often upsetting to a tender stomach. It is better to take the Ginger directly in the mouth. Taken directly, Ginger gives immediate help.

If you have been nauseous for awhile, or even days (i.e., with morning sickness), you may need to take several doses, about 15 minutes apart, before your stomach settles. My pregnant students or students who travel often and tend to get motion sickness carry Ginger powder with them wherever they go. That way they are always prepared. Even when the nausea is from overeating or bad food, Ginger will help clear the stomach and stimulate healthy digestion.

An alternative to taking the Ginger powder plain is to mix it with a little honey or light unsulphured molasses to the consistency of clay. Then roll it into small pellets to swallow or suck on.

TASOLE: Debbie was two months pregnant when she joined my herb class. She looked pale and weak to me, yet I assumed she was regularly consulting her doctor so I did not question her. After the third week she confided to me that she had been having severe nausea, daily, for her entire pregnancy and that her doctor's advice had not helped so far. Her doctor had recently prescribed an even stronger medicine yet she hesitated to take it and inquired if there might be some safe herbal approach she could try first. When I suggested Ginger, she was surprised but willing to give it a try.

At the next class, however, she looked noticeably stronger. The Ginger had virtually ended her vomiting, and she was learning how to adjust the dosage each day depending upon how she felt. Sometimes she needed 1/2 tsp. twice a day or before each meal. On one particularly rough day Debbie started with 1/2 tsp. each hour and kept it up for three or four hours before the nausea went away completely.

The nausea period of her pregnancy finally passed altogether. Over the remaining months she used Ginger occasionally for digestive upset.

Over the years since then I have advised many women about the benefits of Ginger for morning sickness. I have recommended it to both men and women for other types of nausea as well. About one woman in ten will report that the Ginger is ineffective in calming the nausea of pregnancy. If you are one of them, a drop of Peppermint oil in 1/2 glass of water, sipped slowly, will often give the desired relief.

ALSO SEE: *Colds and Flu, Digestion, Fever*

ALTERNATIVE OR SUPPLEMENTARY SELF-HELP: *Cayenne, Comfrey, Garlic, *Peppermint, *Yarrow*

DOSAGE: *Take Ginger as needed. This may vary from once in a day to every hour or so. The amount needed may vary from 1/8 tsp. to 1 tsp. and usually lessens the more often you take it in a single day.*

NERVES: Ginger eases the excitability of nerves and in this way can prove to be quite soothing. I usually take it as a tea for its soothing effect, or soak in a Ginger bath. While it can be soothing to the nerves it is still stimulating to the circulation.

ALSO SEE: *Ginger Bath, Headache, Inflammation*

ALTERNATIVE OR SUPPLEMENTARY SELF-HELP: **Clove, Comfrey, *Garlic, *Peppermint*

DOSAGE: *General*

NIGHT SWEATS: Use 1/2 tsp. Ginger powder or 1 cup of tea two to four times during the day and alternate this with a blood-purifying tea or herbal formula made of one or more of the supplementary herbs listed below.

ALSO SEE: *Circulation, Digestion, Stimulant*

ALTERNATIVE OR SUPPLEMENTARY SELF-HELP: *Chaparral, Comfrey, Yarrow*

DOSAGE: *General or as given*

PERSPIRATION THERAPY: See Circulation and Ginger Bath applications.

SINUS: Because Ginger gets the circulation going so well, it often relieves congestion in many places at once, including in the sinuses. Another form of relief for sinus congestion involves rinsing a mild Ginger tea through the nostrils and/or taking a Ginger tea enema. (See Nasal Rinse instructions in Chapter I, Lesson #2.)

You could easily substitute Cayenne for Ginger in these recommendations, or mix Cayenne with the Ginger in a proportion that gives a stimulating effect at the strength you need.

For a sinus infection, use an oral antibiotic formula from the Garlic or Chaparral chapters (Chapters VI and III). Or, mix 1/8 tsp. Garlic powder with 1/8 tsp. Ginger powder and add 1/2 cup of warm water to make an unbeatable sinus rinse.

ALSO SEE: *Circulation, Congestion, Ginger Bath, Ginger Poultice*

ALTERNATIVE OR SUPPLEMENTARY SELF-HELP: **Cayenne, Comfrey, Garlic, *Onion, Peppermint*

DOSAGE: *General or as given*

SKIN: Healthy circulation is crucial in keeping healthy skin. If symptoms of ill health start showing up on the skin—rashes, boils, pimples, etc.—it often means the body's other eliminative channels cannot keep up with a need to detoxify, and therefore poisons are being released through the skin.

Sometimes a skin symptom can be from a contact poison—like poison ivy—or an allergic reaction to an ingested substance—like eating strawberries. In any case, a Ginger bath or a Ginger soak will often cleanse and alleviate the surface symptoms. This will be only temporary if there is a systemic poison at fault, in which case follow up with daily use of blood-cleansing and blood-strengthening herbs such as Comfrey, Chaparral and Yarrow.

Many of my students have had persistent rashes or other skin irritations that kept to one area of the body, like the hands or elbows. Simply soaking those areas each day in Ginger tea for a few days often took the rash away. One young man had to work with his hands in toxic chemicals every day. Even though he wore hand protection he had a chronic rash and stiffness until he began to soak his hands nightly in Ginger tea.

In general, Ginger baths will bring new vitality to the skin when used once a week. This regular attention to improving circulation, flushing out surface toxins, and sloughing off dead skin cells is what does it!

ALSO SEE: *Circulation, Ginger Bath, Ginger Poultice*

ALTERNATIVE OR SUPPLEMENTARY SELF-HELP: *Chaparral, *Comfrey, *People Paste, Yarrow*

DOSAGE: *General*

STIMULANT: Ginger is invigorating to the circulation and that means all systems of the body are enlivened. Since toxins become trapped and build up in the blood, organs, glands, stomach, intestines, etc., a stimulant is needed to help flush the body.The stimulating powers of Ginger increase vitality, break up toxic mucus and bring a healing warmth. When added to other herbs, Ginger helps bind them together and thus more readily activates their acceptance into the system.

For all of these reasons, Ginger is often used daily as a tonic, especially in the fall and winter months when people tend to get cold and congested more easily.

ALSO SEE: *Circulation, Congestion, Ginger Bath, Ginger Poultice, Inflammation*

ALTERNATIVE OR SUPPLEMENTARY SELF-HELP: **Cayenne, Garlic, Onion, *Peppermint, Yarrow*

DOSAGE: *General*

STOMACH: See Digestion application.

TENDONITIS: See Circulation, Ginger Bath, Ginger Poultice, and Inflammation applications. (NOTE: Ginger poultice is great for tendonitis in animals, even race horses.)

THROAT: For a sore throat mix Ginger powder and Clove powder in equal parts. Take 1 tsp. of this mixture and stir it into 2 Tbsp. of olive oil or sesame oil. Using about 1/2 tsp. of this herbal oil at a time, swallow it slowly so that it can coat the throat. The Clove is an antiseptic and helps numb the throat pain while the Ginger brings blood to the area and helps the throat tissues throw off irritation, inflammation, and infection.

Ginger tea by itself makes a great gargle. Or use the Ginger/Clove mixture, explained above, as a gargle in water instead of in the throat-coating oil version. Also try sucking on small honeyballs (see Chapter I) made from the Ginger or Ginger/Clove powder, to relieve the soreness in the throat.

ALSO SEE: *Colds and Flu, Congestion, Fevers, Ginger Bath, Ginger Poultice*

ALTERNATIVE OR SUPPLEMENTARY SELF-HELP: *Cayenne, *Comfrey, *Clove, *Garlic, People Paste (used as gargle), *Peppermint Oil*

DOSAGE: *General or as given*

URINARY TRACT: Use Ginger internally or externally (as a poultice), or both, for scanty urine, congested or sluggish kidneys, and as a mild to medium-strength diuretic

ALSO SEE: *Congestion, Ginger Bath, Ginger Poultice, Inflammation.*

ALTERNATIVE OR SUPPLEMENTARY SELF-HELP: **Chaparral, *Comfrey, Garlic, Onion, *Yarrow*

DOSAGE: *General*

ONION

BRUISES, SPRAINS, INSECT BITES, CONGESTION... IT'S A GOOD THING I ALWAYS TAKE ONIONS ON MY CAMPING "VACATIONS"!
ONION TONIC
KJohansen

I'LL NEVER LOOK AT AN ONION THE SAME WAY AGAIN....

CHAPTER VIII

ONION

Allium cepa

An Onion pack sat on a bruised and sprained knee,
Then jumped on an earache and shouted, "Whoopee!"
Comes a man using Onion for clogged chest and stuffed nose;
Put a slice on a bug bite and the pain quickly goes!

PERSONALITY PROFILE—Onion

If you take me seriously and try using Onion in the ways I describe, you may never cast a condescending eye on an Onion again. Onions are available everywhere since there is hardly a culture in the world in which the Onion does not play a part in the diet. The juice of the Onion is always ready-to-use which makes it an invaluable self-help remedy. There are no teas to be made, capsules to fill or buy, tricky measurements, harmful side effects, or special utensils needed. This simplicity makes the self-help applications of Onion especially suitable for children to learn and use. I reach first for onion for an antidote to an external poison, as in the case of poisonous insect bites, or for an athletic injury, such as a badly bruised, jammed, or sprained body part—a common casualty in backyard football games all across America.

TASOLE: I once visited a group of friends who lived in the country. I spent most of my time with the children, a group of seven ranging in age from three to seven, teaching them about the healing uses of plants, including the Onion. At one point I had to leave for a few days and when I returned the following story was told (and shown) to me by my young herbistry students.

One day when the entire play-group was running up and down a small hill, one of the five-year-olds took a tumble, rolling fast over some sharp rocks until he reached the bottom of the hill. As the other children ran down to help, one of them remembered learning about putting slices of Onion on bumps and bruises to keep them from getting painful, purple, and swollen (there had been several occasions for me to demonstrate this on them already). So, without consulting any of the nearby adults, one child went into the kitchen and brought out an Onion and a small knife and proceeded to direct everyone to the schoolroom to where he knew he could find tape. The bruised and banged child was helped along by the others. Once settled, the young healers went to work. Every place the injured child pointed to as hurting, including the areas that were already swollen and purple, received a slice of Onion taped over it.

When I arrived back one day later, several of the parents immediately told me to ask the children about their experience of taking care of themselves. Entering the schoolroom I quickly identified the injured child — the one with the numerous patches on his arms, legs, and head. Looking closer, I saw that each patch was a slice of Onion held securely onto the skin with lots of tape. The children told me the story and proudly pointed out that the bruised, swollen and painful spots had gone away after they had applied the Onion. The injured child was now wearing the taped Onion slices as badges, mainly for dramatic effect.

Most interesting to me was that on some especially large bruises there was a narrow outer ring of purple with a normal looking middle area. The middle area was where the round slice of Onion had been taped, and since the slice of Onion was not as big as the circle of injury, whatever part was not covered simply continued with the usual process of bruising or swelling. Any area that was completely covered with the Onion had no remaining signs of trauma.

Those small yet colorful "battle scars" told the whole story of Onion's healing power — a graphic example of how Onion breaks up blood that gathers under the skin when a bruise is forming, and how it also disperses the lymph fluids that gather and contribute to swelling.

The children were all so pleased at their success that they insisted upon keeping the Onion slices over the healed wounds even through one or two carefully orchestrated baths.

Since Onions contain sulphur compounds as one of their active ingredients, they are a superb antiseptic. Like Garlic, the Onion is also used to cleanse the blood and lower high blood pressure. Research done at East Texas State University has identified a prostaglandin compound in the raw Onion. This compound is known for lowering high blood pressure in rats. I offer this bit of "rat information" as reinforcement to my own herbal experience of using raw Onion to lower blood pressure in humans.

In addition to the active ingredients in Onion that help it to break up fluid congestion in body tissues, such as in bruising and swelling, there is also an action that is anti-inflammatory. I have often used an Onion/Salt poultice (see instructions under Applications) for the infamous "water-on-the-knee" injury common to many knee-twisting sports. In every case so far this self-help approach has been successful—breaking up and drawing out blood and lymph fluids with little or no inflammation to the joint. The result has been quicker recovery. The same treatment works wonders on sprained ankles and bruised ribs. You can get newly creative with the old Onion!

In Chapter VI—Garlic, I listed many ways to alter the aroma of Garlic on the breath if this is unwanted. The same methods apply to relieving the aroma of Onion. Be sure to review those suggestions if Onion aroma is a problem for you.

APPLICATIONS AND ATTRIBUTES - ONION

(Quick Reference List)

ANTISEPTIC
ARTHRITIS
ATHLETIC INJURY
BLOOD-BUILDING
BLOOD-CLEANSING
BLOOD PRESSURE
BRUISE
BURSITIS
CONGESTION
COUGH SYRUP
DIGESTION
EARACHE
EYE TEARING (from Onion)
GAS
HEARTBURN
HEMORRHOIDS
HICCOUGHS
HIGH BLOOD PRESSURE
INFLAMMATION
INSECT BITES
JOINTS (injured/aching)
KIDNEYS
LUNGS
ONION/SALT POULTICE
ONION WATER
ORGAN CONGESTION
PARASITES
PNEUMONIA
RIBS (injured/bruised)
RINGWORM
SINUS
SPRAINS
STIMULANT
SURGERY
SWELLING
TONIC
URINARY TRACT
WATER-ON-THE-KNEE
WORMS

FORM:

Use raw Onion. The most common types/colors are white, yellow, and red.

APPLICATION METHODS:

Internally: Use the raw Onion juice (usually diluted with an equal part of water) or the needed amount of the whole raw Onion that has been chopped or blended to a convenient eating form. To get the juice easily, chop or blend raw Onion and squeeze/strain the Onion juice through a cloth or sieve. Also see how to make Onion water in the Tonic application. **Externally:** Use the raw Onion juice, an Onion/Salt Poultice (see that application), or tape a slice of raw Onion onto an area.

AVAILABILITY:

Probably anywhere in the world in grocery stores, gardens, and open-air markets

HINTS/CAUTIONS:

For children or for those who find that taking raw Onion internally is too strong for the present state of their stomachs or taste buds, here are two good tricks.

1) Mix chopped Onion with honey before eating it.
2) Onion juice or diluted Onion juice (with water) is often smoother to take than raw chopped onion. The juice can also be mixed with honey. See the Tonic application for directions.

GENERAL DOSAGE: INTERNAL USE

*PLEASE NOTE: *Although I emphasize using the raw Onion there are several other convenient forms in which to prepare this herb. See the listings for Honeyball, Syrup, Lozenge, and Children's Ideas in Chapter I, Lesson #2.*

Infants to 3 years: Use Onion juice diluted with equal parts of water. Give 1/4 to 1/2 tsp. throughout the day as needed, up to a total of 1/4 cup of the diluted juice in a day.

Children 4 years to 10 years: Onion juice or whole chopped Onion can be given, usually with a little honey or diluted with water if preferred. 1 tsp. of the juice or 1 TBS. of the finely chopped Onion (measurements before water or honey added) from one to six times a day depending upon whether it is being used as a tonic (use smaller dose) or for cleansing toxins of some sort (use larger dose).

Children 11 years to adults: Up to 1/4 cup of the raw Onion juice or 1/2 cup of the finely chopped raw Onion can be divided into 1 Tbsp. doses and taken throughout the day. These amounts are quite variable so adjust them to your liking. Commonly I suggest starting with 1/4 cup finely chopped Onions eaten as a blood strengthening tonic once a day for 10 days or more. This can be mixed with honey if desired.

Pets and Other Creatures: I have never used Onion internally on any animal so you are on your own here.

GENERAL DOSAGE: EXTERNAL USE

Same For All Humans And Other Creatures

Raw Onion, finely chopped or blended or sliced, is used externally as a poultice anytime there is bruising, swelling, insect poison, fluid congestion, or the threat of inflammation. If extra "drawing power" is needed, as is the case with many athletic injuries that swell quickly, you may add about 1/2 part table salt to the Onion "mush." The Onion or Onion/Salt Poultice (see that application) is applied directly to a body part or wrapped in a thin, natural fiber cloth and then applied. The poultice may be warmed (not cooked) in a 350 degree oven. Keep the poultice warm with a hot water bottle or heating pad as desired.

APPLICATIONS AND ATTRIBUTES - ONION

ANTISEPTIC: Onion juice has a good antiseptic action wherever it is applied. If you are out on a picnic and need an antiseptic, there are often Onions handy. (Use only clean and fresh ones, please. No catsup or mustard!) One drawback to using Onion juice is that for some people it may sting, although in my experience this is rare.

ALSO SEE: *Bruising, Inflammation, Insect Bites*

ALTERNATIVE OR SUPPLEMENTARY SELF-HELP: *Cloves, *Comfrey, Chaparral, *Garlic, *People Paste, Yarrow*

DOSAGE: *General*

ARTHRITIS: See Inflammation application.

INJURY: See Bruising, Inflammation, Onion/Salt Poultice, Surgery, and Swelling applications.

BLOOD-BUILDING: See Tonic application.

BLOOD-CLEANSING: See Tonic application.

BLOOD PRESSURE: See Tonic application.

BRUISE: Onion breaks up the congestion of many types of fluids under the skin, including blood which causes bruising, and congested lymph which causes additional swelling and pain. Use Onion as a poultice, finely chopped, blended, or sliced into a convenient form and applied directly to a fresh bruise or to an old one, or use it as a preventive measure on an area that might develop a bruise. If extra fluid-drawing power is needed, mix 1/3 to 1 equal part of table salt into the poultice. For ordinary bruises, Onion usually does the job all by itself.

Think of a slice of Onion as a quick tape-on remedy for most small to medium size bumps and bruises. (Read the TASOLE in the beginning of this chapter.) Use a full-fledged Onion poultice for larger areas of bruising. (See Onion/Salt Poultice application.)

If you are interested in seeing graphically how well Onion works, next time you experience a small area of mild bruising put Onion on half of the bruise and leave the other half alone for comparison.

Since Onion also acts against inflammation and swelling, both of which often go along with bruising, Onion is often all that is needed to speed recovery from physical twists and tumbles.

If you are a person who bruises easily, try Onion as a tonic (see Tonic application). I have had remarkable results in helping many people to lessen their susceptibility to bruising.

Comfrey is a great addition to Onion in any "bruise situation."

ALSO SEE: *Inflammation, Onion/Salt Poultice, Swelling*

ALTERNATIVE OR SUPPLEMENTARY SELF-HELP: **Comfrey, Ginger, People Paste*

DOSAGE: *General*

BURSITIS: See Inflammation application.

CONGESTION: For congestion in the head, chest, or internal organs such as the liver, Onion works "right now," which is what we usually want when we feel awful or can't breathe too well. Congestion with toxins or mucus in any internal organ would result in the organ not functioning optimally and might also cause tenderness in the area.

Make an Onion or Onion/Salt Poultice (see Onion/Salt Poultice application) and apply directly over the congested area, whether it be the lungs, liver, kidneys, etc. A very warm Onion poultice works best in these circumstances, so keep it warm with a hot water bottle or heating pad. Leave the poultice on for at least 30 minutes, although longer is better (i.e., a couple of hours, or even overnight).

Take raw Onion or Onion cough syrup internally, or use some of the excellent choices listed below under "Alternatives," for fast relief from all sorts of congestion.

For congestion in the head, breathing the fumes of an Onion often does the trick. For babies (and for that matter anyone else) another good trick is to put a big chunk of cut Onion next to the child's head at night while the child sleeps. This will make breathing easier. I usually just cut an Onion in half although more cuts make stronger fumes.

TASOLE: Jennifer, a young mother, had a small child who was having great difficulty sleeping because of a stuffy nose. At my suggestion she put a sliced Onion near the child's head, in his crib at night, to help him breathe easier. This worked so well that she continued the treatment for several nights. She did report something odd, however. In the mornings when her child awoke Jennifer could never find the chunk of Onion. After several nights of this Onion mystery, she went into her baby's room one morning a little earlier than usual. There she found him chewing up the last bit of the Onion chunk with his four new baby teeth! Like many of us, she never imagined that raw Onion would be liked by a baby. My experience verifies that many babies love to chew and eat raw Onions!

Jennifer's baby probably thought it was very nice of Mom to leave him a snack every morning. That same chunk of Onion, used both externally and then internally, was a doubly-effective remedy for the congestion symptoms, and the child was soon breathing better both day and night.

ALSO SEE: *Cough Syrup, Onion/Salt Poultice, Tonic*

ALTERNATIVE OR SUPPLEMENTARY SELF-HELP: *Cayenne, *Comfrey, *Garlic, *Ginger, Peppermint, *Slippery Elm, Yarrow*

DOSAGE: *General*

COUGH SYRUP: Onions are an excellent base for cough syrups, and also quite potent even as the sole herbal ingredient. In creating cough syrups, try to aim for a flavor that is not so unusual that the "consumer" refuses to use it! For instance, I once had a student who made a "whocko-socko" cough syrup that worked extremely well both for slowing the cough and healing the cause of it, yet the flavor was so strong (she had mixed several of the strongest congestion herbs, bitter and sweet alike, in an Onion and honey base) that only extremely hardy types would try it. (Yet don't forget that you can be very creative and make your own variations.)

Here are a few of my favorite recipes.

Cough Syrup #1: Chop 1 cup of raw Onion and place in a small stainless steel or glass cooking pot. Absolutely do not use an aluminum pot or aluminum utensils. Add enough raw honey to cover the Onion (perhaps 1/2 cup) and *slowly* simmer the mixture until the Onions have become dissolved into bits, as much as possible, in the syrup. This may take twenty minutes. Cover the pot to lessen the evaporation of nutrients, yet stir frequently to avoid burning it. While simmering, the syrup can be diluted with water, if you like. Strain it (unless you like the Onion bits in there) and store it in the refrigerator. This syrup can be used as frequently as you like. It is commonly taken as needed or up to once every half hour in 1 tsp. doses for smaller children and 1 Tbsp. doses for people 10 years and older.

Cough Syrup #2: Prepare Cough Syrup #1. Depending upon your need add:

- 1 tsp. Cloves (whole or powdered) for pain relief
- 1 to 2 Tbsp. Comfrey root or Slippery Elm (powdered or chopped) for additional decongesting and healing of lung tissues
- 1 to 2 Tbsp. chopped fresh Ginger root — or
- 1 tsp. dried Ginger root powder for increasing overall circulation, warmth, and effectiveness of the syrup

I recommend that you read about these herbal additions in their respective chapters in this book. You will get a better sense of why you would want to choose one herb over another. You may, of course, add all the suggested choices but in lesser amounts, up to 2 Tbsp., total, of additional herbs, keeping aware of the taste preference of the person who will be taking the syrup.

Although I call this mixture a cough syrup, it also provides the helpful qualities of its herbal components to the entire body, thus helping the whole system regain its equilibrium. In this sense you could also call it a tonic (see Tonic application) and it could be used for rejuvenation purposes even when there is no cough present.

ALSO SEE: *Congestion, Onion/Salt Poultice, Tonic*

ALTERNATIVE OR SUPPLEMENTARY SELF-HELP: *Cayenne, *Clove, *Comfrey, Garlic, *Ginger, Peppermint, *Slippery Elm*

DOSAGE: *As given*

DIGESTION: Use finely chopped or pulverized Onions (mixed with a little honey if you need a buffer for its spiciness) and eat 1 or 2 Tbsp. before and after a meal, or use Onion-water, to stimulate efficient digestion and help prevent heartburn, indigestion and gas.

To make Onion-water, soak finely chopped Onions in an equal amount of pure water for 12 to 15 hours and then squeeze out the liquid and store it in the refrigerator. Take this liquid, on the average, in 1/2 to 1 cup doses, two to four times a day, before and/or after you eat. (See more details of how to make and use Onion-Water in the Tonic application.)

Using Onion-water alone sometimes works better than eating the Onion. The Onion-water is potent, yet mild enough to be used even by those people who find eating Onions to cause burning or unrest in the stomach.

However you ingest the Onion, in addition to helping your digestion, you will be giving yourself the tonic advantages of using Onion.

ALSO SEE: *Congestion, Cough Syrup (can be used as a digestive aid!), Tonic*

ALTERNATIVE OR SUPPLEMENTARY SELF-HELP: **Cayenne, Chaparral, Comfrey, Garlic, *Ginger, *Peppermint, *Yarrow*

DOSAGE: *As given*

EARACHE: Cut an appropriate size Onion in half and wrap one half in a natural fiber cloth. Put this wrapped Onion-half on a cooking dish and warm at 350 degrees in the oven until it becomes somewhat softened. Remove the Onion from the oven and cool it just enough that it is still quite warm yet comfortable enough to be applied to the user's head. This warm Onion poultice is placed (flat side to the skin, of course) behind the ear over the mastoid bone (that hump behind most ears) or positioned a little lower or even directly over the ear if that feels better for the type of earache. This poultice can easily be held in position by a scarf tied around the head, also providing you with a good laugh if you catch a glimpse of yourself in the mirror. Sometimes you can keep the poultice in place simply by lying on it. A hot water bottle or heating pad can help keep it warm. Warm Onion helps break up and disperse congestion in the ear and can help relieve the pain quite quickly.

To treat the ear internally along with this external Onion poultice, use Garlic oil. There is a recipe for this in the Garlic chapter (Chapter VI).

Most earaches are quickly relieved or leave altogether (usually within a day) when this internal and external self-help is applied. If an earache is the result of a larger systemic infection or an ear abscess, it will also be useful to do an herbal enema, clean the ear with hydrogen peroxide as necessary, and use a potent infection-fighting formula such as the ones listed in the Chaparral and Garlic chapters (Chapters III and VI, respectively). The enema helps immediately to take the pressure off the detoxifying system so all the body's resources can be concentrated on the areas of acute need. You may be surprised at what a difference this can make.

Remember, whenever you treat an earache in one ear, it is best to give both ears the internal treatment to help prevent a healthy ear from getting involved in the trauma.

ALSO SEE: *Antiseptic, Congestion, Inflammation, Onion/Salt Poultice, Tonic*

ALTERNATIVE OR SUPPLEMENTARY SELF-HELP: *Clove, Comfrey, *Garlic, Ginger (especially a ginger bath), *Peppermint (oil rubbed behind the ear before Onion poultice is applied)*

DOSAGE: *As given*

EYE TEARING: To prevent eyes from becoming over-irritated while cutting Onions:

- Cut the Onion under water, or
- Cool the Onion in the refrigerator for an hour or more before slicing, or
- Burn a candle close to where you are cutting the Onion.

There is a volatile oil in Onions that can be quite stimulating to the delicate membranes of the eyes and nose. The "tricks" suggested above will help to stabilize or evaporate this oil faster than it can bother you.

Many people don't mind the tearing effect of Onions. In fact they rather enjoy it! It is a natural remedy for clearing stuffy heads or for giving your eyes a good flush. I have some students who deliberately cut Onions to get themselves crying when they feel the need. Each to his own!

ALSO SEE: *None*

ALTERNATIVE OR SUPPLEMENTARY SELF-HELP: *None*

DOSAGE: *None*

GAS: See Digestion application.

HEARTBURN: See Digestion application.

HEMORRHOIDS: Cleanse the blood steadily on a daily basis using blood-cleansing teas such as Onion juice (see Tonic application), Yarrow or Comfrey. Topically a raw Onion poultice can give fast relief and is applied (wrapped in a thin gauze) to the anus and any external hemorrhoids, and left on overnight. Another method is to cut an appropriately shaped slice of Onion and directly insert it into the anus, leaving it there overnight. This treatment will help to shrink, cleanse, decongest, and speed recovery from hemorrhoids.

Diet is a very important factor in controlling hemorrhoids. Hemorrhoid sufferers should *absolutely* avoid fried food, refined foods and sugars, caffeine, alcohol, and white (processed) flour products including pasta. All of these foods put a strain on the digestive system resulting in more toxins being dumped into the blood. This toxic condition contributes to the stressing of the anal blood vessels which then erupt into hemorrhoids.

ALSO SEE: *Congestion, Digestion, Tonic*

ALTERNATIVE OR SUPPLEMENTARY SELF-HELP: *Chaparral, *Comfrey, Garlic, *People Paste, *Slippery Elm, Yarrow*

DOSAGE: *As given*

HICCOUGHS: Take raw Onion juice, 1 Tbs. each half hour. If straight juice is too strong for you, review the method for diluting it with water (in the Tonic application) and take it more frequently as needed. To get straight Onion juice, simply blend (do not add water) or finely chop some Onion, place it in a clean cheesecloth, and squeeze out the juice. Blending yields the most juice and is the fastest method. Dilute with water if you need to.

ALSO SEE: *Cough Syrup, Digestion, Tonic*

ALTERNATIVE OR SUPPLEMENTARY SELF-HELP: **Peppermint*

DOSAGE: *As given*

HIGH BLOOD PRESSURE: See Tonic application and the Garlic chapter (Chapter VI).

INFLAMMATION: Onion is famous for reducing inflammations from sprains or similar body twistings. It also has good results on areas bothered by arthritis, bursitis, rheumatism, tendonitis, etc.

Use an Onion poultice, or an Onion/Salt poultice (see Onion/Salt Poultice application), over the inflamed part to help draw out any swelling from congestion of fluids. In addition, take Onion or Onion juice internally or drink anti-inflammatory teas such as Comfrey root or Yarrow.

ALSO SEE: *Antiseptic, Congestion, Onion/Salt Poultice, Tonic*

ALTERNATIVE OR SUPPLEMENTARY SELF-HELP: *Chaparral, *Comfrey, Ginger, *People Paste, Slippery Elm, Yarrow*

DOSAGE: *As given*

INSECT BITES: This is a major use for Onion. Use it for any kind of insect bite or poisonous sting from a wasp, bee, spider, gnat, ant, mosquito, small (non-lethal) snake, etc. It works almost immediately. It is useful for children to learn about the use of Onion, and many times a young student of mine has had the self-satisfying experience of handling his or her own wasp, bee or ant sting.

In case of a sting or bite, slice, chop, or grind a bit of Onion (whichever form suits the shape and site of the bite), and tape it directly onto the site of the bite, covering an area a little larger than the bite/sting itself. All it takes for the smallest stings is to rub the spot with Onion juice from a cut piece of Onion without even bothering to tape it there. **It is important for the onion juice to come into contact with the site of the sting or bite**, so be sure to put the wet, juicy side of the cut Onion onto the skin. (I note this because I once had a student who took a layer of Onion and laid it dry-side down on a bruise. Needless to say this did not get very good results. It was a good lesson for me. I had to be more specific.)

The Onion juice acts as an antidote and draws out most poisons on the spot, even in severe cases. Sprinkle some salt on the Onion Poultice if you want extra drawing power. The sooner you put the Onion on the spot the better, although I have had good results even when I have not attended to a sting until an hour or so later. If you are extremely sensitive to insect stings, drink some Comfrey or Yarrow tea to keep the blood cleansed and prevent harsh reactions. For most people, however, an Onion poultice is enough.

TASOLE: One summer I worked at a healing-arts camp that had several hives of honeybees. One day a hive swarmed to a nearby tree, so the resident bee-keeper took a few volunteers and went to recapture it. The next thing I knew one of the male volunteers was brought to the kitchen with one arm totally covered with bee stings and random stings on the rest of his body. I was told that the swarm had fallen from its branch onto his arm, which was swelling fast. The young man looked un-well, to put it mildly, and was evidently in great pain. We immediately began to pack his arm with Onions. I had never tried Onion on such a large number of stings before, yet within 15 minutes the pain had dramatically decreased and the arm did not appear to be swelling any further (although it was hard to see under all that Onion).

Three hours later when we took off the Onion to reapply a fresh poultice, I was amazed to see that the gigantic mass of stings, redness, and swelling had reduced significantly. There were now only clearly identifiable puncture holes surrounded by light-pinkness, and almost no swelling. We repacked the arm and began giving the man a blood-cleansing herb tea of Comfrey and Yarrow. The large amount of honeybee venom in his system had begun to make him feverish and nauseous. (It probably would have been best to have him start drinking the tea immediately after the accident, yet he didn't seem interested until he started getting feverish.)

By the next morning there was no further need to use the Onion poultice. He continued with 4 to 6 cups of blood-cleansing tea for about three more days, and by then he was totally back to normal.

ALSO SEE: *Antiseptic, Onion/Salt Poultice*

ALTERNATIVE OR SUPPLEMENTARY SELF-HELP: **Chaparral, Comfrey, Garlic, *People Paste, *Yarrow*

DOSAGE: *Put an Onion poultice on the site of sting or bite, and drink 2 to 6 cups of blood-cleansing tea, such as Comfrey or Yarrow, throughout the day if there is a systemic reaction to the sting or bite.*

JOINTS (injury/aching): See Bruising, Inflammation, Onion/Salt Poultice, Sprain, and Surgery applications.

KIDNEYS: See Urinary Tract application.

LUNGS: See Congestion, Cough Syrup, and Tonic applications.

ONION/SALT POULTICE: Onion breaks up congestion and/or toxins under the skin that cause bruising, swelling, inflammation, and pain. It then helps to move the toxins out through the blood, lymph and skin. Salt adds drawing power to the Onion poultice. With this combination I have often had dramatic, overnight results in a large variety of situations, such as water-on-the-knee, twisted or jammed joints and appendages, renewed swelling of old injuries or of surgeries done to repair those injuries, lung congestion, other organ congestion, "bumps-on-the-head" that result in large knots and/or bruises . . . just about any situation where you need the kinds of action Onion provides. In some situations it may be more convenient to use a plain Onion poultice without the salt mixed into it. This can work very well. The salt is mainly for extra drawing power of unwanted fluids.

Here is how to make this poultice. Grind, or finely chop, enough Onion to cover the area to be helped. To this "Onion mush," add salt in the proportions of 2:1, that is, for 1 cup of chopped Onion you would add about 1/2 cup of salt. Sea salt is preferable and in any case it is best to use salt that is not iodized when possible. Pile this mixture on and/or around the joint, bruise, bump, inflammation, sprain, swelling, etc. Place it either directly onto the skin, or wrap the mixture in a thin, natural fiber cloth, if this is more convenient. If put directly onto the skin first, hold the mixture onto the area with a thin, natural fiber cloth and fasten the cloth in place with an elastic bandage or with surgical tape. Since the poultice is wet, and since you will want to keep it that way, wrap the entire area with a plastic bag or plastic wrap. Seal the edges as best you can with masking tape or whatever you have. If you keep the skin around the poultice dry, it works well to tape the plastic wrap to the skin which usually forms an adequate seal. At least it minimizes leakage.

The best time to apply an Onion/Salt Poultice is at night so you can sleep with it on and remove it in the morning. I don't find it worth all the preparation unless it is done at a time when it can be left on for at least two hours. In removing it you may find that the Onions will have a strange odor. This is from the fluids pulled out of the area by the poultice. Have a plastic bag handy to throw the whole thing into for convenient disposal. Some people find the Onion aroma lingers on the skin. If this is unwanted, it is easily removed by washing the skin and then rubbing the affected area with lemon juice.

A one-night poultice is usually enough to clear up most conditions. For stubborn situations, such as a long-term lung congestion or an old injury, you may repeat the poultice as needed.

There are circumstances where a heated poultice is useful, such as for lung congestion. For these times it is a simple matter to put the poultice, cloth and all, into the oven on a baking dish until it is warmed enough. It can be kept warm with a hot water bottle.

Remember, this poultice, without the salt, still works very well. The salt is there for its potent drawing power which is necessary when there is more than a little swelling involved.

Comfrey is an additional supplement to use with an Onion poultice. Take Comfrey internally and soak an injury in Comfrey decoction in between poulticing.

ALSO SEE: *Bruising, Congestion*

ALTERNATIVE OR SUPPLEMENTARY SELF-HELP: **Comfrey, Ginger, *People Paste*

DOSAGE: *As given*

ONION WATER: See Tonic application.

ORGAN CONGESTION: See Congestion application.

PARASITES: Onion is one part of a procedure for ridding the body of many types of common parasites, including ringworm, pinworm, roundworm, and hookworm. Start drinking Chaparral tea in 1-cup doses, 4 cups a day, or take Chaparral powder in a dose of 2 capsules, three times a day. Supplement this by eating plenty of raw Onion and/or Garlic, and do an Onion water enema (see Tonic application) or Garlic water enema (see Garlic chapter, Chapter VI) each day for three days in a row (while still taking the Chaparral). Rinse/rub any external marks of parasites, such as in ringworm, with Onion or Garlic juice (straight—undiluted). Do this routine for about ten days total, taking the enemas on days four, five, and six. When completed, wait seven to ten days, and then repeat the routine if any further parasitic symptoms have returned. Often a second round of parasites will hatch within that seven to ten day waiting period after the first routine, and this is why a second routine is often beneficial.

An even stronger method, for hardier types of people, is to fast, taking only herbal teas on days four, five, and six of the above routine. Throughout the fast, continue to drink the Chaparral tea or take the Chaparral powder as recommended above. Add as much plain water or other enjoyable herb tea of your choice (not more Chaparral than the suggested amount) to equal an intake of at least 10 cups of water or tea on each of those fasting days. Sometime on day six, at least two hours before you take the enema, eat 1/2 to 1 cup raw chopped Onion. Chew well. I find it hard to eat raw chopped Onion plain, so I usually add honey to buffer it. One of my students warmed the Onions briefly in the oven and then put a little catsup on them to make them easier to take. The point of this "Onion snack" on the third enema day is that Onion's high sulphur content, along with its other chemical properties, creates a fine purge for tough parasite cases, especially after the "stage has been set" by the rest of the routine. Remember, this is strong treatment, and I only suggest this addition to the original routine for those who have an otherwise healthy digestive tract.

ALSO SEE: *Tonic*

ALTERNATIVE OR SUPPLEMENTARY SELF-HELP: **Chaparral, *Garlic*

DOSAGE: *As given*

PNEUMONIA: See Onion/Salt Poultice application (for use over the lungs), and see the Comfrey and Garlic chapters (Chapters V and VI).

RIBS (injured/bruised): See Onion/Salt Poultice and Surgery applications, and review the Comfrey chapter (Chapter V).

RINGWORM: See Parasites application.

SINUS: See Congestion application.

SPRAINS: See Onion/Salt Poultice application. Think "Onion" in any situation involving a sprain. Review the Comfrey chapter (Chapter V).

STIMULANT: See Tonic application.

SURGERY: Onion treatment is a useful follow-up to surgeries done to repair connective tissues, bones and joints as a result of athletic injuries, and/or surgeries that involve the placement of metal pins. Many people continue to have random pain and swelling even long after surgery. Others have a weakness in the areas operated upon and so are inclined to strain these areas more easily. Even with a professionally surpervised rehabilitation program, self-help in the form of the Onion/Salt Poultice can do wonders to keep swelling and bruising to a minimum throughout the process

ALSO SEE: *Bruising, Onion/Salt Poultice*

ALTERNATIVE OR SUPPLEMENTARY SELF-HELP: **Comfrey, Ginger, *Slippery Elm*

DOSAGE: *General*

SWELLING: See Inflammation and Onion/Salt Poultice applications.

TONIC: I love it when something as common and easily available as raw Onion turns out to have such potent tonic qualities.
An Onion tonic can:

1) gently and steadily clean the blood
2) build and revitalize the blood
3) help in lowering high blood pressure
4) lower cholesterol
5) enhance digestion
6) gently stimulate internal organs, thus helping to relieve sluggishness
7) supply a high dosage of vitamin C

The simplest Onion tonic involves eating 1/2 cup raw, chopped Onions four times a week. If raw Onions are too spicy for your stomach, start with a smaller amount and work up or use the Onion-water recipe below. The sensitivity will lessen. Also try mixing raw honey with the chopped Onions or Onion-water (whatever amount of honey does the job for you) as this buffers the spiciness, enhances digestion, and tastes great. Other Onion tonics include the formulas listed under the Cough Syrup application. Here is how to make Onion-water.

ONION-WATER

Soak equal parts finely chopped Onions and pure water (some people like it stronger and so use less water) for 12 to 15 hours and then thoroughly strain out the liquid. This liquid is now your Onion-water tonic.

A stronger Onion-water can be obtained by blending the Onions before adding them to the water, letting the mixture stand for 12 to 15 hours, and then straining that mixture through a cloth. Start by drinking 1/2 to 1 cup two to four times a day as frequently as every day if you like. It is best to take the Onion-water tonic half an hour before meals, yet anytime that works for you is fine.

I suggest that you review the examples of how and why Onion works by reading the Personality Profile at the beginning of this chapter.

ALSO SEE: *Antiseptic, Congestion, Parasites*

ALTERNATIVE OR SUPPLEMENTARY SELF-HELP: *Cayenne, *Comfrey, *Garlic, *Yarrow*

DOSAGE: *As given*

URINARY TRACT: The Onion/Salt Poultice (see that application), placed over the kidneys or bladder, can relieve pain and congestion in those areas while encouraging their healing. Also, taking Onion on a daily basis as described in the Tonic application can strengthen and gently cleanse the blood and lymph, which lends good support to the entire urinary tract.

Comfrey is a superb herb for all sorts of urinary tract "glitches," so please be sure to review that herb also.

ALSO SEE: *Antiseptic, Congestion, Onion/Salt Poultice, Tonic*

ALTERNATIVE OR SUPPLEMENTARY SELF-HELP: **Chaparral, *Comfrey, *Garlic, *Yarrow*

DOSAGE: *General*

WATER-ON-THE-KNEE: See Onion/Salt Poultice and Surgery applications.

WORMS: See Parasite application.

PEPPERMINT

I FEEL BETTER ALREADY
RELAX
STIMULATE AND SOOTHE
10 ESSENTIAL HERBS
Hmmm, IT SAYS HERE A LITTLE PEPPERMINT WITH MY CATNIP DOES WONDERS FOR THE DIGESTION!

CHAPTER IX

PEPPERMINT

Mentha piperita

Peppermint Polly smells happy, tastes great!
For digestion or sinus, it's never too late.
She can perk-up or soothe body parts, it's no joke!
If you're out for too long, take her bath for sunstroke.

PERSONALITY PROFILE—Peppermint

One handy trait of Peppermint is that its primary potency comes from its oil, and Peppermint oil is readily available from most health food stores in tiny bottles that fit easily in a pocket, purse, glove compartment, or backpack for immediate use anytime, anywhere. The best oils are available only in health food or herb stores. I recommend a brand named "Aroma Vera," which has a French label but which is distributed out of Culver City, CA. It sells for a reasonable price and has an inverted dropper right in the bottle for convenient use. Without a good dropper, you may become too discouraged with trying to dispense it by the drop. For the purest (strongest) oils, the ability to dispense accurately is important. An overdose of Peppermint oil often results in a temporary gagging experience with occasional nausea. In many places Peppermint oil or extract is still available at regular drug stores, usually in the digestive aids section, and is most often of a more dilute, less potent variety. However, in times of need I have used Peppermint extract, Peppermint essence, Peppermint flavor, or other more dilute variations, and have still gotten fairly useful results (using larger doses).

Some of the most potent ingredients in Peppermint leaves, found in the oil, are Menthofuron, Menthone, and menthol. These components help expel gas, give a strong antiseptic/anti-viral action, and give a mild, temporary numbing and sedative effect. This is effective for digestive distress, laryngitis (inflamed throat), and for teeth and gum pain, especially in teething babies. Although not as potent as Clove oil for relief of certain types of pain, Peppermint oil is generally soothing and offers a convenient, milder alternative to the Clove oil.

You may notice in the applications list that follows that I sometimes call Peppermint a stimulant and at other times I refer to it as a relaxant. This is the "Peppermint Paradox." It means that Peppermint is predominantly *stimulating to the circulation* yet *soothing to the nerves*, thus having both qualities at once. It is possible, however, for one of these qualities to overwhelm the other, depending upon the type of preparation. Peppermint oil is more stimulating and Peppermint tea is generally more soothing. Therefore, in the case of a headache caused by congestion, you might rub a drop of Peppermint oil on the temples or back of the head to encourage better circulation. For tension headache, however, choose a cup of Peppermint tea for its relaxing effect. Experiment with yourself to learn how these different preparations respond in your body. You will then know when it is a good idea to use one or the other—or even both, together.

When you buy Peppermint herb, what you usually get is the dried Peppermint leaf. This herb should have a fresh greyish-green color and a definite aroma of Peppermint. If it is brown or some other suspicious color and/or is lacking in a spritely Peppermint aroma, don't buy it.

Properly dried Peppermint of good quality will have enough volatile oil in it to be quite useful for most needs. Getting the use of this oil depends on preparing the tea properly and protecting the delicate oil from evaporating. This simply means **don't ever boil it, and always steep it in a container with a well-fitting cover**. You should be able to taste and smell the minty-ness in the tea which means the oil is still active. If you ever accidently boil your tea, consider throwing it into the compost and starting over. (This is true for most herbs that call for steeping.) It is worth the practice to learn to become a good herbal tea maker as most of these Ten Essential herbs, including Peppermint, are commonly used in the tea form.

TASOLE: Once while I was staying with my friend Regina, her parents paid us a visit. They wanted to take the whole family out to dinner so they packed up the grandchildren and all went off to find a restaurant. Two hours later they returned home and I immediately noticed that Regina looked concerned. She told me that her mother was having a severe attack of indigestion, a pattern that was common for her. Pain in the stomach and gall bladder would escalate to migraine headache and heart pain, all of which could last for several days. Her mother had a prescription drug for this problem but had left it at home and Regina wondered if I had any ideas that might help.

Since it was late at night and we were far from town, her mother consented to try one of Regina's "herbal things" pending her earliest opportunity to get some "real medicine". Regina cautioned me to think of an idea that would not seem too radical to her mom, since she well knew my "creative" instincts.

My imagination at first went off on its usual humorous tangent and then settled on an obvious and available item of help . . . namely, the tiny bottle of Aroma Vera Peppermint oil which I always carried in my purse. I gave the bottle to Regina and suggested that she give Mom two drops in a half glass of water to be sipped over a five minute period. Then I went back to reading my latest science fiction thriller. Regina went back to the kitchen with my suggestion. At that point her parents were discussing whether they should just go home right then, before the symptoms became much worse. Meanwhile Regina prepared the Peppermint concoction and Mom started to sip it.

Soon the discussion in the kitchen quieted down and ten minutes later Regina's mother came looking for me. She reported her surprise in finding that she was definitely feeling better, and asked me if it would be alright to take some more of my Peppermint. When I assured her it was fine to have more, she took another dose and then went to sleep. Her husband was both surprised and relieved. Apparently, sleeping soon after one of these attacks was not his wife's usual experience. The next morning she was fine and decided to stay around for a few more days.

Over the years, after this, I would sometimes ask Regina about her mom. I found out that the Peppermint oil worked about 70% of the time. I want to emphasize that Peppermint is not a permanent cure-all, and such severe gastric distress suggests the need for professional health advice. Yet for temporary relief I would still call this "significant help worth trying."

Peppermint is the strongest of the mint family. Other mints, such as spearmint, have similar but milder action. Spearmint in particular is a useful alternative when Peppermint is too strong for a situation. With infants or people who have an adverse response to Peppermint's strong minty-ness, I definitely recommend using spearmint instead. While Peppermint can be used safely with children from age two years on, use spearmint to get the similar yet milder versions of Peppermint-style help for babies under two since Peppermint is sometimes a little too stimulating for a baby's system.

Peppermint is very easy to grow both indoors and out. Since mints are notorious for crossbreeding, if you want to keep a pure Peppermint patch don't plant it near any other type of mint. I have brought home wild mints I have found by riversides and all sorts of other mints from friends and mail-order catalogues. I have grown and used them all for pleasure and medicinal uses and have found that any mint will give some measure of the help that Peppermint does yet usually much milder. Peppermint is my mint of choice for most medicinal uses.

APPLICATIONS AND ATTRIBUTES - PEPPERMINT

(Quick Reference List)

ACIDITY
ANTISEPTIC/ANTI-VIRAL
ANTISPASMODIC
ANXIETY
BATH
BREASTS
BREATH
CAFFEINE WITHDRAWAL
CHILDHOOD ILLNESS
CHILLS
CIRCULATION
COLDS and FLU
COLIC
CONGESTION
CONSTIPATION
DIARRHEA
DIGESTION
FACIAL
FASTING
FEVER
GAS
HAIR RINSE
HALITOSIS
HEADACHE
HEARTBURN
HEART PALPITATION
INSOMNIA
INTESTINES
ITCHING
LARYNGITIS
MASTITIS
MENSTRUAL CRAMPS
MORNING SICKNESS
MOTION SICKNESS
MUSCLE SPASM
NAUSEA
NERVES
OVEREXPOSURE
PAIN
PEPPERMINT BATH
PERSPIRATION THERAPY
RELAXANT/SOOTHING
SEDATIVE
SINUS
SKIN
SPASMS
SUNSTROKE/HEAT
TEETHING
THROAT
TOOTHACHE

FORM:

Use Fresh or dried leaves, or Peppermint oil.

APPLICATION METHODS:

Internally use tea, infusion, oil, fresh mint drink, or enema.
Externally use tea, infusion, oil, poultice, soak, bath.

AVAILABILITY:

Herb store, garden, mail order (dried herb or fresh plant starts), many open-air markets around the world

HINTS/CAUTIONS:

Do not use Peppermint for infants up to two years old or anyone with a known hyper-sensitivity to Peppermint as it may be too stimulating and result in temporary nausea or internal irritation. Usually a spearmint substitute works well in these cases. An exception may be in cases of colic where the spearmint substitute is not doing the job. If there are no adverse responses to the spearmint, you can switch safely to mild Peppermint tea.

GENERAL DOSAGE: INTERNAL USE

*PLEASE NOTE: *Although I emphasize using tea, there are many forms of herbal preparations such as Capsules, Children's Ideas, Infusion, Honeyball, Syrups, etc. See these headings and also the Dosage Equivalents in Chapter I, Lesson #2.*

Infants to 3 years: Up to about 2 years of age it is usually best to substitute spearmint for Peppermint in most situations (see note about this in "Hints" above). Start with 1/2 cup spearmint tea two to three times a day before determining if the stronger Peppermint tea may be needed. Peppermint oil or Peppermint infusion is usually too strong for any internal use with this age group.

Children 4 years to 10 years: Peppermint tea 1/2 to 1 cup, one to three times a day; or Peppermint infusion, 1 Tbsp. as needed, taken each 10 to 15 minutes; or Peppermint oil, 1 drop of the pure oil in 1/2 cup water sipped as needed once or twice a day.

Children 11 years to Adults: Peppermint tea 1 cup as needed; or Peppermint infusion, 1 Tbsp. as needed, perhaps taken each 10 to 15 minutes; or Peppermint oil, 1 to 2 drops of the pure oil in 1/2 cup water sipped as needed.

NOTE ABOUT PEPPERMINT OIL: For any internal use of Peppermint oil, the dose may vary according to the strength and purity of the oil you are able to purchase. Also note that I always say "sip as needed." This is to indicate that to drink it all down at once is not always the best way to use it. Sipping over a few minutes gives the oil time to gently begin working. Peppermint oil taken in this way is so effective that in some cases you may find that you don't need to finish the whole dose.

GENERAL DOSAGE: EXTERNAL USE

Same For All Humans And Other Creatures

Try a Peppermint infusion (see Chapter I, Lesson #2) as a wash, soak, or bath for skin, hair rinse, nerves, overexposure, circulation, itching, and other external applications listed below.

Peppermint oil diluted in plain olive oil or water is an alternative for many external uses. To make a Peppermint oil dilution, start with 2 to 5 drops of the strongest Peppermint oil you can find and dilute it in 1/4 cup of dilution material (i.e.,olive oil, water, rubbing alcohol). Experiment with the strong action of pure Peppermint oil in finding the best dilution strength for the job. For instance, I put 15 drops of Peppermint oil in 1/2 cup of olive oil or 5 drops in a tablespoon of olive oil for a stimulating massage rub. As an inhalant, use a steamy infusion or add up to 20 drops of pure Peppermint oil (according to preference) for each cup of steaming hot water. Make a small "tent" over your head with a towel to help hold and direct the steam, lean over the brew, and inhale gently. This is a good method to use for headache, sinus congestion, stimulating facial, tired eyes, etc.

APPLICATIONS AND ATTRIBUTES - PEPPERMINT

ACIDITY: Peppermint will often reduce or eliminate discomfort from an over-acid stomach.

ALSO SEE: *Digestion, Intestines, Nausea*

ALTERNATIVE OR SUPPLEMENTARY SELF-HELP: *Comfrey, *People Paste (taken internally), Slippery Elm, Yarrow*

DOSAGE: *Drink 1 cup of Peppermint tea or 1 drop of Peppermint oil in 1/2 cup water sipped as needed. Also see General Dosage.*

ANTISEPTIC/ANTI-VIRAL: The active ingredients in Peppermint, some of which I described in the Personality Profile, have antiseptic abilities. The oil is the most potent part of the Peppermint and can be accessed either by using a carefully prepared tea or by using the oil alone.

Since there are stronger antiseptic herbs among the Ten Essentials, don't depend solely on Peppermint, especially in severe cases. Note the starred (*) alternatives listed below.

ALSO SEE: *Colds and Flu, Fever*

ALTERNATIVE OR SUPPLEMENTARY SELF-HELP: **Chaparral, Comfrey, *Garlic, Onion, *People Paste, Yarrow*

DOSAGE: *General*

ANTISPASMODIC: See Spasms application.

ANXIETY: See Nerves application.

BATH: See Peppermint Bath application.

BREASTS: See Mastitis application.

CAFFEINE WITHDRAWAL: See Circulation application.

CHILDHOOD ILLNESS: In children 2 years and older, Peppermint tea is a gentle help in easing through many childhood upsets, both physical and emotional. At the first signs of an upset stomach, fever, or cold symptoms it is usually easy to get a child to drink a cup of Peppermint tea sweetened with honey. This is sometimes all it takes to ease a child's body back into balance, or help a child cope with a short-term discomfort.

ALSO SEE: *Antiseptic/Anti-viral, Chills, Colic, Fever, Intestines, Nausea, Overexposure, Peppermint Bath*

ALTERNATIVE OR SUPPLEMENTARY SELF-HELP: *Clove, *Comfrey, *Garlic, Onion, Yarrow*

DOSAGE: *General*

CHILLS: Peppermint stimulates circulation, especially to surface tissues, and also soothes the nerves. Both actions are very useful in helping take chills out of the body. Drink the tea hot or, if you use Peppermint oil, put it into hot water.

Peppermint mixed with Comfrey is a great tea for this use.

ALSO SEE: *Circulation, Colds and Flu, Fever, Peppermint Bath*

ALTERNATIVE OR SUPPLEMENTARY SELF-HELP: **Cayenne, Comfrey, *Ginger, Yarrow*

DOSAGE: *General*

CIRCULATION: The stimulating properties of Peppermint get the blood moving, especially to the surface tissues. Some ex-coffee drinkers swear by having a strong cup of Peppermint tea, or Peppermint oil in water, in the morning to get them going. It is especially useful for those who are just breaking the caffeine habit.

ALSO SEE: *Chills, Cold and Flu, Peppermint Bath, Perspiration Therapy*

ALTERNATIVE OR SUPPLEMENTARY SELF-HELP: **Cayenne, Comfrey, Garlic, *Ginger, Yarrow*

DOSAGE: *General*

COLDS and FLU: Use Peppermint to help soothe the symptoms associated with a simple cold or flu such as chills, fever, aches and pains, etc. For a more severe cold or flu you may need one of the stronger antibiotic herbs such as Garlic, Chaparral, or People Paste (used internally).

Don't forget to use Peppermint tea or oil as an inhalant or chest/foot rub (the oil is best here) during cold and flu symptoms.

ALSO SEE: *Fasting, Fever, Nausea, Peppermint Bath, Perspiration Therapy, Sinus*

ALTERNATIVE OR SUPPLEMENTARY SELF-HELP: *Cayenne, *Chaparral, Clove, *Comfrey, *Garlic, Onion, *People Paste (internally), Yarrow*

DOSAGE: *General*

COLIC: This is one instance where even an infant may benefit from taking Peppermint tea. For children under two years start off by trying milder spearmint tea to help break up gas and other digestive distress that comes with colic. If the spearmint does not seem to do the job, yet there are no adverse responses, move on to trying the Peppermint tea. In either case, for children over one year old, it is alright to sweeten the tea with a little light molasses or honey, if a sweetener seems needed. Do not use honey for children under one year; use molasses instead. Usually Peppermint oil is too strong for an infant, but on rare occasion after trying both types of mint teas, I have gotten good results by using 1 drop of pure Peppermint oil in 1/2 cup water, given on a spoon or by dropper in small (mouthful) doses at 5-minute intervals.

ALSO SEE: *Digestion, Intestines, Nerves, Peppermint Bath*

ALTERNATIVE OR SUPPLEMENTARY SELF-HELP: *Comfrey, *People Paste (Start with 1/16 to 1/8 tsp. doses internally each hour for infants up to 1 year), *Yarrow*

DOSAGE: *General or as given*

CONGESTION: Besides the usual head and chest congestion, Peppermint is also helpful in treating congested circulation, congested bowels, and congested sweat glands.

For head congestion, use Peppermint oil in steaming hot water or Peppermint tea as an inhalant. If you use the tea, be sure to prepare it with a lid on the steeping pot to preserve the essential oils in the herb. While the tea is still hot, hold your head over the steaming pot. Create a tent by covering your head and the pot with a towel to keep the fumes concentrated. Breathe in, taking deep breaths. If your nose is too stuffed to breathe in at all, try drinking a little Cayenne in water before starting this procedure, to help get things moving (see Cayenne, Chapter II). In any case, when necessary you can start by inhaling through your mouth. Mix Peppermint oil, perhaps 1/2 tsp., into 1/4 cup olive oil and use this as a chest and/or sinus rub for children and adults alike.

Hot Peppermint tea taken internally also helps to stimulate the body out of a congested state. A tiny pinch of Cayenne, plain or in the tea, hastens the effect of the Peppermint.

ALSO SEE: *Digestion, Mastitis, Peppermint Bath, Perspiration Therapy*

ALTERNATIVE OR SUPPLEMENTARY SELF-HELP: **Cayenne, Clove, Comfrey, Garlic, *Ginger, *Onion, Slippery Elm*

DOSAGE: *General or as given*

CONSTIPATION: See Intestines application.

DIARRHEA: See Intestines application.

DIGESTION: Peppermint really shines as a digestive aid. Use it to help neutralize acid, relieve gas in the stomach and intestines, soothe heartburn, stimulate digestion when you have overeaten or have eaten food that does not agree with you, counteract nausea, or help with just about any other digestive disturbance you can think of. If you often experience digestive distress, you may want to try a cup of Peppermint tea before you eat, as a preventive. But don't neglect examining your diet, since what you eat and how you eat it are probably at cause here.

If your digestive distress is due to an ulcer, Peppermint can help, yet Cayenne and Comfrey would be even more potent. (See Chapters II and V.)

If you know you have congestion in a particular digestive organ (i.e., the liver or stomach, etc.) rub a few drops of Peppermint oil directly over these areas to stimulate circulation there and help unclog things. Also take the Peppermint internally. Together these applications will enhance digestive capability.

For a digestion-oriented headache, see the Headache application.

I always carry a tiny bottle of Peppermint oil in my purse since digestive distress is such a common experience for so many people. Usually 1 or 2 drops in 1/2 cup water, sipped as needed, is all it takes to make a fast and positive difference in digestive efficiency.

TASOLE: I once worked in a busy candy shop on the main street of a tourist town which attracted people from all over the world. During one record-breaking week, my telephone was used by no less than three different families from three different countries, speaking three different languages, all of whom had gotten locked out of their respective rent-a-cars. During one of these escapades a German family was so anxious about their car situation that they left Grandma sitting in the shop. The old woman seemed in great distress, and through sign language and a few English words told me of her painful and upset stomach. When she realized she had been left "alone" in the shop, she was even further upset.

As we "talked", I understood that the American foods she had been eating on this visit were not agreeing with her at all and that she sorely dreaded the upcoming airplane trip home. Immediately I popped out my little Peppermint oil bottle and put a drop in a half glass of water. I offered it to her and tried to make her understand that she should just sip on it. She sipped once or twice and then drank it down. At first nothing happened but then, after three minutes or so, she began burping like crazy and passing gas occasionally, smiling each time. The Peppermint had really stimulated some movement in a previously "stalemated" situation. Sometimes a few good burps are all it takes!

Her family came back soon and she insisted that I explain to them about where to get some more Peppermint oil to take home with her, especially for use on the airplane ride.

ALSO SEE: *Acidity, Colic, Fasting, Headache, Intestines, Nausea*

ALTERNATIVE OR SUPPLEMENTARY SELF-HELP: **Cayenne, Comfrey, People Paste (taken internally), *Slippery Elm, Yarrow*

DOSAGE: *General*

FACIAL: To help cleanse the pores, stimulate circulation, and enhance a healthy glow in the skin, use Peppermint herb or oil as a cosmetic facial application. Steam the face exactly as you would for sinus congestion, by making a strong pot of Peppermint tea and holding your face over the steaming brew for 15 to 20 minutes. Or use 5 drops (1/4 tsp.) Peppermint oil for each cup of water. Keep your head and the pot enclosed with a towel or something to capture the steam. Another way to do a Peppermint facial is to mix some Peppermint oil with the water needed for a clay facial mask. In this case you would end up with a Peppermint clay mask that would be great for your skin as well as your sinuses! An herbal mask can be made by softening the dried Peppermint leaves in water, or grinding them to make a paste of fresh leaves. Pack this mixture on your face for 15 to 20 minutes.

ALSO SEE: *Hair, Skin*

ALTERNATIVE OR SUPPLEMENTARY SELF-HELP: *Comfrey, *Ginger, *Slippery Elm*

DOSAGE: *As given*

FASTING: Peppermint tea is good during fasting as a stimulating, 1-cup-a-day addition to the day's program. You would not usually want to use Peppermint as the only tea for a fast since it can be too stimulating used alone for that purpose. Yet when used as recommended, it can help to stimulate circulation and organ activity. That means greater energy for you.

My suggestions for the major tea to use for a short (two to three days) cleansing fast would be Comfrey and/or Yarrow (see Chapters V and XI).

ALSO SEE: *Circulation, Digestion, Intestines, Stimulant*

ALTERNATIVE OR SUPPLEMENTARY SELF-HELP: *Chaparral, *Comfrey, Onion, *Yarrow*

DOSAGE: *During a short fast, drink 1 or 2 cups of Peppermint tea a day as an adjunct to the main tea used, as described above. If the Peppermint is mixed with another herb, it is fine to drink as much as you want.*

FEVER: Since Peppermint is soothing to the nerves and stimulating to the circulation, it works well for helping the body deal with fevers, especially if the fever is accompanied by upset stomach. Peppermint tea or oil can be used alone, or Peppermint can be mixed with another herb, such as Yarrow or Comfrey, for potent fever relief.

ALSO SEE: *Antiseptic/Anti-viral, Circulation, Fasting, Nausea, Nerves, Peppermint Bath, Perspiration Therapy*

ALTERNATIVE OR SUPPLEMENTARY SELF-HELP: *Cayenne, Chaparral, Comfrey, *Garlic, Ginger (bath), *Yarrow*

DOSAGE: *General, or when mixed with another herb as suggested, drink as much as you want.*

GAS: See Colic and Digestion applications.

HAIR (and scalp): Peppermint tea as a hair rinse is a stimulating tonic for the scalp and hair. It can either be left on to dry or left on for only a few minutes and then rinsed out with plain water. I have always used Peppermint tea for this purpose but you might want to experiment with the Peppermint oil or Peppermint infusion. Put a few drops of Peppermint oil in some warm water, stir it well, and rinse through your hair.

ALSO SEE: *Circulation, Facial, Skin, Stimulant*

ALTERNATIVE OR SUPPLEMENTARY SELF-HELP: **Comfrey, *Ginger (both herbs used as hair/scalp rinses)*

DOSAGE: *As given*

HALITOSIS: For chronic bad breath, look toward cleansing and strengthening the blood and eliminative functions in the body, perhaps through using some of the supplementary herbs listed below. In the meantime, a tiny drop of Peppermint oil on the tongue can camouflage bad breath well. Also, Peppermint oil as a breath freshener is ideal after eating Garlic, especially if Garlic is not the aroma of choice for the situation at hand. If bad breath is due to a problem with gas in the stomach, use Peppermint according to the Digestion application.

ALSO SEE: *Digestion, Intestines*

ALTERNATIVE OR SUPPLEMENTARY SELF-HELP: *Chaparral, *Clove, Comfrey, Ginger, Yarrow*

DOSAGE: *1 small drop of Peppermint oil on the tongue or, if you need a digestive aid as well, put a couple of drops of the oil in 1/2 glass water and sip it. In this way it does two jobs at once.*

HEADACHE: Headaches are often from indigestion, congested liver, or poor circulation to the head (which is often a side-effect of tension). Taking Peppermint tea or oil internally can help break up congestion while soothing the nerves. Another way to use Peppermint in this situation is to rub a drop of the oil (more if a less concentrated oil is used) onto the temples, or forehead, or behind the ear, or at the big "dent" (greater occipital) in the base of the back of the head. If you know you are having difficulty with a congested digestive system, it can also be helpful to rub a few drops of Peppermint oil directly over the area (for instance over the liver or stomach), in addition to using Peppermint internally as described.

ALSO SEE: *Circulation, Digestion, Intestines, Nerves, Peppermint Bath, Stimulant*

ALTERNATIVE OR SUPPLEMENTARY SELF-HELP: **Cayenne, Comfrey, Ginger, People Paste (used internally), *Yarrow (especially Yarrow Tincture)*

DOSAGE: *General or as given*

HEARTBURN: See Digestion application.

HEART PALPITATION: Peppermint tea or oil gives mild yet steady relief for this situation. For stronger help you may want to use Cayenne (see that Chapter II).

Sometimes chronic difficulty with heart palpitations can be due to indigestion and gas difficulties. You may need to review the Digestion application in this and other chapters.

ALSO SEE: *Circulation, Digestion, Nerves, Stimulant*

ALTERNATIVE OR SUPPLEMENTARY SELF-HELP: **Cayenne, Clove, Comfrey, *Garlic, Ginger*

DOSAGE: *General*

INSOMNIA: See Nerves application.

INTESTINES: Because Peppermint is soothing to the nerves, stimulating to circulation, and somewhat antispasmodic, it can relieve cramping (griping) in the bowels, spastic colon, gas, and light cases of constipation or diarrhea. A Peppermint tea enema will often give immediate relief for sluggish intestines that are tending toward constipation, spastic colon, or griping colon and, on the other hand, it can soothe a nervous bowel and accompanying diarrhea.

Peppermint would *not* be used, however, in any case of badly irritated or bleeding bowels as it can be too stimulating in this circumstance. For these situations you would use the soothing and rehabilitating actions of a Comfrey or Slippery Elm enema and/or tea for powerful and immediate self-help.

ALSO SEE: *Digestion*

ALTERNATIVE OR SUPPLEMENTARY SELF-HELP: **Comfrey, Garlic, Ginger, People Paste, *Slippery Elm, Yarrow*

DOSAGE: *General; for a situation as severe as a very spastic colon, you would want to use 3 to 5 cups of Peppermint tea a day for 7 to 10 days.*

ITCHING: See Skin application.

LARYNGITIS: Peppermint oil has properties (see Personality Profile above) that can temporarily numb an inflamed pharynx or larynx. This is very useful for singers or speakers who are often bothered by this. The oil may also be used for any sore throat, since its good antiseptic qualities may attack the cause of soreness altogether.

ALSO SEE: *Antiseptic, Pain*

ALTERNATIVE OR SUPPLEMENTARY SELF-HELP: *Cayenne, *Clove, Garlic, Ginger, Onion (throat lozenges), Slippery Elm (throat lozenges)*

DOSAGE: *1 drop of Peppermint oil on the tongue, or 1 or more drops of the oil in a little water for a gargle (sometimes helpful to add a pinch of salt to the gargle).*

MASTITIS: This is characterized by an inflammation in the lymph and/or mammary glands in the breast. Since I most commonly come across this situation in nursing mothers, this is who I am predominantly talking about here. Occasionally a nursing mom will develop a soreness and/or a firm, stiff area in her breast that will quickly escalate to major pain, "hardness," and fever (heat) there. It is always best to initiate self-help measures at the first sign of soreness in a breast gland, yet even if it has gone beyond that, I have had success using a Peppermint poultice or fomentation (pack). See the detailed instructions for a poultice or fomentation in Chapter I, Lesson #2.

For a fomentation, make some strong Peppermint tea, soak a cotton cloth in it, and apply it (very warm) to the breast. Re-dip the cloth at 5 to 10 minute intervals and keep this up for 20 minutes or more. Often a hot water bottle on top of the Peppermint pack will help keep it warm enough. An alternative to the tea is to gently apply Peppermint massage oil (see recipe below) to the area, cover it with a clean cotton cloth, and then apply a hot water bottle over the cloth. In between cloth applications, or at the end of a 20 minute series of applications, massage the breast fairly vigorously in the direction the milk should flow, using Peppermint massage oil. (Recipe: 5 drops of the strongest type of Peppermint oil to one tablespoon of olive oil.)

This massage is vigorous and often very uncomfortable at first, especially if the breast is quite inflamed. The idea here is to get the lymph fluids and milk flowing as much as possible which greatly relieves the breast tenderness. Massage will help break up the breast congestion which is causing the inflammation. Be careful to wipe off any mint from the nipple before allowing a child to nurse.

Advise the mother to drink herb tea such as Comfrey, Yarrow, or Peppermint (these are OK for a baby to get through the milk), 2 to 4 cups in a day and, in addition, drink plenty of pure water, at least 2 quarts each day.

ALSO SEE: *None*

ALTERNATIVE OR SUPPLEMENTARY SELF-HELP: **Comfrey, Ginger (used as alternative herb in breast pack), Yarrow*

DOSAGE: *General and as given*

MENSTRUAL CRAMPS: Peppermint tea is a good herb to try for relief of menstrual cramps because of its relaxing qualities and its ability to stimulate circulation and thereby relieve certain types of congestion. Also I find that taking a supplement of calcium lactate regularly before and during menstruation often prevents or relaxes the cramping.

Another good method is to mix about 5 drops of strong Peppermint oil in one tablespoon of olive oil and massage the lower abdomen. All the ideas under the mastitis application can also be applied to the uterine area for menstrual cramping.

ALSO SEE: *Circulation, Mastitis, Nerves, Peppermint Bath, Stimulant, Spasms*

ALTERNATIVE OR SUPPLEMENTARY SELF-HELP: *Chaparral, Comfrey, *Ginger, *Yarrow*

DOSAGE: *General and as given*

MOTION SICKNESS: See Nausea application.

MORNING SICKNESS: See Nausea application.

MUSCLE SPASM: See Spasms application.

NAUSEA: Nausea comes from a variety of situations—ranging from the flu, to pregnancy, to emotionally charged situations like having to face your housemate with the news that you have permanently blackened, warped, and rendered useless her most expensive, and favorite, cooking pot.

Use Peppermint tea and/or Peppermint oil in any situation involving nausea. If there is some reason you cannot use Peppermint, a good alternative is Ginger root tea or powder (especially for morning sickness).

For dry heaves (I dislike those intensely), make a cup of Yarrow/Peppermint tea and take it in doses of 1 Tbsp. every 10 minutes or so. The heaves will usually calm down within 1 to 5 doses, but finish the cup of tea anyway just to "make sure"!

If nausea is chronic due to poor eating or drinking or drug-taking habits, please address the cause.

ALSO SEE: *Digestion, Nerves, Peppermint Bath, Spasms*

ALTERNATIVE OR SUPPLEMENTARY SELF-HELP: **Ginger, People Paste (used internally), Slippery Elm, *Yarrow*

DOSAGE: *General*

NERVES: Peppermint is soothing and relaxing to the nerves and has a mild sedative action for many people. Use it for insomnia, anxiety, and nervous tension. Generally I use Peppermint tea or infusion, as the oil may be too strong and stimulating, thereby negating its possible soothing effects.

Many students tell me that a cup of Peppermint tea in the evening is all it takes to help relax restlessness after a busy day.

ALSO SEE: *Headache, Pain, Peppermint Bath*

ALTERNATIVE OR SUPPLEMENTARY SELF-HELP: **Clove, *Garlic*

DOSAGE: *Tea is usually the best form and can be taken as needed.*

OVEREXPOSURE: Since I have lived most of my life in the southwestern U.S., the majority of my experiences with overexposure to the elements have involved getting too much sun. When I lived for a few years in New England, however, I found that the same herbal treatments applied for overexposure to cold.

Symptoms of overexposure may include one, or any combination of the following:

- complete physical weakness
- headache, especially accompanied by eye discomfort
- frostbite
- sunburn
- faintness
- body trembling
- extreme body temperature (either high or low)
- mental/emotional confusion

The most serious cases of overexposure, especially those involving unconsciousness, will require professional help. In cases of mild to average seriousness, there are many forms of self-help you can apply.

The first thing to do for immediate relief is to take a Peppermint bath (see Peppermint Bath application) of the appropriate temperature for the type of exposure problem. For heat prostration, use a lukewarm bath. For overexposure to cold, use lukewarm to warm bath water. The Peppermint bath temperature should always be comfortable to the person in it. Bathe for 20 minutes or longer as desired, adding more hot water as needed to keep the temperature comfortable.

While bathing, drink some Peppermint tea (room temperature or very warm), or substitute another herb tea made from one or more of the Ten Essentials. Ginger tea, for instance, is a stronger stimulant and works well for cold exposure, and Cayenne is always the thing for shock. For cold limbs before or after the bath, use a few drops of Peppermint oil for each tablespoon of plain oil (olive oil is good) and rub this on the limbs to help normalize circulation.

TASOLE: I once lived in a desert area with a group of friends who were often doing building projects. Pete, a new arrival to our group, decided one day to shave his head. Oiling up his shiny pate, he then went to work on the roof, only to become ill a short while later from heat prostration. His head had begun to get sunburned, not to mention the rest of his light skin, as he had worn no shirt or head covering. By the time he came to me for help, his head was throbbing, he was weak and nauseous, and of course his sunburned head and skin were extremely uncomfortable. I recommended a Peppermint bath right away, but could tell by his expression that he did not think a Peppermint bath sounded strong enough for relief of his present suffering. I also suggested drinking cool Peppermint tea (but not ice-cold tea) during and after the bath. I further suggested that he keep completely covered up when working outside, at least until he became used to the intense desert sun.

Later that same evening Pete returned, beaming and saying he felt great, except for his still tender skin. He had followed my suggestions and was surprised at how quickly he began to recover once he finally got into the Peppermint bath and drank some of the tea.

By the next day he was back at work, well-covered with clothing and sunscreen, and looking much like a walking tomato with hairy legs. But hey, we got our building finished!

ALSO SEE: *Circulation, Headache, Pain, Peppermint Bath*

ALTERNATIVE OR SUPPLEMENTARY SELF-HELP: **Cayenne, Clove, Comfrey, Garlic, *Ginger, Yarrow*

DOSAGE: *General and as given*

PAIN: Peppermint oil, used externally, will often have a temporary numbing effect which is convenient for easing the pain of small bumps and lumps, for teething, or for laryngitis. Peppermint oil is milder in this regard than Clove oil, which is a very potent numbing agent and the one that I recommend for the tougher jobs.

ALSO SEE: *Laryngitis, Teething, Toothache*

ALTERNATIVE OR SUPPLEMENTARY SELF-HELP: **Clove*

DOSAGE: *Rub Peppermint oil onto an affected part or, if oil is too strong by itself (i.e., sometimes for teething), dilute the Peppermint oil by putting 1 to 5 drops in a spoonful of plain oil such as olive oil, and rub this dilution on the affected part.*

PEPPERMINT BATH: After a long day's work, there is nothing like a Peppermint bath to cleanse and strengthen your personal magnetic field. Make Peppermint a part of your daily routine, especially if you work with computers or must deal directly with large numbers of people every day. An herbal bath will enhance your circulation, help lessen the effects of overexposure to the elements (whether from a job environment or from the sun), soothe your nerves and emotions, and otherwise act as a nice rejuvenator at the end of a day.

ALSO SEE: *Facial, Hair, Nerves, Overexposure, Perspiration Therapy, Skin*

ALTERNATIVE OR SUPPLEMENTARY SELF-HELP: **Ginger, *Yarrow*

DOSAGE: *Make 2 quarts or more of very strong (at least triple strength) tea, strain out the herbs and add the liquid to the bath. Or put about 4 oz. of the herb in cheesecloth and immerse it directly in the bath water. Either way you will be sitting in a tub of Peppermint tea and it feels great! Peppermint oil can work well yet it can be somewhat expensive for an entire bath. Depending on what strength of Peppermint oil you have, try 1 tsp. in the tub to start with and see how it feels.*

PERSPIRATION THERAPY: It is through perspiration that the body releases poisons via the lymph glands and the skin during any illness. Use a Peppermint bath and drink Peppermint, Ginger or Yarrow tea while in the bath to promote perspiration. For a much stronger action in Perspiration Therapy, use a Ginger bath. Peppermint is balancing to the circulation as it helps the body sweat out toxins.

ALSO SEE: *Circulation, Fever, Peppermint Bath*

ALTERNATIVE OR SUPPLEMENTARY SELF-HELP: *Cayenne, Clove, *Ginger, *Yarrow*

DOSAGE: *General*

RELAXANT/SOOTHING: See Nerves application.

SEDATIVE: See Nerves application.

SINUS: Use Peppermint oil straight, or mix several drops of it in a spoonful of plain oil, such as olive oil, to rub over the sinus areas. Even just rubbing a drop near the opening of the nostrils, so the oil fumes can be inhaled, is quite helpful. For infants and toddlers, I put the oil on a cloth and lay it by the child's head while he/she is sleeping. I call this the "sinus-opening aroma cloth" method. Peppermint tea inhaled into the nostrils (one nostril at a time, please) is a nice rinse for the nose and stimulating to the sinuses especially after a day of working in a dusty, fumey, sawdust-filled, or otherwise polluted environment. (See Nasal Rinse in Chapter I, Lesson #2.) The tea is also quite useful for sinus congestion and mild sinus irritations.

ALSO SEE: *Colds and Flu, Circulation, Congestion, Headache*

ALTERNATIVE OR SUPPLEMENTARY SELF-HELP: **Cayenne, Comfrey, Garlic, *Ginger, *Onion, Yarrow*

DOSAGE: *General*

SKIN: Peppermint oil and Peppermint tea both help stimulate circulation to surface skin tissues. Used as a bath it is a good skin tonic. Put a few drops of Peppermint oil in massage or skin oil to help tone the skin. Since the oil has antiseptic properties, it can be used whenever this property is called for.

Peppermint tea makes a soothing bath or rinse for itchy skin rashes.

ALSO SEE: *Circulation, Facial, Peppermint Bath, Perspiration Therapy*

ALTERNATIVE OR SUPPLEMENTARY SELF-HELP: **Comfrey, Ginger, *People Paste, Slippery Elm*

DOSAGE: *General*

SPASMS: Peppermint tea or infusion has gentle antispasmodic qualities. Vomiting, menstrual and leg cramps, headache, etc., all respond well to Peppermint treatment. The oil is especially potent for spasms, used externally. You may want to use the tea or infusion internally and the oil externally at the same time.

ALSO SEE: *Bath, Menstrual Cramps, Nausea, Pain*

ALTERNATIVE OR SUPPLEMENTARY SELF-HELP: **Clove, Comfrey, *Garlic, Ginger*

DOSAGE: *General*

STIMULANT: In the Personality Profile I described the "Peppermint paradox"—that this herb is stimulating to the circulation and yet, at the same time, soothing to the nerves. Peppermint oil used alone is more stimulating. A cup of Peppermint tea is more relaxing. The amount of Peppermint oil naturally occurring in a cup of tea is enough stimulant for most circumstances, yet it's nice to have the stronger action of the concentrated Peppermint oil, used alone, when that is needed.

A stimulant may be called for in situations of sluggish digestion, headache, sinus congestion, poor circulation, heartburn, muscle spasm, etc.

ALSO SEE: *Circulation, Congestion, Digestion, Headache, Menstrual Cramps, Overexposure, Sinus, Skin*

ALTERNATIVE OR SUPPLEMENTARY SELF-HELP: **Cayenne, Chaparral, Garlic, *Ginger, Yarrow*

DOSAGE: *General*

SUNSTROKE/HEAT PROSTRATION: See Overexposure application.

TEETHING: Rub 1 drop of Peppermint oil, diluted with 10 drops of olive oil if the Peppermint oil is of the very strong variety, straight onto the painful gums for a temporary numbing action. Clove oil is a much stronger numbing agent and is a good alternative, especially for those who are sensitive to the menthol action of Peppermint. It often depends on what you have on hand when the teething discomfort sets in. Also check out the Homeopathic remedies for teething at your local health food store. They often work with amazing speed and efficiency.

ALSO SEE: *None*

ALTERNATIVE OR SUPPLEMENTARY SELF-HELP: **Clove*

DOSAGE: *As given*

THROAT: See Laryngitis application.

TOOTHACHE: Rub Peppermint oil directly onto the gum. Depending on the strength of the oil that you have and the age of the person needing help, you may need to dilute the Peppermint oil in a little plain oil such as olive oil (perhaps a 1:10 dilution as for teething). For many children or extra-sensitive individuals the dilution will be necessary, yet for the hardy types, using the oil straight will be fine.

Clove oil is much stronger for this application and you may want to use this as an alternative if you have it on hand or mix Peppermint and Clove oils together for an "in-between" strength.

ALSO SEE: *Pain, Teething*

ALTERNATIVE OR SUPPLEMENTARY SELF-HELP: **Clove, Garlic, People Paste*

DOSAGE: *As given*

SLIPPERY ELM

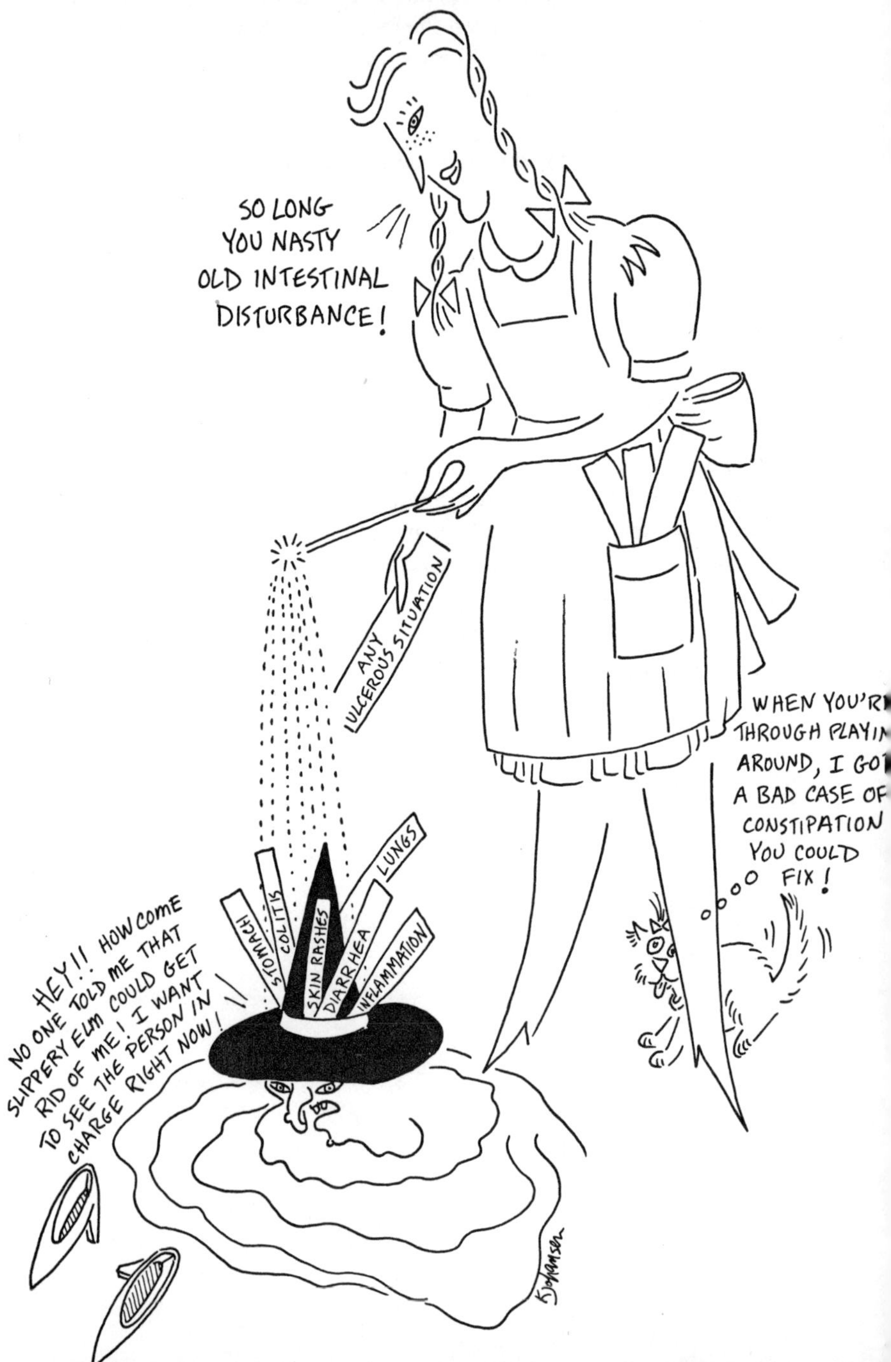

CHAPTER X

SLIPPERY ELM

Ulmus fulva

The Slippery Elm Slider mixed with juice just last week,
For bowels too loose, or colitis relief.
He can soothe, be nutritional, build strength, what a guy!
Skin troubles? Inflammation? He'll spit in their eye!

PERSONALITY PROFILE—Slippery Elm

Have you ever been through a period where the stress level is so high that your intestines give up trying to make any sense of things and go to one extreme or the other—becoming too loose or way too tight? Taking a heaping teaspoon of Slippery Elm powder every two to five hours can soothe the worst digestive inflammation or nervous diarrhea. Slippery Elm can re-establish harmony in inflamed intestines within the day, and I have personally seen it do even more marvelous and seemingly miraculous things than that. These are some of the reasons, among many others, that I have included Slippery Elm among my Ten Essentials. And besides, it tastes good too. Most people enjoy the taste, finding it somewhat nutty.

TASOLE: Hilary, a fifteen-year-old girl, came to see me on the advice of her mother. The girl had battled such severe intestinal difficulties since birth that between malformations of the colon and chronic intestinal inflammations, she had finally ended up having surgery in which several inches of her colon were removed. Her doctors had explained to her that she should never expect to have normal bowel movements again and indeed she dealt with fairly constant diarrhea. As you can imagine, this was a big drawback to her social life and she felt extremely discouraged in having to look forward to a lifetime of embarrassment.

I had used Slippery Elm before in cases involving rejuvenation after digestive surgery—including intestinal surgery for colitis and hemorrhoids. But I had never encountered these problems in anyone so young.

I suggested to Hilary that she start using Slippery Elm powder, drinking 1 tsp. in juice or tea, four or five times a day. I suggested using the powder without capsules whenever possible since capsules cause some people digestive trouble, which slows down the body's use of the herb. As often happens, Hilary thought my idea was too simple to have any real effect on her overwhelming and long-term difficulty, yet she said she "would probably try it". Her hopelessness affected me too. It seemed unrealistic to hope for much relief in her case even though my other similar stories had happy endings.

One month later I received a call from Hilary's mother to say that her daughter had begun at first, to tentatively try the herb in small amounts each day. When she discovered that the taste of Slippery Elm was not going to be an additional torture, she started the suggested dosage. Within three days of doing that, she had a "normal" bowel movement of soft yet "formed" consistency for the first time in many years. (She literally could not remember any bowel movement experience that was unstressful.) The results had continued. At the time of the call, Hilary had often been having unstressful bowel movements of average consistency for three weeks. Several months later I learned that the progress was still excellent. Hilary was able to decrease the dosage to three or less times a day except during times of extreme "teenage stress" where she needed more to balance things out.

The bottom-line is that her self-confidence soared and her social life began to shine.

After my experience with Hilary I had other opportunities over the years to assist people recovering from similar surgeries. The Slippery Elm always had some, and often dramatic, effect. After a while I sometimes suggested mixing 1 part Comfrey root powder with 2 or 3 parts Slippery Elm to speed new tissue growth and enhance the anti-inflammatory action. This is a wonderful partnership of herbs, although not as tasty as the plain Slippery Elm.

Slippery Elm is a mucilaginous herb with many properties similar to Comfrey root yet enough differences that I include it with no worry about repeating herbal actions unnecessarily. Mucilaginous means that a plant contains significant amounts of mucilage, a slippery, sticky and soothing substance, often of high nutritional value (as is the case with Slippery Elm) that coats, protects, and rejuvenates an area from infection, inflammation and other irritants. At the same time it acts as a further deterrent to many toxic substances through its ability to absorb and help them pass harmlessly out of the body. This mucilaginous property is especially useful in any case of inflammation or congestion, such as inflamed mucous membranes of the lungs, digestive tract, or urinary tract including kidneys, and in any ulcerous situation either internal or external. Mucilage is soothing to burns, colitis, lungs, stomach, and skin rashes of all sorts. It helps counter-balance either diarrhea or constipation. Slippery Elm soothes the inflammations associated with diarrhea and protects the intestinal linings from further inflammation, and the fiber it provides helps soften fecal matter and move it easily out of the body.

Whenever you are dealing with what I call an "itis" situation, the mucilaginous and nutritional action of Slippery Elm comes more into play. "Itis" conditions include: arthritis, tendonitis, prostatitis, bronchitis, colitis, conjunctivitis, etc. The "itis" means that the area or organ is inflamed and irritated. The mucilaginous and anti-inflammatory attributes of Slippery Elm definitely come into play here.

Mucilage does not break down or disappear quickly when put to use, which means that you can usually get continuous results from one dosage to the next. Take 1 tsp. Slippery Elm powder with a glass of water or juice (lukewarm liquid makes it work fastest), and it will stir up and start activating the mucilage immediately. This "slippery help" will extend itself to the bowels so that subsequent bowel movements show effects of the mucilaginous quality of Slippery Elm.

There is one note of caution about this mucilaginous action of Slippery Elm. If you find it necessary to use this herb daily for a period of three weeks or more, it would be wise to take a day off from its use once a week. This herb does its job so well that a prolonged use of 2 tsp. or more per day of the plain root powder (herbal mixtures which include

Slippery Elm are exempt) could, in especially sluggish systems, overcoat the digestive tract and temporarily lessen assimilation of some nutrients. If it is helping you, and you want to keep using it for longer periods, simply take a day off once a week or mix it with another herb such as Ginger. In cases of severe colitis or intestinal surgery (as in the TASOLE above), however, the benefits of using it may far outweigh the small benefits of being without it for a day, and in these cases you may continue as usual without a "day-off" break.

I mentioned that Ginger is a good herb to mix with Slippery Elm to insure against an unusual overcoating of the intestines. In fact, Ginger is a good addition anytime because it significantly increases the focus and action of Slippery Elm in every way. I would mix 1/4 to 1/2 part Ginger for each one part Slippery Elm. Most often the powdered form works best for these mixtures, yet chunks of each herb, simmered together, make a potent tea or decoction.

Another word associated with Slippery Elm is "demulcent," which describes the soothing, softening, buffering and (for this herb) poison-drawing qualities that Slippery Elm brings to any herbal formulation. It is often mixed with herbs that otherwise have potent volatile oils or attributes that may act harshly in the system. These include Chaparral, Cloves, Peppermint, Garlic and Ginger. Slippery Elm buffers these strong herbs, binds them together and adds the healing qualities unique to itself.

You may remember that I called Cayenne and Ginger "carrier herbs." Their special function is to help carry the herbal effects of a formula deeply into the body tissues and organs. Slippery Elm, then, could be called a "buffer/binder" herb. By analogy, if we were speaking of a group of people, Slippery Elm would be the diplomat, interpreting even the harshest statements in a tactful and usable fashion so the most aggressive elements in the group could work smoothly together without irritating each other or innocent bystanders.

Slippery Elm also has strong nutritional value (see Nutrition application) and can be used as an addition to oatmeal to increase its protein and give a pudding-like consistency to the cereal while lending its light nutty flavor. When used for making cough syrup, cough lozenges or sore-throat lozenges it is so soothing and tasty that children and other finicky eaters usually like using them. (See Cough application.)

Slippery Elm plays an essential role in People Paste—my all-purpose formula for internal and external use. Consult the People Paste Appendix.

APPLICATIONS AND ATTRIBUTES - SLIPPERY ELM

(Quick Reference List)

ABSCESS
ADHESIVE AGENT
ANTACID
APPENDICITIS
ASTRINGENT
ATHLETE'S FOOT
BLEEDING
BOILS/PIMPLES
BRONCHITIS
BURNS
COLDS AND FLU
COLITIS
CONSTIPATION
COUGH SYRUP
CYSTS
DIARRHEA/DYSENTERY
DIGESTIVE TRACT
DISC (Slipped)
EYES
GALL BLADDER
GASTRITIS
GOUT
HEMORRHOIDS
INFLAMMATION
INTESTINES
LUNGS
MUCILAGINOUS
MUCOUS CONGESTION
NAUSEA
NUTRITION
POISON OAK/IVY
REJUVENATION
RHEUMATISM
SINUS
SKIN
SLIPPED DISC
SOOTHING
SORES
STOMACH
SURGERY
THROAT
TONIC
TONSILLITIS
ULCERS
URINARY TRACT
VAGINITIS
WOUNDS

FORM:

Use dried inner bark, either in powder, or chopped/shredded into small bits for gentle simmering.

APPLICATION METHODS:

Internally: Use powder (plain, in capsules, or mixed in liquid such as juice), tea, decoction, or tincture (least favored form for this herb). **Externally:** Use the powder in poultices, or the decoction as a soothing wash.

AVAILABILITY:

Herb or health food store, mail order. (See Buyers Guide, Appendix D.)

HINTS/CAUTIONS:

For prolonged use (more than three weeks) you may need to take a day off each week from using Slippery Elm, for the reasons described in the Personality Profile. Otherwise I know of no harmful side effects for anyone of any age even if you use it frequently to make special oatmeal for your children (see Nutrition application).

GENERAL DOSAGE: INTERNAL USE

⋆PLEASE NOTE: *Although I emphasize using Slippery Elm powder in water or juice, there are many forms of herbal preparations which are quite effective such as Tea, Capsules, Children's Ideas, Honeyballs, Decoction, etc. See those headings and Dosage Equivalents in Chapter I, Lesson #2.*

Infants to 3 years: Use Slippery Elm tea, possibly sweetened with light unsulphured molasses, as often as needed. Prior to "chewing age" the tea can be fed by dropper or spoon.

If the child is of "chewing age", honeyballs (see Chapter I, Lesson #2), syrups, or lozenges (as described in the Cough and Throat applications below) can be used freely. Young children should take smaller amounts more frequently. For example, an ounce of tea, or 1/4 tsp. of the powder in a "honeyball," might be taken at random intervals during the day until one cup of tea is consumed or 2 tsp. powdered Slippery Elm have been eaten. The powder can be cooked with a little oatmeal or other hot cereal and sweetened in the child's favorite way as often as desired.

Children 4 years to 10 years: Slippery Elm, in any form, can be used as desired. A preferred way to take Slippery Elm is to mix 1/2 to 1 tsp. of the powder with juice or water, or make it into a "honeyball." The powder mixes readily in slightly warmed liquid and I often blend it so as to speed preparation. This herb can be readily cooked with hot cereals such as oatmeal (start with 1 tsp. per cup of cereal and increase according to taste) and flavored according to the child's preference. When the *Most Direct Action* is called for, however, I prefer a straight powder in juice, syrup, lozenge, or honeyball. Capsules are OK for those who can swallow and digest them easily, but this is often "iffy" when digestive distress is already the problem.

Children 11 years to Adults: Slippery Elm, in any form, can be used as desired. A preferred way to take Slippery Elm is to mix one full teaspoon of the powder with one cup of juice or water. The powder mixes readily in slightly warmed liquid and I often blend it so as to speed preparation. This herb can be readily cooked with hot cereals such as oatmeal (start with 1 tsp. per cup of cereal and increase according to taste) and flavored according to the user's taste. When the *Most Direct Action* is called for, however, I prefer the straight powder with juice or water, tea/decoction, syrup or lozenge (see Cough and Throat applications), or Honey-ball (see Chapter I, Lesson 2). Capsules are OK for those who can swallow and digest them easily, but this is often "iffy" when digestive distress is already the problem.

Pets and Other Creatures: I have never used Slippery Elm internally on pets but I see no reason not to. It would be especially good to try for elderly pets with weak constitutions or digestive difficulties.

GENERAL DOSAGE: EXTERNAL USE

Same For All Humans And Other Creatures

Be sure to review the People Paste Appendix (Appendix A) which carefully describes a special use for Slippery Elm. People Paste is a must-always-have-on-hand for every herbal first-aid kit.

In addition to People Paste for all external uses, here are a few other guidelines:

Slippery Elm powder, moistened into a paste, is applied as a poultice to external wounds and rashes for its soothing, anti-inflammatory, astringent (drawing), and mucilaginous (protective) qualities. Often an equal part of an antiseptic herb such as Chaparral, Garlic, Clove, Comfrey or Yarrow is mixed with the Slippery Elm powder when antiseptic action is needed. Common moistening agents include raw honey, aloe vera gel, unsulphured molasses, glycerin, olive oil (not on a fresh wound), and water. Dry powders can be applied to bleeding or oozing wounds. See details of poultice-making in Chapter I, Lesson #2.

Slippery Elm decoction is used to wash or soak skin inflammations and irritations of all types.

Slippery Elm enemas are used for inflammations or congestion in the colon such as might be found with diarrhea, colitis, or constipation. You will need to make a diluted and well-strained decoction for this purpose as the thick mucilage in the herb can sometimes plug up the enema apparatus. See enema instructions in Chapter I, Lesson #2.

APPLICATIONS AND ATTRIBUTES - SLIPPERY ELM

ABSCESS: Slippery Elm soothes the troubled area while it helps draw poisons out of the abscess with its astringent action. When additional potency is needed, mix Slippery Elm with one or more antibiotic or antiseptic herbs such as Garlic, Chaparral, Clove, Comfrey, or Yarrow powders. See brief instructions for poulticing in General Dosage for External Use above. See detailed poultice instructions in Chapter I, Lesson #2.

For internal support in dealing with any abscess, take antibiotic or antiseptic herbs such as Chaparral, Comfrey, or Garlic (see Chapters III, V, and VI). Mix one or two of these powdered herbs with 1/2 part Slippery Elm powder and take with juice, or put the herbs in capsules, honeyballs, etc. Take 1 tsp. of the mixture (for adults) three to six times a day. I recommend working both internally and externally at the same time for any infection, including abscesses.

ALSO SEE: *Adhesive Agent, Mucilaginous, Skin, Wounds*

ALTERNATIVE OR SUPPLEMENTARY SELF-HELP: **Chaparral, Clove, *Comfrey, *Garlic, *People Paste, Yarrow*

DOSAGE: *General*

ADHESIVE AGENT: Think of Slippery Elm as a healing "herbal glue." Slippery Elm is sticky because of its mucilaginous action, and this quality actually helps bind torn tissues together. It is a useful base for a huge variety of other preparations, from poultices of one or more herbs to throat lozenges.

ALSO SEE: *Abscess, Cough Syrup, Mucilaginous, Skin, Throat, Wounds*

ALTERNATIVE OR SUPPLEMENTARY SELF-HELP: **Comfrey*

DOSAGE: *General*

ANTACID: When you are having heartburn, acid stomach, or irritated ulcers (especially from something you just ate), reach for the Slippery Elm instead of trying to coat the stomach with milk or the chemical antacids on the market. Slippery Elm enhances the well-being of the tissues involved, without the build-up of the toxic substances that I have observed with the frequent use of milk products or synthetic stomach antacids.

Slippery Elm works fast for most people. You could make yourself some honeyball or dry (pill type) "stomach pills" (see Honeyball and Pills in Chapter I, Lesson #2) to carry with you to take whenever an acid problem arises. If you'd rather not fuss with making anything, simply take 1 tsp. of the dry Slippery Elm powder directly in the mouth with a cup of juice or water.

Slippery Elm's demulcent (soothing) and mucilaginous actions are brought into play immediately if you activate them before swallowing by blending or stirring the Slippery Elm into one cup of lukewarm (or room temperature) juice or water. Then when the herb hits your stomach it is ready to start to work. All these ideas are fast-acting, so choose the one that is most convenient for you.

ALSO SEE: *Mucilaginous, Ulcers*

ALTERNATIVE OR SUPPLEMENTARY SELF-HELP: *Clove, *Comfrey, Peppermint (oil), Yarrow*

DOSAGE: *General*

APPENDICITIS: Your appendix is a tiny "appendage" of tissue just off the large intestine, right where the large intestine and small intestine come together, usually within the lower right side of the abdomen.

I am speaking here of mild appendicitis, something that you feel can be handled at home. I am not speaking of a severely painful, life-threatening appendicitis attack for which you may need surgery. Now that this is clear, here is some self-help that you may apply:

Fast on water for one day so as not to add any more stress on the intestines and so as to enhance the body's ability to eliminate toxins. Drink at least two quarts of water or herb tea during the day. Take a gentle Slippery Elm enema to cleanse the colon, helping to relieve it of pressure and irritating toxic waste.

Choose one of the strongest antibiotic herbs, such as Garlic or Chaparral; mix with equal parts Comfrey root or Slippery Elm, and 1/4 part Ginger (all herbs in powder form). Take 1 tsp. of this mixture in juice, tea, water, or capsules each two to three hours (less often for less severe inflammation/infection). Drink Slippery Elm or Comfrey leaf tea, about 4 cups each day, especially the day of the water fast. Continue until the inflammation (pain) subsides, and then lessen the herbal intake slowly down to nothing over a period of three to five additional days. The Slippery Elm enema could be repeated after a day or two if it was helpful. Be sure to review the enema instructions in Chapter I, Lesson #2.

ALSO SEE: *Mucilaginous, Nutrition*

ALTERNATIVE OR SUPPLEMENTARY SELF-HELP: *Chaparral, *Comfrey, *Garlic, Yarrow*

DOSAGE: *General or as given*

ASTRINGENT: Slippery Elm firms and tones tissues and draws out poisons (astringent actions) while it soothes. It promotes healthy tissue growth with its potent nutrition. Whenever you experience a flaccid "out-of-tone" feeling or action in an organ, try taking Slippery Elm for its astringent purpose. Perhaps you are trying to re-firm and tone digestive organs as part of an overall program of rejuvenation from habits of chronic overeating and eating of poor foods. (See Rejuvenation application.) Since the digestive organs often get unnaturally stretched, using an astringent herb in conjunction with an overall program of self-help (blood-cleansing, reorienting eating habits, etc.) is quite useful. Review the other astringent herbs mentioned below as alternatives. They can supplement Slippery Elm when more astringency is needed.

ALSO SEE: *Mucilaginous, Nutrition*

ALTERNATIVE OR SUPPLEMENTARY SELF-HELP: *Chaparral, Clove, *Comfrey, Onion, *Peppermint, *Yarrow*

DOSAGE: *General. For this application Slippery Elm is often mixed with other herbs.*

ATHLETE'S FOOT: Follow instructions in the General Dosage for External Use, above, for preparing a paste of Slippery Elm to apply to outbreaks of athlete's foot. For stubborn cases add a fungicide herb such as Garlic or Chaparral to the paste; I suggest taking the mixture internally as well (in tea, juice, honeyball, etc.).

For persistent cases of athlete's foot, use the 21-Day Chaparral Cleanse described under the Blood-Purifier application in the Chaparral chapter (Chapter III). Also see the Athlete's Foot application in that chapter.

ALSO SEE: *Skin*

ALTERNATIVE OR SUPPLEMENTARY SELF-HELP: **Chaparral, *Garlic, *People Paste, Yarrow*

DOSAGE: *General*

BLEEDING: Following bouts of internal bleeding anywhere in the digestive tract, it is wise to use Slippery Elm and continue its use at least three times a day for several days. This continued use protects the tender digestive areas where the bleeding originated and promotes healthy tissue growth while lending strong nutritional support.

ALSO SEE: *Mucilaginous, Nutrition, Skin, Ulcers, Wounds*

ALTERNATIVE OR SUPPLEMENTARY SELF-HELP: **Cayenne, *Comfrey*

DOSAGE: *General*

BOILS/PIMPLES: See Abscess application.

BRONCHITIS: See Cough Syrup, Lungs, Mucilaginous, and Throat applications.

BURNS: See Skin application.

COLDS AND FLU: For severe bouts of a cold or flu, use an antibiotic or antiseptic herb such as Chaparral, Garlic, or Yarrow, in addition to using Slippery Elm for its anti-inflammatory, soothing and mucus-arresting qualities.

For mild colds or mild digestive types of flu, Slippery Elm may be all you need. Eating lightly is always a good idea during these symptoms of toxic overload, so a good way to use the Slippery Elm is to blend the powder in juice. It will fill and soothe you while lessening hunger pangs. Drink at least two quarts of water or herbal tea, choosing some of your favorites from among the Ten Essentials. Comfrey/Peppermint tea would be excellent at such times.

ALSO SEE: *Cough Syrup, Diarrhea, Digestive Tract, Lungs, Mucilaginous, Sinus, Throat*

ALTERNATIVE OR SUPPLEMENTARY SELF-HELP: **Chaparral, *Comfrey, *Garlic, Ginger (especially Ginger Bath), Peppermint, *Yarrow*

DOSAGE: *General*

COLITIS: See Intestines and Mucilaginous applications.

CONSTIPATION: See Intestines and Mucilaginous applications.

COUGH SYRUP: Slippery Elm makes great cough syrup used either alone or as a base for additional herbs. Since it helps to collect and expel mucus, acts against inflammation, and serves to soothe and nourish, Slippery Elm really shines as a cough syrup. Here are a few recipes which can be cooked up when needed and/or stored fairly well in the refrigerator for a few weeks. After a few weeks, to insure potency, it is best to start with a fresh batch when another need arises. An older syrup often still tastes OK and usually wouldn't hurt, however.

COUGH SYRUPS

Recipe #1: In a saucepan, mix 1/4 cup (4 Tbsp.) Slippery Elm powder or Slippery Elm small chunks with 1 cup raw honey or light unsulphured molasses. Simmer and stir gently for 20 minutes. That's it! If you want it thinner, feel free to add a little water. If you started with powder it will be a thicker brew as you do not (cannot) strain it out. If you started with the herbal chunks, you will get a juicier brew as the chunks are strained out after simmering. Some people really like having the herb powder left in for extra potency, while others don't like the texture and so prefer to strain the herb out. It's your choice. This recipe is meant as a basic starting place. I encourage you to experiment freely with proportions to suit your needs.

Recipe #2: Use basic Recipe #1 but substitute an additional herb such as chopped raw Onion (yummy), Comfrey, Ginger, Clove or another herb of your choosing for *part* of the Slippery Elm. If you are flexible about the flavor, you can really have fun experimenting with your mixtures.

Recipe #3: To any finished syrup add a few drops of an essential oil to supplement healing action and taste. Peppermint oil is refreshing when added to Recipe #1. Clove oil would be a fine choice for its antiseptic and pain-numbing qualities.

COUGH LOZENGES

If you were to accidently cook a syrup for too long at too high a heat and cool your "mistake," you would probably end up with a hard herbal candy (lozenge) which would be impossible to remove from the pot!

If you want to make throat (or cough) lozenges on purpose, first cook the honey or molasses to the "hard-crack" stage on a candy thermometer. Then add your herbs for about 10 minutes of simmering or steeping. It won't matter if the honey cools off somewhat when the herbs are added if it was already at the "hard-crack" stage of heat. The reason you add the herbs second is that it takes honey or molasses perhaps half an hour or more to get hot enough, and this might overcook the herbs.

Spread this hot mixture (or place in small blobs) onto a buttered cookie sheet to cool. When the mixture is partially cool it will be easy to score it with lines to facilitate breaking it up later. These tasty, broken bits are your new cough drops!

ALSO SEE: *Lungs, Mucilaginous, Throat*

ALTERNATIVE OR SUPPLEMENTARY SELF-HELP: *Clove (herb or oil), *Comfrey, Garlic (add after cooking), *Ginger, *Onion, Peppermint oil*

DOSAGE: *For children up to about six years, most syrups should be taken 1 tsp. at a time every two hours or as needed. For older children or adults, up to 1 Tbsp. per dose is not uncommon. Take as needed.*

CYSTS: Mix Slippery Elm powder with equal parts of Chaparral and/or Comfrey and/or Garlic powder. Moisten enough of the powdered mixture to make a poultice to cover the cyst about 1/3 inch thick with the paste. Leave the poultice on as much as possible, changing it two to four times a day. There is a good chance this will shrink or remove an ordinary cyst within a week.

I highly recommend also taking the 21-Day Chaparral Cleanse as described in the Blood-Purifier application in the Chaparral chapter (Chapter III).

ALSO SEE: *Abscess*

ALTERNATIVE OR SUPPLEMENTARY SELF-HELP: **Chaparral, *Comfrey, *Garlic, People Paste*

DOSAGE: *As given*

DIARRHEA/DYSENTERY: Some of the causes of common diarrhea are nervous anxiety, poor eating habits, poor food combinations, and certain types of food poisoning. Dysentery is an actual digestive infection and can also be from an infestation of a parasite, usually an amoeba (called amoebic dysentery). Dysentery is such a severe diarrhea that there is often bleeding from the colon; bleeding can also occur in the more common forms of diarrhea.

For common diarrhea, even if it includes some intestinal bleeding, Slippery Elm is the first herb to think of. Mix or blend 1 rounded tsp. of the powdered herb in 6 oz. juice or water (lukewarm temperature is best yet not crucial), and drink this as needed. I have seen one dose stop mild diarrhea. In more severe cases, students of mine have taken a dose after each diarrhea bowel movement until the condition finally slowed and then stopped. It is always a good idea to continue with two or three more doses, after the diarrhea seems finished, to prolong the soothing and protective action of the Slippery Elm and help prevent another flare-up of the diarrhea.

For diarrhea that is in the dysentery category, you may want to add an additional powdered herb to the Slippery Elm and then proceed as above. Parasite/antibiotic herbs such as Chaparral and Garlic are useful here. Comfrey root would assist in stopping any bleeding, and Ginger would bind and carry your formula potently to where it is needed.

An enema using Slippery Elm (or Comfrey, or Yarrow) tea usually speeds recovery from this intestinal distress. Diarrhea of any type or severity generally robs the intestines of friendly digestive bacteria and increases inflammation of the intestines for as long as the situation lasts. In addition, lymphatic fluids carrying their load of body toxins drain into the colon in their work to help the body eliminate waste. Using a

Slippery Elm enema immediately puts a soothing and protective coating over the inner linings of the colon. These linings are constantly being irritated by the harsh diarrhea fluids which prolongs the condition. The Slippery Elm enema quickly rinses out the accumulating lymph fluids, helps stop bleeding, and speeds establishment of an environment where the healthy bacteria can regroup. In the more serious case of amoebic dysentery, you should use a Garlic enema (see Garlic chapter, Chapter VI) to kill the amoebas. Otherwise, however, Slippery Elm is a good enema choice for diarrhea.

Let me re-emphasize that common diarrhea from anxiety or poor food habits usually responds quickly to a dose or two of Slippery Elm powder taken internally. Generally, an enema would not be necessary here.

TASOLE: My friend Jane was going through a particularly stressful time and her nervous system frequently got into such a state that everything "let loose", so to speak, resulting in severe diarrhea. Her psychiatrist would regularly prescribe drugs to calm her nerves, and to sedate her perception of her emotions. Quickly, however, the drugs lost their strength and at the same time themselves added digestive stress to her system.

Jane was leaving the country on business and was worried about how to handle the bouts of diarrhea from that increased stress. (I had long since given up suggesting a change of life-style.) It was obvious to me that we needed to find some symptomatic relief that would not create long-term deterioration in her health, while she addressed the deeper emotional issues.

Since her prescription drugs were optional, I suggested she start using an herbal formula to strengthen and balance the nervous system. For immediate, symptomatic relief, I recommended 1 rounded tsp. Slippery Elm powder mixed or blended in 6 ounces of juice or water after each bowel movement, or at least four times a day. Jane, however, was embarrassed to be seen taking powdered herbs in juice at her business meetings so we settled on using the herb in capsules as a discreet alternative. I stressed that this alternative was not as potent or fast in its result.

When she returned two months later she was excited to report that the Slippery Elm worked. She began to have entire nights of sleep uninterrupted by intestinal difficulties and trips to the bathroom. Jane confessed with delight that she even made the effort to take the herbs without the capsules several times during the day, and her condition improved to the point where the diarrhea was nonexistent. She continued to use Slippery Elm twice a day for prevention. Not only was her anxiety about personal embarrassment greatly relieved, but she was also experiencing a dwindling need for calming drugs as the herbs she was taking for her nerves continued their strengthening effect.

As Jane came to terms with her emotional life through therapy, she made definite steps toward a career change. Eventually she stopped all prescription drugs and was only using the Slippery Elm on the random occasion of digestive distress.

ALSO SEE: *Digestive Tract, Intestines, Mucilaginous*

ALTERNATIVE OR SUPPLEMENTARY SELF-HELP: **Comfrey, Garlic (for amoebic dysentery), People Paste (used orally)*

DOSAGE: *General or as given*

DIGESTIVE TRACT: Use Slippery Elm to soothe any irritation in the digestive tract, promote protection and healing of ulcerated tissues, relieve gas (gastritis), soothe nausea, and help calm cramping. With upheavals in the digestive tract it is common to have trouble assimilating nutrients from food that is eaten. Slippery Elm provides easy-to-assimilate nutrition and what I call "prize-winning-fiber," both of which help rejuvenate while giving symptomatic relief.

For persistent nausea I have used Slippery Elm powder in juice or water, or Slippery Elm tea (the gentlest form) taken by the teaspoon (sometimes even less) until the stomach stays calm and soothed. This works on even the most delicate stomachs and for age groups from infants to the elderly.

ALSO SEE: *Diarrhea, Intestines, Mucilaginous, Nutrition, Ulcers*

ALTERNATIVE OR SUPPLEMENTARY SELF-HELP: **Cayenne, *Comfrey, Garlic, *Ginger, Onion, *Peppermint, Yarrow*

DOSAGE: *General*

DISC: See Slipped Disc and Nutrition applications.

EYES: Use well-strained Slippery Elm tea as a soothing, anti-inflammatory eyewash for conjunctivitis and/or tired, inflamed, scratched, weepy eyes. It is safe even for infants and can be wiped through the eyes with a soft cotton swab when it is not possible to use an eyecup or eye drops.

For additional help with tired or inflamed eyes, apply a poultice of Slippery Elm paste (moisten Slippery Elm powder with water or honey) onto the eyelids of closed eyes. Cover the poultice with warm cloths or cotton balls. These warm cloths are kept warm by repeated dippings in warm Slippery Elm tea or another suitable herb tea such as Comfrey. A Cayenne eyewash (see Cayenne chapter, Chapter II) followed by at least twenty minutes of warm Slippery Elm poultice is a wonderful rejuvenating treatment. If you live in a sunny climate it is enjoyable and quite beneficial to the eyes to sit in the sun for twenty minutes while using the poultice.

With air or chemical pollution I have often seen chronic eye difficulties—the result of toxic substances in the blood and eyeball itself. In these chronic cases I suggest using blood-purifying herbs internally—such as one cup of Yarrow tea each day, or the 21-Day Chaparral Cleanse described under the Blood-Purifier application in the Chaparral chapter (Chapter III).

ALSO SEE: *Mucilaginous, Nutritional, Skin*

ALTERNATIVE OR SUPPLEMENTARY SELF-HELP: **Cayenne, Cloves, *Comfrey, Peppermint*

DOSAGE: *General or as given*

GALL BLADDER: Slippery Elm used three or more times daily has often helped with the release of gallstones and gall gravel deposits that are clogging and persistently irritating the gall bladder. For more specific help in actually dissolving stones and gravel, see *Natural Healing With Herbs* by Humbart Santillo (listed in the Resource Guide, Appendix C).

ALSO SEE: *Digestive Tract, Mucilaginous*

ALTERNATIVE OR SUPPLEMENTARY SELF-HELP: **Chaparral, *Comfrey, Garlic, Peppermint, Yarrow*

DOSAGE: *General*

GASTRITIS: See Digestive Tract application.

GOUT: See Mucilaginous application.

HEMORRHOIDS: See Intestines application.

INFLAMMATION: See Mucilaginous application.

INTESTINES: I have used Slippery Elm for a wide variety of intestinal difficulties including: colitis, diverticulitis, constipation, diarrhea, spastic colon, and hemorrhoids.

In the powdered form (tea is OK, too), Slippery Elm is most often used internally to coat, soothe, and rejuvenate the mucous membranes and other tissues of the entire digestive tract. The tea is used as an enema for inflamed, ulcerated, constipated or diarrhea-prone, and undernourished colon tissues. Slippery Elm suppositories are made for additional direct help with hemorrhoids. Use suppositories at night for greatest convenience. For complete directions in making suppositories, look under the Suppository or Bolus headings in Chapter I, Lesson #2.

Slippery Elm is first aid for diarrhea, and many people fail to realize that it is also a remedy for constipation. Knowing that this herb helps mightily with both bowel extremes is a bit of data that can be put to good use by stay-at-homers and busy travelers alike.

TASOLE: Tom had a fairly constant constipation problem which, I observed, was largely due to his eating and drinking habits. He was, however, unwilling to change his ways. I suggested the standard use of Slippery Elm knowing that this herb would add slippery fiber and a protective coating to his fast-deteriorating digestive tract. I thought there was a good chance that this intervention might "buy him some time", pending the unlikely event that his food, drink, and emotional habits would change.

The Slippery Elm worked so well that Tom, who was a jogger, discovered that he couldn't jog soon after taking the Slippery Elm because he invariably needed a bathroom, pronto! Before he got his timing straightened out, in fact, he had a couple of jogs where he had to take emergency action in the woods. He wasn't having diarrhea at all, but just the normal action he had grown used to "not expecting".

ALSO SEE: *Diarrhea, Digestive Tract, Mucilaginous, Nutrition*

ALTERNATIVE OR SUPPLEMENTARY SELF-HELP: **Cayenne, *Comfrey, *Ginger, Peppermint, Yarrow*

DOSAGE: *General*

KIDNEYS: See Urinary Tract application.

LUNGS: Drink Slippery Elm tea, or use one teaspoon of the powder in juice or water three to six or more times a day. This will soothe irritations in the lungs and bronchials and help clear mucus from the head, throat, and chest. (Review the Cough Syrup application above.) During lung congestion, be sure all your eliminative channels—bowels, urinary tract, sweat glands, and skin — are as open as possible. Many people have found that an enema helps to initially break up the congestion. My students and I have found that Slippery Elm, taken orally, actually gathers up unwanted mucus and packages it for speedy delivery out of the system.

Use an antibiotic herb such as Chaparral or Garlic, along with the Slippery Elm, when lung infection is present. Remember also that deep breathing and exercise help a lot when trying to expel mucus from the body. Comfrey is an excellent addition when there is congestion or bleeding in the lungs. Ginger (1/4 part) will help focus, bind and carry an herbal lung formulation more potently to where it is needed.

ALSO SEE: *Mucilaginous, Mucus Congestion*

ALTERNATIVE OR SUPPLEMENTARY SELF-HELP: *Cayenne, Chaparral, *Comfrey, *Garlic, *Ginger, Peppermint*

DOSAGE: *General*

MUCILAGINOUS: A mucilaginous plant contains significant amounts of mucilage. In herbistry "mucilage" describes a slippery, sticky and soothing substance, often of high nutritional value (as is the case with Slippery Elm), that coats and protects an area from infection, inflammation and other irritants. Mucilage also acts as a further protection from many toxic substances since it absorbs them and helps them pass harmlessly out of the body. This mucilaginous property is especially useful in any case of inflammation or congestion—such as the inflamed mucous membranes of the lungs, digestive tract, or urinary tract (including kidneys)—or any ulcerous situations, both internal and external. This is discussed in greater detail in the Personality Profile at the beginning of this chapter.

This mucilaginous quality is extremely valuable in many situations, including: appendicitis, arthritis, colitis, gout, rheumatism, sinusitis, bronchitis, (almost any "itis" situation), burns, ulcers, skin rashes . . . The list goes on and on. Remember that Ginger is often a good addition to Slippery Elm (use 1 part Ginger to 4 parts Slippery Elm) to catalyze action when herbal help is needed (especially in the intestines).

In the Appendicitis application there is a good internal formula that would be quite useful in most inflammations.

ALSO SEE: *Appendicitis, Bleeding, Nutritional*

ALTERNATIVE OR SUPPLEMENTARY SELF-HELP: **Comfrey, Ginger*

DOSAGE: *General*

MUCOUS CONGESTION: See Cough Syrup application.

NAUSEA: See Digestive Tract application.

NUTRITION: Review the Personality Profile and General Dosage instructions for ideas of how to use Slippery Elm with hot cereals. This herb has such high nutritional value that it is often used just for that reason.

Slippery Elm has the amino acids for building usable proteins and is full of essential minerals. These nutrients are available in an easy-to-assimilate form which is why Slippery Elm is used with all age groups, especially during the recovery period of a debilitating disease. It will often stay in a weakened system even when nothing else will. Slippery Elm supports the building of healthy tissue and nurtures and strengthens the body's systems.

For adding nutritional value, a nut-like flavor, and pudding-like smoothness to cooked cereals, start with 1 tsp. Slippery Elm powder for each cup of water called for in your recipe. After adding the herb you can adjust the amount of water so you end up with cereal of your preferred thickness. The more Slippery Elm powder added, the more water you may need to add also. Add sweetener and spices according to taste.

Slippery Elm gruel is an unbeatable food for persons of any age who are recovering from vomiting or any debilitating illness. Here is my recipe.

SLIPPERY ELM GRUEL

In a medium-sized bowl mix 1 tsp. Slippery Elm powder and enough cold water to make a smooth paste. Slowly add two cups of boiling water, constantly stirring. This makes a thin gruel which can then be flavored, as you like, with lemon, honey, molasses, cinnamon, cloves, nutmeg, etc. Start with these proportions but feel free to experiment and make it as strong as you like. Administer the gruel by the spoonful, or drink by the cup, up to two or three cups in a day.

In addition to this method of making the gruel you could also use this same basic technique but use Slippery Elm chunks which you simmer and then strain out at the end. Some people prefer this texture; however I believe there is higher nutritional value in leaving the herb powder in the gruel as described.

For extremely weak individuals, in addition to or instead of feeding them the gruel, you may want to use a body-temperature cupful of the gruel as a retention enema, i.e., holding the gruel in the colon as long as possible to allow the body to absorb the nutrients. This one cupful is often totally absorbed so there will not necessarily be any evacuation of the bowels.

ALSO SEE: *Digestive Tract, Intestines, Mucilaginous*

ALTERNATIVE OR SUPPLEMENTARY SELF-HELP: *Cayenne, *Comfrey, Garlic, Onion*

DOSAGE: *General or as given*

POISON IVY/OAK: See Skin application.

REJUVENATION: See Nutrition application.

RHEUMATISM: See Mucilaginous application.

SINUS: Use Slippery Elm powder and/or tea internally while at the same time using the tea as a nasal rinse.

A soothing and mucus-drawing nasal rinse is made from a cup of Slippery Elm tea cooled to a still warm, yet comfortable temperature. Gently inhale the tea through one nostril at a time. Always treat both nostrils.

For a sinus infection you may want to add an antibiotic or antiseptic herb, such as Garlic or Chaparral, to the nasal rinse, and also take the antibiotic herbs internally (see Chaparral and Garlic, Chapters III and VI). One teaspoon of table salt added to one cup of the nasal rinse also acts as an additional infection deterrent while the Slippery Elm tea will keep the nasal passages from becoming too dry.

Overall, Slippery Elm has a strong soothing and mucus-gathering effect. For a more stimulating and sinus-clearing action, you can add 1 part Ginger herb to 4 parts of the nasal rinse herb before preparing the rinse. Some people enjoy the effect of adding the tiniest drop of Peppermint oil to the nasal rinse. It is quite stimulating.

ALSO SEE: *Lungs, Mucilaginous, Mucus Congestion*

ALTERNATIVE OR SUPPLEMENTARY SELF-HELP: **Cayenne, Chaparral, Clove, *Comfrey, Garlic, *Ginger, *Peppermint*

DOSAGE: *General and as given*

SKIN: Slippery Elm mixes into a convenient paste for external application to skin irritations, poison ivy/oak, wounds, or burns. It is also a great base in which to mix other herbs. Use one teaspoon of the herb powder, whether it is plain Slippery Elm or a formula, and mix it with a wetting agent such as raw honey, glycerin, aloe vera gel, olive oil (not on fresh burns or fresh wounds), or plain water (dries fairly hard, however). Powder can be applied dry to a bleeding wound or oozing skin condition.

It doesn't take much wetting agent to make Slippery Elm into a paste; a common mistake with beginners is to end up with a soup, instead of the intended paste consistency. You can always add more herb powder if this happens to you.

Poultices should be changed at least twice a day and the skin washed with Slippery Elm tea or an antiseptic substance such as Chaparral tea or hydrogen peroxide.

Slippery Elm tea makes a soothing wash for larger areas of skin that may be covered with a rash or lots of bug bites. You can always take a bath in Slippery Elm when there is widespread skin irritation. For a bath use a double-strength tea made from powder or herb bits. Make two quarts tea, strain out drain-clogging bits, and add it to the tub.

With a skin fungus, add a fungicide herb such as Chaparral or Garlic, and for chronic skin troubles I recommend a blood purifier such as the 21-Day Chaparral Cleanse described in the Blood-Purifier application in the Chaparral chapter (Chapter III).

For burns that do not involve major tissue damage, mix Slippery Elm powder with Comfrey powder and wet this with raw honey to make a paste. Apply this poultice to the burn and wrap in a gauze bandage. The herbs can be gently soaked off the burn once or twice a day. Do not vigorously scrub the burn as this will disturb new tissue growth. If some herbs stick to the burn after a gentle soaking, this is OK. Simply apply a fresh poultice on top of this. Rinsing with hydrogen peroxide is effective in removing the old poultice gently if this concerns you.

Be sure to review the Burn application in the Comfrey chapter (Chapter V). And don't miss the instructions in the use of People Paste (Appendix A), for state-of-the-art skin and wound care.

ALSO SEE: *Mucilaginous, Nutrition*

ALTERNATIVE OR SUPPLEMENTARY SELF-HELP: *Chaparral, *Comfrey, Garlic, *People Paste, Yarrow*

DOSAGE: *General, and as given*

SLIPPED DISC: Take Slippery Elm internally three to six times a day to add needed nutrition for repairing and strengthening a slipped disc. Additionally it is quite useful to prepare a Slippery Elm poultice to be applied directly over the disc area. This can be left on overnight and/or for long periods during the day.

I have used these methods successfully on a few slipped discs and several old bone injuries. If it is working, you should notice strengthening within a week or two of consistant Slippery Elm use. Use Slippery Elm in conjunction with Comfrey, both internally and externally, for a doubly potent treatment for a slipped disc or for any other bone weakness or injury.

ALSO SEE: *Mucilaginous, Nutrition*

ALTERNATIVE OR SUPPLEMENTARY SELF-HELP: **Comfrey, People Paste*

DOSAGE: *General*

SOOTHING: See Skin and Mucilaginous applications.

SORES: See Abscess and Skin applications.

STOMACH: See Digestive Tract, Mucilaginous and Ulcers applications.

SURGERY: When recovering from surgery, especially of the digestive tract, Slippery Elm can speed recovery. (See the TASOLE in the Personality Profile.) Simply use a cup of the tea, or take 1 tsp. powder in 6 oz. juice or water (capsules are hard on the digestive tract, especially after digestive surgery) three or more times a day. This will soothe and rejuvenate body tissues, especially in the digestive tract, while balancing bowel action and increasing important nutritional components. For a strong mixture use equal parts of Slippery Elm and Comfrey with 1/4 part Ginger (all herbs are powdered) and take 1/2 to 1 tsp. three times a day with a glass of water or as a honeyball, etc.

Check with your surgeon before using these suggestions.

ALSO SEE: *Digestive Tract, Intestines, Mucilaginous, Nutrition, Slipped Disk, Ulcers*

ALTERNATIVE OR SUPPLEMENTARY SELF-HELP: *Cloves, *Comfrey, People Paste, Peppermint, Yarrow*

DOSAGE: *General*

THROAT: Make a basic gargle by mixing 1 tsp. Slippery Elm powder in warm water (warm salt water is also good). Or, simply use 1 cup Slippery Elm tea, strained of herbs, for your gargle. Slippery Elm is excellent by itself, or you can add 1/8 tsp. Cayenne, 1/4 tsp. Ginger or Clove powders, or 1 or 2 drops of Peppermint oil or Clove oil to increase its pain-relieving, mucus-clearing, and antiseptic action.

Slippery Elm gargle would be a good thing for tonsillitis, laryngitis, post-nasal drip, strep throat, and those generic sore throats that creep up on you from public speaking, singing, or daily stress.

Make yourself some customized Slippery Elm throat lozenges. Use the throat lozenge procedure listed under the Cough Syrup application using any herbs you like.

ALSO SEE: *Cough Syrup, Mucilaginous*

ALTERNATIVE OR SUPPLEMENTARY SELF-HELP: *Cayenne, *Clove (oil or powder), Ginger, *Peppermint oil*

DOSAGE: *Use one cup of tea by itself or add 1/8 tsp. Cayenne, or 1/4 tsp. Ginger or Clove; or add 1 or 2 drops Clove or Peppermint oil. Use as a gargle.*

TONIC: See Nutrition application.

TONSILLITIS: See Throat, Mucilaginous, and Cough Syrup applications.

ULCERS: Use a skin poultice of Slippery Elm for external ulcerations (see Skin application) and "specialize" it for specific needs by adding an antibiotic herb such as Garlic or Chaparral, a cell-proliferating herb such as Comfrey, or an antiseptic herb like Yarrow or Clove.

Internally, for ulcers, use Slippery Elm two to six times daily according to the General Dosage instructions. This will coat, protect, soothe, slow or stop bleeding, and speed healing of the ulcerous condition anywhere from the mouth on through to the anus.

For chronic bleeding ulcers, use Cayenne daily (see Cayenne chapter, Chapter II) if the Slippery Elm is not enough. Also, Comfrey is a good addition in treating internal or external ulcers.

I have found that diet plays a major role in handling internal ulcers. For starters, I would recommend eliminating fried foods, processed foods and caffeine.

Also give particular attention to the Mucilaginous application.

ALSO SEE: *Digestive Tract, Intestines, Mucilaginous, Nutrition, Skin*

ALTERNATIVE OR SUPPLEMENTERY SELF-HELP: **Cayenne, Chaparral (for use with ulcers, always mix Chaparral with an equal part of Comfrey or Slippery Elm to buffer it), *Comfrey, Garlic, People Paste*

DOSAGE: *General*

URINARY TRACT: Slippery Elm aids relief of inflammation, gravel deposits, burning urine, and otherwise irritated urinary tract membranes.

An alternative to plain Slippery Elm is to make a decoction using 2 oz. Slippery Elm and 1 oz. Comfrey. Add 4 cups of water and simmer this mixture for 30 minutes with the pot-lid half off. Strain out the herbs and add 1/2 tsp. Cayenne to the liquid. Drink 3 oz. of this decoction every two to three hours until inflammation subsides and then lessen the frequency of the dosage to three times a day for three to six more days. If you need to, make this into a powdered formula by mixing 2 parts Slippery Elm, 1 part Comfrey Root, and 1/4 to 1/2 part Cayenne. Put the mixture into size "00" capsules and take 1 or 2 capsules each three hours. Or, you could simply take 1/2 tsp. of the powders directly into the mouth, without the capsules, using juice or water to swallow it. Always drink a full glass of water with each dose of the dry powdered formula.

A Ginger fomentation over the irritated part of the urinary tract (i.e., kidneys, bladder, etc.) is useful. (See Ginger chapter, Chapter VII.)

ALSO SEE: *Antacid, Mucilaginous, Nutrition*

ALTERNATIVE OR SUPPLEMENTARY SELF-HELP: **Chaparral, *Comfrey, Garlic, Peppermint, *Yarrow*

DOSAGE: *General*

VAGINITIS: Use Slippery Elm tea as a soothing and Ph-corrective douche for irritations in the vagina. If there is infection present, make a few vaginal boluses (see Chapter I, Lesson #2) using Slippery Elm powder with an equal part of an antibiotic or fungicidal herb such as Garlic, Chaparral, or Yarrow. Mix the herb powders with some melted cocoa butter (available at drug and health food stores) to a clay-like consistency. Form lozenge shapes from teaspoons of the mixture. Cool/harden them in the refrigerator. Insert 1 bolus into the vagina several times a day. There will be an herbal discharge that can be absorbed on a thin pad or panty-shield. Gently cleanse the vagina with a Slippery Elm tea douche if necessary. If you have no cocoa butter you can wet the powders with water, dry the bolus shapes in a 120 degree oven, and use them. They are a little rougher than the ones made with the cocoa butter and you may want to insert them with a small amount of hypo-allergenic lotion or olive oil.

Use the Enhanced Garlic Formula (see the Antibiotic application in the Garlic chapter, Chapter VI) or an antibiotic formula from the chaparral chapter, orally whenever vaginal infection is present.

ALSO SEE: *Mucilaginous*

ALTERNATIVE OR SUPPLEMENTARY SELF-HELP: **Chaparral, Comfrey, *Garlic, Yarrow*

DOSAGE: ***Internally, use General dosage. Use douche no more than once a day for the shortest period of time possible. Use boluses (as described) two to five times a day.***

WOUNDS: The most famous, prize-winning, amazing and efficacious way to use Slippery Elm for healing wounds of all types is to make it into People Paste. This mixture is so extraordinary that I have devoted a full appendix to it. Consult that for wounds. (See People Paste, Appendix A.)

Lacking People Paste, Slippery Elm powder, either by itself or with another herb or two of your choice (Comfrey and Chaparral are good ones), can be moistened to a paste-like consistency with raw honey (plain water will work but it can dry quite hard), and applied directly to a wound. Cover the wound with an appropriate bandage, and change the poultice two or more times a day as necessary. Wash the wound gently (so as not to disturb new tissue growth) when changing the poultice, using an antiseptic herbal wash such as Chaparral or Yarrow, or use hydrogen peroxide.

Slippery Elm pulls torn tissues together, soothes raw nerves in wounds, offers protection against infection, and feeds new tissue growth, making it a superb choice for most wounds—from an infected mosquito bite to a cut from a slip of the saw in the woodshop. I have literally "pasted" severed fingertips back together with Slippery Elm concoctions (see People Paste, Appendix A), and 90% of the time they have grown together beautifully.

It pays to keep a dry mixture of Slippery Elm, with another herb or two mixed in it, on hand for immediate use. It takes only a moment to moisten it and "paste" it onto/into a wound.

Also see the detailed poultice instructions in Chapter I, Lesson #2.

ALSO SEE: *Mucilaginous, Nutrition, Skin*

ALTERNATIVE OR SUPPLEMENTARY SELF-HELP: *Chaparral, Clove, *Comfrey, Garlic, Onion, *People Paste, Yarrow*

DOSAGE: *General and as given*

YARROW

BLOOD-PURIFIER, FEVER,
ANTISEPTIC AND FLU—
ANY WAY YOU LOOK AT IT,
IT'S SO GOOD FOR YOU
RUN FOR YOUR LIVES BOYS!
THAT YARROW WILL GET YOU
FOR SURE!!!
FEVER
LIVER DISTRESS
DIRTY BLOOD
INDIGESTION

CHAPTER XI

YARROW

Achillea millefolium

Yarrow sings of fevers, of cold sores, and of flus,
And to intestinal pain he certainly rues.
Songs of rashes and scratches, clean blood and short fasting,
For help with all these, Yarrow tea is quite lasting.

PERSONALITY PROFILE—Yarrow

Yarrow is a medicinal herb with a strong mystical history. The stems of the yarrow plant have been used for thousands of years, starting in the Orient, for the divination of fortunes through the use of the *I Ching*. Forty Yarrow stalks would be gathered, cut to the proper length, and dried. Then the process of "throwing the stalks" would be used to determine which hexagram (explanation of forces at play in a situation) should be applied to the user's question. The use of plants for physical healing often has an esoteric counterpart. In any case, it is good to remember that "A Yarrow in the hand is worth two in the bush", or "Some Yarrow each day keeps the doctor away", or "Here today, gone with Yarrow" . . . or however those old sayings are supposed to go (my friends say I often get them a little mixed up). The point of all this is that in addition to its mystical roots, Yarrow is so effective in practical, everyday matters that it has a permanent place on my Ten Essentials list!

Yarrow is often put in the category of "bitter herbs" because of the powerful, volatile oil it contains. This oil, called Achillein, together with tannin (tannic acid), gives a stimulating, astringent, and bitter edge to the flavor and action. These properties, along with many others, act on the liver to strengthen its efficiency and stimulate bile production. Yarrow also functions as a strong antiseptic and viral inhibitor. Yarrow's action as an astringent means that it firms and tones tissues, including the tissues of internal organs that might have become flaccid, inefficient, or tired out by abuse from unhealthy habits and/or a toxic environment. While Yarrow tones the tissues, its stimulating property also rehabilitates the body's systems into renewed alertness and immunity. As an antiseptic and antiviral agent, Yarrow kills many harmful microorganisms upon contact. Its volatile oil collects and absorbs many impurities (I think of it as gathering the toxins into little packets) and then, somewhat like a detergent, breaks down these "corralled" toxins into forms much easier for the body to eliminate without the usual illness symptoms. In many ways, Yarrow's inhibiting action is similar to an oil spill cleanup job.

The best way to activate the healing properties of Yarrow is to make a water extract, otherwise known as tea. If you want the most potent results from any bitter herb, including Yarrow, it is best not to add any sweetener to it. But, if you have not yet developed a taste for Yarrow and feel you need to sweeten it, please use a little raw honey and forego the use of any other type of sweetener. When you are steeping the Yarrow to make tea, be sure to do this in a covered pot to preserve the volatile oils and protect them from evaporating. If you start with freshly gathered undried Yarrow blossoms or leaves, you must simmer them (rather than steeping them) as slowly as possible, covered, to make the tea. The active properties in Yarrow can also be extracted in an alcohol-based tincture (a way of making a concentrate) that may be convenient for use with children, while traveling, or for immediate use when making tea is not possible. If you want to experiment with a Yarrow tincture to see the pros and cons of these different forms, see the basic formula under the Yarrow Tincture application in the list below.

I have always gathered and dried the Yarrow blossoms for my own use and this is the part of the herb that is commonly found in an herb store. However, the leaves and stems are also potent and could be used medicinally if you gathered your own. Since I am able to gather my own Yarrow easily nere in Arizona, I use the stems and leaves for making a wonderful Yarrow bath and I save the blossoms for internal use because of their flavor and action. In New England and Arizona I find and gather white blossoms. In Colorado, Yarrow blossoms are often yellow, and there is even a pink blossom that I have only seen growing cultivated.

Yarrow grows all over the United States and in many parts of the world. A friend of mine who went mountain climbing in Austria told me that even at timberline he found tiny Yarrow plants growing close to the ground—a little sideways because of the winds, yet strong and lovely with their perky white flower tops.

Some people find that there is an herb that is "their" herb—the one they immediately reach for to rebalance the whole system if anything feels as if it might be going wrong. Yarrow works like that for me, and many of my students have also found this to be the case. I use one cup of Yarrow tea a day as a tonic.

TASOLE: My friend Cynthia once told me about her regular bouts with "the death and dying disease." In general, Cindy had excellent vitality, energy and apparent health, yet every month when her menstrual cycle was beginning she would suddenly get extremely nauseous, feel faint, have trouble walking, and suffer diarrhea, painful cramps, and heavy bleeding. Bodily shaking, together with everything else, would commonly leave her collapsed on the floor. Cindy was always certain that she was about to die, and no matter what help she sought, the problem stubbornly continued. Occasionally a month would go by without this happening and she would think that perhaps it was gone for good. But the next month it would surprise her again—and I do mean surprise. It could happen at a moment's notice.

Cindy learned from me that Yarrow greatly strengthens and cleanses the blood and acts as a powerful tonic for female organs — actually balancing the menstrual cycle — so she joined me one day to gather some. Taking some Yarrow home with her, she began my favorite regimen of having one cup of Yarrow tea each day. Several weeks later she reported to me that there had been a dramatic and pleasing change in her monthly cycle. She had not had the drastic menstrual experience that month and was experiencing many of the tonic (strengthening) actions of Yarrow,including greater vitality, better digestion, healthy skin, and stronger immunity to the common colds and flu. She reported that the only thing she had done differently that month was to have that one cup of Yarrow tea each day. She admitted that she had started using Yarrow mainly out of curiosity and had not really hoped for a change in her menstrual difficulties. The enhancement of her general well-being was very welcome, however, and she intended to continue using Yarrow as a general tonic on the basis of all the benefits she had experienced so far.

The next month also passed with no menstrual upheaval and we began to hope that there might be a real change in this long-standing problem. During the third month there were mild signs of the old trouble, yet she found that drinking an additional cup or two of Yarrow tea, taking doses of calcium lactate, and drinking some electrolyte-balancing juice helped to remedy this right away, and the "death and dying syndrome" never got under way again.

Yarrow has become "her herb". Although she may occasionally skip her cup of tea, if she ever feels discomfort around the time of her menstrual cycle she brews up her Yarrow tea and takes extra calcium and some electrolyte juice (easily found at a grocery store, as athletes commonly use this) to give her body what it needs. These simple measures worked, I believe, because Cindy had toned and strengthened the functioning of her internal organs and her blood chemistry with the Yarrow—exactly what a "bitter tonic" is supposed to do!

I had rarely seen a case as dramatic as Cindy's, and this experience broadened my view of the possibilities for the slow steady use of Yarrow as a tonic.

Another use of Yarrow that has been especially helpful to me is as an aid in waking up alert and "ready-to-go" in the morning. For many years I was one of those people who has difficulty in being alert in the morning; since I was not willing to become a coffee drinker or take harsh stimulants, I just put up with it. This morning lethargy is a typical symptom of hypoglycemia (low blood sugar) that can occur for a variety of reasons which I won't elaborate here. Suffice it to say that hypoglycemia is a common dilemma in our Western culture.

I began to drink a cup of Yarrow tea at night, the last thing before going to bed. The Yarrow strengthened my body's ability to maintain a balanced blood sugar level throughout the night, and I would wake up alert and clearheaded in the morning. Yarrow strengthens and encourages the natural action of important internal organs, including the liver and pancreas, which in turn leads to more optimal functioning, alertness, and available energy in a body that is otherwise in generally good health. So give this Yarrow tea a try if you have any trouble waking up alert in the morning.

Struggling with a caffeine addiction? Use Yarrow tea at night and Cayenne herb in the morning. Look in the Cayenne chapter (Chapter II) under the application "Caffeine Withdrawal," and add this use of Yarrow to those instructions.

APPLICATIONS AND ATTRIBUTES - YARROW

(Quick Reference List)

ALLERGY
ANTISEPTIC
ARTHRITIS
ASTRINGENT
BATH
BLEEDING
BLOOD-PURIFIER
BURSITIS
CHILDHOOD DISEASES
CHILLS
CIRCULATION
COLDS and **FLU**
COLIC
CONGESTION
DIGESTION
DIURETIC
EYES
FASTING
FEMALE ORGANS
FEVER
GALL BLADDER
GAS
HEMORRHOIDS
HEPATITIS
HYPOGLYCEMIA
IMMUNE SYSTEM
INFECTION
INFLAMMATION
INSECT BITES
INTESTINES
ITCHING
LIVER
LUNGS
LYMPH SYSTEM
MENSTRUATION
NAUSEA
NIGHTSWEATS
PERSPIRATION THERAPY
REPRODUCTIVE ORGANS
SINUS
SKIN
SPASMS
STIMULANT
STOMACH
TEETHING
TONIC
TONSILLITIS
URINARY TRACT
VARICOSE VEINS
WAKE-UP TEA
WOUNDS
YARROW BATH
YARROW TINCTURE
YEAST INFECTION

FORM:

Use blossoms (most commonly used), leaves, stems—all parts used either dried or fresh, and Yarrow tincture.

APPLICATION METHODS:

Internally: Use Yarrow as a tea, powder, infusion, tincture, or enema.
Externally: Use Yarrow tea, powder, or infusion as a wash, soak, bath, or poultice.

AVAILABILITY:

Herb store, grow your own, gather wild, mail order seeds (for growing), and dried herb

HINTS/CAUTIONS:

Many midwives advise against using Yarrow during pregnancy as it belongs to a family of plants that are known to be extra stimulating to the uterus. I have not found this to be the case with Yarrow itself, yet it seems best to be cautious just-in-case.

GENERAL DOSAGE: INTERNAL USE

⋆PLEASE NOTE: *Although I emphasize using tea, there are many forms of herbal preparations such as Capsules, Children's Ideas, Infusion, Honeyball, etc. See these headings as well as Dosage Equivalents in Chapter I, Lesson #2.*

Infants to 3 years: Yarrow tea or infusion offered in a bottle or cup, by dropper, or by teaspoon, usually 4 oz. (for tea) or 2 oz. (for infusion), two to four times per day. Use Yarrow tincture according to manufacturer's instructions, or see Yarrow Tincture application below.

Children 4 years to 10 years: Yarrow tea, 1 to 4 cups daily. Yarrow infusion, 2 to 4 oz., one to four times a day. Yarrow powder, 1/2 tsp. in honeyball or capsule, etc, up to 8 times a day. Yarrow tincture according to manufacturer's instructions, or see Yarrow Tincture application below.

Children 11 years to Adults: Yarrow tea as needed, usually not more than 8 cups per day (largest dose would be for fasting or extreme illness in an adult). Yarrow infusion, 4 oz. as needed, usually not more than eight times per day. Yarrow powder 1/2 to 1 tsp. in capsule, honeyball, or plain; up to 8 times a day. Yarrow tincture according to manufacturer's instructions, or see Yarrow Tincture application below.

Pets and Other Creatures: Probably best to use Yarrow tincture (see Yarrow Tincture application below) on animals as it is a little difficult to administer this bitter tea to them. You can try spooning the tea into the mouth of a smaller animal, or use Yarrow powder in pills or capsules (See Chapter I, Lesson #2).

GENERAL DOSAGE: EXTERNAL USE

Same For All Humans And Other Creatures

Yarrow tea or infusion can be used to cleanse, soak, or poultice any external situation where there is a need for antiseptic, soothing (as in itching), enhanced healing and/or anti-inflammatory action. Yarrow tincture can be used in the same way, yet it is often more efficient to make the tea in quantities rather than use up your tincture. Use Yarrow powder or fresh plant for poulticing.

APPLICATIONS AND ATTRIBUTES - YARROW

ALLERGY: Many allergy symptoms such as itching, sneezing, eye irritations, and scratchy throat are greatly helped by using Yarrow tea. Drink 1 to 4 cups daily. It can be used as a very soothing eyewash or skin wash.

If your allergy symptoms are seasonal, Yarrow can be used as a preventive method by starting a 1-cup-per-day regimen ahead of time.

For food allergies that may result in hives or swollen face, etc., Yarrow works well taken as a tea, or used as an herbal wash and/or enema.

ALSO SEE: *Circulation, Congestion, Digestion, Fasting, Perspiration Therapy, Tonic, Yarrow Tincture*

ALTERNATIVE OR SUPPLEMENTARY SELF-HELP: **Cayenne, *Chaparral, Comfrey, Onion*

DOSAGE: *Use 1 cup per day as a preventive method; 2 or more cups during symptoms as needed. Tincture can work well—use as directed by manufacturer, or as given in Yarrow Tincture application.*

ANTISEPTIC: Be sure to read about how and why Yarrow works as an antiseptic in the Yarrow Personality Profile. You can use Yarrow tea internally or externally to help kill or inhibit growth of harmful bacteria for anything from intestinal flu to an itchy insect bite.

ALSO SEE: *Colds and Flu, Infection, Inflammation, Insect Bites, Itching, Perspiration Therapy, Skin, Tonic, Yarrow Bath*

ALTERNATIVE OR SUPPLEMENTARY SELF-HELP: **Chaparral, Clove, Comfrey, *Garlic, Onion, *People Paste, Peppermint*

DOSAGE: *General*

ARTHRITIS: See Inflammation, Tonic, and Yarrow Bath applications.

ASTRINGENT: As an astringent use Yarrow internally and externally for situations such as: bleeding, weepy skin rashes, hemorrhoids, wounds, out-of-tone liver and digestive functions, and anytime you need a "drawing" action (pimples, splinters, abscesses, etc.).

As an astringent Yarrow firms, tones, and draws toxins out of body tissues, including the tissues of internal organs that might have become flaccid, inefficient, or tired out by abuse from a poor diet, use of addictive substances such as caffeine, alcohol, or nicotine, and/or a toxic environment. The firming, "tightening" action of Yarrow contributes to its efficacy in bleeding.

ALSO SEE: *Digestion, Hemorrhoids, Liver, Tonic, Yarrow Bath*

ALTERNATIVE OR SUPPLEMENTARY SELF-HELP: **Chaparral, Clove, Comfrey, Onion*

DOSAGE: *General*

BATH: See Yarrow Bath application.

BLEEDING: Used internally and/or externally, Yarrow tea helps the blood coagulate.

Externally, use Yarrow powder or infusion as a poultice or fomentation on a wound, scrape, bite, etc. For a small amount of bleeding simply sprinkle Yarrow powder, 1/8 inch deep, onto the affected part. (See poultice and fomentation instructions in Chapter I, Lesson #2.)

Internally, use Yarrow tea, infusion, or powder for bleeding in the lungs, stomach, intestines, mouth, etc.

Anytime you use Yarrow for bleeding you can enhance it, if necessary, by mixing it in equal parts with another "bleeding herb" such as Comfrey or Cayenne and then applying it as described here.

ALSO SEE: *Astringent, Tonic*

ALTERNATIVE OR SUPPLEMENTARY SELF-HELP: **Cayenne, *Comfrey, People Paste*

DOSAGE: *General*

BLOOD-PURIFIER: See Tonic application.

BURSITIS: See Inflammation application.

CHILDHOOD DISEASES: Most common childhood diseases—chicken pox, mumps, measles, German measles, colic, whooping cough, bronchitis, tonsillitis—respond well to Yarrow. Use it specifically for fevers, itching, lymphatic cleansing, inflammation (all the words ending in "itis" fit in this category), calming the stomach, and fighting many types of infection. It is easy to see why you should think of Yarrow first where childhood diseases are concerned.

Be certain to review the Children's Ideas in Chapter I, Lesson #2, for easy ways to offer herbs to children.

ALSO SEE: *Colic, Congestion, Fever, Infection, Inflammation, Itching, Lymph, Perspiration Therapy, Skin, Tonic, Yarrow Bath*

ALTERNATIVE OR SUPPLEMENTARY SELF-HELP: *Clove, *Comfrey, Garlic, *Peppermint—and actually any of these Ten Essentials have some good use for childhood illness.*

DOSAGE: *General*

CHILLS: Chills are commonly associated with fever, poor circulation, and those "pre-illness twinges" we have all experienced. In any case, Yarrow is a #1 balancer of circulation. Along with its tonic qualities, Yarrow flushes out the cause of many fevers and/or prevents the chills and twinges of pre-illness from going any further.

Yarrow is a good tonic for those who often tend to feel cold.

ALSO SEE: *Circulation, Colds, Fever, Perspiration Therapy, Tonic, Yarrow Bath*

ALTERNATIVE OR SUPPLEMENTARY SELF-HELP: **Cayenne, Garlic, *Ginger*

DOSAGE: *General*

CIRCULATION: When a health problem persists, it is often the circulation that needs to be strengthened. Accumulated toxins in the organs and body systems result in an overall sluggishness. Nerve, blood, and lymph circulation/energy are then greatly slowed down and this in turn contributes to an even greater build-up of toxins. The body thus becomes an inconvenient "Sludge Monster". Since this syndrome is inherent in most illnesses, anything that will flush out the "sludge" and stimulate renewed circulation to these areas can turn the illness around. Yarrow is a potent and persistent help in this, especially since it stimulates the pores of the skin to open and release body waste.

ALSO SEE: *Perspiration Therapy, Skin, Stimulant, Tonic, Yarrow Bath*

ALTERNATIVE OR SUPPLEMENTARY SELF-HELP: **Cayenne, Chaparral, Garlic, *Ginger*

DOSAGE: *General*

COLDS AND FLU: If 1 or 2 cups are used each day as a tonic, Yarrow can often prevent a cold or flu from "getting you". So if there is a cold or flu going around your neighborhood, don't sit idly by and wait for the symptoms to start. Try Yarrow as a preventive.

If it is too late for prevention, eat light and easy-to-digest foods (perhaps miso broth) or fruit, and then flush yourself out by drinking 4 to 8 cups of Yarrow tea each day. For those who want the fastest possible results, use a Yarrow tea enema along with the drinking of the tea. Most of my students find this combination knocks out a cold or flu (especially stomach or intestinal flu) within a day. If there are any lingering symptoms, however, just continue with the tea for a while to finish them off. I usually advise drinking the tea for one full day past the ending of all symptoms of illness.

Although Yarrow is usually strong enough on its own, also review the uses of Garlic, Chaparral and Ginger for help with colds and flu symptoms. A Ginger bath can take the ache out of your body while Garlic and Chaparral are potent antibiotics when that is needed.

TASOLE: I can't tell you how often I get phone calls from people with symptoms of the common colds and flu, especially in the winter months. Usually, each person feels that his/her case is unique, unusual, never-before-dealt-with, and surely requires the most complex treatment I can think up. This was definitely the case with Ruth, a college professor friend who called for help.

Ruth reported waking up one day feeling "the beginnings of something". By the next day the aches, pains, fever, scratchy throat, and queasy stomach were full-blown. Looking over her stash of antibiotics left over from previous illnesses (just in case she might decide to try some) and preparing herself for the usual $60 doctor appointment, she decided to check with me first: Could she save her money and avoid more prescription drugs? Were there a few herbs she could use instead?

When I told her to stop eating for the day, drink Yarrow tea and take a Yarrow enema, I could tell from the sound of her voice that she did not believe this could possibly be enough to stop the forward march of her collapsing health.

The next day she called me again, this time more ill than the day before. She wanted to know if I thought she should go to the doctor. I emphasized that she needed to make her own decisions and added, "By the way, did you try the Yarrow idea?" "Not yet," she meekly responded. "I may be too ill for that." After a moment's pause, she admitted that my recommendation just sounded too simple and that she had no confidence in her ability to take care of her own health.

We talked about this for a while, and I hung up assuming that she was going to see a doctor. The next day, however, she called to say that she couldn't get an appointment for several days and so had decided to try the Yarrow treatment in the meantime.

Within one day of using the Yarrow in the way I had suggested, Ruth had such positive results that she called me back overjoyed. The best part of the whole treatment for her was that she had an experience of being able to help herself in a simple and efficient manner. She completely recovered before the day for her doctor appointment arrived.

This story repeats itself so regularly that I tell it here in hope that it may give a boost of confidence to first-time users of herbs.

ALSO SEE: *Antiseptic, Chills, Circulation, Fever, Infection, Inflammation, Intestines, Perspiration Therapy, Stimulant, Tonic, Yarrow Bath*

ALTERNATIVE OR SUPPLEMENTARY SELF-HELP: **Cayenne, *Chaparral, Clove, *Comfrey, *Garlic, Ginger*

DOSAGE: *General*

COLIC: Yarrow tea or tincture (I prefer tincture in this case) can break up gas in the digestive tract while gently stimulating the liver and digestive functions. This strengthens the child's whole system and relieves the painful stress of colic. Yarrow can also work as a preventive method for colic because of its tonic application.

In severe cases of intestinal colic in babies, a gentle injection of Yarrow tea into the colon, using a bulb syringe, can give instant relief. Simply inject the Yarrow tea gently into the rectum until the child's own automatic sphincter reflex ejects it. This may require one to three uses of the bulb syringe. A bulb syringe holds about 1/2 cup of liquid. (See Enema instructions in Chapter I, Lesson #2.)

ALSO SEE: *Circulation, Digestion, Gas, Liver, Stomach, Tonic, Yarrow Tincture*

ALTERNATIVE OR SUPPLEMENTARY SELF-HELP: **Peppermint*

DOSAGE: *Use Yarrow Tincture (my preference) as described in that application or try 1/2 cup or more Yarrow tea or 2 oz. infusion given in a bottle, spoon, or by dropper, and sweetened slightly if needed (light molasses is good for this).*

CONGESTION: Congestion can happen in any internal organ, not just the lungs, sinuses, or colon. Congestion is often a function of poor nerve, blood, and lymph circulation which is where Yarrow comes into play. In the Personality Profile above, I described how Yarrow gathers up toxins and "packages" them for more efficient elimination. That is exactly the action needed for breaking up many kinds of congestion.

For head congestion, try rinsing the sinuses by gently snuffing warm Yarrow tea up through the nostrils, one nostril at a time. (See Nasal Rinse instructions in Chapter I, Lesson #2.)

For common illnesses in which many of the internal functions feel sluggish or overwhelmed with toxins, try a Yarrow tea enema. (See Enema instructions in Chapter I, Lesson #2.) Also drink the tea.

For digestive congestion in the stomach or intestines, try Yarrow tea, infusion, or tincture (see Yarrow Tincture application). If more help is needed, use a Yarrow enema. Yarrow is great for any type of intestinal congestion, not as a laxative but as a detoxifying stimulant to restore proper functioning.

For congestion in the lungs, use Yarrow tea and/or a Yarrow enema. Comfrey is good with Yarrow as a tea for chest congestion.

An Onion poultice (see Onion chapter, Chapter VIII) applied directly to any area of congestion (i.e., ears, chest, liver, gall bladder) is an effective external aid along with drinking Yarrow tea.

ALSO SEE: *Circulation, Colds & Flu, Perspiration Therapy, Tonic, Yarrow Bath*

ALTERNATIVE OR SUPPLEMENTARY SELF-HELP: *Cayenne, Chaparral, *Comfrey, Garlic, *Ginger, *Onion, Peppermint*

DOSAGE: *General*

DIGESTION: Yarrow stimulates the liver and gall bladder to produce the digestive juices which assist the digestive process to work more smoothly. It also operates as an astringent to firm and tone the tissues of the digestive organs themselves which speeds their rejuvenation. What this means is less gas, less stomachache, better assimilation of nutrients, and a feeling of renewal rather than the typical "dragged-down" feeling that accompanies poor digestive functioning. Use Yarrow tea for any digestive distress, especially for painful gas anywhere in the stomach or intestinal area.

Drink a cup of Yarrow tea about 10 minutes before eating to set the stage for good digestion. For travelers, Yarrow tincture is often convenient for the times when you cannot make a cup of tea. If you have mistakenly eaten bad food, a timely cup of Yarrow tea or use of the tincture can often prevent the usual results of severe indigestion.

If indigestion or even some types of food poisoning have already begun, you can still use a Yarrow tea (or tincture) and Yarrow enema combination to set things right. This duo can often shortcut even the diarrhea from many of these digestive misadventures.

ALSO SEE: *Circulation, Congestion, Stimulant, Tonic*

ALTERNATIVE OR SUPPLEMENTARY SELF-HELP: **Cayenne, Comfrey, Garlic, *Ginger, *Peppermint, Slippery Elm*

DOSAGE: *General*

DIURETIC: Drink cool Yarrow tea for its best diuretic effect, although it is still usable if taken warm.

ALSO SEE: *Tonic, Urinary Tract*

ALTERNATIVE OR SUPPLEMENTARY SELF-HELP: *Chaparral, Comfrey, *Ginger*

DOSAGE: *1 to 3 cups of cool Yarrow tea in a day is usually enough for this use, but more can be taken according to need.*

EYES: Use Yarrow tea as an eyewash for tired, irritated, or inflamed eyes. Use it at a comfortable temperature. I find that warm tea is good for tiredness, and cold tea is good for itching.

ALSO SEE: *Allergy, Inflammation*

ALTERNATIVE OR SUPPLEMENTARY SELF-HELP: *Cayenne, Comfrey*

DOSAGE: *Make average strength Yarrow tea, strain well, and use as an eyewash either warm or cold.*

FASTING: Under the supervision of a health professional you may find your body enjoys great benefits by taking 1 to 3 days off from eating. Replace food with drinking 4 to 8 cups of Yarrow tea each day. Using Yarrow in this way has had the effect of rebalancing and rejuvenating many students and friends who were bothered with chronic weakness (i.e., indigestion, infection, skin symptoms, congestion, etc.) or who simply wanted to do a yearly cleaning of their physical apparatus.

ALSO SEE: *Circulation, Congestion, Perspiration Therapy, Tonic*

ALTERNATIVE OR SUPPLEMENTARY SELF-HELP: *Chaparral, *Comfrey, Peppermint*

DOSAGE: *Drink 4 to 8 cups of Yarrow tea per day. It is often good to alternate the Yarrow tea with a cup of pure water. Including both water and tea, it is suggested that you drink at least 2 quarts of liquid each day, and preferably more.*

FEMALE ORGANS: See Menstruation and Reproductive Organs applications.

FEVER: Yarrow is the first herb you should think of when you want to do something about a fever. As I described in the Personality Profile, some of the active principles in the herb actually help gather up toxins in the body and package them for elimination. This helps the body handle its own rebalancing quickly, without the need for prolonged or high fever.

If the fever is particularly severe, use Yarrow tea or Yarrow tincture as much as needed and add the use of a Yarrow enema. In some cases, where nausea or intolerance of drinking much liquid is a difficulty, it may be necessary to take the tea in spoonful doses every few minutes; usually, however, a cup of the tea can be drunk easily.

Continue taking the tea—4 to 8 cups in a day — in severe illness. For milder fever or illness however, you can end the body's need for a fever (as a means of purifying) by simply drinking 1 or 2 cups of tea, eating lightly, and perhaps taking a Yarrow enema.

A Yarrow bath can also work wonders. Make 2 quarts of triple strength tea, strain, and add the liquid to a basin or tub of bath water.

ALSO SEE: *Childhood Diseases, Circulation, Colds & Flu, Congestion, Infection, Inflammation, Perspiration Therapy, Tonic, Yarrow Bath*

ALTERNATIVE OR SUPPLEMENTARY SELF-HELP: *Cayenne, Chaparral, Comfrey, *Garlic, *Ginger, Onion, Peppermint*

DOSAGE: *As given or general*

GALL BLADDER: Yarrow tincture, tea or infusion is useful as a stimulant for the flow of bile, as an anti-inflammatory agent, and as an efficient, long-term liver and gall bladder tonic. For severe gall bladder congestion, you may want the help of a Yarrow enema. (See Enema instructions in Chapter I, Lesson #2.)

ALSO SEE: *Circulation, Congestion, Digestion, Fasting, Perspiration Therapy, Tonic*

ALTERNATIVE OR SUPPLEMENTARY SELF-HELP: **Cayenne, Chaparral, *Comfrey, Garlic, *Onion (poultice over gall bladder)*

DOSAGE: *General*

GAS: Yarrow enhances bile output and digestion efficiency which can help prevent stomach and intestinal gas from forming, or it can help break it up quickly. Use any form of Yarrow, including a Yarrow enema.

ALSO SEE: *Congestion, Digestion, Tonic*

ALTERNATIVE OR SUPPLEMENTARY SELF-HELP: *Cayenne, *Ginger, *Peppermint*

DOSAGE: *General*

HEMORRHOIDS: Use Yarrow tea as a tonic (see Tonic application) to cleanse and strengthen the blood, blood veins, and vessels. Daily use of Yarrow can steadily cleanse and shrink swollen hemorrhoids (and other varicose veins). Immediate self-help can be given for severe symptoms by using a double strength Yarrow tea as a sitz bath, and/or by using about one cup of the tea as a retention enema. Hold it in for as long as possible before ejecting it. (See Enema instructions, Chapter I, Lesson #2.)

As most herbalists know from their own experience and observation, a healthy diet and decreased emotional stress play an important role in healing hemorrhoids.

ALSO SEE: *Circulation, Congestion, Tonic, Varicose Veins, Yarrow Bath*

ALTERNATIVE OR SUPPLEMENTARY SELF-HELP: *Cayenne, Chaparral, *Comfrey, *Garlic, *Slippery Elm*

DOSAGE: *General*

HEPATITIS: Because of its strong tonic qualities, Yarrow is a good preventive for the type of hepatitis that is commonly contracted from contaminated food or water. In my experience, Yarrow encourages rehabilitation of the liver while a person is recovering from hepatitis. It does this by enhancing blood-purifying and digestion processes while lessening inflammation.

Yarrow and the other herbs listed under "Alternative Self-Help" below, are all useful as external poultices over the liver in addition to their internal use.

A Yarrow enema (together with the drinking of Yarrow tea) is a further boost toward a speedy recovery from hepatitis.

ALSO SEE: *Congestion, Infection, Inflammation, Perspiration Therapy, Tonic, Yarrow Bath*

ALTERNATIVE OR SUPPLEMENTARY SELF-HELP: *Chaparral, *Comfrey, Garlic, Onion, People Paste*

DOSAGE: *General*

HYPOGLYCEMIA: One cup of Yarrow tea before bed keeps my blood sugar balanced during the night. Its powerful tonic qualities also strengthen my body during this important healing time. This enables me to wake up clearheaded without experiencing the sluggish "sugar low" that encourages many of us to leap for the coffee or other stimulants.

I have also found that drinking 1 or 2 cups of Yarrow tea during the day lessens the blood sugar "ups and downs" and the related hypoglycemia symptoms. At the same time it gives me ongoing strength. This is not an uncommon experience among my friends and students, too. We have also learned that avoiding stressful foods—like processed foods and refined sugars—magnifies the benefits of Yarrow tea for beating the All-American "Hypoglycemia Blues."

ALSO SEE: *Blood-Purifier, Congestion, Digestion, Tonic*

ALTERNATIVE OR SUPPLEMENTARY SELF-HELP: **Cayenne, Chaparral, Comfrey, Garlic, *Ginger*

DOSAGE: *General*

IMMUNE SYSTEM: See Blood-Purifier and Tonic applications.

INFECTION: The tannic acid and volatile oils (including Achillein) in Yarrow are two of its main infection-fighting properties. Whether you use Yarrow internally or externally, you are getting this infection-fighting power. I use Yarrow for infections anywhere in the body — e.g., for conjunctivitis (eyes), colds, flu, wounds, staph, vaginal yeast, and even infected splinters and insect bites, to name a few.

Read more details on how this herb works in the Personality Profile at the beginning of this chapter.

ALSO SEE: *Antiseptic, Circulation, Colds and Flu, Congestion, Fasting, Inflammation, Insect Bites, Perspiration Therapy, Tonic, Yarrow Bath*

ALTERNATIVE OR SUPPLEMENTARY SELF-HELP: **Chaparral, *Garlic, Onion, *People Paste*

DOSAGE: *General*

INFLAMMATION: Especially concentrated in the flowers of Yarrow are carbohydrates and proteins that some observers, including myself, feel are retained at a site of inflammation to enhance the quick repair of damaged, inflamed tissue. In addition these nutrients, along with Yarrow's volatile oils and tannic acid, break down and eliminate irritating (inflammatory and/or infectious) toxins in the blood, lymph, and tissues themselves. There is an interesting note about this action of Yarrow in the book *Herbal Pharmacy* by John Heinerman (see Resource Guide, Appendix C). Consult it for more details.

Use Yarrow as an herbal soak or Yarrow bath for inflamed athletic injuries, arthritis, bursitis, etc. At the same time use Yarrow internally, preferably as a tea.

Also remember that Comfrey is a great herb for soothing inflammation and is doubly potent in combination with Yarrow. Use internally and externally as poultice, soak, or tea.

ALSO SEE: *Circulation, Congestion, Infection, Perspiration Therapy, Tonic, Yarrow Bath*

ALTERNATIVE OR SUPPLEMENTARY SELF-HELP: *Cayenne, *Chaparral, Clove, *Comfrey, Garlic, Ginger, Onion, *Slippery Elm*

DOSAGE: *General; Yarrow is best taken on an empty stomach, but this is not essential.*

INSECT BITES: Since Yarrow grows fresh in many different climates, it is a good herb to learn to identify in the wild. I always teach my children's classes to identify Yarrow so they can begin using it right away. They grab a few leaves or blossoms and chew them into a poultice for quick relief from any type of insect bite they might receive while at play. You simply take the wad of chewed up or well-crushed, moistened leaves and/or blossoms, and rub it, tape it, or hold it on the insect bite. Do the same thing when using dried Yarrow, or activate the herb with boiling water if you like. Yarrow tea or a Yarrow bath is good for soaking, bathing, or washing any bite or other skin irritation, and drinking the tea will often stop a reaction to insect bites. Many children from my herb classes have stopped painful reactions from ant bites, bee stings, spider bites, etc., on themselves and/or playground friends by knowing this Yarrow trick.

ALSO SEE: *Circulation, Itching, Skin, Tonic, Yarrow Bath*

ALTERNATIVE OR SUPPLEMENTARY SELF-HELP: **Chaparral, Clove, *Comfrey, Garlic, *Onion, *People Paste*

DOSAGE: *General*

INTESTINES: Use Yarrow tea and/or a Yarrow enema for many types of intestinal distress, including intestinal flu and other types of diarrhea. It can also help relieve griping in the colon.

ALSO SEE: *Congestion, Digestion, Gas, Hemorrhoids*

ALTERNATIVE OR SUPPLEMENTARY SELF-HELP: **Comfrey, Ginger, *Slippery Elm*

DOSAGE: *General*

ITCHING: Drink Yarrow tea or use a Yarrow bath, salve, or poultice for itching from allergies, insect bites, and even poison oak or poison ivy.

ALSO SEE: *Allergy, Insect Bites, Skin, Tonic, Yarrow Bath*

ALTERNATIVE OR SUPPLEMENTARY SELF-HELP: *Chaparral, Clove *Comfrey, *Ginger, Onion, *People Paste, *Slippery Elm*

DOSAGE: *General*

LIVER: Yarrow tea or tincture helps to stimulate healthy functioning of the liver and increases bile production in the gall bladder. Its tonic actions strengthen, tone, and rehabilitate the liver tissue itself.

For chronic liver difficulties, try Yarrow daily as a tonic, drinking 1 to 2 cups of the tea during the day. For a liver crisis, drink Yarrow tea as needed and place a poultice of Yarrow directly over the liver to help eliminate liver blockages and stimulate bile. A Yarrow enema and/or a short (1 to 3 day) Yarrow tea fast can also relieve an acute liver situation. It is best to fast under professional supervision.

ALSO SEE: *Circulation, Congestion, Fasting, Gall Bladder, Infection, Inflammation, Perspiration Therapy, Tonic*

ALTERNATIVE OR SUPPLEMENTARY SELF-HELP: **Chaparral, *Comfrey, Garlic, Onion, Peppermint*

DOSAGE: *General or as given*

LUNGS: Yarrow is highly recommended for bleeding in the lungs as well as for lung congestion. Use as a tea and/or an enema. You may think it odd to suggest an enema for something that is wrong in the lungs, yet the large intestine will readily absorb fluid and herbal actions into the body. Also, the colon is a major avenue of elimination of lymphatic wastes and other bodily wastes. Even when there is no apparent constipation or diarrhea in the colon, an herbal enema will usually catalyze a draining of congestion from the lungs and other internal organs. Try it.

ALSO SEE: *Congestion, Perspiration Therapy, Tonic*

ALTERNATIVE OR SUPPLEMENTARY SELF-HELP: *Cayenne, *Chaparral, Clove, *Comfrey, Garlic, *Onion*

DOSAGE: *General*

LYMPH: Lymph fluid surrounds and saturates every cell in the body. It brings nourishment to the cells and picks up waste products for elimination which is a crucial process of healing during any health crisis. Lymph glands, located at junctures throughout the lymphatic system, collect these wastes. "Pumping" the lymph glands through general exercise and physical activity encourages the elimination of these accumulated wastes from the body via the skin, blood, and other eliminative channels. When you work up even a mild sweat, lymph fluid cleanses out through the skin in the perspiration. Anything that helps to open the pores in the skin, stimulate circulation, cleanse the blood, and strengthen the function of internal organs will improve the healthy functioning of the lymphatic system.

Yarrow promotes all these actions and is an efficient herb to think of for supporting the lymphatic system during any illness. When the lymphatic system is functioning well, the body will easily make short work of any health crisis, restoring itself to normal quickly.

Chaparral is another major lymphatic helper. See the Lymph application in the Chaparral chapter (Chapter III).

ALSO SEE: *Circulation, Colds & Flu, Congestion, Fasting, Fever, Perspiration Therapy, Tonic, Yarrow Bath*

ALTERNATIVE OR SUPPLEMENTARY SELF-HELP: *Cayenne, *Chaparral, *Comfrey, Garlic, *Ginger, Onion*

DOSAGE: *General*

MENSTRUATION: Look over the TASOLE at the beginning of this chapter. If I were inclined to spend my time peddling tonics or elixirs on street corners, I'd put up a stand and strut around shouting, "Git yer menstrual cure-all right 'ere, folks!" while holding up beautifully packaged bundles of Yarrow. Well . . . maybe in my imagination I might.

Use Yarrow, 1 to perhaps 4 cups of tea a day, as a continuing tonic to promote menstrual health and balance. A Yarrow poultice placed on the abdomen over ovaries and uterus, one to three times a week, is an additional aid. If menstrual cramping is a problem, a calcium lactate or calcium gluconate supplement, added to the diet on a daily basis or at least during the week before and during the menstrual flow, further enhances the benefits of the Yarrow herb. Many women find that adding an electrolyte juice of some sort during and/or just prior to the menstrual flow lessens or stops menstrual pain. However these last two are are only suggested in addition to the Yarrow as helpful "extras."

Yarrow can be used for: menses that are too heavy or too light; spotting between cycles; erratic cycles; weakness/faintness; hot or cold flashes corresponding with ovulation or menses, and persistent menstrual cramping (helpful to add calcium for this last one).

Chaparral is another major herb for balancing the female organs and menstrual cycle.

ALSO SEE: *Congestion, Reproductive Organs, Tonic*

ALTERNATIVE OR SUPPLEMENTARY SELF-HELP: *Chaparral, Comfrey, *Ginger*

DOSAGE: *General or as given*

NAUSEA: See Stomach application.

NIGHTSWEATS: Drink a cool to cold (but not iced) cup of Yarrow tea before bed and at one other time during the day. Daytime tea can be any temperature.

ALSO SEE: *Circulation, Lymph, Perspiration Therapy, Tonic*

ALTERNATIVE OR SUPPLEMENTARY SELF-HELP: *Chaparral, Clove, Comfrey, Ginger (bath)*

DOSAGE: *As given*

PERSPIRATION THERAPY: There is a technical word for this action which is diaphoresis. It means the action of an herb that helps open the pores, balance circulation, and induce perspiration, thereby helping the internal and external (i.e., skin) organs of elimination cleanse the body of toxins more actively and efficiently. Take hot Yarrow tea for this purpose. In opening the pores, Yarrow encourages increase of circulation to surface tissues which promotes a healthy and cleansing sweat, helps clear up skin troubles, breaks up cold blockages (internal chills), encourages body warmth, dispels fever, and stimulates the eliminative functions of the lymph and skin, thereby increasing the speed at which the body may cleanse and heal itself.

I don't want to give you the idea that every time you drink Yarrow tea you will break out into a massive sweat, as this is not the case at all. Opened skin pores will naturally release toxins through mild perspiration. When a more active sweat is needed, as might be the case with a dry fever for instance, you can sit in a hot bath or wrap yourself in warm blankets in a warm room, and drink Yarrow tea. During the course of using Yarrow as a daily tonic, you will probably notice that whenever you are exercising, you will break into a sweat much more easily, which greatly enhances the body's cleansing and rejuvenating ability.

ALSO SEE: *Circulation, Congestion, Fasting, Lymph, Tonic, Yarrow Bath*

ALTERNATIVE OR SUPPLEMENTARY SELF-HELP: **Ginger, Peppermint*

DOSAGE: *Use as a tonic, 1 cup Yarrow tea a day. For a more active perspiration effect, take 2 or more cups hot tea. For greatest action during illness, drink the hot tea while sitting in a hot bath—a Yarrow Bath or Ginger Bath is perfect for this purpose although plain hot water alone will do.*

REPRODUCTIVE ORGANS male/female: All the actions of Yarrow as a tonic come into play here, so please review the Tonic application.

For male organs, Yarrow is used in a sitz bath and/or taken as tea for prostate, testicle, and penis irritations and swelling. It also has good results with epididymitis.

A sitz bath is a tub of tea or plain water that is big enough to sit in with the water covering only up to and including the entire hip area. While a warm Yarrow sitz bath can work wonders by itself, it is more potent to alternate between warm and cold. Sit in a tub of ice cold water/tea for 1 minute followed by 5 minutes in a warm-hot bath of Yarrow. Alternate between the hot and cold for a cumulative total of 20 minutes. This will greatly increase circulation to the affected parts. Sitz baths can be used frequently, from once a week to twice a day depending on the situation.

For female organs, sitz baths are also recommended for chronic problems including inflammation and infection of reproductive organs. Use Yarrow tea as a douche for vaginal discharge—including unhealthy types of mucus and yeast infection. Also take the tea internally, drinking 2 to 6 cups a day.

Chaparral is another specific herb for self-help with reproductive organs.

ALSO SEE: *Circulation, Congestion, Fasting, Infection, Inflammation, Menstruation, Perspiration Therapy, Tonic*

ALTERNATIVE OR SUPPLEMENTARY SELF-HELP: **Chaparral, Comfrey, Garlic, *Ginger*

DOSAGE: *General or as given*

SINUS: See Congestion application.

SKIN: See the Perspiration Therapy application. Anytime something goes wrong with the skin you can be fairly sure that the other organs of elimination are getting overloaded and the skin is having to take up the slack. This is very inconvenient!

Use Yarrow tea as an herbal wash, soak, or bath while also taking advantage of its tonic and infection-fighting qualities by using Yarrow internally in the form of tea, infusion, or tincture. This internal/external usage helps the body cleanse more efficiently (especially supporting the liver), takes the pressure off the skin, and further helps the skin recover its health by promoting new cell growth. When used as a wash and/or tea, Yarrow has fungicide effects which can work on fungus infections of the skin. Yarrow will soothe itching.

ALSO SEE: *Antiseptic, Circulation, Infection, Itching, Perspiration Therapy, Tonic, Yarrow Bath*

ALTERNATIVE OR SUPPLEMENTARY SELF-HELP: **Chaparral, *Comfrey, Garlic, *Ginger, Onion, People Paste*

DOSAGE: *General*

SPASMS: See Intestinal and Stomach applications for explanation of Yarrow's help with stomachache and intestinal pains, two common types of spasms.

STIMULANT: Yarrow's tonic qualities gently stimulate the internal organs, especially the liver, kidneys, and gall bladder, to cleanse and strengthen themselves. That means rejuvenation for the whole body. I use Yarrow for stimulation whenever I'm feeling sluggish and need a pick-me-up or need help recovering from dietary excesses.

ALSO SEE: *Circulation, Congestion, Digestion, Gall Bladder, Liver, Lymph, Perspiration Therapy, Tonic*

ALTERNATIVE OR SUPPLEMENTARY SELF-HELP: **Cayenne, Chaparral, *Ginger, *Peppermint*

DOSAGE: *General*

STOMACH: If you need something to quickly settle an upset stomach, improve digestion, or quiet the symptoms of a stomach flu, Yarrow is probably the herb for the job. Even when vomiting has been persistent and nothing at all will stay down, you can often alleviate it by taking Yarrow tea, 1 tsp. at a time each 5 or 10 minutes. It often stays down better if taken cool or at room temperature, so it may be necessary to experiment with the temperature of the tea in extreme cases. The idea is to take these small doses at regularly spaced intervals, even though the first 1 to 3 doses may be vomited up. In most cases the vomiting reflex will stop very quickly. I say "in most cases" just to avoid exaggerating by saying "always." Yet in my experience this way of using Yarrow has worked every time. I have used Yarrow for infants and 90-year-old friends.

As the tea begins to stay down, you can begin to take a little more in each dose and the doses can be taken closer together. When the first inkling of an appetite starts to return, it is wise to begin taking a mild food or broth, 1 tsp. at 5 or 10 minute intervals, until you are certain the stomach can handle it.

Yarrow itself is nourishing, so it is fine to depend on the herb alone for awhile before starting to eat simple foods again. Slippery Elm "gruel" (see Nutritional application in Chapter X) is a good and mild rejuvenating broth for a tender stomach.

If there is an upset stomach without constant vomiting or dry heaves, you probably don't have to be so particular about measuring and timing the doses but can simply drink the tea as you find convenient.

If you feel "queasy" after eating, feel you have gotten food poisoning, have nervous digestion, get frequent heartburn, or find your stomach just isn't at its best for any reason, Yarrow is really worth a try. Ulcerous conditions often respond well to Yarrow as well, especially if used as part of a daily regimen that includes the use of Cayenne once or twice a day.

Be sure to review Yarrow's Tonic application.

TASOLE: My good friend Donna called me one day to say that her 9-year-old son had been vomiting all day and having dry heaves for a few hours. Nothing she tried would calm it and he couldn't even keep water in his stomach. He had a slight fever, yet no other symptoms.

Her son, Joey, had been an herb student of mine when he was six years old and was familiar with using herbs. When I arrived he was just beginning another bout of vomiting. When it was over he lay down, exhausted. We talked a little as I rubbed his back and when I suggested using Yarrow, he said he remembered it well from our previous herb classes. He had used it often for insect stings and small injuries while out playing. It was not a tea he was used to drinking because of its mildly bitter taste, yet he knew it "could fix lots of things", as he put it, and so was willing to give it a try.

We started with the one-teaspoon-of-tea-every-five-to-ten-minutes routine, and the first teaspoon he vomited up very quickly. The second teaspoon stayed down a few minutes longer before it came up, and the third teaspoon stayed down completely even though he felt a little nauseous. Soon after that, he and his mom stopped timing the doses and he just sipped on a cup of tea, feeling much better although still very weak. His fever was gone by evening and the vomiting stopped completely. He continued with two cups of Yarrow tea each day for a day or two since he still didn't feel exactly right. By the third day he was fine. Since many of his neighborhood friends were suffering from the same stomach flu, he began to call them and tell them about his amazing new "find"—Yarrow!

I tell Joey's story because it is a good example of how children really appreciate learning how to take care of their own health. It gives them a sense of well-being and the confidence to help their friends.

Another young student of mine used Yarrow tea to help his sick grandfather. The child simply picked some Yarrow in the backyard, cooked up some tea, and started the teaspoon doses on his initially skeptical, but later appreciative, grandfather.

ALSO SEE: *Colds and Flu, Digestion, Fasting, Inflammation, Perspiration Therapy, Tonic*

ALTERNATIVE OR SUPPLEMENTARY SELF-HELP: *Cayenne, Comfrey, *Ginger, People Paste, *Peppermint, Slippery Elm*

DOSAGE: *Use as given here or use General Dosage.*

TEETHING: To make an unbeatable teething solution, soak equal parts of Yarrow and brandy together in a glass jar for 10 days. Strain well. To apply to baby's gums, dip your finger in the mixture and rub on the gums. If there is an objection to using alcohol, you may substitute glycerine. Glycerine, a clear sweet substance with a consistency somewhat like honey, is available at drug stores.

The addition of Clove oil to any teething mixture gives extra pain relief. See the Clove chapter, Chapter IV.

ALSO SEE: *Yarrow Tincture*

ALTERNATIVE OR SUPPLEMENTARY SELF-HELP: **Clove, Peppermint*

DOSAGE: *As given*

TONIC: Yarrow is an extraordinary tonic herb. It has essential oils, tannic acid, carbohydrates, and proteins that, together with other constituents, can catalyze the following actions:

- Yarrow stimulates the liver and gall bladder to produce bile and other digestive substances.
- It strengthens the ability of the liver, lymph system, and skin to cleanse the blood.
- It "packages" toxins in the body for more efficient elimination.
- Yarrow has strong infection and inflammation-fighting abilities.
- It is an excellent agent for promoting opening of the pores, circulation to surface tissues, and perspiration for release of body toxins.
- It breaks up "cold blockages" and chills in the internal organs so they can resume the rejuvenation process.
- It strengthens the immune system.
- Yarrow balances menstruation.
- It acts as an astringent to tone, firm, and cleanse the tissues of the body, including the internal organs.
- It helps balance blood-sugar upheavals common to hypoglycemia.
- Yarrow promotes the healing of wounds.

The way I use Yarrow as a tonic is to drink 1 cup of Yarrow tea each day, usually right before bed, as this helps me wake up clearheaded and alert. Any time of the day, however, is good for taking Yarrow as a tonic. If I feel I need to do a short cleansing fast of perhaps two or three days, Yarrow is often the rejuvenating herb tea I use.

Yarrow connoisseurs will want to learn to identify and gather the herb themselves in order to get the most potent "raw material" to work with.

ALSO SEE: *All the other applications*

ALTERNATIVE OR SUPPLEMENTARY SELF-HELP: **Cayenne, *Comfrey, *Garlic, Onion, Slippery Elm*

DOSAGE: *Using 1 cup each day is a common way to use Yarrow as a tonic, yet more can be used as needed. See General Dosage.*

TONSILLITIS: See Inflammation application.

URINARY TRACT: Yarrow tea can often reverse a bladder infection and help to strengthen the kidneys. Simply drink a cup of the tea three to six times a day. If you tend to get chronic bladder infections, you may want to try a cup of Yarrow tea each day for ongoing prevention.

ALSO SEE: *Circulation, Infection, Inflammation, Lymph, Perspiration Therapy*

ALTERNATIVE OR SUPPLEMENTARY SELF-HELP: **Chaparral, *Comfrey, *Garlic, Ginger, People Paste (used internally), Slippery Elm*

DOSAGE: *General*

VARICOSE VEINS: Use Yarrow as a tonic, 1 to 3 cups a day, to cleanse and help rehabilitate varicose veins. Sometimes it helps to put a Yarrow poultice on the more severe areas of varicosity.

Diet plays an important part in self-help for severe varicose veins. I find it quite helpful to avoid processed food, red meats, fried foods, processed sugar and sugar substitutes.

ALSO SEE: *Hemorrhoids, Inflammation, Perspiration Therapy*

ALTERNATIVE OR SUPPLEMENTARY SELF-HELP: *Cayenne, Chaparral, *Comfrey, Onion, People Paste*

DOSAGE: *As given*

WAKE-UP TEA: See Hypoglycemia application.

WOUNDS: Use Yarrow tea as an antiseptic wash. Use Yarrow alone, fresh or dried, in a poultice for wounds or mix it with other herbs such as Comfrey. Drink the tea as additional reinforcement to prevent infection.

ALSO SEE: *Antiseptic, Infection, Inflammation, Skin*

ALTERNATIVE OR SUPPLEMENTARY SELF-HELP: **Chaparral, *Comfrey, Garlic, *People Paste*

DOSAGE: *General*

YARROW BATH: To make a Yarrow bath, use one full cup of Yarrow blossoms and/or leaves. Bring one gallon of water to a boil, remove from heat, add Yarrow and steep for at least 30 minutes, covered. Strain and add this concentrated brew to a bathtub of very warm water. Soak for at least 30 minutes.

This bath will soothe a tired and aching body, calm emotions, and promote relief of inflammation both internally and externally. It also provides antiseptic action for skin difficulties, soothes itching, and imparts Yarrow's tonic qualities to the whole body through the skin.

Yarrow baths provide a good incentive for gathering your own Yarrow. It is the best way of getting a large quantity of the finest quality Yarrow blossoms and leaves for the least expense. Gathering Yarrow is also quite pleasurable. If you must buy your Yarrow for baths at an herb store, ask for the commonly given discount for buying a pound or more.

Take a Yarrow bath as often as you like.

ALSO SEE: *Antiseptic, Childhood Diseases, Circulation, Fever, Inflammation, Itching, Lymph, Perspiration Therapy, Tonic, Wounds*

DOSAGE: *As given*

YARROW TINCTURE: There are many ways to make a tincture. Here is a basic recipe, using Yarrow as the example:

YARROW TINCTURE RECIPE

This tincture is made in two stages.

STAGE 1) Make a strong infusion with either fresh or dried Yarrow using 3-5 tsp. Yarrow for each 1 cup water. If you start with fresh herb, then you must chop it finely and simmer it as slowly as possible, covered, for 30 minutes (no more). If you start with dried herb, steep it in a covered pot for at least 30 minutes. Covering the pot helps to preserve the delicate essential oils in the herb. Let the infusion cool (still in a covered pan), and then strain this infusion to continue protecting essential oils. (I usually simply let the brewed mixture sit, covered and unstrained, until it cools to room temperature.) However, after the 30-minute brewing time, you may cool it more quickly in a refrigerator if you like. DO NOT USE ALUMINUM POTS OR ALUMINUM UTENSILS OF ANY KIND.

STAGE 2) Cool this infusion to room temperature, measure it, and put it into a glass jar with a well-fitting lid. (A canning jar works well.) Add strong red wine in the proportions of 2 parts infusion to 1 part wine. To these combined liquids add enough Yarrow flowers, either dried or fresh, to equal about 1/2 the volume. Let this combination sit in the covered jar in a sunny room for twenty-one days. Gently shake the jar each day.

At the end of the twenty-one days, strain the mixture and press out as much tincture as possible from the herbs. Sometimes I use a cotton cloth for this and press the herbs thoroughly with my hands. Store the tincture in 4 to 6 oz. amounts in small glass bottles that seal tightly. Sealing with wax over the corks or lids is a very good idea. Store the tincture in a dark, cool, dry place, like a rarely used cupboard. Keep an opened, unsealed bottle (the one you are currently using) in the refrigerator. If prepared, sealed, and stored properly, this tincture will maintain its potency for a year or more.

A tincture is particularly handy for use with children and infants, while traveling, at the office, as a quick digestive aid, or for relief of many types of abdominal pain. Use the Yarrow tincture when a concentrated liquid would be convenient instead of making the tea. However, keep in mind that the freshly made tea or infusion is generally the best form for using Yarrow. Alternating use of tea and tincture also works well.

ALSO SEE: *None*

ALTERNATIVE OR SUPPLEMENTARY SELF-HELP: *None*

DOSAGE: *Average dose is 1/2 to 1 tsp. in a little water for children and adults. For infants use 5 to 10 drops. Use Yarrow tincture as needed throughout the day. (One dose is enough for many circumstances.) After any dose, wait about 15 minutes to see what action you are getting before determining the need for another dose.*

YEAST INFECTION: For vaginal yeast, douche with Yarrow infusion and drink 2 or more cups of Yarrow tea each day. Also, using a vaginal bolus of People Paste, Chaparral, Yarrow, or Garlic can be quite useful. (See Bolus instructions in Chapter I, Lesson #2.)

For any external yeast infection, use a Yarrow infusion wash or soak, a Yarrow poultice, and/or drink Yarrow tea.

ALSO SEE: *Menstruation, Reproductive Organs, Tonic, Yarrow Tincture*

ALTERNATIVE OR SUPPLEMENTARY SELF-HELP: **Chaparral, *Garlic, People Paste*

DOSAGE: *As given or see General Dosage. Yarrow tincture is also good as a douche. Only a small amount of water is needed, to carry tincture to the vaginal tissues. Do not put undiluted tincture in the vagina. Dilute 2 Tbsp. tincture in 1 cup water.*

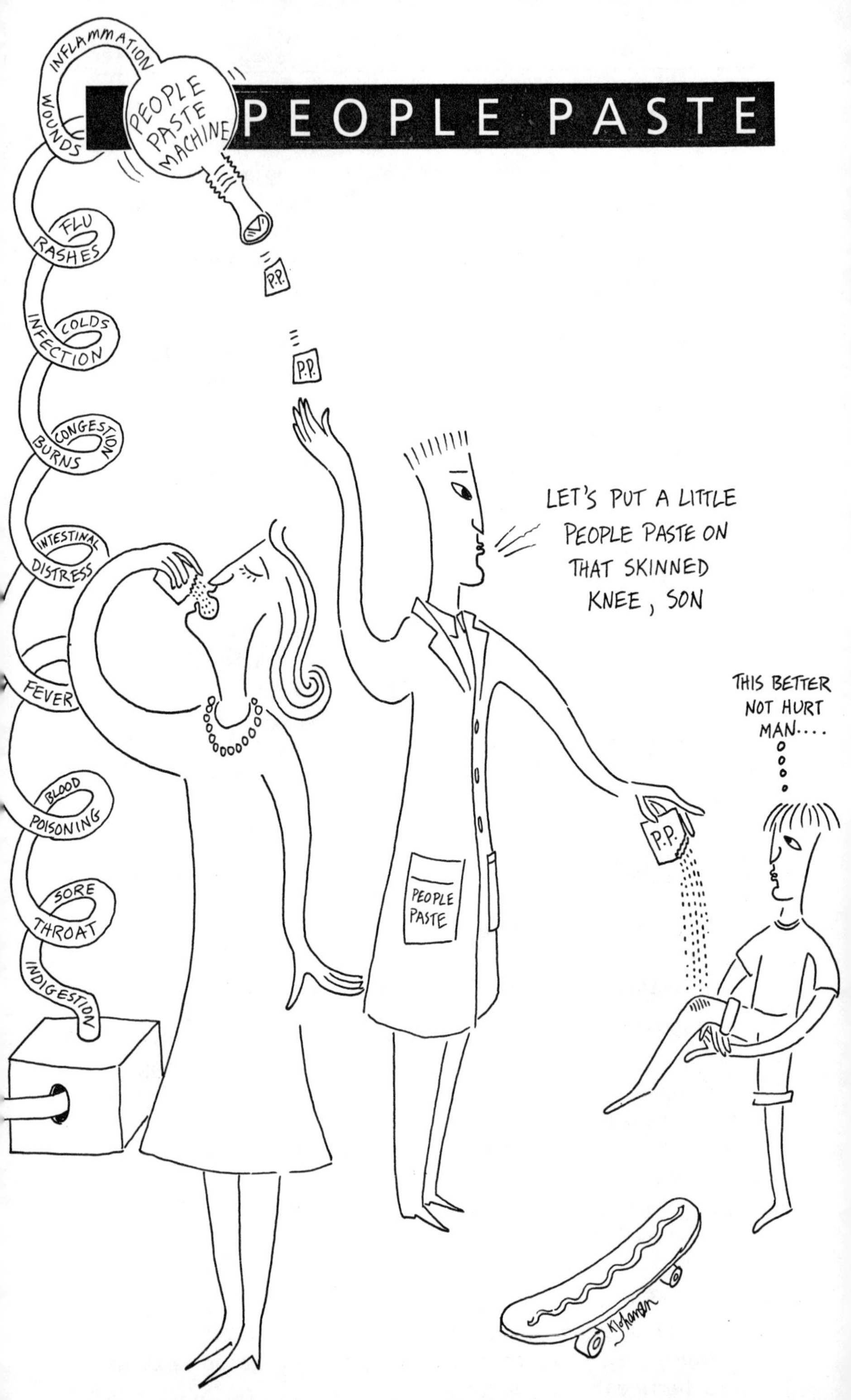
PEOPLE PASTE
PEOPLE PASTE MACHINE
INFLAMMATION
WOUNDS
FLU
RASHES
COLDS
INFECTION
CONGESTION
BURNS
INTESTINAL DISTRESS
FEVER
BLOOD POISONING
SORE THROAT
INDIGESTION
P.P.
P.P.
LET'S PUT A LITTLE PEOPLE PASTE ON THAT SKINNED KNEE, SON
PEOPLE PASTE
P.P.
THIS BETTER NOT HURT MAN....

APPENDIX A

PEOPLE PASTE

People Paste can be used for all manner of needs.
For cuts, wounds, or rashes, it's just the right speed.
For digestive upheavals, for flu or for eyes,
It's a traveler's delight used in any disguise.

People Paste does far more than simply "paste" things together. It is appropriately named for its profound ability to put the body back in place when it seems to be falling apart,in small or large ways, either inside or out. It's the perfect thing for pets and livestock, too.

The first (and so far best) People Paste formula I ever used (I have since "invented" others) includes Slippery Elm as a major ingredient. It is a simple formula to learn about and to make since it has only three ingredients, which are readily available at herb or health food stores. It would be a good idea to make some People Paste in advance of travelling since I am not certain you can find these herbs easily everywhere in the world.

The formula for the "original" PEOPLE PASTE is:

Mix equal parts of powdered

SLIPPERY ELM, GOLDENSEAL, and **MYRRH.**

Slippery Elm:

Anti-inflammatory, demulcent (soothing), contains protein for building new tissues, mucilaginous (see Slippery Elm chapter, Chapter X)

Goldenseal:

Antiseptic, antibiotic, cell proliferant, blood-cleanser, astringent, pulls tissue together for effective wound healing. Consult one of the two-starred (**) reference volumes cited in the Resource Guide, Appendix C, for details on the chemistry and seemingly endless uses of this herb.

Myrrh:

Antiseptic (quite powerful), antacid, digestive aid, expectorant, stimulant (mild), breaks up gas, encourages tissues to heal. Consult one of the two-starred (**) reference volumes cited in the Resource Guide, Appendix C, for details of the chemistry and uses of this herb.

If you want to stick to the Ten Essentials or they are the only ones you have on hand in a moment of need, you can easily substitute two or three of the other Ten Essentials for the Goldenseal and Myrrh. (Keep the Slippery Elm, an essential ingredient.) Two excellent substitutes would be Comfrey root and Chaparral, but do not hesitate to use any herb, mixed with the Slippery Elm, that has the properties you need for the situation. By being creative with this basic idea, you can "invent" new types of People Paste as is convenient.

For the purposes of this appendix I will be using the "original" People Paste formula (the one I use most), as my example. **Clove** powder is always an optional addition when stronger **pain relief** is needed, although the original People Paste is already quite good in this regard.

Internally People Paste is used for flu, indigestion, fever, colds, blood-poisoning, intestinal distress, sore throat, congestion, inflammation, infection and much more. It is usually taken in 1/4 to 1/2 tsp. doses in water, capsules, or honeyball (see Chapter I, Lesson #2), yet an adult in "dire need" could take up to one teaspoon.

Externally, People Paste is famous for help with wounds, rashes, infections, and burns. In my experience this amazing formula prevents infection while it pulls wounds together and greatly decreases the chance of scarring. Even on larger wounds the use of People Paste has led many to think that the wound had been stitched by an expert.

The dry powder can be used directly for an external need yet it is most often "activated" by moistening the powders.

MOISTEN PEOPLE PASTE WITH:

Honey (raw, uncooked): Honey is all-purpose, and usually the best choice for any need. It has its own antiseptic and enzymatic qualities, is high in healing minerals, keeps the wound and paste from drying out, is soothing, and penetrates well. Safe when taken internally too! (See Honey, Appendix B.)

Aloe Vera Gel: High in minerals, somewhat antiseptic, tends to dry out in the paste after a while, good for the skin (especially with burns), safe internally as well.

Glycerin: a clear and sweet sticky fluid of the consistency of honey, easily purchased at drug stores and many health stores, highly emollient, carries herbs well, safe internally.

Olive oil (or a seed oil such as Sesame): Use with older wounds that tend to get too dry, or for dry irritations of the skin. DO NOT USE OIL ON NEW BURNS OR NEW (STILL OOZING OR OPEN) WOUNDS. The oil could slow the tissues' ability to reconnect and oil can also hold heat in the tissues of a burn.

Molasses (unsulphured, blackstrap): High in minerals and iron to enhance healing of tissues, carries herbs well.

Water (or your own saliva for self-use): Water, especially pure mineral water, is fine for mixing People Paste, yet it usually dries out after a while, leaving the herbal paste quite hard. I have used this fact to great benefit when I wanted an antiseptic, herbal "cast" for a broken finger or for another "drier" type of wound that needed protection.

For any external use, first wash or soak the area with an antiseptic herb such as Chaparral, Garlic, Clove, Comfrey, Onion juice, or Yarrow. I often use honey to clean a wound by pouring/dripping (not rubbing) the raw honey directly onto the area. The body heat will warm it and get it runny, and then the honey will actually lift out any dirt or debris from even the tiniest crevices of the wound. Hydrogen peroxide is a good choice for old infected wounds, especially if the wound is draining from an opening on the surface.

After the wound or rash, etc., is properly prepared, apply the People Paste dry, or moistened with one of the agents mentioned above, according to need. The bandaging technique is up to you, depending upon the situation.

For most external needs, a People Paste dressing can be easily soaked off in an antiseptic herbal solution or hydrogen peroxide. Then a fresh dressing can be reapplied, as needed, usually at least twice a day.

For fresh wounds that should be undisturbed while the torn tissues reconnect, and especially where stitching is not an option, I have soaked the entire area, People Paste-bandage and all, in an antiseptic herbal solution two to four times a day for up to two days before attempting to unwrap it. This will keep the People Paste strongly activated. You must, however, have knowledge of how to carefully and frequently check for signs of infection. I have never cared for a wound (or heard of a wound) that developed an infection while People Paste was being used. It is a powerful antiseptic/antibiotic. In extreme cases, however, it pays to be "overly" cautious and regularly check for fever, increased swelling or heat in a wound, red lines of blood-poisoning, etc. Old infected wounds should be treated with regular cleaning and changing of the dressing two to four times a day.

Students sometimes ask me if People Paste poured directly into a wound will keep the tissues apart and therefore delay its natural healing. The answer is "NO." Even on large wounds I don't hesitate to put the herbs directly into the torn tissues, as the People Paste pulls wounds together from the bottom up and partially dissolves into the tissues themselves. As this process continues, the wounds close up perfectly with less and less room for the People Paste. On some severe wounds I have actually taped People Paste into the wound, perhaps 1/16 to 1/8 inch thick, using "butterfly tapes" which I often cut myself. I then cover the entire wound with another layer of People Paste which I soak off and replace at least twice a day.

There are so many variables to the use of this formula; I want to give you a good sense of its flexibility so that your confidence in using People Paste will develop quickly.

"Proud flesh" is a clumsy and unnecessary growth of new tissue that sometimes forms on the surface of a wound, contributing to slow healing and thick scarring. To me it often looks, at first glance, like a layer of pus forming. Then, when I touch it, I see that it is not pus at all but a layer of fairly thick, firm white tissue that has not yet formed into a permanent scar. If a wound develops "proud flesh" as part of its healing process, I pack the wound for one day with the mashed white insides of an ordinary banana. Within twenty-four hours, or at the most forty-eight hours, this generally removes all or most of the proud flesh and slows or stops the further forming of the extra tissue. The next day I clean the wound and resume with the People Paste. Occasionally a severe wound, during its healing process, might again form proud flesh. If this happens, you can repeat the banana poultice treatment.

TASOLE: One afternoon my friend Betsy and I were out chopping wood when she missed the wood with the axe and chopped her arm instead. This left a big flap of muscle just hanging there off her arm and we gave each other the "Holy S---" look. I managed to get her to the kitchen where I cleaned the wound with honey, pouring it over the open wound and letting it lift out the dirt and float it away. We then filled the open wound with a People Paste/Honey combination. We did not consider getting stitches because our experience had told us that with People Paste and correct bandaging, stitches are rarely needed except in the most extreme cases. We wrapped the entire wound with a gauze bandage and left it undisturbed for twenty-four hours to let the tissue begin to reconnect. Every day after that we took off the gauze and gently soaked the wound (so as not to disturb the healing tissue) in an antiseptic herbal infusion. Chaparral, Comfrey, or Garlic worked well for this. We soaked it long enough to clean out most of the People Paste and thoroughly and gently patted it dry with a clean gauze or cloth. Whatever small amounts of the herbs were remaining we left undisturbed, and covered the wound with a new dressing. Day by day we watched with interest as the wound pulled together and the tissues perfectly matched themselves up leaving, at first, a thin "hairline" scar which went away over a few months time.

I have personally been involved in many similar experiences. Other People Paste testimonies have been told to me by my students. Whether it was the case of the man who got his hand mangled in a chain saw or the five-year-old who shut his toe in a door, the same basic procedure was used with the same amazing results.

APPENDIX B

HONEY

Pure raw honey can be used internally in honeyballs, syrups, lozenges, teas, etc. It is used externally in poultices with powdered herbs, or alone.

Pure raw honey:

1) is antiseptic.
2) is an emollient.
3) is a preservative.
4) is soothing.
5) used externally, encourages growth of new skin.
6) enhances the action of an herb or herbs with which it is mixed, because of its enzymes and trace minerals.
7) carries herbal actions quickly into the blood, when used internally, because of its enzymes and simple sugars, levulose and dextrose.
8) binds together the actions of the herbs with which it is mixed, thereby increasing the efficiency of an herbal formula.

One memorable account of how honey acts as an antiseptic was reported by Murray Hoyt in his book *The World Of Bees* (Bonanza Books, 1965).

Mr. Hoyt recounts how Dr. W.G. Sackett, a bacteriologist, set out to prove that honey was fertile ground for growing bacteria and ended up proving the opposite! Dr. Sackett inoculated honey with typhoid and dysentery bacteria. Within 10 hours the dysentery bacteria were all dead and within 48 hours the typhoid bacteria were dead! Dr. Sackett continued the testing with other bacteria and found that this antiseptic activity was repeated over and over.

Historically, honey has been used as an effective preservative for food, cosmetics, and even mummies. Honey is immune to spoilage because its simple sugars, texture, and self-contained enzymes do not support most microorganisms.

In the cosmetic and medical industries, honey has long been known for its emollient, preservative, and antiseptic properties, along with its ability to encourage the growth of healthy skin. These properties and others come into play in honey's well-known ability to speed the healing of burn injuries.

The simple sugars in honey — levulose and dextrose — and honey's trace minerals are quickly and easily absorbed into the blood and are slow-burning fuels for the body's needs. Pure raw honey does not commonly create the stressful blood sugar extremes and glandular imbalances many of us have come to associate with fast-burning refined sugars (commonly sucrose).

Throughout *Ten Essential Herbs* I mention the use of pure raw honey as an enhancement to many forms of herbistry. Honeyballs, People Paste, poultices, teas, syrups, lozenges — all are improved in their efficiency and action with the addition of honey.

Honey is a permanent part of my herbal first-aid kit.

APPENDIX C

RESOURCE LIST

Boston Women's Health Book Collective. *Our Bodies Ourselves.* New York, New York: Simon & Schuster, 1985. 383 pp., paperback.

Christopher, Dr. John R. *Herbal Home Health Care.* Springville, UT: Christopher Publications, 1976. P.O. Box 412, Springville, Utah 84663. 205 pp., hardcover. 1-800-453-1406

* Christopher, Dr. John R. *Capsicum*. Springville, UT: Christopher Publications, 1980. P.O. Box 412, Springville, Utah 84663. 167 pp., paperback. 1-800-453-1406

** Christopher, Dr. John R. *School of Natural Healing*. Springville, UT: Christopher Publications, 1976. P.O. Box 412, Springville, Utah 84663. 653 pp., hardback. 1-800-453-1406

Crook, William, G. *The Yeast Connection: A Medical Breakthrough*. New York, NY: Vintage Books (Random House Inc.), 1991. 201 E. 50th Street, New York, New York 10022. 434 pp., paperback.

Folk Medicine Journal, P.O. Box 11471, Salt Lake City, UT 84147. *Alternative Health Care Quarterly* (64pp) edited by John Heinerman, PH.O. $25/yr.

** Grieve, Mrs. M. *A Modern Herbal* (2 volumes). New York, NY: Dover Publications, 1971. 180 Varick Street, New York, New York 10014. 427 pp., paperback.

Heinerman, John. *Heinerman's Encyclopedia of Fruits, Vegetables, and Herbs.* Englewood Cliffs, N.J.: Simon & Schuster/Prentice-Hall, 1988. Order from: Dr. John Heinerman, PO Box 11471, Salt Lake City, UT 84147. 400 pp., paperback. $17.95 (postage included).

** Heinerman, John. *Herbal Pharmacy*. Englewood Cliffs, N.J.: Simon & Schuster, 1990. Order from: Dr. John Heinerman, PO Box 11471, Salt Lake City, UT 84147. $19.95 (postage included).

Herbal Gram, a quarterly international journal about medicinal plants published by the American Botanical Council and the Herb Research Foundation. P.O. Box 201660, Austin, Texas 78720. $25/yr. 1-800-373-7105.

* Hills, Lawrence, D. *Comfrey: Fodder, Food & Remedy*. New York, NY: Universe Publishers, 1976. 381 Park Ave. South, New York, New York 10016. 212-387-3400. 253 pp., paperback. (Note: this book presently out of print, but well worth searching out.)

Jensen, Bernard. *Chlorophyl Magic from Living Plant Life*. Escondido, CA: Bernard Jensen Enterprises, 1981. Rt. 1 Box 52, Escondido, California, 92025. 153 pp., paperback.

Jensen, Bernard. *Doctor-Patient Handbook*. Escondido, CA: Bernard Jensen Enterprises, 1981. Rt. 1 Box 52, Escondido, California, 92025. 80 pp., paperback.

Kloss, Jethro. *Back to Eden*. Santa Barbara, CA: Woodridge Press, 1975. P.O. Box 6189, Santa Barbara, California, 93111. 689 pp., paperback.

Mendelsohn, Dr. Robert. *How to Raise a Healthy Child in Spite of Your Doctor*. Westminster, MD: Ballantine Books, Random House, 1987. 400 Hahn Rd., Westminster, Maryland 21157. 304 pp., paperback.

Moore, Michael. *Medicinal Plants of the Mountain West*. Sante Fe, NM: Museum of New Mexico Press, 1979. P.O. Box 2087, Sante Fe, New Mexico, 87503. 200 pp., paperback.

* O'Brien, James Edmond. *Miracle of Garlic and Vinegar*, Boca Raton, FL: Globe Communication (Mini Mag.), 1992. 5401 N.W. Broken Sound Blvd., Boca Raton, Florida 33487. 514-849-7733

Santillo, Humbart. *Food Enzymes: The Missing Link to Radiant Health*. Prescott, AZ: Hohm Press, 1987. P.O. Box 2501, Prescott, Arizona, 86302. 602-778-9189. Paperback.

Santillo, Humbart. *Energetics of Juicing* (cassettes with a booklet). Prescott, AZ: Hohm Press, 1991. P.O. Box 2501, Prescott, Arizona, 86301. 602-778-9189.

** Santillo, Humbart. *Natural Healing With Herbs*. Prescott, AZ: Hohm Press, 1984. P.O.Box 2501, Prescott, Arizona, 86302. 602-778-9189. 370 pp., paperback.

Spellenberg, Richard. *Audubon Society Field Guide to N. American Wildflowers* (several volumes by region). New York, NY: Alfred A. Knopf, 1979. 862 pp., paperback.

Travis, John and Ryan, Regina Sara. *Wellness Workbook*. Berkeley, CA: Ten Speed Press, 1988. P.O. Box 7123, Berkeley, California, 94707. 237 pp., paperback.

** Wren, R.C. *Potter's New Cyclopaedia of Botanical Drugs and Preparations*. Woodstock, NY: Beekman Publishers, 1980. P.O. Box 888, Woodstock, New York, 12498. 914-679-2300. Hardcover.

* Excellent resource on a single herb.
** Excellent over-all resource.

APPENDIX D

HERB BUYER'S GUIDE

Blessed Herbs, Rt. 5 Box 1042, Ava, Missouri 65608, 417-683-5721. Wildcrafted and organically grown herbs, fresh or dried, cut, sifted, or powdered. Cottage industry, careful attention, good reputation.

Custom-Made Formulas, P.O. Box 1623, Salt Lake City, Utah 84110-1623. Specializing in personalized formulating for individual health needs. Formulas made to order only upon request. No mass-produced products at all.

Frontier Cooperative Herbs, Box 3021, 78th Street, Norway, Iowa 52318, 319-227-7991. Extensive inventory of medicinal and culinary herbs, herbal preparations and supplies of all sorts, good printed matter, newsletters and books. Wholesale/retail.

Gaia Herbs, 62 Old Littleton Road, Harvard, Massachusetts 01451, 508-456-3049. This company makes potent and carefully prepared fresh plant extracts, tinctures, oils, elixirs, salves, you-name-it. Wholesale/retail.

Herb Pharm, P.O. Box 116, Williams, Oregon 97544, 1-800-348-4372. Excellent quality "concentrated herbal drops" (tinctures/extracts). Educational product catalogue mailed upon request.

Lotus Light, P.O. Box 1008, Silver Lake, Wisconsin 53170, 1-800-548-3824. Huge variety of body care and health products including herbs and herbal prepartions.

Meadowbrook Herb Garden, Rt. 138, Wyoming, Rhode Island 02898, 401-539-7603. Culinary and medicinal herbs, seeds.

Nichols Garden Nursery, 1190 N. Pacific Highway, Albany, Oregon 97321, 503-928-9280. Live herb plants, dried herbs, spices, and seeds.

Pacific Botanicals, 4350 Fish Hatchery Road, Grants Pass, Oregon 97527, 503-479-7777. Mark and Marggy Wheeler grow organic medicinal herbs and also gather "wild herbs". This is a source of dried and fresh plant materials for discriminating herbalists. $25/min.

Reevis Mountain School of Self-Reliance and Reevis Mountain County, HCO2 Box 1534, Roosevett, Arizona 85545, 602-467-2536. Prime quality organic wildcrafted herbs and tinctures from the southwest U.S. are their specialty. Their founder and director, Peter Bigfoot, teaches excellent herbistry, lifestyle, and self-reliance courses. This is the best source for buying Chaparral.

San Francisco Herb Company, 250 14th Street, San Francisco, California 94103, (U.S.) 800-227-4530, (CA) 800-622-0768. Major herb importer, source for dried bulk herbs and herb seeds. Wholesale to the public.

Taylors Herb Gardens Inc.,1535 Lone Oak Road, Vista, California 92083, 619-727-3485. A Wonderful source for live herb plants and seeds.

Turtle Island Herbs Inc., Gold Hill-Salina Star Rt., Boulder, Colorado 80302, 303-442-2215. High quality herbal extracts, salves, syrups, massage oils, herbal formulas and herbal first aid kit. Their catalogue is informative.

APPENDIX E

TRAVEL KIT GUIDE

Here are two fabulous herbal travel kits made from the Ten Essentials System. I find it convenient to use empty 35mm film containers for transporting herbal items, especially the powdered ones, as these containers are airtight, waterproof, unbreakable, and made of plastic that is stable enough that it does not deteriorate into the herbs. However any container with these qualities will do and I have also used extra-tough zip-lock baggies. I *ABSOLUTELY AVOID* glass or aluminum containers or anything that would rust, deteriorate or break easily.

Regular size kit:

one small container Clove oil, with dropper
one small container Peppermint oil, with dropper
one or two ounces dry People Paste powder
one or more ounces Slippery Elm powder
one or more ounces Enhanced Garlic Formula
one or more ounces Ginger powder (for bath or ?)
small container Cayenne
"breathable" surgeon's adhesive tape

a few sterile gauze pads of various sizes
small container non-iodized sea salt
(for gargle and nasal rinse)
small container of raw honey
small container of Aloe Vera Gel
(These last two are for mixing with People Paste.)

For this regular size herbal travel kit I also stuff, here and there in my baggage, small packets of dry herbs or tea bags that I might want to use for tea.

"Bare Necessities" travel kit:

small container Clove oil, with dropper
small container Peppermint oil, with dropper
People Paste *OR* Enhanced Garlic Formula
(enough for internal and external uses)
small container Cayenne
"breathable" surgeons' adhesive tape
sterile gauze pads

In this "bare necessities" category I find that I can almost always find fresh Garlic, Onion, salt (for gargle and nasal rinse) and Ginger root in small shops or open-air markets even in obscure places. These on-the-spot additions are valuable to your travel kit. If you are familiar with the many ways to use the herbs on the list, and especially if you take this book (or just a copy of the Appendix F chart) with you, you will be able to handle the most common travelers' health needs such as colds, flu, fever, indigestion, toothache, sore throat, nausea, insect bites, infection, minor injuries, diarrhea, food poisoning, insect repelling, even bedbugs and much more!

It's extra fun traveling just to try out these herbs!

APPENDIX F

GENERAL USE CHART

This appendix is intended as a quick reference chart. I have selected many of the most common daily applications of the Ten Essentials and included them here. ***Primary herbs*** *for each application are indicated on the chart* ***by large and small dots***. Further information about finding an application is indicated by the size of those dots.

FOR IMMEDIATE USE, when no further information is needed, go straight to the herb chapter indicated for an application and follow the directions for General Dosage.

Large Dots tell you that you will find further information on this particular application by referring in the indicated herb chapter to the ***specific*** application title you see on the chart. For example, if you are looking on the chart under the heading "Digestion," you will find a large dot in the Peppermint column. Turn to Chapter IX, Peppermint, and you will find instructions under "Digestion" in the Applications and Attributes list.

Small Dots indicate that you will ***not*** find, in the indicated herb chapter, the specific application title listed on this chart. You ***will*** find one or more ***related*** applications to the one you are seeking. Look on the Applications and Attributes (Quick Reference List) in the indicated herb chapter for related applications. For example, you may consult the chart in this apppendix for help with a stomachache. Under the heading "Stomach" on the chart, a small dot will refer you to the Peppermint chapter, Chapter IX. Peppermint is a primary herb for help with all sorts of digestive upheavals, including stomachache from indigestion. However, these various digestive upheavals are all covered under the heading "Digestion," in the Peppermint Applications list. There is no separate, specific application labeled Stomachache in that list.

If you refer to Headache on the Apppendix F chart, for another example, you will see a small dot referring you to the Clove chapter, Chapter IV. A headache is a type of pain. In the Clove Applications list there is an application titled "Pain," but no separate, specific application titled "Headache."

For each application listed on this chart, there are other herbal choices among the Ten Essentials, in addition to those named here. The chart simply points out the primary choices for quick reference. For further references, or for extensive references to additional applications not listed in Appendix F, see the complete Index at the back of the book.

If you travel light and don't have room to pack the entire book *Ten Essential Herbs*, at least ***make a copy of Appendix F and take it with you while traveling*** (for a memory jogger). This General Use Chart (Appendix F), along with one of the travel kits described in Appendix E, make a useful combination for taking care of your health when you are on the road.

CHAPTER XI **YARROW**	CHAPTER X **SLIPPERY ELM**	CHAPTER IX **PEPPERMINT**	APPENDIX A **PEOPLE PASTE**	CHAPTER VIII **ONION**	CHAPTER VII **GINGER**	CHAPTER VI **GARLIC**	CHAPTER V **COMFREY**	CHAPTER IV **CLOVE**	CHAPTER III **CHAPARRAL**	CHAPTER II **CAYENNE**	GENERAL USE CHART APPENDIX F
			•			●			●		ABSCESS
				●	•		•				ATHLETIC INJURY
●					●		•		●		ARTHRITIS
●		●			●	●		●			BATH
	●						●			●	BLEEDING
	•						●				BONES
			•	●	•		●				BRUISES
	●		•				●				BURNS
●					●					●	CIRCULATION
●			•		●	●	●		●	●	COLDS and FLU
				●	●	●	●				CONGESTION
	●				●					●	CONSTIPATION
				●		●	●				COUGH

continued

CHAPTER XI **YARROW**	CHAPTER X **SLIPPERY ELM**	CHAPTER IX **PEPPERMINT**	APPENDIX A **PEOPLE PASTE**	CHAPTER VIII **ONION**	CHAPTER VII **GINGER**	CHAPTER VI **GARLIC**	CHAPTER V **COMFREY**	CHAPTER IV **CLOVE**	CHAPTER III **CHAPARRAL**	CHAPTER II **CAYENNE**	GENERAL USE CHART APPENDIX F
	•		•								DIARRHEA
●		●	•		●		●			●	DIGESTION
				●		●		●			EARS
	●						●			●	EYES
●						•	•		●		FEVER
						●			●		FUNGUS
	●	●			●						GAS
			•			●		●		●	GUMS
•		●			●			•		•	HEADACHE
				●		•				●	HEART (Blood Pressure/Tonic)
●	●						•				HEMORRHOIDS
●			•						•	•	HYPOGLYCEMIA (Tonic)
●			•			●	●		●		INFECTION (Antibiotic/Antiseptic)
●	●						●				INFLAMMATION
●				●		●	●		•		INSECT BITES
•	•		•	●		●	●		●		KIDNEYS
●			•				•		●		LIVER
●	●	•		●			●	●	•		LUNGS
●	●	●			●						NAUSEA
		●				●		●			NERVES
		●	•					●			PAIN
•			•				•		●	•	POISON
●					•				•		REPRODUCTIVE ORGANS
		●						●			SEDATIVE
										●	SHOCK
		●		●						●	SINUS
●	●		•				●	●	●		SKIN
		•				●		●			SLEEP
		●				●		•			SPASMS (Antispasmodic)
				●	●		●			•	SPRAINS
●	●	•			●		•	•		•	STOMACH
		●						●			TEETHING
	●	●						●		●	THROAT
			•			●		●			TOOTHACHE
	●		•				●			●	ULCER
●	●		•			●	●	•	●		WOUNDS
●						●			●		YEAST INFECTION

INDEX

C